The Republican War Against Women

Updated Edition

THE REPUBLICAN WAR AGAINST WOMEN

AN INSIDER'S REPORT FROM BEHIND THE LINES

TANYA MELICH

UPDATED EDITION

BANTAM BOOKS
NEW YORK   TORONTO   LONDON   SYDNEY   AUCKLAND

THE REPUBLICAN WAR AGAINST WOMEN
A Bantam Book

Publishing History
Bantam hardcover edition published February 1996
Bantam trade paperback edition / January 1998

Cover design by Belina Huey.

Library of Congress Catalog Card Number: 95-43111

ISBN 0-553-37816-3

Published simultaneously in the United States and Canada

Bantam Books are published by Bantam Books, a division of Bantam Doubleday
Dell Publishing Group, Inc. Its trademark, consisting of the words "Bantam Books"
and the portrayal of a rooster, is Registered in U.S. Patent and Trademark Office
and in other countries. Marca Registrada. Bantam Books, 1540 Broadway, New
York, New York 10036.

PRINTED IN THE UNITED STATES OF AMERICA
BVG   10   9   8   7   6   5   4   3   2   1

To my Utah and New York families
with love

CONTENTS

Prologue

They were beautiful children—a honey-haired boy about four and his older sister with similar golden locks. They were dressed in white shirts, cutoff jeans, and dirty white sneakers. Wide-eyed and sweet-faced, they reminded me of my own two. They stared vacantly from the curb across the street. I smiled. They pretended not to see me.

The Texas sun seemed too hot for so early in the morning. Their skin was pale and fragile. They had no hats, nothing to protect their arms, their legs. They'd be sunburned soon.

I wondered where their parents were. Didn't anyone over there care?

The adults standing around them paid no heed. They were busy saving the unborn; they had no time for children standing on curbs.

I hurt inside. I didn't like being there any more than those children. Something was terribly wrong—children being forced to watch their elders preach hate, police with holstered guns treating demonstrators like criminals, ordinary people shouting crude epithets and threats.

It was no place for children. It was no place for anyone.

·   ·   ·

We'd already been standing there an hour. When I'd arrived at seven A.M. from the convention hotel with other pro-choice Republicans, the lines were already forming. We stood three deep in front of the doors of the Planned Parenthood clinic locking arms with pro-choice Houstonians. Before us were blue sawhorses, while fully armed Houston police patrolled past us up and down the block.

Across the street were more sawhorses. Leaning against them were the children, the brother and sister and others, and behind them were the adults. Unlike their children, the adults were not beautiful. Their faces were contorted, and for the last hour they'd been calling on us to "stop killing God's children! Repent your sinful ways!" Accompanied by two women beating a bass drum, we had drowned them out with our own chant: "Not the church, not the state, women must decide their fate."

At first it had been a game, the exercise of free speech. We were chanting, they were chanting—though with an edge. Then it turned ugly; the threats came, the yelling started, and some of the Operation Rescue men broke past the police officers to get to the doors of the clinic.

They failed, but it was no longer just another demonstration of opposing views. This was deadly serious. A fight could break out, a knife could flash, a gun could go off—and then, as always happens when grown-ups forget children, the children would be hurt. The same pattern, old as history, would play out once again.

Suddenly the shouting stopped, and thirty-four-year-old Randall Terry, leader of Operation Rescue, moved to the center. His microphone popped with static. An array of ministers in their shapeless brown and gray summer suits, all white men except for one lone black among them, began to sing "Amazing Grace." I saw some of the twisted faces of the women relax, and they joined in. I felt an urge to join in too.

For a few moments both sides were caught up in the beauty of the hymn; we could all have been standing together at a Fourth of July celebration. We weren't. We were soldiers in a deadly war. My colleagues and I were in Houston to prove our strength not only to Terry and his followers but to the delegates of the Republican National Convention and to George Bush. And worst of all, I thought, I'm one of those delegates and I'm in the middle. I'm here pledged to nominate the man who's encouraging these people even as I stand here against them.

I can't remember Randall Terry's exact words, but I remember that he spoke quietly at first as he exhorted us to love others as Jesus had said, to turn the other cheek. I, who had gone to Baptist Sunday school almost every week from childhood until college, recognized the Scriptures he quoted. Then his tone changed. The biblical words of love turned sour. He became an avenger. The microphone crackled. The hate spewed forth: "Baby-killers! Murderers! Scum of the earth! Destroyers of precious life!" He shook his finger at us.

I found myself trembling. I could feel the arms of my newfound friends on either side stiffen as the diatribe grew shriller. Our side called back: "Not the church, not the state, women will decide their fate." We too were shouting now. The sun grew hotter. More police arrived. My stomach turned over. I felt sick.

Where were the two children? I strained to find them. No one was on the curb. They had been taken home. At least someone over there had sense.

Then I saw them, each perched on a man's shoulders. The girl was easier to spot. Her hair glinted in the sun as before, but her pretty face was twisted like the grown-ups'.

Her little brother sat on the shoulders of a smaller man and stared blankly at his sister. He watched her as she raised her delicate finger and pointed it directly at me, screaming, "Stop killing the babies! Stop killing the babies! Murderer, murderer!" The little boy picked up the rhythm and in a high singsong voice joined his sister: "Murderer, murderer! Baby-killer, baby-killer!" It was as if their hatred were a match for Terry's.

My nausea gave way to anger. The call to hate, the paranoia, the conspiracy theories, the manipulation of decent people's emotions, the robbing of those children's innocence, the gratuitous violence, were all being justified in the name of religious faith. This was not the religion of my childhood. This was not generous, loving, compassionate.

I'd deluded myself. The tacit approval of the President of the United States was being used to shatter the nation's tranquillity, to tear away at its Constitution, to shackle women, and to stifle dissent—all in the cause of winning elections. George Bush and the other leaders of the Republican party were to blame for giving respectability and power to this movement of hate, this sickness of the soul. And I too was to blame. They'd encouraged this firestorm and I'd gone along. I'd let cleverness overwhelm good sense. I'd not been willing to let go, to leave the party of my roots, my ambition, my life's work, my dreams. I'd been wrong, very wrong.

The noise diminished. The other side was packing up. For today, the confrontation was over. My friends and I left the picket line to go to the hotel to plan our next move. I glanced back. Terry and his troops roared one last time, "You traitors, you traitors to life!" as the children singsonged, "Baby-killer, baby-killer!" I didn't yell back. The bigger problem lay elsewhere.

PART ONE

How It

Happened

1

The Conflict of Principle and Expediency

I cannot remember a time when the Republican party was not part of my life. I grew up in a family where political talk dominated daily meals and weekend picnics in the red rock desert surrounding my hometown of Moab, Utah. My mother and father constantly reminded us that public service is an honorable calling, that we had a duty to participate in the nation's political life, and that we could do this best by working for the Republican party.

I started that "working" early on. As a preschooler, I remember standing with my dad outside the Grand County High School auditorium handing out Willkie for President pamphlets. By the time I entered first grade, I'd stuffed envelopes, licked stamps, and passed out literature for Dad's campaign for the state senate. After he was elected, the family went to Salt Lake City for the three-month legislative session; and for the next eight years I witnessed in a modest way Utah's political life.

I went to school in Salt Lake City when the legislature was in session, and after school I would wander the halls of the state capitol, sit in the legislative chamber watching the men debate, and occasionally be allowed on the senate floor to sit in my father's chair. I was fascinated by the political jockeying and relished the stories about what the Republicans and Democrats were doing to each other. To me at that young age, politics seemed not only a worthwhile endeavor but the most exciting action around.

The values I was taught as a child were the values my family respected so highly in the Republican party: Lincolnian compassion and championing of equal opportunity for all Americans; Theodore Roosevelt's vision of a responsible capitalism held in check by a caring government; and Herbert Hoover's ethic of self-reliance, in which individuals turned to government for help only as a last resort. For much of my life, I not only believed that this was what the party stood for, I worked to further those ideals. I organized campaigns for Republican candidates, recruited new members, and did a wide variety of tasks directed toward increasing its power. As for the Democrats, I thought they stood for big government that obstructed individual freedom, and that Franklin Roosevelt and his New Deal had undermined America's remarkable free enterprise system. It was unimaginable to me that I could have much in common with the values of the Democratic party.

But beginning in 1964, the national Republican party changed. It turned its back on the Lincoln tradition and gradually embraced a presidential electoral strategy that reinforced resistance to the civil rights movement. Over the years, the party that had so majestically led the nation through the Civil War betrayed its founding principles of freedom for all. By 1980, this strategy had further expanded to embrace a deliberate policy of hostility toward women. The shift was subtle—in the late twentieth century, no major American political party could openly admit it opposed opportunity for 53 percent of the nation's citizens. But the preceding decade had produced some scattered gains for women; and in reaction, the Reagan and Bush administrations actively sought to dismantle those gains. A different Republican agenda came into play.

This book is in the main the story of that changed and changing agenda. Only peripherally is it about the party's racial strategy introduced in 1964, a tale that has already been told well and in detail elsewhere. But bigotry is bigotry, regardless of who the objects of hatred or ridicule may be. While the focus in these pages is on gender, the fates of women and blacks in America have been intertwined since the nation's beginnings; no change in the political life of one happens without affecting the other.

Second, this book is about the struggle between the women's movement and its political opponents. It is about the feminist women of the Republican party: how we sought to turn our party's commitment to individual freedom into concrete action, and how we fought those who embraced the messages of misogyny. The dictionary defines *misogyny* as hatred, dislike, or mistrust of women. While the majority of the Republicans who opposed us weren't misogynists, those who sought to control the party's agenda discovered that the women's liberation movement—stimulated in 1963 with the publication of Betty Friedan's *The Feminine Mystique* and born in 1966 with the founding of the National Organization for Women (NOW)—was generating a backlash not unlike the racist backlash to the civil rights movement. Growing numbers of women were challenging the traditional roles expected of them; more and more they were entering the work force, whether out of choice or necessity; and many were raising their voices demanding to be heard. For some Americans, these changes were unsettling or even frightening, and fear bred resistance. In 1980 the national leadership of the Republican party adopted a misogynist strategy that deliberately exploited this backlash to win votes. It has pursued this strategy ever since.

The third and overarching story in this book is the age-old conflict between principle and expediency in pursuit of political power. By playing on fear and hatred in its quest for votes and discovering that this paid off, the national leadership of the Republican party has sown a cancerous divisiveness across the land.

To understand the misogynist strategy, it is necessary to return to the nation's founding, for the root cause of this division over gender springs from a defect deep within American culture. It derives from an enduring belief that women should not have equal opportunity because their "natural" sphere is the private world and their judgment in public matters cannot be trusted. The division also springs from political greed. It is the interplay of philosophical belief and "practical" politics that has deprived American women from fully sharing in their nation's promise.

That promise was articulated in the Declaration of Independence, which committed the nation to the ideal that all Americans are guaranteed equal opportunity to life, liberty, and the pursuit of happiness. Yet in 1788, twelve years after proclaiming this grand promise, the propertied white men of America ratified a Constitution that ignored women and accepted slavery. To have given white women and black slaves constitutional protection at that time would have required a philosophical leap that most of these men could not have made. Most found it impossible to accept women and blacks as equals. It also would have placed a serious roadblock in the way of the Constitution's ratification, since giving either of these groups the vote would have upset the delicate political balance that bound southern slaveowners and northern business owners in common cause.

Thus began the carousel of American racial and gender politics. Still, it was only a few decades later that the new nation's propertied white males were challenged. The movement for freedom for those left out of the Constitution grew slowly and quietly through religious and intellectual revival meetings. By 1829, when New York State abolished slavery, it had begun in earnest. By 1848, women had organized. Gathering in Seneca Falls, New York, on July 19 and 20, 1848, these women and a few male friends, under the leadership of Lucretia Mott and Elizabeth Cady Stanton, issued the Declaration of Sentiments. Patterned after the Declaration of Independence, it called for a woman's right to divorce and to ownership of her property after marriage; an end to the double standard of morality between men and women; full political participation; and equal opportunity in education and employment. It declared that woman is "man's equal—was intended to be so by the Creator, and the highest good of the race demands that she should be recognized as such."

The declaration spoke eloquently, in words that are still timely today. Six years later, male acquaintances of the women who supported the Seneca Falls declaration took their own action. In July 1854, united in their opposition to slavery and angered by the passage of the Kansas-Nebraska Act, which opened the western territories to the "peculiar institution," a coalition of Whigs, Free-Soilers, and antislavery Democrats met in Ripon, Wisconsin, to propose the formation of a new party that would turn its back on all the existing political parties—the Whigs, the Free-Soilers, the Know-Nothings, and the Democrats. Within a week, similar meetings in other states followed suit, and the Republican party was born.

The cause of liberty for the slaves was what brought these men together. The leaders of the recently born women's movement were not present at the party's founding, but they were confident that with the abolition of slavery would come freedom for their sex as well. Although women lacked the formal political franchise to participate in the new party, movement leaders did all they could to help it.

Within six years of its founding, this upstart, passionate freedom movement had turned into the most powerful political force in the country, and in 1860 its candidate for president, Abraham Lincoln, was elected, setting the nation in a different direction that promised new opportunities for all Americans.

Accepting the abolitionists' arguments that eliminating slavery must be the party's first priority, the women put aside organizing for women's rights and threw themselves into the Civil War effort, expecting that their cause would be enthusiastically embraced by the Republicans once the war was won and the slaves were freed.

It was not to be. The war ended in 1865, and the Thirteenth Amendment, ratified in December, abolished slavery. But only a few short years after the terrible conflict ended—before the wounds had healed and the weariness of war had receded—Republican leaders broke their pledge to further women's rights. In 1869 the Republican-controlled Congress sent the Fifteenth Amendment to the states for ratification. The amendment gave the vote only to black men and not to women—a betrayal that was the most destructive action the party was to take against women until the days of Reagan–Bush.

The women who had embraced the Seneca Falls declaration were bitterly disappointed. The arguments they now heard from Republican leaders, such as Horace Greeley and Wendell Phillips, and from black leader Frederick Douglass were familiar—the need for national tranquillity justified the party's action. The 1868 battle to impeach Lincoln's successor, Andrew Johnson, in part because of his willingness to placate southern landholders and merchants, had split the Republicans and the nation. Many Republicans claimed America could not stand the additional stress that would come from giving women and blacks the vote at the same time. What was needed most was stability. Besides, they said, the Civil War had been fought to free the slaves, and this was the "Negroes' hour." The freedman must have the vote first. Women could wait a little longer.

In the end, as in 1787–88, practical politics determined what happened. The goal of these men was to maintain Republican party power. At the time when suffrage for blacks and women was debated, the still-young party controlled the Congress, the White House, and the majority of the state legislatures and was riding an immense tide of popularity after the Union's victory. It had the political clout to pass a constitutional amendment giving both women and blacks the vote, but a combination of lack of interest and practical politics stopped it.

As the men in charge saw it, to give women the vote at the same time as black men would substantially undercut the broad new power the Republicans had achieved. The men assumed that if southern white women in the former Confederate states were allowed to vote, they would vote against the party whose efforts had defeated the Confederacy. Their vote would cancel out the new black vote that would go to the Republicans, possibly losing them control of Congress and the White House. Women's suffrage would have to be put aside to maintain Republican power.

Despite this decision, the Republican party's record toward women was still much better than that of the Democrats. But it certainly did not match the myth perpetuated by the Republican faithful that the party of Lincoln and individual rights automatically produced a record of achievement and gains for women. Of the fifty years between 1870, when the Fifteenth Amendment was ratified, and 1920, when the Nineteenth Amendment finally gave women the vote, the Republicans controlled the White House for thirty-four, and for most of that time they controlled the Congress as well. They could have delivered women's suffrage, but they did not believe it would bring them any political advantage.

Not until 1912 did the political environment significantly change for women. Angered by the direction in which his handpicked successor, William Howard Taft, was taking the nation, former president Theodore Roosevelt bolted the Republicans, formed the Progressive party, and ran against both Taft and Democrat Woodrow Wilson. Roosevelt had not been a champion of women's rights, but now he enthusiastically embraced "equal suffrage for men and women." He had two practical reasons for his conversion: Progressives were strong advocates of women's suffrage; and six normally Republican western states had granted women the vote and might come into his camp. Roosevelt's gamble did pay off in the West, where he won, but not nationally. He came in second to Wilson in both the popular and electoral votes.

Still, despite his defeat, Roosevelt's experience with women voters had shown Republican leaders that backing women's suffrage might be politically astute after all. Democrats now held an electoral grip on the South, due in large part to their success in intimidating black males and keeping them from the polls. Adding southern women to the voting rolls would probably not change Republican prospects there, but in the rest of the country the women's vote could be organized for Republican candidates. By 1916, Roosevelt had returned to the Republican party. The Progressive movement was attempting to break up the urban Democrat machines, and there seemed a chance that urban women, even if their husbands were loyal to the Democrats, might be amenable to a party that had welcomed back a reformer like Roosevelt.

So at its convention in 1916, for the first time in its history, the Republican party passed a platform that included a plank favoring "the extension of the suffrage to women." Ambivalence on the issue was still plentiful, however, as was clear from a waffling addition "recognizing the right of each state to settle the question for itself." Two weeks later, the Democrats too passed a platform plank endorsing women's suffrage. Although their wording lacked the Republicans' equivocation, theirs was an empty promise. They could not deliver on it because their voting base was too dependent on those who opposed suffrage—the saloonkeepers, the liquor and brewery industry, and the hierarchy of the Catholic Church. Five times over the next three years, three Democrat-controlled Congresses voted down suffrage legislation.

Then in 1919 a newly elected Republican Congress easily endorsed the Nineteenth Amendment, mandating that "the right of citizens of the United States to vote shall not be denied or abridged . . . on account of sex," and sent it to the states. It was ratified in 1920, and twenty-nine of the thirty-five state legislatures that approved it were controlled by Republicans.

Fifty-one years after they betrayed America's women, the Republicans had finally rectified their bad faith. But it would be wrong to deduce that the country's political parties had finally awakened to the cause of women's suffrage because of belief in the promise of the Declaration of Independence. Suffrage came about because women had finally developed enough grassroots muscle to force the politicians to take notice. They won the vote in spite of the parties.

For the first time in American history, women of all classes, backgrounds, and ages had worked together in common cause, despite outrageous harassment. They organized spectacular parades and demonstration after demonstration, even though they were spat on and physically attacked. They were thrust into prison cells with "wormy food, open toilets that could only be flushed from outside their cells, dirty sheets and blankets washed once a year, cockroaches and rats, quarters shared with syphilitics, fetid air, filth, drinking water in an open pail. Some women were put into solitary confinement . . . [and] were held incommunicado, without counsel." The battles were prolonged and the outcome by no means certain, but the suffragists ultimately prevailed.

After the Nineteenth Amendment was ratified, both parties immediately sought to win the women's vote by passing legislation they thought women wanted, but these efforts quickly dissipated when their support for such legislation brought no rewards at the ballot box. Soon after suffrage was enacted, for example, Congress passed what was thought to be a major "women's law," the Sheppard–Towner Act. At the time, it was the most ambitious maternal and child health program ever enacted, but when a women's voting bloc failed to materialize in gratitude, Congress refused to renew funding for the program.

The lack of attention to women's concerns could not be blamed entirely on the men in power, however. After suffrage, the activists who had fought so vigorously for the vote were unprepared to use the electoral power they had won. Their vaunted political prowess crumbled when the remarkable unity they had achieved in the years just before their victory disintegrated. They did not use the exceptional organizing skills they had learned during the suffrage struggle to seek large numbers of appointments or nominations for public office. They did not vote as often as men or become politically active; and those who did go to the polls tended to vote like their husbands or other male family members. Battle-weary from the stresses of World War I and the suffrage fight, and flush with their newly won right to vote, most women retreated into the social and domestic life of the twenties and left political life to the men.

They were following a long tradition. Before 1920, women's public experience had been primarily outside organized politics. They'd worked for the vote, for peace, for maternal and child health and child labor legislation, for conservation and other progressive issues. They had not worked for Democrats and Republicans, and in the years that followed few women joined political parties. With rare exceptions, they didn't prod the men in power to initiate a systematic plan to increase the number of women in politics.

Most of the women who did go to Congress, like Republican Margaret Chase Smith, the nation's only woman U.S. senator for twenty-four years, began their political careers by filling seats vacated when their husbands died. Of the seventy-five women who served in the House between 1916, when Republican Jeannette Rankin of Montana became its first woman member, and 1971, when the modern women's political movement was founded, only a handful were elected in their own right, among them Republican Clare Boothe Luce and Democrat Helen Gahagan Douglas. During this long time, the number of state and local women officeholders remained minuscule as well.

It was not until 1938 that the Republican National Committee founded the National Federation of Republican Women; and even then its motives were mixed. Fairness to women mattered less than the urgency of finding new, sorely needed sources of support for a party that had been badly crippled by its disastrous electoral defeats in 1932, 1934, and 1936, when FDR reigned supreme. A similar motivation underlay the 1940 Republican mandate that women hold equal positions on the party's national and executive committees, and its decision that same year to put the Equal Rights Amendment in its platform—it needed their support. (The Democrats did not require women's equal participation on their committees until 1972, and it did not put the ERA in its platform until four years after the Republicans.)

The Republicans' claim that theirs was the party more supportive of women had begun to fade with the political ascendance of Eleanor Roosevelt and FDR's appointment of Frances Perkins to be Secretary of Labor, the first woman to serve in a federal cabinet post. But neither party had an impressive record of appointing women between 1932 and 1960. In 1953 President Eisenhower named Oveta Culp Hobby to his cabinet as secretary of the newly created Health, Education and Welfare Department. He rewarded Ivy Baker Priest, the Utah GOP national committeewoman who in 1952 ran the party's first organized effort to mobilize women for a presidential candidate, by appointing her U.S. treasurer. He also responded to Priest's call that because women had served the country well in the Second World War and in his campaign, they deserved to be a part of his government, by giving several low-level appointments to women and naming Clare Boothe Luce as ambassador to Italy.

Whether the intention was well-meaning, self-serving, or both, these appointments in no way represented shared political power, and as the nation entered the sixties, both parties clung to a tacitly accepted code that women were to be given "full equality" but few significant roles. Those in power saw little political advantage in changing the status quo. The grand dreams of the early feminists that the vote would be an effective tool for bettering the lot of women and granting them full political participation had not materialized.

The era of comparative stability that followed World War II came to an end in 1964, soon after the assassination of John F. Kennedy. It was a time of ferment—and in racial terms, the culmination of events that had begun in 1948, when some southern Democrats bolted their party after Harry Truman had courageously proposed a civil rights program to end segregation and the party's 1948 convention had passed a civil rights plank endorsing it. These "Dixiecrat" Democrats nominated South Carolina governor Strom Thurmond to run for president on a States' Rights ticket, with a platform that glorified "segregation of all the races." Thurmond won Alabama, Louisiana, Mississippi, and South Carolina, victories that encouraged the Dixiecrats to try and develop a new political base outside the Democratic party.

By 1964, the nation was forced to confront its never-fulfilled pledge of equity for all its citizens. African-Americans were demanding the rights they had lost after Reconstruction. The civil rights movement was in full swing, frequently punctuated by violent efforts to subdue it, that a shaken nation saw played out on its television screens.

That year the Republicans nominated Barry Goldwater to be their presidential candidate, precipitating the greatest ideological shift in the party's history. The genesis for this shift grew out of a recognition by some conservative Republicans that the South was ripe for a Republican takeover. They formed themselves into the Draft Goldwater movement.

In a February 12, 1963, article in the conservative magazine *National Review,* its publisher, William Rusher, outlined how Goldwater, who strongly opposed the federal government's encroaching on states' rights, could carry enough southern and border states to offset President Kennedy's advantage in the North. (Kennedy would be assassinated on November 22 of that year, and Lyndon Johnson would become president.) Known as the theoretician of the Goldwater movement, Rusher never directly said that the party should oppose the goals of the civil rights movement. Yet as the Goldwater campaign unfolded, it was clear that its southern strategy was based on the premise that Republicans could win votes by playing to the backlash against the movement's goals and against the federal government's actions to end segregation. The strategy was blatantly racist, an attempt to use bigotry to wrest the South from the Democrats.

The Republicans' shift represented a frontal assault on the Lincoln legacy. Although the party was no longer the black man's protector, the legend that it was remained a lively part of its mythology. The Goldwater campaign set out to court the Dixiecrat Democrats—soon to be called the Wallace Democrats, after Alabama governor George Wallace. In 1963, the governor had vehemently opposed the integration of his state's schools, and then taken his case to the nation's voters by running for president in the 1964 Democratic primaries against Johnson.

Goldwater had let southerners know his thoughts on civil rights issues long before Wallace made his stand. In November 1961, at a meeting of southern Republicans, Goldwater said that the party should not "outpromise the Democrats" on civil rights. "We're not going to get the Negro vote as a bloc in 1964 or 1968, so we ought to go hunting where the ducks are." He kept to this southern strategy. When Congress passed Johnson's civil rights legislation in June 1964, Goldwater voted against it. After Wallace's candidacy faded, Goldwater was the de facto leader of Wallace's states' rights philosophy, and during the fall campaign Strom Thurmond, who had become a Republican, stumped the South for him.

Johnson swamped Goldwater, winning 486 electoral votes to Goldwater's 52. The Republicans' southern strategy's themes against busing and the Civil Rights Act helped Goldwater carry all four of the states won by Thurmond in 1948—plus Georgia. It was the highest number of former Confederate states to vote Republican since Reconstruction.

In 1968 Johnson, overwhelmed by opposition to his championing of the Vietnam War, announced he would not seek reelection and the Democrats nominated Hubert Humphrey. The Republican presidential nominee, Richard Nixon, built on Goldwater's southern success. Instead of rejecting racism outright, as the last Republican president, Dwight Eisenhower, had done by federally enforcing school desegregation, Nixon expanded the southern racial strategy into a national strategy. He targeted traditional northern Democrats in urban neighborhoods, where battles were being fought over school and housing integration, and those suburbanites who had recently fled the cities to escape racial tension. He also competed for the votes of the Dixiecrats, who now had a new candidate in George Wallace, running for president as a third-party white supremacist.

Nixon's message was subtle but understandable to those who were listening. Under the guise of attacking big government, he let voters know that he would slow down the civil rights movement. The federal government had gone too far in school desegregation and other civil rights legislation. It was intruding excessively into the lives of ordinary people.

His racial strategy succeeded. The backlash white vote in the South helped him wrest South Carolina, North Carolina, Virginia, and Florida away from Wallace and gave him several states in the North, where many blue-collar Democrats, angry over their party's championing of civil rights, voted Republican for the first time.

Nixon won, but the election was much closer than it appeared from his 301 electoral votes to Humphrey's 191 and Wallace's 46. The Vietnam War was the most incendiary issue, but race also divided the American people. These divisions were vividly illustrated by the popular vote: Nixon's 43.42 percent barely beat out Humphrey's 42.72 percent. Out of more than 73 million votes cast, Nixon's plurality was slightly over half a million. His victory was not so much a mandate for a new beginning as an anguished cry from confused voters.

Nixon knew how precarious his success had been, and he set out to fashion a strategy that would guarantee a solid victory in 1972. First, he had to solidify his Republican base, which consisted of old guard and moderate Republicans. The old guard supported a private economic system unfettered by government regulation, with low taxes and minimal government spending. They were foreign policy isolationists. The moderates were also fiscal conservatives, but they had embraced some New Deal government programs and were internationalists on foreign policy issues. Nixon's first challenge was to ensure that the old guard and the moderates would work with the new conservatives who had backed him: not only the Draft Goldwater group but former Wallaceites and other Democrats who had deserted their party in 1968. Second, he had to find issues that would convince still more Democrats to desert their party.

The electoral approach he seized on was one his campaign had pursued imperfectly in 1968. It was named and articulated by Kevin Phillips, an assistant to Nixon's campaign manager John Mitchell, in his 1969 book, *The Emerging Republican Majority*. This New Majoritarian strategy maintained the old guard fiscal conservative message that had been the centerpiece of the Republicans' opposition to the Democrats since the New Deal, while it kept the southern strategy and added something new. Through meticulous analysis of demographic and voting data, Phillips demonstrated that the New Deal coalition that had kept the Democrats in power since 1932 was falling apart, and that a new Republican majority could be built by joining the white southern conservatives Rusher had identified for Goldwater's 1964 campaign with blue-collar Democrats and independents who were social conservatives. Phillips also postulated that these Democrats and independents, whose economic level had improved beyond that of their parents and enabled them to leave the cities and settle in suburbia, were ripe for the old guard economic philosophy.

Phillips wrote: "The upcoming cycle of American politics is likely to match a dominant Republican party based in the Heartland, [the] South, and California against a minority Democratic Party based in the Northeast and Pacific Northwest (and encompassing southern as well as northern Negroes). With such support behind it, the GOP can easily afford to lose the states of Massachusetts, New York, and Michigan and is likely to do so except in landslide years."

The social elements of Phillips's strategy were grounded in taking advantage of the growing backlash to the changes of the sixties. The Republican party would win on the basis not of what it stood for but of what it would be against. New Majoritarian adherents wanted the civil rights agenda slowed and, in the case of busing, ended; they believed the opening of the country's culture and institutions to more egalitarian ways was unsound; and they considered opponents of the Vietnam War to be unpatriotic.

Nixon's new conservatives embraced this strategy, but moderate and old guard Republicans were unhappy with the racist nature of its premise and the way it was writing off large northern cities for the party, just as Republicans had written off southern voters in the past.

Women's issues did not enter into the New Majoritarian strategy at this point. With a few exceptions, in fact, no political analysts were paying attention to women. Rusher and Phillips ignored them in their writings, as did Richard Scammon and Ben Wattenberg in their 1970 book, *The Real Majority*, which also analyzed the disintegration of the New Deal coalition. Scammon and Wattenberg devoted half a page in their 333-page book to describing how women voted like men. Since electoral data showed that men and women of similar demographic backgrounds did vote alike, the analysts assumed that women voters would continue to follow men's voting behavior. They did not conceive that an increasing number of women would oppose the political parties' traditional line of paying lip service to women's issues and go on to develop their own gender-based politics.

It was not that the Republicans showed hostility as such to opportunities for women. They simply accepted the status quo, not only Goldwater conservatives but moderates as well. Women who later became leaders in their own right, such as Pat Hutar and Phyllis Schlafly, were part of the Goldwater movement's inner circle and played an important role in its early success. Republican women were no more shut out of the deliberations of their party than were Democratic women out of theirs. The Goldwater and Nixon campaigns may have been pursuing a racist electoral strategy, but neither was guilty of constructing an anti-women strategy. At the 1968 GOP convention, 17 percent of the delegates were women; at the Democratic convention, the proportion was only 13 percent. The 1964 Goldwater platform included a commitment to equal rights for women, although in Nixon's 1968 platform, women's equal rights were subsumed in a catchall phrase of concern for citizens "long disadvantaged by race, color, national origin, creed, or sex." The Democrats, on the other hand, bowing under pressure from labor leader George Meany, who feared the ERA would wipe out protective legislation for women workers, had withdrawn their platform support for women's rights in both 1964 and 1968.

But after 1968 the traditional Republican stance began to change. The new conservatives gradually embraced a different philosophy toward women's rights because another opportunity to raid the Democratic party's electoral base opened up. Phillips's analysis showed that Catholics, a major linchpin of the New Deal coalition, could form a substantial part of a new socially conservative Republican party. The offspring of mainly Irish, Italian, and Polish Catholic immigrants would not only be amenable to the party's traditional call for lower taxes and fewer government programs, but were ripe for a different social message than the one they were hearing from the Democrats. Many were upset about the loosening of sexual mores, and when the National Conference of Catholic Bishops moved publicly to stop the legalization of abortion, the new conservatives quickly embraced the anti-abortion issue as another way to win over Catholic Democrats.

"As early as 1970," academic Timothy Byrnes reported in his 1991 book, *Catholic Bishops in American Politics,* "Republican registrars in California gathered outside Catholic churches to accommodate any parishioners who might want to switch their partisan affiliation in response to the California Democratic party's support of legal abortion. This registration drive, according to *Commonweal,* was a political experiment engineered by the Republican State Central Committee to see if the abortion issue could be used to cause a mass defection of Catholics from the Democratic party."

Many states had laws that limited the use of contraceptives and banned abortion. A campaign to liberalize such laws had been under way for many years, and the lobbying was beginning to bear fruit. In 1965 the Supreme Court had ruled in *Griswold v. Connecticut* that Connecticut could not prohibit married couples from using contraceptives or doctors from prescribing them because the Constitution guarantees a right to privacy for such reproductive matters. This first major step in opening up reproductive freedom for women was followed two years later by California's legalization of abortion, and in 1970 by New York's.

The liberalization of reproductive health laws set off a strong counterreaction from the Catholic Church, which had long opposed abortion and contraception. In the late sixties, more than five years before the Supreme Court legalized abortion in *Roe v. Wade,* its bishops in the United States started an organized anti-abortion movement, unlike its previous scattershot efforts. The bishops became politically active nationally in a manner never before witnessed in America.

In moving toward a changed policy on reproductive rights, Byrnes points out that the new conservatives didn't believe the bishops could deliver a "Catholic vote" per se. But they did "enjoy access to millions of voters," and "through their traditional relationships with urban machines across the country, the bishops had come to embody the strong, traditional ties that bound the Catholic church and the Democratic party together." The new conservatives intended to break those ties by tightly linking the Republican party to the Church's position on abortion.

There was arrogance in the conservatives' assumption that American Catholic women would automatically vote for the party supported by the hierarchy of their church even if this conflicted with their personal dilemma over unwanted pregnancy. These women would now have a painfully difficult choice. The new conservatives also seemed oblivious to the damage that would be done to the nation's religiously tolerant climate if a major political party decided to champion one faith's doctrine on women's issues to the exclusion of other faiths' views. They showed not an inkling of recognition that opposing women's right to choose was a direct attack on women's freedom.

The newly invigorated women's movement blossomed in 1971. The movement had never died, but after the mid-twenties, when the suffragists had split into two factions, it had remained dormant. Occasional successes for women had been brought about by the efforts of individual women and their allies and by the constant optimistic prodding of Eleanor Roosevelt. And in the early sixties, stimulated by the civil rights movement, *The Feminine Mystique,* the strong leadership of Women's Bureau director Esther Peterson, and the persistence of Michigan congressmember Martha Griffiths, women began to wake up and organize. The National Organization for Women (NOW) grew out of a meeting held in 1966 over concern that the sex discrimination provisions in the 1964 Civil Rights Act were not being properly enforced. NOW focused on eliminating sexism in American society and lobbying for legislation. But its major arena was not electoral politics, and as the 1972 elections approached, feminists needed a purely political arm to further their goals.

The National Women's Political Caucus (NWPC) became that arm. Formed in Washington, D.C., on July 11, 1971, to "fight for the rights and needs of women and of all under-represented groups," it was the first organized, serious effort to bring more women into politics since the late twenties. Out of the twenty-one members elected to the policy council of the newly formed caucus, eleven were Democrats, two Republicans, and the rest unaffiliated.

At the founding of the New York arm of the NWPC that fall, I represented the New York State Republican party and was swept up like everyone else by the optimistic rhetoric and the exhilaration of starting a new political movement. I found the women friendly except for the few, upset over the Vietnam War, who turned hostile when they found out I belonged to Nixon's party. Others, however, were glad to have experienced Republicans on hand to help launch the modern feminist political movement.

I had been living in New York City for thirteen years by then, and during that time had worked for many Republican candidates. The party's success—not women's—had been my principal political interest; but when I learned about the feminist agenda of the NWPC, I had joined on the spot. What the women spoke about didn't seem at all radical. I saw it as a logical next step in my political life, with my intent now to elect Republican women who believed in feminist goals. The objectives of the NWPC were an extension of my own personal and political values.

The 1972 presidential election was NWPC's initial focus. I had no idea that as we Republican feminists began to scour the country for women to run for office and become delegates to the 1972 GOP convention in Miami Beach, the new conservatives were forming a national strategy to stop us. Admittedly, Nixon's administration had been a mixed bag in terms of women's concerns—some of his actions had been supportive, while others suggested the new conservative agenda was making ominous inroads. We expected to have problems in Miami Beach. But as we prepared for the convention, we were confident that we would be successful in getting a women's plank that committed the party to address our goals. After all, we belonged to the party of Lincoln and liberty, the party that had given women the vote. How could it not be in everyone's best interest to join us in this new endeavor?

2

TWO EMERGING AGENDAS

Soldiers equipped with gas masks and assault guns were scattered around the roofs of the buildings surrounding the Miami Beach Convention Center. They seemed oddly out of place to us—saturation security was not the kind of presence we Republicans expected at our national convention. Although we certainly remembered the violence of the Chicago Democratic convention four years earlier, we'd never felt the need for battle-ready troops to protect us from the demonstrators and proselytizers who always showed up at our quadrennial gatherings.

But times were different now. This was August 1972. It was nearly four years since Nixon had taken office, and the Vietnam War that had made Chicago so incendiary still raged. The antiwar demonstrations were even worse than under Lyndon Johnson. Kent State, My Lai, and the Pentagon Papers had exacerbated the rage. The war fed ugly domestic unrest and a student revolution on campuses across the country. Drug use was widespread among the young, millions of them angry, defiant, and estranged, their elders baffled by the disintegration of the stable world they had known.

In July the Democratic party had nominated George McGovern in a tumultuous convention, in which the platform endorsed immediate withdrawal from Vietnam, abolition of the draft, and amnesty for draft resisters. The Democrats were also torn apart over proposed reforms in convention rules and delegate selection procedures, and by efforts of feminists to include reproductive rights language in the platform.

The Republican National Convention in Miami Beach that summer was not a happy one either, despite the sumptuous yacht parties, elegant receptions, and superficial gaiety that the planners of the Committee to Re-Elect the President (CREEP) were trying to orchestrate. Every day when we came out of the convention halls, we faced belligerent men and women shouting at us, from behind the chain-link fence that confined them, to stop the bombing, stop the killing. Every day we faced the poignant sight of Vietnam vets in their worn bemedaled uniforms, some on crutches, others in wheelchairs, gathered in front of our hotels. Even as Vietnam haunted us, we tried to act as though it did not exist. Since Nixon held the cards in Miami Beach, we felt we could do little about the war, so we went about our political business and focused on issues we thought we *could* do something about.

I'd come to Miami as an alternate delegate-at-large from New York pledged to Nixon. It was not my first national Republican convention. I vividly remember hearing, as I lay awake in my bed late on election night in 1948, my parents' outbursts of disbelief as the radio announced that Harry Truman had defeated Tom Dewey for the presidency. They had sworn then that they would do all they could to see a Republican elected in 1952. That year Dad became a Utah delegate for Robert Taft, and he and my mother took my brother, my sister, and me with them to Chicago for the convention.

That experience was a defining moment in my life. On the Fourth of July weekend, as we drove through the green rolling Iowa hills and across the Midwest toward Chicago, I believed we were on a glorious mission to save the country from the Democrats who were ruining it. Each American flag flying from the porches and community flagpoles in the towns we drove through increased my pride in my beautiful country.

I'd recently read Whittaker Chambers's anticommunist book, *Witness,* and knew just how lucky I was to live in a nation free from communism. It was important, I thought, that Robert Taft be elected to protect not only America but the world.

Instead the Republicans nominated Dwight Eisenhower, and I learned to accept him as a reasonable substitute for the man I thought was better. What came first, however, was one of the most turbulent nominating conventions in Republican history. The memories are many. I became angry over a political slight, hitting an Eisenhower delegate on the head with my Taft sign when he asked how much I'd been paid to demonstrate for Taft. (The thought that someone would pay others for expressing their political feelings was alien to my young heart.) I was sitting near the podium when one of my heroes, Illinois delegate Everett McKinley Dirksen, pointed his finger at Tom Dewey and blamed him for "leading us down the road to defeat." I met Granddad Snyder's old mining engineer friend, former president Herbert Hoover, and was proud when he told me how impressive it was to see a girl so young interested in politics. I could barely speak when Granddad introduced me to Douglas MacArthur, fresh from touring America after his firing by Harry Truman. I wanted to ask him if he thought we'd beat the Communists in Korea, but I was too shy.

Above all, I remember my first brush with the ugly side of politics, finding screeds under our hotel-room door attacking Taft's honesty, and listening to the abusive comments Eisenhower supporters made to me when they saw my Taft button. It was my first contact with the fury and hatred that politics can unleash. When Taft lost and I shared in the sorrow of my parents and their friends, I swore to myself that one day I would go to New York and help defeat that awful Tom Dewey and his "eastern crowd" that the Taft people kept saying were to blame for the destruction of a good man.

There'd been other conventions. In 1956 I went to San Francisco as a page for the Utah delegation and met Bill Rusher, Clif White, Bob Bauman, Stan Evans, and other leaders of the fledgling Goldwater movement that was beginning to form within the Young Republican National Federation (YRNF). White and Rusher became my friends. I was active in the University of Colorado Young Republicans and at their urging became an officer in the national Young Republicans. I agreed with their views on the need for balanced budgets and maintaining a hard line against communism, and I shared their belief that less government was better government.

Four years later I would run into them at the 1960 convention in Chicago, where they told me they were engineering a vanity vice-presidential nomination for Arizona senator Barry Goldwater, to launch their effort to nominate a "true conservative" to be president. Four years later in San Francisco, they succeeded in nominating him, leaving behind traditional politics for the politics of ideology. They were on a crusade that I couldn't share. I regretted that my friends no longer had room in their politics for a moderate Republican like me.

By 1968, the ideological lines had been drawn. The convention was in Miami, and I went as a member of the Rockefeller for President staff. Rusher and White were there for Ronald Reagan. Both our candidates lost to Nixon, and now in 1972, here we all were again, back in the same uncomfortably hot and humid Florida city, this time pledged to the Nixon–Agnew ticket. This convention was not about nominating a candidate for president. We had our candidate. Republicans—moderates and liberals, the old guard and the new conservatives—had come to shape the future direction of the Republican party.

There had already been a few fights between us. In New York in 1970, Clif White had managed the U.S. Senate campaign of James Buckley, brother of *National Review* founder and editor William F. Buckley, Jr. The Nixon White House had decided it wanted Buckley, running as the nominee of the Conservative party, to defeat the incumbent Republican senator, Charles Goodell. The Conservative party had been formed in the early sixties to push New York's Republican party to the right, and with the president's support, the new conservatives now had the opportunity to prove they could undercut the state GOP.

Goodell, who had been in the House, had been appointed by Governor Nelson Rockefeller to fill the unexpired Senate term of the assassinated Robert Kennedy, and I was acting as his campaign's director of research. The goal of the new conservatives was to destroy Rockefeller's power in his own state. Nixon professed to be against Goodell because of Goodell's opposition to his Vietnam policies. But this was only part of the story. New York was to be a test case for trying out the social agenda messages of the new conservatives. If they could knock off delegate-rich New York, with its moderate Republican governor and liberal Republican senators Javits and Goodell, they would have eliminated one of the major forces standing in the way of taking over the party.

Vice President Spiro Agnew was the hatchet man for the president. It was unusual to find a Republican vice president attacking an incumbent Republican senator in a general election, but Agnew's behavior fit the new conservatives' script. Agnew lashed out at what he considered Goodell's embrace of the Democrats' liberal "new politics," and armed with the biting words of his speechwriter, Patrick Buchanan, he called Goodell the "Christine Jorgenson of the Republican party." (Jorgenson had made headlines nationwide for undergoing a sex-change operation.) It was harsh language, going well beyond the bounds of standard hard-nosed political give-and-take.

Buchanan's using the Jorgenson analogy to describe Goodell's change from an old-line conservative to a liberal Republican was unsettling. The sexual terminology signaled that Goodell was somehow immoral, that he sanctioned aberrant sexual behavior. It was a New Majoritarian tactic that was to become all too familiar in the decades to come.

Buckley won handily, defeating Goodell by a margin of 39 to 24 percent, with Democrat Richard Ottinger coming in second with 37 percent. The victory communicated to other Republicans that an ugly attack on a moderate incumbent Republican was an acceptable practice. Somehow California governor Ronald Reagan's often-quoted Eleventh Commandment, that no Republican should speak ill of other Republicans during a general election campaign, didn't faze his fellow conservatives Buchanan and Agnew. The Goodell lesson was not lost on Republicans around the country: Nixon favored the new conservatives. The White House was not interested in a Republican party that welcomed various views and types. Loyalty to the party meant loyalty to Nixon *and* the new conservatives' view of the world.

Buckley's victory stimulated the growth of the New Majoritarian strategy nationally. By defeating Goodell, the new conservatives had proved that the party could reach beyond old guard Republicans and attract Democrats by using selected social issue messages—for example, patriotism in the case of the Vietnam War, implying that only degenerate types like hippies would oppose their own government at war; or sexual "abnormality," as the Jorgenson analogy connoted. They had succeeded brilliantly in undermining the moderates in New York State.

Nelson Rockefeller was elected to an unprecedented fourth term as governor that same November, but the new conservatives had established a beachhead in the nation's most populous centrist Republican state. When Rockefeller couldn't even protect his own nominee for U.S. Senate from his former nemesis the Goldwaterites, the tide shifted against him. He was never again to wield major influence in a national party convention. It was a major blow to the moderate wing of the national Republican party, crippling its ability to mount a serious counterforce to the new conservatives in California, Texas, and Florida.

Still, despite the conspicuousness of the New York upset, most of the changes favoring the new conservatives came about gradually, and much of their agenda, both political and social, remained obscure to the general public. As the Republicans convened in Miami two years later, we who were members of the new National Women's Political Caucus arrived filled with optimism. In 1972 old guard conservatives like Congressmembers Gerald Ford and John Rhodes and Kansas senator Robert Dole supported women's rights, as did moderates such as Illinois senator Charles Percy and the GOP leader of the Senate, Hugh Scott of Pennsylvania. None of us dreamed that before long the party would deliberately embrace a political strategy directly hostile toward women.

To the uninitiated, political conventions often seem like a circus where people wearing silly hats and sporting campaign buttons spend hours going to parties, falling asleep during political speeches, and giving interviews to reporters about the merits of their state's most famous product and its candidate of the moment. This characterization is wrong. Behind the fluff and nonsense, deadly serious business takes place that affects not only the party's future but the nation's destiny. No matter how many times candidates engage in what sound like nitpicking debates over wording or make light of platforms, these statements of the party's promises and dreams set the tone for campaigns and, if the party wins, for how it will govern. Not every promise is kept, but those that are fought over and triumph at the convention—the ones that attract the most attention—are invariably translated into the party's governing agenda.

Rules are also important in determining who gets political power. Some rules govern how the party recruits its members and how the convention operates, but the lifeblood for determining the party's presidential nominee springs from rules that set the number of convention delegate votes for each state. The Republican party determines this number by a formula that awards bonus delegates to states that have voted for the Republican presidential candidate and elected Republican governors, members of Congress, and state legislators. The formulas are set at each national convention for the presidential campaign four years hence. Thus the 1972 convention mandated the formulas for the delegates to be chosen in the party's 1976 presidential primaries, state conventions, and caucuses. Those who control the national convention have a built-in advantage in influencing the delegate numbers for their candidate four years hence. To some extent, therefore, they can develop formulas that play to the potential electoral strengths of their candidate.

For most of their party's history, Republicans used delegate formulas rooted in traditional balancing strategies similar to those adopted by the Founding Fathers when they established a states-based U.S. Senate and a population-based House of Representatives. But beginning with Goldwater's nomination in 1964, delegate apportionments at national conventions were increasingly skewed in favor of the more conservative states in the South and West. In 1971 the Ripon Society, a national policy group of moderate Republicans, sued the Republican National Committee to redress this imbalance. The society's aim was to break the ideological slant of the formulas, to attract more participants from urban areas, and to establish a starting place after each election that would open the process more fairly to all ideologies, interests, and regions. In other words, the suit aimed to level the playing field for each new set of Republican presidential contenders.

Robert M. Pennoyer, the society's lawyer who had served in the Eisenhower Justice Department, argued that the formulas by which the party's convention delegates were selected discriminated against the large states and favored the small ones. For example, at the 1972 convention eight states with 49 percent of the country's population were allotted only 37 percent of the delegates, even though Nixon had won 52 percent of these states' votes in 1968. Ripon claimed that to be fair, the delegate formula should balance more equitably a state's population and its Republican voting strength.

The reality underlying the Ripon suit was not arcane: It was about presidential politics. The new conservatives opposed the suit. Led by White and Rusher, they wanted to maintain the formulas favoring the more conservative southern and western states because it would help them secure the 1976 presidential nomination for Spiro Agnew or Ronald Reagan. The potential moderate candidates—New York's Rockefeller, Michigan's George Romney, and Illinois's Charles Percy—came from states with majority Democratic registrations in their cities, yet they had won impressive numbers of votes in these cities. If the Ripon suit succeeded, it would help the moderates, since it would mean counting in the formulas more people from urban areas who were new to the party, were not necessarily conservatives, and had demonstrated that they would vote for GOP moderates.

Four months before the Miami Beach convention, a federal district court ruled that the old formulas were unconstitutional and placed the convention under injunction to draft new ones. Just before the convention opened, Justice William Rehnquist, who had been a strong Goldwater man before Nixon appointed him to the Supreme Court, stayed the injunction based on an appeal from six western Republican state chairmen. Nevertheless, party rules required that the convention must revise the formulas to fit with the election returns of the past four years, so even as the Republican National Committee was appealing the court's decision, the Miami convention would be deciding the formulas for 1976.

Nixon's people were furious about the suit. They wanted a smooth-running convention. They certainly wanted no trouble from their fellow Republicans. What with the Vietnam War and domestic tumult, the administration was having enough problems. It needed an uncontentious nomination in Miami—a coronation, as some perceived it. But for the moderates looking beyond Nixon to 1976, the stakes were too high to accede to the president's wishes. The battle over the rules formula had to be fought.

It was also a do-or-die proposition for the new conservatives. To agree to Ripon's fair-play approach could easily give moderate Republicans a fighting chance to stave off the conservatives' domination of the national GOP. If the moderates won, they too would seek out the defecting Democrats that Kevin Phillips had identified, but their message would not be antiurban, racist, and sexist, as the new conservatives' was becoming. Their policy for addressing the nation's domestic ills would be to respond to the needs of the cities, minorities, and women.

The formula battle in Miami, called the Rule 30 fight, pitted moderates Romney, Rockefeller, and Percy against new conservatives Reagan of California and John Tower of Texas. It was not a big states–little states confrontation, as it was described by some of the press. In fact, California, Texas, and Florida, three of the most populous states in the union, opposed the big states formula. Although officially Nixon took no position, the full force of the White House was used to crush the moderates, including tapping the telephones of the Ripon operatives —a dirty-tricks practice that, the nation was to discover over the next year, had not been confined to Miami.

From the committees to the convention floor, the Rule 30 fight was hard-fought and harsh. In the end, the moderate reformers were no match for Nixon and his team. The convention turned them down, 910 to 434.

If there was any doubt as to what the Rule 30 battle had been about, one had only to note that new conservative ideologue New York congressmember Jack Kemp, whose state would gain if the convention adopted the moderates' formula rules, was a leader for the small-state, new conservative–backed rules. Needless to say many New York delegates, regardless of their ideology, considered Kemp a Benedict Arnold.

The delegate-formula rules adopted by the convention were advantageous for the southern conservatives because they favored states that had no established Republican party. Thus, the New York Republican party, which at the time of the 1972 convention had the governor, both U.S. senators, twenty-three congressmembers, and majorities in both houses of the state legislature, would get fewer bonus delegates for winning elections than would Louisiana, which had no Republican governor, senators, congressmembers, or state legislature majorities.

Under the new Rule 30, if Nixon won Louisiana by a one-vote margin in 1972 and lost New York by one vote, Louisiana would get at least eleven bonus delegates for the 1976 convention, while New York (with four times the population of Louisiana) would get a maximum of two—and then only if it retained its governor and U.S. senator in the 1974 midterm elections. So much for a level playing field, where presidential contenders of all ideological casts would have a fair chance to slug it out.

The new Rule 30 established the primacy of the new conservatives in delegate selection. In 1976 all Republican challengers for the presidency would still compete in state conventions and primaries, but if they were not part of the new conservative movement, they would now be starting their campaigns with a built-in handicap.

While our moderate friends leading the Rule 30 fight were getting pummeled by the Nixon operatives, the Republican feminists concentrated on passing a set of rules, called DO8, that would broaden participation in the party. DO8 was recommended by a special committee headed by feisty Missourian Rosemary Ginn, a street-smart politician who disarmed her opposition with her wit. Underneath that proper midwestern style, however, was a woman with a feminist streak that would have made Elizabeth Cady Stanton proud.

We thought Nixon's people were too busy with Rule 30 to bother with DO8. Not so. Led by Ginn and Pat Bailey, an Arkansas feminist with a sense of humor that endeared her to even our most tenacious opponents, we struggled through nine days of guerrilla warfare to get DO8 added to Rule 32, known as the convention's antidiscrimination rule. Rule 32 said that the party would "take positive action to achieve the broadest possible participation in party affairs" and that participation could not be limited because of race, religion, color, or national origin. Aha! Sex had been left out.

We chuckled only briefly, however. Instead of pulling off what should have been a relatively easy exercise in adding a few words, we were attacked by new conservative Clarke Reed of Mississippi for applying undemocratic and unfair "quotas." "The broadest possible participation" didn't even remotely mean the imposition of quotas, but Reed and his southern allies were paying no attention to logic. As we would discover with later efforts to bring more women into the party, the rhetoric of the "party of the open door," as the Republican party described itself in the 1972 Rules Committee report, was just that: rhetoric.

During several days of debate in a hot, stuffy, too-small room, Clarke Reed and his Florida friends William Cramer and Paula Hawkins repeatedly declared that there was no need to reform the party. Then a strange thing happened. Gremlins gummed up the proceedings. Each time the Rules Committee voted on a change in DO8, the new version would be sent out to be copied for all the committee members. The phrase "take positive action," which appears in Rule 32, had both a legislative and a legal history related to affirmative action; yet when the copies returned from the Xerox room, the phrase "take positive action" had been mysteriously eradicated and in its place was "strive to achieve," a phrase that had no legal history behind it and thus weakened the rule considerably. The dirty tricksters were at work yet again.

When we found out what happened, Ginn forced another vote to put "take positive action" back into the rules. This time our side won the votes not only of the reformers but of those who were angry that someone was trying to double-cross the committee. Six days later, the convention voted for a new Rule 32 that expanded the "positive action" directive to cover delegate selection that would ensure the broadest possible participation of women, young people, minority and heritage groups, and senior citizens. A separate section singled out women, saying that "each state shall endeavor to have equal representation of men and women in its delegation to the Republican National Convention." The convention also adopted the DO8 suggestion that a committee be created to work with the states to come up with ways to broaden the party under the new Rule 32. This committee became known (somewhat confusingly) as the Rule 29 Committee.

We thought we'd won, even though the new conservatives claimed victory too, since the rules provided no mechanism for enforcement. For the next four years, we would fight with them over how to enforce these rules.

I am often asked why we fought so hard for tiny changes such as these, and what difference it made, since no machinery was in place to enforce Rule 32. But it was through these rules battles that both women and the new conservatives were gathering recruits and power. These skirmishes won us new friends among the women delegates; in turn, the new conservatives made inroads against the old guard and moderate power brokers. In conventions to come, as in the Rule 32 battle, the new conservatives used our efforts to win equity for women as an excuse to label us as not true to conservative principles and thus not to be supported.

But even given its opposition to DO8, the Nixon White House was much friendlier in Miami to the feminist Republicans than to our moderate friends in the Rule 30 fight. Before the convention, Republican National Committee chairman Bob Dole had had no problem in urging the state Republican parties to make half of their delegations women, and CREEP campaign manager John Mitchell had been glad to boast that the Nixon campaign would specifically court women voters. We were glad to hear this, although we observed that these officials provided no party resources to increase the number of women delegates to Miami. It was aggressive organizing by Republican feminists and their sympathetic male colleagues in the states that made the difference. Women constituted 30 percent of the delegates in Miami, an impressive gain over the 17 percent of 1968.

In his first term, Nixon had responded to the demands of the newly vocal women's movement by giving women more opportunities. Barbara Franklin was named to direct the first White House "women's desk"; the president appointed more women to high governmental positions than in any time in U.S. history; and Anne Armstrong, co-chairman of the national party, gave the convention's keynote address, a first for either of the major parties. But when it came to women's issues that might conflict with the goals of the New Majoritarian strategy, the White House was less sympathetic.

What had alerted us to the likelihood of trouble in Miami had come ten months earlier, when Nixon had vetoed the Comprehensive Child Development bill. It was the first major effort by Congress since the Second World War to respond to the nation's child care needs. This Javits–Mondale bill had had broad bipartisan support and was a genuine attempt to come to grips with the nearly twelve million mothers with children under eighteen who had recently joined the labor force. If the president had vetoed the bill solely on grounds of cost, the anger of women and child advocates would not have been quite so strong, but that was not the only reason he gave. Child care threatened family stability by encouraging women to work, Nixon said, and provisions for child care would move the nation away from a family-oriented society.

Republican feminists were startled. We were in the middle of formulating our "wish list" of women's issues to submit to the president's campaign, and here was the president opposing the right of women to choose whether they would work. What also irritated us was that the *Ripon Forum* editorialized strongly in favor of the veto. Many of us were Ripon Society members, and some were officers. We angrily challenged George Gilder, who had written the editorial and eight years later would become the intellectual celebrity of the Reagan administration. We wrote Gilder that "child care should be available for all women who choose to work.

To confine the mobility of one segment of the population, and indeed the majority of the population . . . on the supposed logic that there is not now sufficient employment for the males in our society is rank discrimination and ignores the very cornerstone upon which our democratic society is based.

Child care enhances family stability, we said; it does not destroy it. Feminists all across the country expressed similar outrage at the veto.

This Ripon Society exchange was the first indication many of us had of how difficult our task was to be. It was one thing to hear Strom Thurmond opposed to child care. It was another to learn that not only the president but members of the leading moderate Republican organization thought child care would "destroy" the family.

As noted earlier, abortion had also become an important political issue before Miami. Even though the legalization of abortion in *Roe v. Wade* lay a year and a half in the future, the national leadership of the Catholic Church was pressuring Nixon to do something to curtail it, and he did.

In April 1971 the president put limits on liberalized abortion rules in military hospitals. In May 1972, when a Commission on Population Growth that he had established recommended that states make abortion accessible and family-planning services widely available to teenagers, Nixon rejected these recommendations. He then stepped into New York State politics, directly confronting Governor Rockefeller, who with Republican assemblywoman Constance Cooke had been a prime mover in passing New York's legalized abortion law in 1970. In an unusual step for a president, Nixon sent a public letter to Terence Cardinal Cooke, who was leading a campaign by the New York Archdiocese to repeal the New York law. "I would personally like to associate myself with the convictions you deeply feel and eloquently express," he wrote the cardinal. ". . . Your decision, and that of thousands of Catholics, Protestants, Jews, and men and women of no particular faith as defenders of the right to life of the unborn, is truly a noble endeavor."

Rockefeller, who was Nixon's New York State campaign manager, was furious at this inappropriate meddling in state affairs but circumspect in his public anger. Constance Cooke was not, accurately describing Nixon's letter as a "patent pitch for the Catholic vote."

While Nixon had commented publicly on state and federal judicial decisions on school busing and integration, this was his first public foray into state abortion politics. It signaled that anti-abortion politics was now securely ensconced not only in the New Majoritarian arsenal but in the White House. The genie was out of the bottle. If feminist Republicans hadn't been aware of what was happening when Nixon vetoed the child care bill, his unprecedented interference in New York's abortion law fight should have tipped them off.

Under Nixon's tutelage, the national Republican party was now adopting Phillips's New Majoritarian strategy, using control of women's decisions about whether to go to work or to have a child as a way to win votes from Catholics and conservative southerners, the old New Deal Democratic stalwarts. The strategy deliberately exploited the fear that some of these New Deal Democrats felt about empowering women, just as earlier it had played on their fear of minorities. Fear was the foundation on which the new Republican coalition would be built.

About other issues of concern to women, the White House seemed schizophrenic. It was not quite sure where this new women's force was going. The administration was in bed with the new conservatives but was flirting with us. Indeed, before the convention actually opened, Nixon moved to cooperate with us on the party platform.

NWPC member Bobbie Kilberg was a staff assistant to Nixon's domestic policy chief, John Ehrlichman, and worked with Martin Anderson, who was preparing the draft platform. In a memo written to Anderson two months before the convention, she urged that the president "commit himself to name a woman to the Supreme Court and . . . to the Cabinet . . . [to] pledge the Administration and the Republican Party to an active role" in ratifying the ERA, to accelerate the appointment and promotion of women at all levels, and to commit to day care (despite his veto) and to other recommendations for which we had been lobbying. Her memo made no mention of reproductive rights.

Most male Republican leaders in the northern states responded positively to our call to support the ideas in Kilberg's memo. Our feminist agenda was more comprehensive than that, however. Equity for women was its core. We also wanted support for reproductive rights, extension of the Equal Pay Act, equalization of Social Security benefits, temporary disability benefits for pregnancy and childbirth, and party rules changes that would encourage fuller participation of women and minorities. It was a list that we would find ourselves presenting over and over in the years ahead to an increasingly unresponsive party.

By the time the Miami convention opened, our colleagues in Washington had convinced Nixon's campaign team that supporting opportunities for women was a plus. The printed convention program touted the president's 1972 State of the Union message that "while every woman may not want a career outside the home, every woman should have the freedom to choose whatever career she wishes with equal chance to pursue it." (His comments about the consequences of encouraging women to work when he vetoed the Comprehensive Child Development bill were not included.) The program cited his "unprecedented" leadership in appointing more women to top-level policy positions "than ever before in the nation's history," his support for the ERA, the passage of the 1972 Equal Employment Opportunity Act, the expansion of the 1964 Civil Rights Act to cover sex discrimination, the requiring of affirmative action plans for hiring and promoting women in firms doing business with the government, and the filing of sex-discrimination charges against 350 higher education institutions.

It was a solid list, and the reason we had come to Miami feeling hopeful despite his veto of the child care bill. It seemed to us that by laying out these accomplishments in the program, the campaign team was confirming that the president planned to support many of the goals we were lobbying for.

Moreover, he delivered in Miami. The convention adopted a plank supporting equal rights for women, endorsement of the ERA, commitment to federally aided public and private day care services, equal pay for equal work, and a national commitment to full women's participation at all levels in the political process.

The adoption of the child care provision in the plank was a major achievement. It was the only change made in the Nixon-dictated platform, and it came about because Massachusetts congressmember Margaret Heckler and the rest of the Republican feminists, including Betsy Griffith, Pat Bailey, Connie Newman, Pamela Curtis, Chris Topping, Bobbie Kilberg, Jill Ruckelshaus, and myself, pushed so hard. We got tremendous help from some of the women delegates whom we met for the first time that week. Its passage was a belated recognition by the administration that supporting child care could help the Republicans attract women voters. We hoped they also recognized that the issue went beyond votes—that child care was a problem in serious need of the nation's attention.

The 1972 women's plank is a classic example of how a political party caught up in the throes of a new movement's ideas tries to incorporate them without unduly disturbing the status quo. Since help for child care was the issue George Bush would use in 1988 to win women's votes, it is also worth noting that the 1972 plank, which was both more comprehensive and less specific than Bush's, represented the party's general attitude on the subject until the Religious Right became a significant power in the party eight years later.

The plank's language on child care read:

> We believe the primary responsibility for a child's care and upbringing lies with the family. However, we recognize that for economic and many other reasons many parents require assistance in the care of their children. To help meet this need, we favor the development of publicly or privately run, voluntary, comprehensive, quality day care services, locally controlled but federally assisted, with the requirement that the recipients of these services will pay their fair share of the costs according to their ability. We oppose ill-considered proposals, incapable of being administered effectively, which could heavily engage the Federal Government in this area.

There was, however, a major omission in the plank—reproductive rights were nowhere to be found. A Gallup poll taken around the time of the convention showed that 68 percent of Republicans believed abortion was a decision that should be left to a woman and her doctor, and that omitting it from the platform was consistent with the sense that abortion was a private matter, better left out of politics.

Omitting it from the platform was certainly the wish of Nixon's campaign team, which hoped the issue would go quietly into the night. It didn't, and the Platform Committee heatedly debated the issue but ultimately took no position.

We were new to the politics of women's liberation and thought we should be grateful for what we had won, so we didn't push our pro-choice friends on the Platform Committee to issue a minority report that would have brought the issue to the convention floor and a debate on national television. We certainly had the votes for a minority report. But our big-hitter allies were engaged in the Rule 30 conflict and had no time to help us organize a floor fight. Several pro-choice supporters on the committee told us that while they agreed with us, they didn't want to embarrass the president. (This was a refrain—and an excuse—we were to hear at every convention for the next twenty years.)

Nor were we feminists of one mind on what to do. Some argued that if we succeeded in getting to the floor, we would thereby give "right-to-life" advocates a chance to show their bottles of fetuses on national television, which would hinder the efforts at abortion reform under way in the states. My instinct said this argument was specious, yet I'd spent enough time in Albany the previous May being battered by the right-to-life demonstrators' gruesome props to know my friends had a point. The pro-choice political movement was still in its infancy, and we, along with most of America, hadn't yet gotten used to the ugliness of anti-choice tactics. Nor did we want to scare off potential supporters with a rancorous debate on television. We were still not secure in our own arguments, still uncomfortable talking briskly and openly about women's right to abortion.

I was conflicted. It was one of many times I have found myself torn between making practical political arguments and wanting to stand up for an unwinnable principle. It seemed to me that the individual freedom of women to make their own reproductive choices was bedrock Republican philosophy, yet I truly could not justify taking our fight to the floor only to lose.

We were also becoming vaguely aware that many of our moderate male leaders felt uncomfortable defending women's reproductive freedom. We were not happy with Nixon's position, but we had won an impressive women's plank that refuted his own policy on federally supported child care, while our friends, who included many of the prominent leaders of the party's moderate wing, had suffered a major defeat in the Rule 30 fight. For a neophyte movement, it was a genuine accomplishment.

It was also an illusion. Nixon had already begun to put the social issues agenda of the New Majoritarian strategy in place, but we weren't aware he had done this because, except for reproductive rights, he'd supported all the women's issues we wanted.

Those who were not watching carefully no doubt thought the 1972 Republican convention a rather dull affair, with the party's nominees for president and vice president settled and Nixon's campaign team dictating the party's platform. They were wrong, dead wrong. Two forces of major importance to the nation's future were sparring in the Miami convention arena: the new conservatives and the Republican feminists. Both groups tried different tactics to enhance their strength. Neither was always sure who their friends were, but both were optimistic that the majority of Republican delegates supported their cause. In the middle were Richard Nixon and his team, trying to keep the undercurrents of difference from affecting his reelection, even as he orchestrated the new conservative agenda.

The Rules Committee's preamble said, "Ours is the party of equality for all—favoritism for none." We believed it. We also believed we had time. We resolved to build the Republican women's movement over the next four years and return to the next national convention to make that preamble a reality.

3

THE LINE IS CROSSED

From August to November 1972, Republicans put aside the differences of Miami. Although the term was not yet in wide use, Nixon succeeded in keeping us together under what was truly a big tent, unlike the artifice that Lee Atwater would try to force us under in 1989. In the campaign, the new conservatives and the old guard approvingly watched the president ridicule George McGovern's "new politics" of, in Charlie Black's words, "acid, amnesty, and abortion." (Black, who was one of the architects of the New Right, became a major player in the politics of misogyny in the seventies and eighties.) In fact, Nixon did such a skillful job of attacking the Democrats that the University of Michigan Center for Political Studies concluded that America was more polarized ideologically by Election Day than at any time since the thirties.

Everyone worked for the Nixon–Agnew ticket. It was the last time that a Republican presidential nominee would be enthusiastically embraced by all wings of his party. Nixon kept Republicans unified by giving something to everyone, though some got more than others. The new conservatives were pleased he privately backed their social agenda. The old guard and moderates believed they had a foothold in international trade issues and foreign policy, and feminists thought he would implement the promises of the women's plank.

Nixon achieved a knockout victory. His electoral vote margin—520 electoral votes to McGovern's 17—was greater than FDR's historic 1936 landslide and Lyndon Johnson's in 1964. His popular vote, a truer barometer of the country's enthusiasm for a candidate, was also impressive: 60.59 percent, compared with 60.79 percent for FDR in 1936 and 61.05 percent for Johnson.

Having won so decisively, the president now believed he had a mandate to implement the policies of the New Majoritarian strategy: to take the nation in a more conservative direction—at least on social issues—and to build a new, more conservative Republican party. Immediately after Thanksgiving, he removed all those in his administration who he thought might stand in his way, weeding out moderate and old guard Republicans.

This move for ideological purity proved to be politically foolish. Back in June, five men linked to his campaign had been arrested for breaking into the Democratic National Committee's Watergate headquarters. Headline news for a while, it had faded from attention during the fall; but it was now turning into a major national scandal. By Christmas, Nixon and his immediate staff were obsessed with covering up the White House's engineering of the break-in. They needed those they had fired not only to run the government but to help present a respectable face to an American public shaken and confused by this man it had just reelected in a landslide to the highest office in the land.

The efforts at cover-up did not succeed, and on May 17, 1973, the Senate Watergate Committee, chaired by North Carolina Democrat Sam Ervin and Tennessee Republican Howard Baker, began nationally televised hearings on the break-in. For the next fourteen months, the country was mesmerized by the unraveling scandal and more and more disillusioned at each new revelation of Nixon's disregard for the public trust.

Watergate was not the only betrayal, however. As we Republican women were discovering, Nixon's backing for the women's plank had been a facade—pragmatic politics that he had no intention of implementing.

In March 1972, five months before the Miami convention, congressional Republicans had joined their Democratic colleagues in overwhelmingly approving an Equal Rights Amendment and starting the process for ratification by the states. Regardless of party, the majority of the nation backed women's equality. Nixon acknowledged this reality in Miami. To oppose the feminists at the convention—with the exception of the abortion issue—would have disturbed his carefully constructed unity tent and given Democrats grounds to label him anti-women.

But as soon as the election was over, the facade collapsed. Nixon did not implement the women's plank. The new conservative movement had always had a subculture of New Right men and women who opposed women's rights, but they had not been in charge. With the president moving the Republican party in a more conservative direction, they now began to play a major role.

Not everyone in the New Right was hostile to women's rights; far from it. Many were pro-choice. Others backed women's equity in credit, employment, and education and in retirement and insurance benefits. But they now put aside their personal feelings in support of the New Right's advancement and vigorously opposed the ERA, affirmative action, and reproductive rights.

The New Right is an amalgam of individuals and structures that Ripon Society founder Jack Saloma aptly termed the conservative labyrinth. Its activist arm—the political action groups—did the nitty-gritty organizing in the Republican party and were most directly responsible for bringing the New Right to power. They raised large sums of money through direct mail that not only funded their work but made some of the organizers millionaires. The most initially successful of the New Right leaders was Richard Viguerie, a former fund-raiser for the Young Americans for Freedom. (YAF had been started by William F. Buckley and Rusher to recruit young people into the new conservative movement.) Viguerie had raised "about $7 million" to retire George Wallace's 1972 presidential campaign debt, and in the mid-seventies, with other new conservatives, would try to "create a Reagan–Wallace third party ticket" to seduce conservatives into leaving the Republicans. He originated the direct-mail operations for the New Right, and the huge, brilliantly targeted mailing lists that he built brought in a continuing flow of money. Other financial support came from corporations such as Dart Industries and the Adolph Coors Brewery, and wealthy individuals like Richard Mellon Scaife and William Simon, who was to become Gerald Ford's treasury secretary.

Intellectual ammunition for the misogynist messages came from the New Right's think tanks. The Heritage Foundation, founded in 1973 by Joseph Coors and Paul Weyrich, who was a younger, more radical version of Bill Rusher, became the most influential of these think tanks, offering New Right views on a wide variety of subjects, from why child care is wrong to how affirmative action undermines the integrity of women and minorities. The think tanks packaged these messages for New Right public officials like North Carolina senator Jesse Helms and Illinois congressmember Henry Hyde, who in turn introduced them into Republican policy through legislation or party platforms at state and national conventions.

All this gave momentum to the New Right early in Nixon's second administration, but its incursions slowed, and the Republican party's moderate and old guard wings got a break when in yet another scandal Vice President Spiro Agnew, a New Right idol, resigned on October 10, 1973, and pleaded nolo contendere to a charge of tax evasion for money he had been paid by building contractors when he was governor of Maryland.

In the months before his resignation, the Watergate investigation had exploded with devastating new revelations and charges of obstruction of justice. By now, Nixon recognized that he needed a friend who was respected in a Congress that might try to impeach him, and two days after Agnew's resignation, he appointed Michigan congressmember Gerald Ford to be vice president.

Ford had solid old guard credentials and brought in like-minded pragmatists for his staff. Over at the Republican National Committee (RNC), another old guard type, George Bush, became chairman and did what he could to counteract the damage Watergate was inflicting on the party. The Republicans needed fresh sources of support, so Bush reopened the "positive action" debate by appointing Wisconsin congressmember William Steiger to head the Rule 29 Committee mandated at the 1972 convention. It was the second act of Rosemary Ginn's DO8 work to broaden the party. The much-maligned reforms for which we'd taken so much heat in Miami were now being given another chance because some positive image–building was needed.

All through the spring and summer of 1974, as the Senate Watergate Committee and the special prosecutor closed in on Nixon, Rule 29 Committee meetings were held to learn grassroots Republicans' thoughts on how to broaden the party's base.

But if the New Right's momentum had slowed, it was not quiescent during those meetings. The party's door was not closed, new conservatives maintained, so there should be no rules to mandate its opening.

We argued that while the door had not been locked, it did not look sufficiently inviting, and that the Steiger committee should seek ways to show that all Americans were welcome. The conflict between these two points of view came to a head at a Rule 29 meeting in St. Louis in mid-June. Margaret Heckler and Missouri governor Christopher Bond led our group in looking for ways to attract women, minorities, and young people to the party. As Heckler pointed out, the dusted-off DO8 proposals were not quotas but a way "to provide an 'internal mechanism' so that the GOP can see itself as others see it. If we have a party of white middle-aged males, we should be the first to recognize it, rather than to have someone else point it out to us."

This was not what New Right leader Clarke Reed was interested in hearing. He tried to stop us, joined by his comrade-in-arms, Maryland academic Donald Devine, who had already shown a zest for sexist invective and who, during the Reagan administration, would execute one of its first attacks against affirmative action. Raising the same arguments that their side had perfected in Miami, Reed and Devine warned that "positive action" measures would "McGovernize" the party and impose quotas.

As Lou Cannon of *The Washington Post* reported, this argument was absurd. But as he also pointed out, the Rule 29:

> proposal would, if adopted, thrust the Republican party into active recruitment of minority groups whose affiliation with the Democratic party is now taken mostly for granted.

That was indeed the point. The chief target of the New Right's scare tactics on "quotas" was white males, whom they wished to convince that they would lose power if new groups won party leadership. Women were one of the groups to be feared, though the New Right was too canny to spell this out. Heckler's logic fell on deaf ears. Steiger's Rule 29 Committee deadlocked and postponed further action until December.

Until the 1976 convention, the New Right fought with the Republican feminists over the differences between sincere outreach efforts and the definition of quotas. *Human Events,* a longtime far-right publication, claimed the reformers wanted to move the Republican party to the left. We didn't care about left or right or center; we simply wanted it opened to people who weren't white, male, and middle-aged. It apparently never occurred to the New Right that some of these people—women and minorities, young and old—might actually support their views. But the New Right was not interested in sharing power—all that mattered was holding on to what they had.

In later years some New Rightists would come to see the value of including women and minorities in their leadership. Thomas Sowell, a black academic, became an accepted and respected voice for them during the Reagan–Bush years. The appointments of Sandra Day O'Connor to the Supreme Court and Jeane Kirkpatrick as ambassador to the United Nations were of a similar vein. But back in 1974, it was hard to find anyone in the New Right who was interested in bringing women into leadership positions in their movement. The one exception was Phyllis Schlafly. By dint of her strength, perspicacity, and close association with the Catholic hierarchy, she forced her colleagues to pay attention to her. Still, not even Schlafly ever got the high-level appointment in the Reagan administration that her hard work and contributions to the New Majoritarian revolution warranted.

On July 27 and 29, 1974, the House Judiciary Committee recommended three articles of impeachment against Richard Nixon. On August 9 he resigned, leaving the nation with a sorely damaged faith in the presidency. Gerald Ford was sworn in immediately but one month later pardoned Nixon unconditionally for all crimes he "committed or may have committed" while president. It was more than the emotionally battered nation could take. Voter turnout for the midterm elections that November was the lowest since 1946, and the results for Republicans were disastrous.

But it was an interestingly selective disaster, as more careful scrutiny suggests. The ax fell chiefly on old guard and new conservatives. As Charles Bartlett of the *Chicago Sun-Times* wrote, "The lesson of the election for Republicans is that the truck hit almost no one who was standing in the middle of the road. . . . Republicans running on moderate records won crucial struggles for the votes of middle-class suburbanites."

Bartlett's overall analysis was correct, but there was one loss for moderates that was indeed disastrous. By a margin of 51 to 49 percent, Democrat Jerry Brown defeated moderate Republican Houston

Flournoy for the California governorship. With Flournoy's defeat, the leadership of the California Republicans reverted back to those rightists who had gained power over the state party when Goldwater had won the California GOP primary in 1964.

This 1974 election marked the political women's movement's first serious venture into electoral politics. Its gains were modest. Feminists of both parties battered their heads against the cold reality of modern political life—incumbency. Outsider women had no more success defeating incumbents than outsider men. We had preached that women would jar loose the hold that incumbents had on elected offices. Our message was wishful thinking. Women, it turned out, did not have the magic formula after all. Watergate and individual scandal were the only issues that seemed to defeat incumbents in 1974. Gender was a minor factor at most.

Incumbency was not the only cold political reality. Although women had a far better chance of winning office for open seats—ones not held by incumbents—most of the nominations for open seats in both parties did not go women's way. If you were a Republican woman, it didn't matter where you hailed from: the new conservatives, the old guard, or the party's moderate wing. The guys in power treated you identically—they were glad to have you on board, but only for the seats they knew were unwinnable.

There were occasional exceptions, of course. Out of fifty women running for statewide office in November 1974, nineteen were winners, all in open seats. Connecticut Democrat Ella Grasso won her gubernatorial race and became the first American woman elected governor in her own right. Two Republican women, both with long professional experience, were elected to Congress, also in open seats: Millicent Fenwick, a sixty-four-year-old New Jersey feminist who would emerge as a Republican leader for ERA and abortion rights, and Virginia Smith, sixty-three, an old guard Nebraska conservative who had led the American Farm Bureau Women for twenty years.

Infuriating as they were, the 1974 elections were instructive. Afterward, the women's political movement became smarter. We expanded our infrastructure. We had begun to build it after 1972, when those of us who had worked to recruit women delegates and candidates discovered that except for a few who had worked in partisan campaigns over the years, the newly activated women knew nothing about the mechanics of politics. To educate these women and to teach them how to win elections and public appointments, the bipartisan National Women's Education Fund (NWEF), an offshoot of the NWPC, was formed in 1973.

We believed in the importance of a bipartisan women's movement to accomplish our goals. Democratic and Republican women had their differences, and in 1973 and 1974 we Republicans found ourselves in frequent debate with some of our Democratic feminist colleagues, who in their anger over Watergate, Vietnam, and Nixon's attacks on abortion often had a difficult time accepting our arguments. Some of them helped us raise money and provided other resources for our Republican effort. Others wouldn't. Before long, we found it advisable to set up our own party task forces within the bipartisan structure to accommodate our different ways of doing things. But basically our differences lessened over the years; it was a waste to fight among ourselves when we needed all our time and energy for the ERA and abortion battles.

After 1974, to the bipartisan NWPC and NWEF, we now added the Women's Campaign Fund (WCF), with Betsy Griffith leading the Republican effort. The WCF's sole purpose was to raise money so women could run their campaigns independent of party bosses and, when necessary, run primaries. In addition, the Center for the American Woman and Politics, a nonpartisan think tank and resource center that had been formed in 1971 under the able direction of Ida Schmertz, expanded and selected the equally able Ruth Mandel to be its first executive director. The think tank would become a vital intellectual center for our political movement, chronicling the rise of women's political power.

While this array of organizations can begin to sound like alphabet soup, an infrastructure is in fact indispensable to an effective political movement. We were creating ours. The New Right had grown out of the new conservative movement, which in turn had sprung from the Goldwater campaign. They had the advantage of a ten-year head start on us. They had publications, membership organizations, an impressive direct-mail operation, a think tank, wealthy contributors, and a team of operatives who had been working conventions since their early days in Young Republican politics. If we were to contend with them effectively and build women's political power, we had a lot of catching up to do.

.   .   .

Under Gerald Ford, the New Right was not doing well. Their progress toward taking over the party skidded to a halt with Nixon's departure. Now they had not only Gerald Ford to contend with but his vice president, the loathed Nelson Rockefeller. On top of that, George Bush, who'd always made it his business to be cordial to every wing of the party, had walked away from the chairmanship of the Republican National Committee before the 1974 election debacle and gone off to China to head the newly opened U.S. liaison office in Beijing. His successor was the RNC co-chairman, moderate Mary Louise Smith. None of these leaders had any sympathy for the New Right's agenda.

Smith had the unenviable task of trying to salvage what little political goodwill was left for Republicans. It was a no-win situation, a fact that had surely not been lost on George Bush when he had cut and run. A salvage operation was not a challenge that a future presidential candidate like Bush wanted on his résumé.

A longtime Iowa Republican, Smith had served the party honorably for more than forty years. As a close friend of Bush, Ford, and other members of the old guard establishment, she sprang from the party's pragmatic tradition and was not an ideologue. She was experienced, professional, and skilled and was respected for her astute political sense. The establishment thought she could do a capable job of negotiating around the demands of the zealots and keeping the party together.

When Smith, a trim woman with a neat halo of gray hair, arrived in Washington in September, she promptly confronted a sexist press. Her Democratic counterpart, Robert Strauss, was about the same age as she, but he was always described in dynamic, youthful terms. Smith was routinely identified as the gray-haired grandmother from Iowa, and at an early press conference, she was asked whether she had ever thought of dyeing her hair and why her husband had let her come to Washington alone. Nor was the sexist nastiness limited to the press. After the elections, when the Republicans were angered at the losses they'd sustained, a White House aide speaking off the record said that "the Republican National Committee needs to get back its manhood." No one remarked that it wasn't Smith who had caused Watergate, or noted that Bush had sped off to China just as the fall campaign was gearing up.

Would Republicans have gotten their first woman RNC chairman if Watergate hadn't happened? I doubt it. The truth is that the party was lucky to have such a willing soldier to step in and stanch the bleeding. It was a sacrificial role that women had been performing for a long time.

Smith's job proved to be very difficult. It would seem logical to expect those who had backed her selection to support her in the Herculean task of turning the party around. Not so. Smith, for example, saw changing the party's image as an urgent priority; a Market Opinion Research poll had indicated that only 18 percent of the American public were Republicans. So she announced a $2 million advertising program to begin the process. But instead of applauding her efforts, the moderates and old guard—her own constituency—carped that the money should be spent for other things.

Even worse, Smith was surrounded by a New Right, bloodied but unbowed, that had managed to staff the leadership of the RNC with their own people. Virginian Richard Obenshain, a strong advocate of the New Majoritarian strategy, had become co-chairman, and the general counsel was Floridian William Cramer, who had argued in opposition to Ripon's delegate litigation. Streetwise new conservative operative Eddie Mahe, Jr., an original Draft Goldwater man, was executive director.

Gerald Ford might have been more helpful to Smith had he not had his own hands full with the New Right. They were moving in on their ideological opponents with a vengeance, and women were a particular target. Pat Buchanan proclaimed that "the people . . . are unenthusiastic about militant women," while Bill Rusher criticized Ford's "recent cordial nods toward the black caucus, women's lib, and the draft-dodgers." A New Right colleague of Viguerie, Howard Phillips, even attacked the League of Women Voters, an organization generally thought to be too sedate, too above-the-fray, to warrant ideological criticism. Under these assaults, the harried president found himself juggling counterpressures from women and the right: He backed the ERA and encouraged Republican women to participate in the 1975 International Women's Year (IWY) Conference in Mexico City, while quietly opposing abortion and Steiger's Rule 29 Committee reforms.

As the attacks on women escalated, feminists of both parties decided it was time to organize independent power bases within the parties themselves. The idea had developed out of discussions we'd had with our Democratic counterparts on the National Women's Education

Fund board. We had the same goals, but we were all finding our work on interparty problems to be strained and difficult within the NWPC. The Democrats had their way of doing things, and we had ours. We found them more disorganized and raucous; they found us more formal and staid. We tended to be less confrontational and more structured.

The result was the formation of the Republican Women's Task Force in Washington on April 18, 1975. The Democrats formed a similar group. These task forces would be affiliated with the NWPC, but each would set its own goals and strategies for its party. This splitting-off was a necessary recognition that feminists had to fight their own battles within their parties in their own ways. It was a sign that the political women's movement was maturing. Sisterhood didn't require being nonpartisan. We could acknowledge our party differences in culture and style without forfeiting our shared commitments.

Our Republican tigers from the Miami wars, Heckler and Ginn (whom Ford would later appoint ambassador to Luxembourg), convened the birthing of the NWPC Republican Women's Task Force. Thirty-eight of us came from all over the country to elect Pat Goldman as chair and lay out plans to confront the New Right and storm the Republican establishment. But we did our planning quietly: We made no attacks against Rusher, Viguerie, and Buchanan, used no shrill rhetoric. We'd elect women delegates to the 1976 national convention, find women to run for office, see that the party kept an effective Rule 32, back the Steiger committee, and above all work for the ERA. Our approach was deliberately low-key. We announced we'd work with existing Republican groups—a signal meant to let the National Federation of Republican Women know we were their partners—and reach out to those "not now involved in partisan politics." We had no intention of giving the New Right ammunition to label us radical "women's libbers." They may have been out to stop us, but as Clarke Reed told Bobbie Kilberg, "women are the only ones who give me a run for my money."

It was urgent, we knew, to get organized. The political landscape was now ready for the New Right to begin their presidential campaign for Ronald Reagan.

4

AN EMBOLDENED NEW RIGHT

Gerald Ford announced his presidential candidacy on July 8, 1975, and one week later the Reagan for President Committee was officially formed in Reagan's home state of California, an ideal base from which to launch his delegate hunt in a challenge to President Ford.

From the time he appointed Nelson Rockefeller vice president, Ford had been politically hamstrung by Reagan's operatives. Not even the power of the presidency could protect him from the New Right's stratagems. The crowning insult came when his own campaign manager, Howard "Bo" Callaway, an original member of the Draft Goldwater team whom Ford had deliberately brought in to be his link with the New Right, told Ford that if he wanted to appease them, he should drop Rockefeller from the 1976 ticket. Rockefeller protested. Ford wavered. First he asked him to stay, then he changed his mind. Rockefeller handled the ignominy with dignity and took himself out of the running for vice president after the November 1975 elections.

Many New York Republicans were shaken by Ford's capitulation. His unwillingness to stick with Rockefeller, they believed, would only encourage the right to demand still more. Maryland senator Charles Mathias charged that Ford had become "a captive of the Reagan right." But Ford's yielding made no difference to the right. Two weeks after Rockefeller withdrew, Ronald Reagan declared his candidacy.

Those of us who lived outside the Beltway found the increasing New Right influence on the party far more unsettling than did our feminist colleagues in Washington. They were working for Ford's nomination and for a platform endorsing the ERA and other women's issues (except for reproductive rights), and they were encouraged by the number of high-level women in his administration. Carla Hills was HUD secretary; Air Force general Jeanne Holm was special assistant to the president for women; Bobbie Kilberg was an associate White House counsel; Jill Ruckelshaus was presiding officer of the nation's IWY commission that Ford had established after the 1975 UN-sponsored women's conference in Mexico City, and her husband, Bill, was rumored to be a serious contender to be Ford's running mate.

All these appointments led the Washington women to believe that Ford would be even more supportive of women's issues at the 1976 Kansas City convention than Nixon had purported to be in 1972. Look at Ford's record, they said. And through the task force's activities and the continuing national interest of women in women's issues, we reasoned, we ourselves would be a greater political force at the 1976 convention than in 1972. Ford would help us, because drawing public attention to our agenda would bring him women's votes in November.

Well, maybe. We did have doubts. Ford wasn't Nixon—far from it —but it was hard to forget that the promises made in the 1972 plank had been abrogated as soon as the election was over. But none of us had any doubts about Betty Ford; we all agreed we had a strong ally in this remarkable and refreshing first lady. The previous August she had endeared herself to much of the nation, not only to feminists, with a forthright *60 Minutes* interview, in which she had taken to task some of the New Right's social stands. She made it clear that she supported legalized abortion and the ERA, suggested premarital sex might cut the divorce rate, and said she would not condemn her daughter if she had an affair. She was lively, engaging, and blunt, so different from the withdrawn Pat Nixon, and she clearly had no compunction about taking controversial positions. But much as her outspokenness was admired, it also made her an easy target for the New Right and their constituency. As the weeks passed and Ford continued to acquiesce to New Right pressures, we realized that his honest wife was being used against him. A subtle but distinct message was coming through from the right that if the president would tolerate "that kind of woman," just how "moral" could *he* be?

They attacked her unmercifully. One of the nation's most extreme and vitriolic New Rightists, New Hampshire newspaper publisher William Loeb of the *Manchester Union-Leader,* said that "the immorality of Mrs. Ford's remarks is almost exceeded by their utter stupidity." To his credit, Ford never apologized or refuted his wife's opinions, and she never stopped speaking out or actively working for women's issues. Years later, when the same right-wingers started in on Hillary Clinton, I remembered what they'd tried to do to Betty Ford.

There was no question that Gerald Ford was under siege within his own party. The stakes for 1976 had greatly changed. The New Right had an attractive candidate in Ronald Reagan. If they got the political upper hand, they would demand acceptance of their social agenda. What they needed was a hot-button social issue that they could use to differentiate Reagan from Ford.

One inflammatory issue had evaporated in April 1975, when Americans were evacuated from Saigon and the war finally ended. Another New Right tactic, making frequent insinuations about World War II naval officer Ford's patriotism for suggesting amnesty for draft evaders, faded with the end of the war as well. The New Right's support of the National Rifle Association (NRA) position on gun control was not a source of controversy, since Ford and the party supported it too. That left women and race as the hot-button issues. No matter what Ford's personal feelings were on women's equity, no matter how much he respected his wife's views, he would have a hard time helping our cause when the New Right continually baited him for it.

The race issue would not surface until the presidential primaries of 1976. The attack on women came first, and it was formidable. In the off-year elections of 1975, the women's movement suffered a fateful defeat, one that enhanced the New Right's growing power and pushed Ford even further into their camp.

There were two ERA struggles going on at this time. One was the campaign to convince state legislatures to ratify the constitutional amendment that had been passed by the House in 1971 and the Senate in 1972. The other was to get states to pass their own ERA laws—with the wording differing from state to state but their essence similar—to prohibit government discrimination on the basis of sex. The New Jersey and New York legislatures had easily ratified the national ERA in 1972, and when both states put referenda for their state ERAs on the ballot for Election Day 1975, the conventional wisdom was that these would pass just as easily.

Instead, the campaigns in both states turned into circuses. The New Right, with Phyllis Schlafly—now the unchallenged national leader of the antiratification forces—a solid player on their team, was out to prove that opposing women's rights could win votes, further erode moderate Republican power in these states, and consolidate their own power. Schlafly also worked to defeat the ERA because she believed it would undermine the family and women's roles as homemakers.

Perversely, Schlafly herself fit the feminist model of a self-assured woman with a cause, who speaks out and organizes for what she believes regardless of traditional constraints. Gender was no impediment to Schlafly. She personified the feminist ideal that a woman can take charge of her life and follow her dreams. It didn't matter that her actions and her beliefs stood in harsh contradiction. The logical extension of her fierce convictions that women should stay home would have been to hew to the role of homemaker. If she had truly succeeded in achieving her political goals, she would have had no place in American politics.

Schlafly had recognized astutely that fear of the women's movement—and the ERA—was rooted in its position that women should be free to choose their own destinies. Unleashing the traditional constraints, she observed, was a first step toward the destruction of the family and ultimately the nation. Her first public attack on the ERA had come in her national newsletter in February 1972, one month before the Senate approved the ERA and sent it to the states for ratification. "Women's lib is a total assault on the role of the American woman as wife and mother and on the family as the basic unit of society," she wrote. "Women's libbers are trying to make wives and mothers unhappy with their career, make them feel they are 'second-class citizens' and 'abject slaves.' " Schlafly polished this family values theme to a high sheen, and as the years passed it became part of Republican rhetoric.

According to Schlafly's husband, Fred, the idea to mount an attack on the ERA originated with him. Their marriage was a strong one, not only in the bonds of traditional domesticity but in its intellectual vitality. A Harvard-trained corporate lawyer, Fred Schlafly had married Phyllis when she was twenty-four and he thirty-nine. Her political gifts had already been in evidence before she reached twenty-one. She had graduated from Washington University in three years and had a master's degree from Radcliffe by the time Schlafly sought her out. He had read a bank newsletter that she wrote describing the possible socialist tendencies of Illinois senator Paul Douglas, and he shared her alarm.

Phyllis Schlafly has always maintained that her sole occupation is housewife, yet Fred Schlafly has been the perfect feminist husband, freeing her to follow her nonhousewifely ambitions. He supported his wife financially, psychologically, and intellectually in what she wished to do. *Chicago Tribune* political reporter Dorothy Collins summed up their relationship: "He married her for her spunk and he let her do her thing and she's very fond of him."

It is not surprising, then, that he launched his wife's antifeminist career. "At first she did not see it [the ERA] as a threat," Fred Schlafly said. "She was more concerned about the military threat of the Soviet Union. But as it raced ahead I was able to convince her of its dangers. . . . The Amendment has a very good name—I think girls ought to have equal rights, too. But in the entire history of the world nobody has won any wars using female soldiers."

As early as September 1972, Schlafly had organized anti-ERA workshops, for which she recruited fundamentalist and evangelical women, some of them John Birch Society members. As the years passed, these workshops expanded into state conferences and chapters of Schlafly's national STOP ERA organization. Long before the birth of the Moral Majority, Schlafly's women of the Religious Right had become fixtures in the capitols of southern states, where they clutched their Bibles and exhorted legislators to understand that "women weren't meant by the Lord to be equal." At that time, these women *were* the organized Religious Right.

Conventional wisdom links the entrance of the Religious Right into national politics with the presidential nomination of born-again Christian Jimmy Carter in 1976. But it was Schlafly, with her authoritarian leadership and expert grassroots organizing, who made the Religious Right a political player in the three years preceding Carter's nomination.

It was Schlafly, first of the Goldwater and then the New Right team, who unearthed the political gold of misogyny. It was Schlafly who translated fear of women's liberation into a political force in the Republican party and thereby extended the foundation of the Republican southern strategy. Now not only did the strategy flourish on the back-lash of the civil rights movement, but it was broadened to include a backlash against the women's movement too.

Not surprisingly, Schlafly's greater effort and greatest successes came in the South: Not a single southern state legislature ratified the ERA. Money to finance the activities of her religious women came not only from individuals but from their churches—the same churches that would later swell the coffers of the Religious Right armies of Jerry Falwell and Pat Robertson.

Before 1976, New Right leaders gave Schlafly little help or attention, but well before that she had a most important ally in North Carolina senator Sam Ervin, the Democrat of Watergate fame and a household symbol of unimpeachable integrity.

A hero to many Americans, Ervin was hailed by one Schlafly activist as "one man who stood against the fanatic, mindless, angry temper of the times." As chairman of the Senate Watergate hearings, he had confronted the corruption of the Nixon White House and won. Even without Watergate, his honorable reputation required that one listen to his views with respect. It was out of genuine conviction that Ervin rejected the feminist notion that women were restricted in their opportunities because of stereotypes; instead, he glorified those stereotypes as the essence of womanhood. His arguments were seductive to those women who didn't wish to give up what they perceived to be their privileges as women. To them, he made decent sense out of a confusing time. He seemed a moral man. With his courtly, grandfatherly ways, he looked and sounded like the very opposite of a misogynist. The perplexed women and men who didn't want to find themselves defined as anti-women did not consider themselves bigots because they opposed the ERA. Ervin provided assurance that hostility to the ERA was a respectable stance; he gave them peace of mind.

Ervin was not a New Rightist. In principle and style, he was the antithesis of that other senator from North Carolina, Jesse Helms—a onetime Democrat turned Republican who used rabble-rousing words in a deliberate effort to frighten people. Ervin was civil and courteous and used logic to make his points.

His early assistance to Schlafly was invaluable. Donald Mathews and Jane Sherron DeHart, who wrote about the ERA struggle in North Carolina in their book *Sex, Gender, and the Politics of the ERA,* said he "even placed his franking privilege at her disposal," and Ervin's office became a "national clearing house" for anti-ERA propaganda to state legislators and STOP ERA activists. According to their analysis, Ervin's philosophy toward women encapsulated the attitude of many who opposed the ERA. "As he expected politicians to act like gentlemen, he expected women to act like ladies. . . . When he tried to inscribe their 'proper' role—'homemakers and mothers'—into the Constitution, he did, to be sure, betray an insensitivity to women's position as great as that relating to blacks, but he meant it as a tribute."

Ervin's arguments touched on a central problem for the feminist cause, not only in the South but in all parts of the country where race had become an open political sore. From the evangelical preachers of Oklahoma to the sheriffs of Alabama, many viewed the fight for women's equal rights in the same framework as they had viewed the civil rights battles of the sixties: "The minister who argued that his church's tax-exempt status would be endangered if he would not perform 'homosexual marriages' under ERA was thinking of the Internal Revenue Service's policy of denying such status to all-white 'Christian' academies." Those ERA opponents who believed family life had been undermined by government's "forced busing" in the name of equality now "feared the government would come further into the family under cover of sexual equality." During the ERA hearings in North Carolina, one woman pleaded not to "desexegrate us," while another had said, "forced busing, forced mixing, forced hiring. Now forced women. No thank you." The road to gender equality sounded too much like the road to racial equality.

The pro-ERA message was misinterpreted by many southerners, who thought the federal government was destroying the things they held most dear—their families, their wives and husbands, their homes, their traditional way of life. After ten years of painful racial strife, some women were particularly frightened of what government would do to their daughters and to themselves. They could not comprehend—or didn't want to—that constitutional protection against gender discrimination could help them improve their lives. They were frightened to face an unknown future that might offer new opportunity but at an unknown and unknowable cost. No matter how unsatisfactory the present might be, it seemed safer not to change it. These women didn't consider themselves sexists; they just preferred things the way they were. There were haters too, but they were the minority. Most of those Schlafly recruited were simply afraid.

In 1976 Ervin announced his retirement from the Senate, and Schlafly shifted her working allegiance to Helms. With this partnership, Schlafly brought Religious Right women and their male allies under the New Right's umbrella three years before Weyrich, Viguerie, and Howard Phillips formed a political alliance with Jerry Falwell and his coreligionists, resulting in the Moral Majority. While she kept her organization independent from them and did not share her mailing lists, she had performed a powerful organizational feat by linking her movement to theirs. Accounts of the marriage of the New Right with the Religious Right have never given Schlafly the credit she deserves. It is ironic indeed that an antifeminist woman would be a prime mover in strengthening a movement aimed at keeping down women like her and then would not even receive adequate recognition for doing so from her ideological comrades.

In New York and New Jersey that fall, all the elements of the misogynist strategy came into play, and Schlafly was a prime mover. Just as in the South, the strategy in these states targeted those alarmed by the changes they were seeing in the traditional roles of men and women. It stirred up fear of the unknown—always easy to do in a campaign—by warning that a legal guarantee against gender discrimination was the first step in depriving women of their "special" place in society. It was a much thornier task for proponents of state ERAs to convince frightened voters that the ERAs would benefit women and harm none of them.

As the campaigns began, public opinion surveys in both states showed ample support for their ERAs, echoing the national polls on the Equal Rights Amendment to the Constitution. But polls reflect support for a concept, an abstraction. This struggle wasn't about abstractions. It was about what the ERA would actually *do,* how the lives of women would be changed by its passage. It was in the specifics that the real debate over the goals of the women's movement unfolded and the messages of misogyny were spelled out.

The anti-ERA campaign's first line of attack was to distort how the ERA would affect the rights that women presently had, as well as how it would affect the family. Annette Stern, a suburban New Yorker who called herself a traditional housewife in the Schlafly mode, organized a coalition called Operation Wake Up, whose mission, she said, was to defend women from the avalanche of broken homes the ERA would bring. You'd lose custody of your children in a divorce, she told them. Your husband wouldn't be required to support you, and if you got a divorce, there'd be nothing to force him to give you alimony. And if you were already getting alimony, you'd lose it because the ERA would get rid of all the laws that have been set up to protect women.

This message was terrifying to many women who had spent their lives as homemakers. They truly believed that if their marriages fell apart, the ERA would leave them nothing to live on. We argued that their fears were misplaced; that rather than take away the protections they enjoyed, the ERA would ensure that women were treated equally before the law. But when people are frightened, facts are not necessarily convincing.

Second, the anti-ERA forces used scare tactics—in abundance. One opponent dressed up "as an outhouse labeled THEIRS to dramatize her claim that the ERA would lead to unisex toilets." Another warned that "the ERA would mean the end of femininity." Others claimed that mother/daughter school banquets would be eliminated, that women's colleges and sororities would become illegal. They charged that the ERA would legalize homosexual marriages and the right of gay couples to adopt children, thus encouraging sexual deviance. They predicted chaos in the courts, with the law so unsettled that it would be used to the detriment of women.

Every one of these charges was dead wrong as well as absurd. The experience of states that already had equal rights laws in place confirmed this. Women's colleges didn't go out of business. Mothers still enjoyed banquets with their daughters. No state required unisex toilets; the owners of restaurants and office buildings were free to decide how they would deal with the public's needs. As for gay marriages, the ERA's legislative history plainly indicated that states could decide their own policies.

Third, the anti-ERA forces argued that the ERA would bring "Big Brother" government into everyone's lives, take away states' rights, and give too much power to the federal courts. Journalist Jane O'Reilly answered these charges:

It is because half the population of the United States is not equal under the law and never will be equal in this lifetime if we progress state by state, case by case (always subject to reversal). Without a federal ERA we have no universal legal definition of equality of the sexes. . . .

No society has ever had sexual equality, and the Equal Rights Amendment, if it succeeds, will be for that reason a leap into the unknown. But it will not be an immediate, revolutionary leap beyond the restraints of law and custom. The ERA would cause change, but it is also an attempt to deal with the changes that have already taken place.

The fourth line of attack was to link the ERA to reproductive choice. Here the New Right's political strategy would tolerate no dissension among their supporters. Before the Supreme Court's ruling in *Roe v. Wade* in January 1973, some who embraced the New Majoritarian strategy had been ambivalent about the ERA. But then came not only *Roe* but a determination by the Catholic bishops that the ERA could require the government to protect the right to choice. That would make it more difficult to achieve the Church's goal of passing a constitutional amendment banning abortion—the so-called Human Life Amendment, backed by the National Conference of Catholic Bishops. So ambivalence on the ERA became unacceptable: If the ERA hindered the anti-abortion forces, then the ERA would have to be opposed. While polls consistently showed that Catholics were more likely than Protestants to support the ERA, and just as likely as other Americans to support women's reproductive choice, the New Right leaders put their faith in the capacity of the bishops to deliver their flocks against both the ERA and choice.

It didn't seem to matter that there were no legal links between *Roe* and the ERA—no state court decisions that documented the bishops' view. No matter how many times we cited legal precedent to confirm this, the anti-choice movement didn't believe us. In fact, the women's movement itself began to link the two when, over the years, lawyers and judges started citing equal protection under the law in discussing federal funding of abortions.

Not surprisingly, Phyllis Schlafly also entered the religious fray. She argued in 1975 that if the ERA were passed, the "Catholic church could be required to admit women to the priesthood and to abandon its single-sex schools . . . or else lose its tax-exempt status." Her interpretation was based, she claimed, on a Supreme Court decision, *Bob Jones University v. Simon,* that allowed the IRS to revoke the university's tax-exempt status because it had racially discriminated in its admissions policies. Schlafly insisted the ERA would put sex discrimination on a similar footing with race discrimination—an interpretation, wrote *The New York Times,* that "was disputed by Catholic lawyers who said that the Bob Jones case was purely a procedural one . . . the substantive issue of the validity of the revocation of tax exemption was not decided."

Tax exemptions translated into dollars. Money as well as morals influenced the Catholic hierarchy's fears of reproductive rights. The National Conference of Catholic Bishops took no official position on the ERA itself, but individual priests lobbied legislators in the states where the ERA had not yet been ratified. Other denominations also got into the act. A few evangelical Protestant churches, such as the Church of Christ, organized rescission campaigns in Texas and New Mexico, which had passed state ERAs, because they believed the ERA "would make abortion and looser sex standards more prevalent."

In New York and New Jersey, both major parties and every major state civic group backed the ERA. Opposition organized at the grassroots opposition came from the Knights of Columbus, the John Birch Society, the Mormon Church, Baptist fundamentalist churches, the New York Conservative party, and Schlafly's STOP ERA partners, Annette Stern's Operation Wake Up, and the states' anti-choice movement. On Election Day the referenda lost, in New York by 57 to 43 percent and in New Jersey by 51 to 49 percent.

Voter turnout had been light. Fewer than one in three eligible voters went to the polls in New York State. Despite an aggressive but underfunded get-out-the-vote campaign, voters in New York City, the center of ERA support, didn't turn out in large numbers. Proponents said afterward that they hadn't bothered to vote because the press and polls had convinced them the referendum would easily pass.

The New Jersey turnout was proportionally higher than New York's, and was reflected in the state's much closer vote. But the four supposedly most progressive counties in New Jersey—all in suburbia, where prosperous Italian- and Irish-Americans had settled after fleeing the cities, and all targeted by the New Right—defeated the ERA by much larger margins than the rural areas, which were thought to be culturally more conservative. The misogynist strategy had worked. Analysis showed that the messages on family life, alimony, child support, child custody, and abortion, along with the scare tactics, played a considerable part in getting anti-ERA women and men to the polls.

The New Right was exuberant. The year before, they had defeated the ERA in Arizona, but this was a conservative state in many respects, so the victory was not completely unexpected. Prevailing in the large moderate states of New Jersey and New York, however, was a major upset. (Despite the reputation of New York City as a liberal bastion, New York State is as culturally conservative as New Jersey and much less liberal than such states as Vermont and Oregon.) From then on, misogynist messages were an integral part of the New Majoritarian strategy for winning elections.

As the nation's bicentennial year dawned and the primary season loomed, Gerald Ford was in deep trouble. Given the New Right's success in the November 1975 elections, their continuing incursions into the party structure, and their endorsement of Reagan, the once-inconceivable began to look like a real possibility: The Republican party might not nominate him. Forceful action was urgent.

Ford's campaign managers decided the president must take a vigorous stand against legal abortion. If abortion had been so potent an issue in New York and New Jersey, it might also work in the crucial early primaries, where New Right–leaning Republicans would be coming out to vote. In general, Ford had not been a backer of abortion. When he was in Congress, he had sponsored a "local option" abortion amendment—an action that had helped make his appointment as vice president acceptable to the new conservatives after they lost Spiro Agnew. But hitherto his opposition to abortion had been subtle. Politics now dictated he be outspoken.

In February, shortly before the New Hampshire primary, he chose a nationally televised interview with CBS newsman Walter Cronkite to prove the strength of his anti-abortion commitment. He did not agree with *Roe v. Wade*, he announced; the Supreme Court had gone "too far." He insisted that his was a "moderate position" because he opposed a constitutional amendment outlawing abortion. Instead, Ford said, "each individual state should decide what it wished to do."

The press was astounded that he had made abortion a major national issue. *The Washington Post* editorialized that the abortion issue has "got somewhat overblown and out of hand." In what seemed like something of a stretch, *The New York Times* speculated that Ford had hoped his statements would *lessen* the attention given to abortion in the campaign. But the reverse was true. The Cronkite interview put the issue at the forefront, and it energized pro-choice Republicans outside Washington. For our part, we were angered by Ford's attempt to label his position "moderate"; at best, it was only slightly less belligerent than that of Reagan, who had endorsed a constitutional amendment. We decided it was essential that we fight for *Roe* at the national convention.

In the New Hampshire primary, Ford beat Reagan by a meager 1,317 votes. No one was certain what part, if any, the Cronkite interview played in this outcome, but Ford stuck to his strong anti-choice position, and New Hampshire proved to be his low point in the primaries. The campaign gathered strength through the spring; he won by wide margins in all states except North Carolina, where Jesse Helms delivered his state to Reagan, 52 to 46 percent, by using racist and sexist themes. Helms's most blatant piece of racist fear-mongering was a flyer that quoted Ford as suggesting that GOP senator Edward Brooke of Massachusetts, a black, "should be considered" for the vice presidency. The flyer carefully failed to note that Brooke was one of a number of prospects on the president's list.

The New Right's bigotry strategy burst forth fully in the Texas presidential primary on May 1, where voters were not bound by party affiliation and could select any candidate they wanted. There were two candidates for the Democratic presidential nomination on the ballot: Jimmy Carter and George Wallace. The Reagan camp saw this as an opportunity to pull conservative Democrats over to their man and away from Wallace. Reagan media man and New Right consultant Arthur Finkelstein recruited a Wallaceite to create television commercials to attract these voters. (Finkelstein later became the key strategist behind New York senator Al D'Amato's rise to power.) The spots used an approach like this: "I've always been a Democrat. As much as I hate to admit it, George Wallace can't be nominated. So for the first time in my life I'm gonna vote in the Republican primary. I'm gonna vote for

Ronald Reagan." Simultaneously with these airings, mailings went out identifying Reagan with all the hateful parts of Wallace's social agenda.

The maneuver worked. Reagan swept the state against Ford, winning all ninety-six Republican delegates.

Emboldened by Texas, the New Right transformed their guerrilla efforts against the moderates into open civil war. Pat Buchanan laid out the strategy:

> There is a deep, fundamental split on the political right, an expanding conflict among "conservatives." Ford is a conservative. But . . . it is a conservatism marked by wariness of conflict, resistance to change, and an abiding ambition to conserve the status quo. . . . It is a don't-rock-the-boat conservatism exemplified . . . by what Mr. Ford calls the politics of cooperation, conciliation, compromise and consensus.
>
> Reagan is leading a diverse army of political have-nots: Democrats with nowhere else to go, Independents who believe the parties have become both similar and corrupt by long association, and Republicans *who believe that conflict, not compromise, is the essence of politics.* . . . [emphasis added]
>
> The Reagan campaign is becoming a vehicle for a provincial revolution against the Republican as well as the national establishment. . . . The liberal wing of the Republican party is a spectator now. It lacked the numbers to advance its own candidate, or the will to save its own champion, the Vice President. The civil war in the GOP is between conservatives—militant and moderate.

The New Right's tactics were spelled out for all to see. Conflict, not compromise and conciliation, was their battle cry. Their weapon was fear.

The Reagan onslaught subverted our strategy for winning more women delegates to the convention. Ford's team was unable to help us; to overcome Reagan in the primaries and at the state conventions, it had to field prominent, widely recognized Republicans, and in most cases that didn't mean women. We were trapped. We couldn't be delegates because we weren't well known. We couldn't become well known because the party wouldn't back us, yet to challenge Ford's delegates would defeat our cause, since he was unquestionably more sympathetic to us than Reagan.

We would be lucky to match our 1972 record of 30 percent women delegates, we realized. For whatever consolation it might give us, the Democratic women were also having trouble, but for different reasons. We were contending with a right-wing assault against women. They were seeking a fifty-fifty rule requiring their delegations to be half men, half women and were dealing with traditional opposition. They were proposing; we were on the defensive.

Steiger's Rule 29 Committee had fallen on hard times. After persistent and intense bombardment from Reed and Devine, the proposed mechanisms for enforcing the "positive action" measures had been watered down. We would have one more chance to change them at the national convention. Pat Bailey told the task force women to keep a record of the state parties that had failed to follow Rule 32 to bring women into the party. At the convention we planned to challenge the credentials of delegates from those states.

In the spring and early summer, task force members testified on our issues at platform hearings in Los Angeles, Des Moines, and Washington, D.C., but by July, it was clear that we would get no more help from the president's campaign on these issues than we had on women delegates. In July, very angry, we went to the press. A public charge seemed to be our only leverage. On behalf of the Republican Women's Task Force, Pat Goldman released a letter she'd sent to Mary Louise Smith at the RNC complaining about the small role women were slated to play in Kansas City. Republican women "will be allowed to vote, occasionally, to be seen and hardly ever heard," she wrote. "How are you—how are we—going to respond to the better than 700 women who were elected as delegates? How can you explain to them that only five of them were found capable of leadership from the entire convention?"

Our protests got modest results. A few women speakers were added to the convention program. Smith said she shared Goldman's frustrations but added that she thought the party's problem was that Republicans "don't have women positioned correctly." It was the circular game yet again.

In July, anticipating that her husband might be selected as the vice-presidential nominee, Jill Ruckelshaus resigned as presiding officer of the IWY commission and delivered a 391-page report to the president. When Ford accepted the report, ". . . to Form a More Perfect Union," which included 115 recommendations on how to improve the lives of American women, he directed the attorney general to review the U.S. Code "to determine the need for revising sex-based provisions that are not justified." He also stated that while he supported the ERA, "injustice cannot wait upon politics, nor upon the lengthy public discussion which has already delayed ratification of this Constitutional Amendment. The time to act is now." He called on the nation's governors to initiate similar reviews of their states' laws.

On the surface, the president's directive sounded supportive. Beneath the surface, however, was the insinuation that perhaps equity could be achieved by a method other than the ERA. It was a clever move—it might temper the right's antagonism to his ERA stand while keeping us happy. Four years later, when Reagan became the GOP nominee, he adopted his own version of this approach, purportedly supporting equal rights for women even as he was rejecting the ERA.

Eleven days before the convention opened in Kansas City, *The New York Times* reported that Ford had 1,108 delegates to Reagan's 1,027. The number needed for nomination was 1,130. There were still 124 uncommitted delegates, enough to put either man over the top.

Many Ford supporters were stunned. They could not believe that Reagan had become so strong. A sitting president was on the verge of losing his party's nomination. Not since Taft and Ike had fought bitterly for the Republican nomination in 1952 had the party been so split. Fervent though each side was in support of its candidate, insiders in both camps realized that an emotional confrontation at the convention could easily cost the Republicans the election. The Watergate debacle, still vivid in memory, had made the party suspect around the nation. A show of unity was essential if it was to win in November.

But other forces were at work that the insiders could not control. Our burgeoning Republican feminist movement was determined to march to its own drum. So were the new conservatives, led by the leaders of the American Conservative Union, YAF, and the *National Review,* who would soon join up with the New Right. Reagan had Helms pushing him to hold to the New Right's views on a strong anti-Soviet foreign policy, busing, and abortion. Ford had the feminists pushing him to back the ERA, make no mention of abortion in the platform, commit to federal financing of quality day care, and beef up the Steiger committee's recommendations. For their standard-bearer, the New Right had Ronald Reagan, a pure ideologue who had no political reason to modify his views. For our standard-bearer, we had Gerald Ford, who was compromising on our goals in order to save his candidacy.

The Ford campaign was determined to convince the conservative delegates, who were pledged to Ford but hankered for Reagan, that their loyalty was merited. The campaign characterized its draft platform, passed around before the convention opened, as a conservative agenda. Our insider friends, all male except Mary Louise Smith, wished us well in our upcoming hand-to-hand combat with the New Right on the platform, but they insisted their priority must be Ford's nomination. As for the rules fight, they said we'd have to wait and see what happened when we got to Kansas City for the committee deliberations a week before the convention. Maybe, they said not very persuasively, something could be done.

5

A TIME OF ACCOMMODATION

Kansas City was no Miami Beach. Less glitzy and with more style, the former capital of cow towns had transformed itself into "the city of fountains" and was in the middle of an urban facelift. The privately financed $350 million Crown Center, "a city within a city" as the tourist brochures described it, exemplified this new look and was thought to be the appropriate place for the President of the United States to stay. Even so, the much older Radisson Muehlebach housed the convention headquarters. The hotel had been Harry Truman's midwestern White House, and despite recent renovation, still had a comfortable, old-fashioned air and seemed more suitable to Gerald Ford's civil brand of politics.

Kansas City straddles Kansas and Missouri, and I found this symbolic. Kansas had been an early supporter of women, giving them the vote long before the nation got around to passing the Nineteenth Amendment. Kansas had ratified the ERA and was home to Republican Nancy Kassebaum, who would become the only woman in the U.S. Senate when she was elected in 1978. It was an old-line, moderately conservative state, as would be proven once again a week later, when it cast 30 votes for Ford and only 4 for Reagan.

As Kansas represented our hopes, Missouri represented the backlash: the fear of change, the fear of giving a fair shake to women and minorities. Out of Missouri had come the Dred Scott decision, loathsome racial incidents, and, consistent with its history, rejection of the ERA. Although its governor, Christopher Bond, was a moderate, well-meaning man, Missouri was fertile ground for the misogynist strategy. The Missouri delegation would deliver 31 votes to Reagan and 18 to Ford.

As a protest against Missouri's failure to ratify the ERA, the Republican Women's Task Force booked hotel rooms across the Missouri River in Kansas City, Kansas; but like everyone else who wanted to influence the delegates, we had an office at the Muehlebach. As we hoped, it became the rallying point for women at the convention.

Communication was our biggest organizational problem. The delegates were housed all over town and were difficult to locate. We had no money for walkie-talkies and extra phone lines, but we needed a way to share information and lobby the delegates on the Platform and Rules committees. We took to heart the advice of Susan McLane, a task force founder and New Hampshire legislator who cooked breakfast for her legislative colleagues in Concord to glean valuable information and cement relationships. Although we didn't cook for the women delegates on the Platform and Rules committees, we ordered breakfast for them; and each morning we strategized together on ways to get our agreed-on women's plank into the platform. Many lasting friendships grew out of these foxhole experiences.

The apprehensiveness, even fear, that many of us had felt in Miami was gone. Even though we'd joined Nixon under his big tent, we were never at ease with his leadership, certain about his aims, or sure exactly what his staff might do for us or to us. Despite its frustrations, working with the Ford White House was an improvement. We knew the convention in Kansas City would be more competitive and bloodier than 1972, but we were better prepared to do battle.

We were out to win a platform supporting our feminist goals, to protect what was left of the "positive action" proposals of the Steiger committee, and to get women into the party's leadership and our issues to become its policies. We wanted to be recognized as partners. As it turned out, we increased the number of women delegates slightly—from just under 30 percent in 1972 to 31.5 percent—so at least we'd held our own. (It did not escape our notice that the Democratic women had slipped from 40 percent in 1972 to 34 percent at their convention in July, when Jimmy Carter had been nominated for president and Walter Mondale vice president.)

We were not ignored in Kansas City—far from it. Over and over we were reminded that what we did could determine whether Ford would win the nomination. The press kept saying that Ford had the votes, but we all knew better. This convention was too volatile. In Ford's camp were closet Reagan delegates who were pledged to him only out of a sense of duty to the presidency and to his long years of service to the party. The slightest miscalculation by Ford, and they would shift to Reagan.

The New Right, knowing this, was following a strategy that they called "purposeful conflict on substantive issues." So were we. Reagan's campaign manager John Sears pursued a different strategy—purposeful conflict over a rules change. He was leaving policy issues alone because a convention blow-up over ideology would make it nearly impossible to unify Republicans for the fall campaign. The Ford and Reagan people had negotiated a loose arrangement for the platform that he hoped would hold. Ford's delegate team, led by George Bush's good friend James Baker, was nailing down the last of the uncommitted delegates, and like Sears, he wanted no major ideological disturbance.

We had originally planned to stay above the Ford and Reagan fray and we welcomed women from both camps to our cause, but it was difficult for the Reagan women to join us because the New Right had decided to use our issues as a wedge to unhinge the Ford machine. The women delegates who worked with us were chiefly for Ford, although Reagan's daughter Maureen, who was not a delegate, joined us too.

We were there for the Rules, Platform, and Credentials committee meetings, which generally start a week before the convention officially opens. This is a particularly crucial time for those challenging the status quo. It is then that the convention battles begin and outsiders can change the party's direction. The action usually starts in subcommittees, often the birthplace of new ideas, then moves to the full committees, and if the issue is not resolved, blossoms into a fight on the convention floor.

Our Rules Committee strategy quickly became entangled in the Ford–Reagan competition. Pat Bailey, who headed the task force's Rules Committee effort, determined we could not challenge the gender composition of the delegations without jeopardizing Ford delegates. While there were more women in the Ford delegations than in Reagan's, there were still not enough to be in full compliance with the "positive action" rules. We had to be consistent. Any disruption of the Ford campaign script—"don't rock the boat"—would be disastrous for Ford, so we dropped the challenge.

But Sears wished to rock the boat; that was his path to Reagan's nomination. His team tried to convince the Rules Committee to pass a rule, 16C, requiring presidential candidates to announce their vice-presidential choices before the balloting for president. No one was fooled. Sears's proposal was transparently a challenge to the Ford campaign's ability to hold its delegates, but Ford showed he could do it, beating back the 16C proposal by a vote of 59 to 44. The Reagan–Ford competition then shifted to the main convention hall, where on the second day of the convention, the Reaganites, armed with a minority report allowing the convention to revisit the issue, would ask the delegates to vote on 16C.

The 16C fight in the Rules Committee cheated us out of our chance to try to put enforcement machinery behind Rule 32. After several days and nights of acrimonious debate over 16C, the members were tired. The convention had already opened by the time the enforcement discussion came up on the committee's agenda, and most members weren't interested in sitting around for what they knew would be a hot debate over a subject that made many feel uncomfortable. A majority agreed with us on principle—the party should take positive action to attract women and minorities—but principle was no longer the point.

The Ford camp, it turned out, had made a deal not to touch the issue, in exchange for which some of the more conservative delegates would vote for the Ford position on 16C. In addition, the Ford team wanted to placate Clarke Reed, who two weeks before had infuriated his Reagan friends by endorsing Ford, but then angered the Ford campaign by saying that even though he was chairman of the Mississippi GOP, he couldn't deliver his state's delegation for Ford. This inability was a critical matter, because the nomination now hinged on Ford's winning two states, Mississippi and Pennsylvania. There was no way Ford's team was going to deep-six Reed's "pet project," the emasculation of the proposed enforcement measures. The Ford campaign pleaded with us not to embarrass the president. Your cause is just, they said, but we can't deal with it now. We need Mississippi. So we folded our rules fight before it began.

·   ·   ·

The platform was different. Sears had reached a compromise with the Ford campaign, but Reagan's New Right flank, led by Schlafly and Helms, weren't compromising. Our platform battle would be with them.

There were loosely four sets of players in this platform drama, each with its own delegates: the Ford campaign, the Reagan campaign, the New Right ideologues led by Helms, and the Republican Women's Task Force. The Helms delegates were for Reagan, although if they didn't get what they wanted in the platform, some threatened to bolt to a third party that Viguerie, Rusher, and others were organizing. They demanded a militant anti-Soviet foreign policy statement that undercut Ford's more flexible policies, and opposition to abortion and the ERA. While we supported Ford, we feared the convention would abandon the ERA, legal abortion, and federal help for child care. Like the Helms people, a few task force members said they too would leave the party if the convention abandoned its positions on these women's issues.

Some of our issues—equal pay, federal help for locally controlled child care, elimination of discrimination toward women in the Social Security system, displaced homemakers' aid, flexible work schedules, and rewriting of the widow's tax—didn't seem to raise the hackles of the New Right, and the convention included them in the platform. But abortion and the ERA were another story.

For me, abortion was the most crucial question concerning women that the convention faced. A woman's right to determine whether she has a child strikes at the core of her being, affecting how she lives and what she does, who she is and what she will be. It seemed particularly hypocritical that Helms and his team supported a policy of government control over women that was just as despotic as the despotism they claimed to hate. These self-anointed champions of freedom elsewhere in the world were ready to limit the freedom of more than half their country's citizens.

The Republican party's abortion battle in Kansas City was the textbook case for all the battles to come on this issue. Not since the days of the party's fancy footwork on women's suffrage had the contradiction between its principles and political expediency been so stark.

The same arguments as always came into play. First, states' rights had to be considered. Back in 1972, although Nixon had already embraced the anti-choice view and the movement to legalize abortion was sweeping the country, *Roe v. Wade* lay a year in the future. At the time, some felt it was reasonable to omit abortion from a national party platform because change was confined to the state level. This argument was misleading, however, because until such time as all states gave women legal protection to make their own childbearing choices, abortion was a national issue. National political parties have a responsibility to tell American voters their position on national issues. Abortion was already in play in politics in 1972, but in Miami we had chosen to ignore it.

Second, some argued that because abortion is a private matter and therefore doesn't belong in politics, it shouldn't be in the platform. As long as abortion was not a matter of political contention, this argument was valid, but as soon as the reproductive health movement and then the anti-choice countermovement grew strong, the argument made no political sense. For pro-choice people, a position of not taking a position—that is, of keeping the status quo—defeated their purpose because keeping the status quo before *Roe v. Wade* meant abortion remained illegal. After *Roe,* the pro-choice advocates backed the status quo and the anti-choice people wanted to change it. "Abortion is a private matter" became a shibboleth used by both sides. Sometimes in Kansas City we would use it; at other times our opponents would. The truth is that abortion will remain a political issue in America until the country agrees on a policy that a majority can comfortably accept and its public officials will uphold.

Third, there were the equivocal arguments: "I'm for choice, but now's not the time to take a stand," and "We do think women should have that right, but in the overall scheme of practical politics, it can't be a priority."

Then came the loyalty arguments, the ones we kept encountering over our rules strategy. They were always the most difficult to respond to—the ubiquitous "Don't embarrass the president" and "Don't hurt the party or we'll lose in November."

In Kansas City the Ford campaign pitched the equivocal and loyalty arguments, and most of the Washington task force leadership embraced them. Our group split. Chris Topping, the women delegates from outside the Beltway, and I couldn't go along. We believed the party must take a stand for abortion rights. If the Republican party was going to give up on women's freedom, there had at least to be a fight. We weren't about to hand the New Right a gift.

The first struggle surfaced in the Human Rights and Responsibilities in a Free Society Subcommittee, whose actions thoroughly contradicted the grandeur of its title. Stacked with the approval of the Ford campaign in consultation with Reagan's staff, its fifteen members included three pro-choicers, nine strong anti-choicers, and three men who were supposed to be with us but never did anything. Massachusetts congressmember Silvio Conte, thought to be a friend, was absent most of the time. Illustrating a technique we would learn to anticipate in later years, antifeminists chaired this subcommittee, whose province was women's issues, and dominated its membership. Not so mysteriously, our so-called male allies in the Congress, with the exception of Connecticut senator Lowell Weicker, never seemed to want to fight for specific women's causes. They always turned up on the economics and foreign policy subcommittees instead.

The convention organizers had deliberately selected a room for the subcommittee's meetings that was too small to hold all those who wished to participate. Security was strict. Private guards patrolled the entrance. Hot from the television lights, crowded with photographers and reporters, the room reinforced the hostility between the two sides.

Attention rested on the anti-choicers, whose sound boxes played the cries of babies and whose hands held pictures of bloodied fetuses. Several women were pregnant; others cradled infants and grabbed for toddlers with their free hand. It was an unsettling exploitation of children. They testified that pro-choice people were "mass murderers and baby-killers," terms that stepped over the bounds of civil public discourse. They didn't care. The more epithets they shouted at us, the happier they seemed. For many pro-choicers, it was the first time they'd been treated to anti-choice zealotry. Our testimony was thoughtful and reasonable. We didn't want to dignify their crude wrath by shouting back, but now I believe we should have.

The right-wing delegates ran roughshod over all the moderate positions. Not only did the "Human Rights" Subcommittee approve a constitutional amendment to ban abortion, sponsored by member Bob Dole, by a vote of 13 to 1, but it adopted the old 1972 Wallace agenda— no "forced" school busing, no federal aid to schools, no gun control, and mandated school prayer. It showed its independence from Ford by voting 8 to 7 to drop support for the ERA.

In the Platform Committee itself, the New Right had the votes to pass the anti-abortion plank. Committee members Barbara Gunderson of South Dakota and Ann Peckham of Wisconsin were convinced that a sizable number of committee members would speak out against it. Millicent Fenwick, the committee's only feminist officeholder, would lead the debate to delete the plank.

Of all those on the committee who backed the plank—they included Joseph Coors and several New Right members of the House and Senate—Bob Dole had the most at stake. He had survived the Watergate backlash in 1974, fighting an emotional reelection campaign against pro-choice obstetrician Bill Roy and winning 51 to 49 percent. Dole credited much of his victory to his strong right-to-life stance and help from the anti-choice movement. Now he was positioning himself to be Ford's running mate. A strong anti-abortion position would enhance his ideological credibility among the New Rightists. Dole realized that if Ford were nominated, they would try to convince him to pick Reagan as his vice president but might agree to Dole as a backup.

The debate began in another hot room, again filled with a profusion of television cameras and right-to-life and pro-choice partisans, and a surfeit of security guards. Tempers were barely under control.

Fenwick made her case with the traditional Republican conservative argument that abortion was a personal matter and didn't belong in politics and thus in the platform. Then came hours of emotional back-and-forth about the sanctity of the unborn child and the sanctity of a woman's right to choose. Chris Topping and I had surveyed the committee members beforehand and found that the majority agreed with Fenwick, but her motion to eliminate the plank failed 26 to 65. Ford's managers were not going to let the members vote their conscience.

To soothe the pro-choicers, the committee added a few innocuous paragraphs acknowledging that the abortion question was "difficult and controversial" and saying that the party respected the views of everyone. The paragraphs were meaningless. The plank was a forthright statement: The Republican party had firmly endorsed the official position of the right-to-life movement and its religious allies.

But when we analyzed the vote, Chris and I realized we had the potential to take our fight to the convention floor. Of the 106-member committee, only 91 had voted and 26 of them were with us. We needed 27 members to sign a minority report to get us there, insuring a debate by all the delegates before a national television audience. It could be the hottest action of the convention once Ford and Reagan settled 16C, which the convention would take up before the platform.

Forty hours were all we had. It was late Saturday afternoon, and the signatures had to be turned in at the final meeting of the Platform Committee early Monday afternoon.

Barber Conable, an upstate New York congressmember who sat on the Platform Committee and whose wife, Charlotte, was a task force founder, helped me phrase the minority report. It said:

> There is no wide public consensus on this issue. It is felt by some to be a moral issue and by others to be an issue of personal choice, but most agree that it should not be included in a political party's platform.
>
> We support the right of individual party members and candidates and officeholders to contribute to the continuing dialogue on this personal, difficult question, but we think that the Republican party platform, like those of years past, should not attempt to commit its candidates and officeholders, as well as members, as though this were a traditional political issue.

Armed with lists of committee members, hotels, and a couple of rented cars, eight of us set out to find our twenty-seven signers. It was to be a stealth operation. We had agreed that under no circumstances must the press know what we were doing. If it found out, its attention would force the Ford campaign to stop us. At the moment, fortunately, the campaign was too busy organizing the 16C fight to pay much attention to us.

We scoured Kansas City. Like guerrillas engaged in an insurrection, quiet, quick, and discreet, we tracked down committee members at parties and bars and staked out the Muehlebach lobby. Driving for more than an hour to an airport hotel, we woke up a delegate at midnight, who signed in his pajamas. We were having no difficulty at all getting the members' signatures once we found them. What surprised us most was their warmth and goodwill. "Glad you're doing this, thank God someone's concerned." "This is right." "What's gotten into Ford?"

Around three-thirty A.M. on Monday we had our twenty-seventh signature. Outside the Muehlebach's coffee shop five hours later, two more added their names to the dog-eared document before they headed in for breakfast.

Nineteen women and ten men signed: three members of Congress —Fenwick, Conable, and John Anderson—two male doctors, several doctors' wives, and four Reagan delegates. They represented every section of the nation but one. It was as though we were reliving the Civil War. No one from the South or the border states was represented except Faye Chiles of Tennessee, and Tennessee had been on the Union side.

The Ford and Reagan operatives were astounded when Ann Peckham, the first signer, presented our handiwork. With no help from the White House and without the knowledge of the press, we'd accomplished what we'd set out to do. There would be a convention debate on a woman's right to choose. The nation would know where the Republican party stood. It was a high point for us. We'd proved it was possible to stand up to the New Right's blackmail.

The debate was scheduled for Tuesday night after the 16C vote. If Ford won the 16C roll call, he would have secured the nomination by the time our vote came up. His campaign could then loosen up and encourage dropping the abortion plank by releasing delegates to follow their conscience. A CBS delegate survey reported that a majority favored keeping the plank out of the platform. There would be two minority-report platform amendments on the floor that night—ours and Helms's "morality in foreign policy." Helms's amendment was a veiled attack on Ford's foreign policy as developed by his secretary of state, Henry Kissinger. It attacked the Helsinki Pact, so-called unilateral concessions in nuclear testing, détente with the Soviet Union, Ford's "snub" of Alexander Solzhenitsyn, and the signing of "secret agreements," which was code for the Panama Canal treaty that would turn the canal over to Panama in 1999. Our amendment would be first.

We continued to stay away from the press. If we were to have any chance to get the plank dropped, it was important not to force Ford to move against us. What relieved and amazed us was how the press had missed the story until we went to them just before the debate started. It confirmed what we'd often guessed but now knew—a lot of work can be accomplished in politics if you're willing to keep your mouth shut.

. . .

The noise in the hall was deafening. It was Tuesday night, and the 16C debate was about to begin. I was in the New York alternates section, across the aisle from the VIP boxes on the mezzanine, where Betty Ford and Happy Rockefeller were sitting. I had a panoramic view of the floor action and had already heard a test of which partisans—Reagan's or Ford's—could cheer the loudest when Betty Ford and Nancy Reagan were introduced to the crowd. Reagan's partisans sounded noisier, but that was because the convention planners had placed the strongly pro-Reagan Texas delegation just below us and the other big Reagan delegation, California, across on the other side of the hall. In between were the Michigan and New York Ford delegations. The placement muffled the shouts of Ford's delegates. It also proved that much of the convention's machinery was in the hands of Reaganites. Outshouted by Reagan's chorus, the Ford delegates felt under siege, their side not in control.

Every fifteen minutes or so, the Texas delegation would yell in unison, "Viva Olé!" and the California delegates would yell back, "Viva Reagan!" From where I sat, their chanting sounded like a cross between a Big Ten college football game cheer and a Mexican bull-ring hurrah. The Ford delegates in the middle yelled "Ford! Ford!" but they couldn't compete. I felt sorry for Betty Ford and Happy Rockefeller, who sat with fixed smiles as the Texans and Californians whipped up the frenzy.

For some five hours the 16C debate went on, punctuated by whistles, catcalls, and a few scuffles. When it finally came to an end after midnight, Ford had won by 111 votes. He would be the nominee. There was little left that Sears could do to change the outcome.

The first abortion debate at a national political convention started at one-fifteen A.M. Central Daylight Time—after America had gone to bed and just as the Ford campaign wished. Each side had twelve minutes. The pro-choicers used two speakers, the opposition six.

Ann Peckham went first. The delegates were restive and weary, but they settled down as soon as she spoke. It was the quietest the hall had been since the opening prayer many hours before. They seemed receptive when she began, but unfortunately her words were too reasonable, too conciliatory. "The inclusion of an anti-abortion plank . . . would be a tragic mistake for our minority party and for our candidates," she said. Abortion was a moral and legal issue that the party "must permit each Republican candidate to proceed from his or her own personal conviction." There was no passion, no ringing call to arms to arouse the tired delegates. My heart sank. She hadn't directly addressed the issue. She'd only talked about the good of the party.

Mississippi state senator Charles Pickering, Clarke Reed's friend, attacked the Supreme Court for *Roe* and said young women shouldn't have abortions. His oratory was hot and to the point. Ohio's Ralph Perk quoted Ford and Reagan, saying that the party and the government "have the responsibility to protect the lives of all human beings, born and unborn." In jackhammer spurts, Alabaman Frances Wideman, who had led the anti-ERA fight in the Platform Committee, shouted her defiance of our proposal, and Mike Antonovich of California described a "pre-born baby's heartbeat" and quoted Albert Schweitzer that "evil consists in destroying life."

I held my breath, hoping for sparks from our side's other speaker, Dr. George Wood III of Maine. He gave a pleasant description of his life as a family physician in a small New England city. He mentioned abortion only obliquely, referring to it as "a medical decision and not a political decision." He pleaded with the convention: "I am sure there are families which you represent that have already faced or will face this very personal crisis. Please allow your friends and their physicians the alternative to resolve it. It is the least we can do for them at this moment." He was so civilized and tentative and so deadeningly dull.

I was disgusted. Here we'd had a chance on national television to explain why abortion should be legal, why women must be given the same freedom as men—and our side was pleading that the plank would hurt the party and gently asking that we "allow our friends and their physicians the alternative to resolve it."

All that work to get to this? Were the moderates, as our critics said, constitutionally unable to be passionate about anything? I had believed this a silly charge, but I began to wonder as I listened to the fiery words of the next anti-choice speaker. Maryland congressmember Bob Bauman, a devout Catholic and one of the New Right's most virulent antifeminists, let us have it. He compared abortion to slavery, predicting America could "follow in the path of Nazi Germany and consign people to death because they are too expensive to let them live." He was crude, and he was effective. He took no prisoners. As if to let the world know that not all anti-choice people were zealots, mild-speaking Georgia Peterson of Utah followed, saying in a tone similar to Wood's that the convention should reject our amendment.

Then, as if to send a signal to those who might not know how Bob Dole stood, Pickering again took the podium. "Senator Dole recently said, 'I feel very strongly that the majority of those who identify with our party's philosophy, if not with its name, want the abortion issue settled.' " With a grand flourish, Pickering ended the debate. "The issue is a constitutional amendment for living life. Let's have a living Constitution. The issue will not go away." He sat down. The sleepy delegates started talking noisily.

We had seven states lined up for a roll-call vote on our amendment. Conable had warned me that in order to obtain a roll call, convention chairman John Rhodes would have to recognize our floor leader's motion for such a vote. This could be done only by sending a written request to Rhodes. As soon as Pickering finished, Fenwick sought recognition from Rhodes. He ignored her. A phalanx of people surrounded him, and several strong-armed men blocked our page from giving him Fenwick's note. Rhodes called for a voice vote. From where I was standing on the convention floor, the ayes were louder. *New York Times* reporter Chris Lydon was more ambivalent, writing about "the roar of 'ayes' and 'noes' that Mr. Rhodes interpreted against any change in the platform." Rhodes declared that our request for a roll call had lost. With a parliamentary maneuver that few in the convention hall grasped, the party had officially dropped its support for women's liberty without the delegates having to declare themselves on national television.

Now Rhodes moved to start the foreign policy debate. Lo and behold, there was no debate. Led by Richard Obenshain, three delegates argued for Helms's amendment. The Ford side had capitulated. This exercise was a charade. On a voice vote, the convention passed the morality in foreign policy amendment. Ford had won the war and lost the peace. His campaign had negotiated away many of his administration's foreign policy positions and turned its back on a woman's right to freedom.

The ERA did stay in the platform. After the subcommittee had rejected the ERA, the Washington task force women and the pro-ERA women delegates, led by Pamela Curtis, got the attention of the Ford campaign with their intense lobbying. Then, with its modest help the task force engineered what *The New York Times* described as "the best and most skillfully waged political contest on view here." By a vote of 51 to 47, the Platform Committee reversed the subcommittee and returned the ERA to its rightful historic place in the GOP. It was an impressive victory for our young movement. Schlafly threatened a floor fight, but Sears interceded and she capitulated. "I consider it immensely more important that Reagan be nominated," she said. "If Reagan is nominated, the platform is irrelevant because Reagan is against ERA and Mrs. Reagan is against ERA. If Reagan is nominated, we've won."

Ford and Dole were the party's candidates for president and vice president. The New Right had not nominated Reagan or won on the ERA, but they got everything else they wanted. Steiger's plea for a special committee of officeholders and political scientists to review party rules died.

The delegate-formula rules that had brought the new conservatives and now the New Right to power would remain. Between national conventions, only the RNC, which the New Right now controlled, would have the power to review how the party picked its delegates. The old formulas that the Ripon Society had challenged so aggressively were frozen into place, guaranteeing that the smaller and southern states would continue to have greater proportionate influence over party policy than their population or GOP vote warranted. As for the Ripon suit, it had been lost before Kansas City.

Women fared no better. A requirement that women hold half the seats on the party Finance Committee was ignored. Our "positive action" victory of 1972 was swept away. The Rules Committee undercut the rule that states should "endeavor" to give women equal representation on their delegations by ensuring there would be no enforcement procedures.

Ms. magazine quoted White House counsel Bobbie Kilberg as saying that "the Task Force's dissociation from abortion was 'politically wise.' They would not have had Ford's support for the ERA if they had supported abortion." Those of us who'd fought the abortion fight said publicly we weren't bitter. We didn't mention that we believed Ford's man Rhodes had intentionally precluded a roll call. We didn't want to appear disloyal.

Three weeks after the convention, each of the presidential nominees met separately with a panel of Catholic bishops. The bishops said they "were encouraged" although not totally satisfied by Ford's stand. They made it clear that Carter had disappointed them. Betsey Stengel, associate director of the Religious Coalition for Abortion Rights, summed up the significance of these exchanges. "What I really fear is, for instance, the reports that we have had that Ford's staff member said they [the Ford campaign] are going to play on the Catholic vote, and more, they are going to play on . . . the 'cultural dichotomy' between the Catholics and Baptists." This last was an allusion to Jimmy Carter's southern Baptist affiliation. It sounded as though the campaign hoped to use the abortion issue to exploit the animosity between Catholics and southern Protestants that had been an undercurrent in presidential politics ever since the nineteenth century, when Catholic immigration had significantly increased the number of Catholic voters.

Ford's campaign manager James Baker reinforced this that same week, when he told the press that abortion was "a campaign issue because the bishops came out on our side" and that it would "bring in votes for Ford."

The Ford accommodation on reproductive issues was extreme. In Kansas City, we had assumed it was limited to abortion. It wasn't. A broader strategy became clear in the fall, when the campaign ran ads indicating Ford believed that giving information on the use of contraceptives to minor children without parental consent was a "serious blow to the very fiber of the family unit." This statement was a response to several court decisions that had recognized that teenagers who were unable to communicate with their parents because of incest and other abuses should not be prohibited from obtaining abortions and contraceptives.

It would be unfair to say that the Ford campaign and the national Republican party adopted a misogynist strategy in 1976. However, Ford and the party's support for an anti-choice platform and the campaign's ads did prove that both were willing to accept the creeping integration of this strategy into GOP policy.

Ford was not a misogynist. He stood by his feminist wife. In his two years in office, he had shown an admirable concern for specific women's issues and demonstrated it in in his appointments record. Yet his selection of Dole as his running mate rather than Howard Baker, Bill Ruckelshaus, or Anne Armstrong documents that he believed he could not win without embracing the New Right's abortion stand.

The campaign was hard fought, but it got little help from Reagan. In some of his campaign appearances, Reagan lauded the GOP platform and never even mentioned the president. His followers did even less. Whether or not this was a calculated strategy, as Lyn Nofziger said later, "I'm still not sure that things didn't work out for the best in the long run. The nation needed Jimmy Carter in order truly to appreciate a Ronald Reagan."

The election was exceptionally close. *The New York Times* wrote, "Had Mr. Ford carried Delaware and Ohio from the [Ford campaign's] swing list, which would have required the reversal of fewer than 10,000 votes, the final Electoral College breakdown would have been 269 to 269, throwing the election into the House." Carter won 49.9 percent of the popular vote to Ford's 47.9 percent.

The electoral vote—Carter's 297 to Ford's 240—illustrated what had happened to the New Majoritarian strategy. The boost that an anti-choice stance was supposed to bring in Democratic states with large Catholic ethnic populations did not materialize. Carter won 57 percent of the Catholic vote and Ford 53 percent of the Protestants. Ford was saddled with his too-conservative platform. Its anti-labor tone hurt him among the blue-collar Democrats he had hoped to attract. New York, Ohio, and Pennsylvania remained, although narrowly, with the Democrats. As a southerner and born-again Christian, Carter destroyed the right's southern strategy, winning all of the border and southern states other than Virginia. In spite of Reagan, Ford carried California and the rest of the West.

The crucial issue in Ford's defeat, overshadowing all others, was his pardon of Richard Nixon. For too many people, Watergate had been too calamitous a betrayal for forgiveness. For Republicans, Ford had offered little to commit to except loyalty to a party that had disgraced itself with Watergate. It wasn't enough. To that extent the Reaganites were right: It is the commitment to the issues that gets the juices running and makes people work harder and stay longer to fight. Ford didn't give Republicans the fire.

As for women, a majority remained with the Republicans: 51 percent voted for Ford and 48 percent for Carter. Nonetheless, 1976 showed the first glimmer of a women's voting consciousness separate from that of their male family members, which in pre-seventies voting studies had been a key indicator of how women would vote. By large margins, Massachusetts voters adopted a state ERA and Colorado voters rejected an attempt to repeal the ERA that it had adopted in 1972. In both states, women organizers and voters brought about these victories. The fledgling women's movement was raising women's consciousness about the connection between their lives and politics, and the state ERA legislative struggles were bringing into politics women who had never before considered participating.

More women were giving money to candidates and running for office themselves. The number of women state legislators increased to 9.1 percent from 8 percent in 1974. Two more Democratic women joined the sixteen women incumbents in Congress, five of whom were Republicans. Democrat Dixie Lee Ray of Washington became the nation's second woman governor, and Republican Norma Paulus was elected Oregon's secretary of state. While many more women ran and lost, often in no-win districts, those of us in the NWPC, the National Women's Education Fund, and the newly formed Women's Campaign Fund were encouraged.

Ford had nearly won—there was enough blame for his loss to cover everyone. Many analysts noted that if Rockefeller had been left on the ticket (a hypothesis that assumed that Ford would have been able to win the nomination with Rockefeller), Ford would have won New York—and the presidency. Others suggested that Anne Armstrong would have been an even stronger candidate and would have delivered her home state of Texas. Republican feminists outside Washington wondered what the outcome would have been if Ford had been braver in Kansas City. Certainly, alienating pro-choice people in the Midwest and northeast had not helped him; and the vote clearly proved that the Catholic hierarchy did not dictate how the Catholic laity voted. In New York's U.S. senatorial race, for example, pro-choice Catholic Daniel Patrick Moynihan had defeated the leader of the anti-choice movement in the U.S. Senate, Catholic James Buckley. Like Americans of all faiths, most Catholics made their own decisions on how they would vote. Despite the machinations of the New Right, separation of church and state was secure for the moment.

But dark clouds were looming on the horizon for Republican moderates and women. The New Right felt they could do well in the Republican race for power. The next few years would test them—and the women's movement as well.

6

THE BACKLASH BREAKS OUT

For many American women, 1977 was the year they joined the feminist movement. For the New Right, 1977 was the year they moved in on the RNC. For believers in reproductive rights, it was the year a cruel and hateful law eroded a right granted women by the Supreme Court. And for Phyllis Schlafly, it was the year she proved to Republicans who were paying attention that being against the women's movement meant votes and money.

A growing social revolution was changing America. By the fall of 1977, nearly 49 percent of American women were employed full-time outside the home, compared with 34 percent in the early fifties. Their flocking to jobs predated 1977, the year the women's political movement began to take off nationally, but once large numbers of women experienced discrimination on the job, found no adequate child care, couldn't get credit independent of male sponsorship, and discovered other injustices endemic to their gender, they looked for ways to solve their problems.

The majority embraced the feminist message without identifying it as such. Most didn't join the movement but accepted its goal: that they could have a choice in determining their future and need not sit passively by accepting the traditions and mores of a male-dominated society. They could shape the world more to their liking. Their destiny wasn't immutably set because they were women. The feminist slogan, "The personal is political, the political personal," made sense to them whether they were Republicans or Democrats. But even as they were embracing this concept, Schlafly was organizing a movement that would make the Republican party the enemy of women's equality. The movement would grow quickly after Ford's defeat, and its doctrine would become Republican doctrine when Reagan became president.

More than anyone in the party, Schlafly, a devout Catholic, shaped the Republican misogynist strategy. By recruiting large numbers of Catholic and fundamentalist churchwomen to stop the ERA, she showed the New Right how to expand the party base in a direction compatible with their ideology. She proved that not all women agreed with the feminist message and that for some it was actually immoral. For the New Right, Schlafly's cause was a strategic investment toward capturing the White House in 1980 and winning seats in Congress. They welcomed women attacking women's liberation to their ranks, which gave them valuable cover from those who said they were against women. Just as significant for her success was the willingness of New Right members of Congress, such as Jesse Helms, Orrin Hatch of Utah, Phil Crane and Henry Hyde of Illinois, and Bob Bauman of Maryland, to help her.

The New Right men were moving to take over the RNC's machinery. The first skirmish for the 1980 Republican presidential nomination came over the selection of a new national chairman. The winners would have an inside track in planning the 1980 convention and giving their candidates numerous tactical advantages. Even though Ford had said publicly in Kansas City that he wanted her to stay, Mary Louise Smith announced she would retire when her term ended in January to go home to take care of her seriously ill husband. A month after Ford lost the election, he called a GOP summit meeting to pick her successor. In a remarkable exhibition of incivility, Chairman Smith was not invited to the meeting. Among those who were were Vice President Rockefeller, Ronald Reagan, and Democrat-turned-Republican John Connally, who had not even been able to deliver Texas for Ford.

Watergate and Ford's defeat had seriously damaged the morale of the old guard and moderates, but the New Right was not in bad shape; the president's loss meant they could build their own Republican revolution. This accorded with classic revolutionary theory: The old structures had to be destroyed before the revolutionaries could take over. Reagan made it clear that this was the direction he wished to go when he wrote immediately after the election that the majority of

Americans consider themselves conservatives: ". . . [J]ust below the surface, the Republican party is hankering to be reborn. . . . [I]t should reshape itself into a clear-cut alternative to the Democrats. I intend to be in the thick of that effort."

Whatever clout Ford and the old guard might have had in choosing a new RNC chairman collapsed when his candidate, Texan Jim Baker, withdrew at the last minute. In mid-January 1977, with Ford's blessing, the RNC picked recently defeated Tennessee senator Bill Brock over hard-line Reaganite Utah state chairman Richard Richards. It wasn't lost on us that Brock came from the original Draft Goldwater group and that the New Right considered him one of theirs. With Brock's election, the party moved out of the control of the old guard conservatives, never to return.

This was not apparent at the time, however, because Brock picked Arizonan Mary Dent Crisp to be RNC co-chairman, choosing her from a list of women prepared by the Republican Women's Task Force. Crisp had gotten her start in politics working for Goldwater, and both moderates and the old guard were pleased. The New Right didn't seem to care, or maybe didn't notice, that she was an ardent ERA advocate. It appeared to be a good mix—an old guard conservative linked up with a new conservative.

In March, task force leaders Pat Goldman, Pat Bailey, and Alice Tetelman presented an agenda to Brock and Crisp laying out the way the Republican party could finally put its professed belief in women's equity into practice. The agenda was inclusive. If it had been effectively implemented, a new power would have been brought into the party that would have helped maintain the influence of the moderates and old guard. Moreover, the full participation of women would have staved off the shift in women's voting patterns from a preference for Republicans to a preference for Democrats, a shift that first showed up in 1980.

The agenda was a model of how to develop a new political force. It included:

- organizing regional meetings of elected and other Republican women in which women would be brought into party activities and recruited for office
- hiring women for positions at all levels of the party and particularly as state and regional organizers

- establishing a women's speakers bureau that reached out beyond the few well-known GOP women to others in the professions and business
- retraining the GOP field staff to understand the nuances of the new women's issues
- an energetic effort by the RNC, through speeches, testimony, and calls to GOP legislators, to pass the ERA
- highly visible backing of the forthcoming International Women's Year (IWY) Conference in Houston
- continued outreach as defined by the Rule 29 Committee, and to that end printing of the Rule 29 guidelines in the national party rules

But the RNC staff was too busy responding to the pressures of the New Right to work with the Republican women's movement on this agenda. The clout of the New Right was growing both financially and ideologically. They were being funded by Coors, Scaife, and Simon, while Viguerie's direct-mail money machine was raking in millions for political action, accompanying its letters to potential contributors with anti-ERA, anti-abortion, and anti–"women's lib" messages. In 1976 Viguerie had raised close to $5.6 million for congressional candidates. (In contrast, the new conservatives working through the American Conservative Union, *National Review,* and *Human Events* had raised a small fraction of that; and the Republican Women's Task Force was struggling to raise money for its plans from its members and receiving modest hundred-dollar contributions from a few wealthy Republicans.) In 1977 Viguerie was bringing in at least $25 million annually for his clients, which included the National Rifle Association, Conservative Books for Christian Leaders, No Amnesty for Deserters, Congressmember Robert Dornan, and the National Conservative Political Action Committee (NCPAC), the newly organized most virulent and visible political organization of the New Right.

The New Right's financial reach was becoming a source of friction with the new conservatives. The new conservatives focused on policy; they were less interested in making money from politics. Louis Ingram, a former member of the Capitol Hill chapter of the new conservatives, expressed their frustration: "I am convinced that these people put economic and egotistical self-aggrandizement ahead of national interest."

James Buckley noted that "the Viguerie people address only those issues which tend to stir up hostilities among lower-middle-class whites." The three red flags of abortion, gun control, and busing he was referring to were the New Right's biggest direct-mail moneymakers.

The fact that these issues were tactically profitable was what mattered. Arthur Finkelstein, one of the New Right's strategic gurus and a NCPAC founder, described their approach succinctly: "It is not reality that counts so much as the perception of reality." Guided by this smoke-and-mirrors philosophy, the New Right operatives set out to create whatever perception was needed to win.

But it was not a good idea to let internal rivalries fester between the party's conservative factions, and RNC chairman Brock took a crucial step toward taming them when he appointed Charlie Black to be the committee's political director. A North Carolinian whose mentor and political employer had been Jesse Helms, Black had been a field organizer for Reagan's 1976 presidential bid and one of the Reaganites assigned to integrate the Reagan apparatus into the Ford campaign after Kansas City. Black was also co-founder and former president of NCPAC, which had raised millions for the New Right's 1976 campaign activities. In his new role in the RNC, Black effectively became Brock's chief political aide. In this position, he was ideally located to manipulate the committee for the New Right's ends.

This Black–Brock arrangement symbolically established the powerful new coalition of the New Right, the new conservatives, and the old guard, who grudgingly went along. All of them champions of the New Majoritarian strategy, they essentially ended the influence of moderate and some stubborn old guard officeholders over RNC politics.

The factions in this new coalition also ended any productive action for women's rights in the national GOP. The Republican party as a party might not yet have decided to wage active war against women, but it abandoned its acceptance of women's equity as a principle to be achieved as well as a tactic to be used to win political power. Brock made some effort to be even-handed and to welcome the Republican feminists and their message, but he wasn't about to ignore the New Right's strength, and with Black encouraging their goals, Brock was hard-pressed not to cooperate with them.

One of those goals was the eradication of women's reproductive rights. The New Right's onslaught came not only in campaigns but in

Congress. The battle over federal Medicaid funding for abortions for poor women illustrated how powerful they had become. In 1976 the Senate had opposed and the House had been bitterly divided over Henry Hyde's amendment to the HEW and Labor appropriations bills that abolished the use of federal money for poor women's abortions except when a woman's life was endangered. But the Democratic House had passed Hyde's amendment, and the majority of pro-choice senators finally gave in to the House and let the amendment pass. They assumed it was illegal and would be overturned by the courts; and when Judge John F. Dooling, Jr., of the federal district court in New York ruled that the law discriminated illegally against poor women, they were hopeful that the issue was settled.

It was not. The following February the New Right showed their muscle again. The Hyde Amendment came up in the House a second time and passed 201 to 155. Hyde and Bauman had organized the successful outcome—98 Republicans and 103 Democrats for the amendment, 134 Democrats and 21 Republicans opposed—a vote presaging the formation of a women's backlash coalition in Congress that crossed party lines. The vote mirrored the same kind of social issues coalition politics between New Right Republicans and conservative Democrats that was forming in electoral campaigns.

On June 20, 1977, the Supreme Court held 6 to 3 in *Maher v. Roe* and two other cases that neither the Constitution nor existing law required states and localities to pay for poor women's abortions through Medicaid, and it further ruled that public hospitals had no obligation to provide them. The majority argued that the issue "should be resolved by the representatives of the people, not by this court." It was a judicial straddle that initiated a tortuous, zigzag progress toward outlawing abortion that would reach crisis proportions by 1989.

In sharply worded dissenting opinions, Justice William Brennan wrote that "none can take seriously the Court's assurance that its conclusion signals no retreat." In Justice Harry Blackmun's words, "the Court's decision [is] reminiscent of Marie Antoinette's let them eat cake attitude toward the poor during the French Revolution." He added, "There is another world 'out there,' the existence of which the Court, I suspect, either chooses to ignore or fears to recognize. And so the cancer of poverty will continue to grow."

Justice Thurgood Marshall added his own searing dissent: "The court also well knows its decisions will have the practical effect of preventing nearly all poor women from obtaining safe and legal abortions, and will brutally coerce them to bear children whom society will scorn for every day of their lives." He was "appalled at the ethical bankruptcy of those who preach a 'right-to-life' that means, under present social policies, a bare existence in utter misery for so many poor women and their children." Cartoonist Herblock summed up the New Right's philosophy: "It's simple—if you could afford children, you could have abortions."

While the Supreme Court had not ruled specifically on the constitutionality of a ban on federal funding of abortions, the opinions indicated such a ban was probably constitutional; and eventually this led to a reversal of the Dooling decision in New York. With the Court having thrown the issue of Medicaid abortion coverage back to Congress, all hell broke loose in both houses. Although the Democrats held majorities in both, in the House the Republicans led the battle to impose the ban and in the Senate to stop it.

Poor women got no more support from the White House than they had received from the House. President Carter endorsed the Court's ruling, saying, "As you know, there are many things in life that are not fair, that wealthy people can afford and poor people can't. . . . But I don't believe that the federal government should take action to try to make these opportunities exactly equal, particularly when there is a moral factor involved." It was an extraordinarily sanctimonious comment, and it met with widespread distaste.

In accord with the president's endorsement, HEW secretary Joseph Califano announced he would move to cut payments for abortions to poor women. Democratic women issued a statement in response that said, "It simply cannot be in the national interest to force women on welfare—the poorest, least healthy, least educated segment of our population—to bear and rear children they do not want, or alternatively, be made to produce children for others to adopt." Other Democrats criticized Carter for backing a policy that would "impose the moral views of a minority on the majority" and create "more misery and hopelessness for poor and powerless women and their families." They cited President Kennedy's philosophy that in a pluralistic society each person must follow his and her own conscience.

In the Senate, the most passionate advocates for women were

Republicans. Their courage and tenacity led to a five-month struggle with the House that tied up operational funding for the HEW and Labor departments by holding up the $60.1 billion Labor–HEW appropriations bill, threatening a cutoff of paychecks for workers in both departments. The struggle had enormous implications for the direction of America's women's movement, and it was this battle—as much as the 1980 presidential campaign—that proved how strong were the forces aligned against it.

Two months into the stalemate, the National Conference of Catholic Bishops announced a public drive to end abortion. Many members of the New Right were Catholics and many weren't; but the nudge from the conference, following in the steps of the self-righteous preaching of the president, gratuitously reinforced the New Right's sense that they alone spoke for the virtuous.

At about the same time that the bishops declared open war on pregnant women, nearly a hundred thousand women and men marched on Washington in support of the ERA. Abortion was not their focus. The Medicaid battle and its import had become an insiders' game. Most American women were paying little attention to Congress that summer and fall as they held their IWY meetings and worked to pass the ERA.

Republican senators Edward Brooke and Robert Packwood led the fight opposing the ban. Packwood told his colleagues that "to deny abortions to the poor because we disapprove of them is a disdainful, haughty arrogance that should not demean this Congress." Brooke called the ban "nothing but a means test saying who's allowed to have an abortion." Seeking to protect poor women's rights, the two senators saved what they could. The Senate passed a modified Hyde Amendment in a 56-to-39 vote that gave poor women Medicaid funding for abortion not only in cases of life endangerment, rape, and incest but when "medically necessary."

Hyde lashed out at once, calling the legislation "a Christmas tree of exemptions and loopholes. It permits abortions for everything including athlete's foot." And just in case the Senate hadn't gotten his point, the House rejected the Senate bill 252 to 164, sticking with the full ban.

By now, three months had passed. As the deadlock dragged into its fourth month, everyone's nerves were frayed, and anger was universal. Not since the days of the civil rights battles had Congress seen tactics as vindictive and self-righteous as those displayed by Hyde and his New Right allies. These reached new heights when he offered to break the stalemate by allowing financing of "medical procedures" such as dilation and curettage for some rape and incest victims. It is hard to conceive of a more grotesque scenario, or one with so gross an invasion of personal privacy and medical professionalism. Here was one of the nation's great institutions tied in knots as it specified what procedures would be allowed and discussed, and what caps should be placed on a rape or incest victim's bills. Here was a male-dominated Congress debating women's most intimate gynecological and sexual problems.

Finally, Hyde and his House colleagues outmaneuvered the Senate. They called a three-week recess and left town. Their desertion forced the Senate to act—either to pass the appropriations bills with the ban or to face the wrath of the HEW and Labor department employees who would not get paid and the half-million people who relied on grants and contracts from the two departments for their livelihood.

The Senate buckled under, agreeing in essence to the House's "compromise" language. In the end, America's poor women had been held hostage by the zealots of the House and lost. For the next thirteen years, the Hyde Amendment was never seriously challenged. When an effort was made in that direction in 1993, at a point when the number of pro-choice women in the House had increased, it failed. The House Democratic leadership failed to give these members the rules support they needed, and the defeat of the amendment was lost on a parliamentary maneuver.

This debate over the public funding of abortions illustrates various conceptual elements of the misogynist strategy, some of which fit and others of which conflict with traditional Republican philosophy. The elements in the strategy are the cost to taxpayers, the morality of abortion, and the fairness of discriminating against poor women.

The Republican party had traditionally been opposed to government funding of social programs since the days of the New Deal. But after Eisenhower's election in 1952, national Republicans began grudgingly to accept the value of many of the New Deal programs. Nixon and Ford continued this practice, and government support of social programs was accepted public policy by both major parties even as Republicans preached they were the party of less government and tended to be less generous with funding.

The New Right's ascendance changed this acceptance. They argued and gradually cajoled the old guard over to their own view that such programs were morally wrong as well as too expensive for the taxpayers. The cost issue was not a problem for the old guard, for whom the extravagance of federal spending had been a long-standing conviction. Linking the idea that it was morally wrong for women to have abortions with the idea that the government shouldn't pay for immorality was a more difficult leap for them to make. But as the years passed and the New Right grew stronger, old guard Republicans either agreed or went along in order to avoid another ordeal like the 1977 deadlock.

Co-opting the moderate Republicans was harder. They believed poor women had a right to have their medical procedures covered just as poor men did, and they held that one's personal view on abortion should not preclude those services. It was a given that public policy be tolerant of an individual's religious convictions and respect the constitutional separation of church and state. What seduced these moderates into the Hyde camp was the so-called "compromise" notion put forward by the New Right's allies that it was acceptable for women to have abortions but that the taxpayers should not pay for them. It was an insidious argument, and it proved to be an effective one because it gave moderates the rationale to have it both ways. They could keep government expenditures down appearing to condone a particular religious view; and they would not be seen to be anti-women, since they didn't oppose abortion. A poor woman would simply have to find the money on her own. We called people who held this view, multiple-choice.

This is, in fact, one of the most profoundly anti-women arguments in the entire panoply of such New Right messages, for it sets up a double standard of government policy that not only favors the rich and well-off over the poor but singles out women as targets. A woman is punished for becoming pregnant because she is poor, has had failed contraception, is young, or is in a bad relationship or marriage. The argument is puritanical, unforgiving, shortsighted, and wretchedly cruel. Yet the Hyde Amendment continues to be the law of the land even as the U.S. Constitution, through *Roe v. Wade*, ostensibly guarantees all women the right to determine their own reproductive destiny.

Even if one reduces the conflict solely to what is best for the taxpayer's wallet, the proposition that denying poor women public funding for abortions will save the government money is fraudulent. Numerous studies have shown that the cost to government of paying for unwanted children whose care from the prenatal months through age eighteen will be borne by the government is staggeringly higher than the cost of an abortion.

The morality of abortion was a genuine concern for those New Right advocates and their allies who sincerely believed abortion was a sin and therefore should not be funded by the government. But to the vast majority of Republican members of Congress, the Medicaid issue was strictly an opportunity to win New Right support. Brooke and Packwood were exceptions. Their courageous stand was respected but eventually discounted by many national Republican leaders who decided the most pragmatic course would be to accept the New Right's agenda on reproductive rights.

Tallying its victories over numerous moderates and liberals in both parties, the New Right coalition recognized its clout and set its sights on 1980. Jimmy Carter and his administration were generating widespread disaffection. It was time to aim for the presidency. The question now wasn't how, but when.

The defining moment for the American women's movement came in mid-November, at the International Women's Year Conference in Houston. As Megan Rosenfeld wrote in *The Washington Post,* Houston proved that "the woman's movement . . . is no longer a small group of intellectuals. . . . It has developed into a force considered socially acceptable by presidents' wives and housewives from South Dakota, by the middle-aged and older women as well as the young." Rosenfeld was right. The IWY brought feminism to mainstream America.

The conference grew out of a first-ever meeting of the world's women in the summer of 1975 in Mexico City under sponsorship of the UN International Year of the Woman. The Mexico City conference adopted a plan of action for women, and the UN transformed the International Women's Year into the Decade for Women (1975–1985). Mirroring the goals of Mexico City, the Congress then passed legislation funding state IWY conferences as well as the Houston IWY conference, to take place in 1977. Women were to hold an eleven-month series of local and then state meetings to assess how much progress was being made toward women's equality. Each state conference would adopt a plan of action for America's women, and state delegates would then meet in Houston to approve a national plan.

President Ford, a strong proponent, appointed a bipartisan governing commission for the IWY, and through 1975 and 1976 Republican women were the official leaders, first preparing for the Mexico City meeting and then for the Houston conference. With Republicans in charge, the IWY had a less radical image than it would have had with Democrats. They gave the women's movement a centrist cachet and a mainstream legitimacy that was needed, for most Americans knew little about the movement beyond the more radical headlines it had attracted in the early seventies. Headed by Jill Ruckelshaus, these Republicans in charge were as dedicated to feminist ideals as Democrats were, and they had as well the advantage of informal connections to Republican officeholders. Not surprisingly there were those who charged the IWY was radical, but given the support of Ford—by no stretch a radical—these attacks had little credibility.

After Carter's victory in 1976, responsibility for the IWY shifted to the Democrats, and the new president appointed liberal New Yorker Bella Abzug to replace Ruckelshaus. It was an unfortunate change. The image of IWY "respectability" that had been reassuring to those for whom the women's movement was a new concept was blurred; Abzug was outspoken and intense and moderation was not her style. The New Right increased their attacks on the IWY state meetings, labeling them "an affront to womanhood, women's good, and family stability." This onslaught also affected the polite but valuable backing IWY had been receiving from Republican officeholders. Illinois senator Charles Percy, whom Ford had appointed to the bipartisan IWY commission and Carter had reappointed, discovered that the New Right had targeted him for defeat in the state's 1978 primary; there were press reports that Phyllis Schlafly would be the challenger. Percy's response was to drop out of the women's rights movement. He didn't go to Houston. His cop-out worked. By 1978, he'd made peace with the Illinois right, and Schlafly announced she was too busy overseeing STOP ERA to run against him.

But despite the New Right's attacks on the state IWY meetings, Schlafly quickly realized the Houston conference was going to be a spectacular success. It was coming at the end of the ERA ratification fight, and she knew the Houston delegates would endorse the amendment. Thirty-five states had ratified, three more were needed, and the ratification deadline was just sixteen months away. It was essential for Schlafly's anti-ERA strategy that she destroy the credibility of the IWY delegates' claim that they represented the majority of America's women.

Back in 1967, after Schlafly had been defeated in her bid to become president of the National Federation of Republican Women, she formed an organization called the Eagle Forum, whose mission was to back conservative candidates for the 1968 elections. The forum now became her tool to build a counterforce against the IWY. She and her followers would boycott the official IWY meeting and hold their own rally in Houston. (As it turned out, Schlafly sympathizers from Utah, Indiana, and Mississippi went to the IWY conference itself and dominated the official delegations from these states.)

For eleven months, from the first IWY state meetings to Houston itself, American women underwent a vast consciousness-raising session. For the first time in the nation's history, women in each state came together to talk about their lot and to articulate their dreams of how they wished to change it. For the majority of those attending, these IWY meetings constituted their first contact with women's politics and the feminist message. They found it an exciting, exhilarating experience, if sometimes a bewildering one. Women from all walks of life got together —doctors and laborers, Catholics, Jews, and Protestants, blacks, Native Americans and Asians, housewives and teachers. They argued about ways to obtain equal pay for equal work and better child care, about abortion and sex education, and the stereotyping of women into traditional roles. "How can I stop my husband from beating me?" they asked. "What will the ERA really mean?" The questions they raised were as varied as the range of their experiences.

Mormon, Catholic, and fundamentalist Protestant women went to these meetings to fight against feminism. Many changed their minds when they got there. The New Right lambasted the IWY in the *National Review* and *Human Events,* but none of this sniping diminished the ardor and camaraderie that the often chaotic IWY gatherings were evoking. Helms held ad hoc Washington hearings against the IWY. Schlafly women crowded into meetings in Montana, Hawaii, and Washington to drum up support for STOP ERA but to little avail. The state

IWY meetings continued to pass resolutions for the ERA, for choice, and for other issues of concern to women whether or not they were feminists. Other than national elections, it was the greatest demonstration of grassroots democracy in U.S. history.

As the November national conference in Houston neared, however, the tone grew meaner. The Imperial Wizard of the United Klans of America said his group would be in Houston with Klan lawyers "to protect our women from all those militant lesbians who are going to be there." The press warned of possible violence between the Klan and IWY delegates on the streets of the city. As the conference opened, *The Washington Post* editorialized that it "was a poor idea" and feared a brawl confirming the "public's most harmful stereotypes of women in politics . . . such an outcome would misrepresent the real social and political changes that have occurred in the past several years."

The predictions of doom and disaster were wrong. Houston turned out to be an energizing and uplifting experience for the majority of the twenty thousand women attending.

First Ladies Rosalynn Carter, Betty Ford, and Lady Bird Johnson sat sedately on the dais on the opening day, the first time three presidents' wives had shared the same stage in support of the women's movement. The delegates truly represented the nation's diversity. The Sam Houston Coliseum was full of American women of all ages, races, religions, occupations, ethnic groups, and classes. More than two-thirds were married and had children. Some were feminist, some antifeminist, some didn't know how they felt about feminism; but all wanted to be in Houston to express their feelings about the future of women.

"Human rights apply equally to Soviet dissidents, Chilean peasants, and American women," exhorted Barbara Jordan, the remarkable congressmember from Texas who had been so impressive a presence during the House Nixon impeachment hearings in 1974. Another Texan, Liz Carpenter, brought everyone to their feet when she described the spirit of Houston:

> So here we are, the faces and voices ignored and silenced too often by the decision makers. . . . Unafraid, uninhibited, let us speak to the future well-being of America. . . .
>
> For, Mr. President, members of Congress, until the women of the United States are full equal operating citizens, your cry

for human rights around this globe will have a very hollow ring.

Who are "we the people" gathered here in Houston? We are the female people left out in Philadelphia. And the irony—the real irony—is that there would have been no America without us. So we are here to state our claim on its past and its future. We have been necessary to it from the beginning. . . .

We crossed the Atlantic to Boston and Jamestown. . . . Across the open plains we trudged every weary foot of it, embraced the majesty of the American Rockies, wrote about it, sang songs about it, helped build the log cabins, light the lanterns of the frontier. . . . [W]e founded the churches and Sunday schools, and with homespun simplicity nurtured the population with faith and spirit.

Once settled, we have seen our own dreams sometimes shattered, often shortchanged, doors closed, or half closed by insecure men and women fearful of a world of equality. . . .

We mothered this nation. Are we to be penalized for it forever? We have no intention of abandoning our role as nurturer or wife, mother, responsible sisters, loving daughters, taxpaying citizens. Some of us are homemakers, some breadwinners. Most women are both. . . .

Are we to be forever shackled by the unending audacity of elected men? . . . America, look at us. Listen to us. Have faith in us. Help us. Love us as we loved you.

We applauded. We cheered. We hugged each other. We were one with the women of Seneca Falls, with the campaigners of 1869, with the suffragists. Carpenter touched our sense of each other, our linkage and necessary dependence on other women. As the days went on and the delegates considered the plan of action, her sentiments kept us together during a few difficult moments, as when a Pennsylvania delegate challenged the all-white Mississippi delegation with its five male members, allegedly Klan members, for failing to include blacks. The Mississippians angrily justified their being there as valid representatives of the women of their state and said that only the husband of one of the women delegates belonged to the Klan.

Votes supporting the ERA and abortion rights touched off intense demonstrations. Unfurling banners with giant color photos of fetuses, anti-choice delegates rushed to the podium singing, "All we are saying is give life a chance," only to have their song drowned out by the chanting of "Choice! Choice! Choice!" Yet through the dissension and the raucousness, we stayed together.

One poignant moment underscored the sense of family that enveloped us. When a resolution crafted by a coalition of racial and ethnic minority delegates calling for the improvement of living and working conditions for women suffering the double discrimination of sexism and racism passed unanimously, the entire hall rose spontaneously and sang "We Shall Overcome." Television cameras caught a loving embrace between Coretta Scott King and members of the Utah delegation. The anger some black and other minority women had had toward feminism as a "white racist tool" had been confronted and briefly dissipated.

Rights for lesbians were the most difficult issue many delegates faced. For some it was the first time they had ever met an acknowledged lesbian. Before Houston, pioneer feminist Betty Friedan had opposed a resolution in the plan that called for protecting homosexuals' civil rights. She feared that emphasis on that issue would diminish the chance to pass the ERA, since an overriding argument by the STOP ERA people was that the amendment sanctioned lesbianism. In Houston, Friedan changed her mind.

In an article about the conference, Friedan wrote,

I never had been opposed to civil rights for homosexuals: the right of sexual preference seemed to me a private right, like the right of religious freedom—and, as such, certainly a women's issue, a women's right. But I had strongly objected to the confusion of feminism with lesbianism and to a focusing on lesbian rights to the neglect of equality common to all women. But now I objected even more strongly to the way the right wing was trying to fan a hysteria of hate and fear against homosexuals to cloak their real economic and political objections to the Equal Rights Amendment. It would have been immoral, wrong, to sacrifice the civil rights of lesbians to appease the right wing. It would not have appeased the right. It would not make the issue go away. It would only increase the bitterness and division that for too long dissipated the energies of the women's movement.

And so Friedan, who had fought for so many years against the inclusion of the lesbian issue in the women's movement agenda, stood before the delegates and urged them to vote for a separate civil rights statement for "our lesbian sisters."

The debate was heated, but the resolution passed with a comfortable majority. Still, the issue stayed thorny and would not be resolved as easily as in Houston, and for years it was often difficult for many women active in the women's movement to confront it.

The final plan of action was a remarkable document, outlining the cutting-edge issues of concern to American women. It included recommendations for helping battered women and children and eliminating discrimination against women in the arts, business, education, employment, and the media. It called for fair credit standards, equal pay, equal treatment in insurance coverage, reproductive rights, aid to displaced homemakers, equal partnership in marriage, fair divorce laws, and more and better child care. The ERA was the most emotionally popular issue, and its inclusion in the plan set off the loudest and longest cheers from the delegates.

Inside the cocoon of those four days of Houston, we women found sisterhood—that universal sense of being together honorably for a great cause. Even now, twenty years later, women who don't know each other will find themselves reminiscing about Houston in the same way war veterans, strangers on sight, quickly become close as they talk about Normandy, Inchon, or Hue.

The Houston conference touched me deeply. On September 28, volunteer women runners holding the IWY torch had set out from Seneca Falls, New York, for Texas. At the November 18 opening ceremonies in Houston, Susan B. Anthony's grandniece accepted the torch. As I ran in the light rain beside the runners those last hundred yards before the torch was passed to the 1977 Susan B. Anthony, I felt a kinship with the women of Seneca Falls. I knew why I had endured the frequent defeats and occasional soaring hopes the last five years. I knew I would work all my life for the changes those women had sought. I understood them. During those few days in Houston, I found many others who felt as I did. We would not forget, we said, and we haven't.

Outside the Sam Houston Coliseum, much of America saw our women's conference in a different light. The nation had had more to watch on television than us. Some eleven thousand people had gathered with Schlafly on the other side of the city for her rally "for the family" the afternoon of the opening IWY session. The press reported they were mainly white, southern, and members of fundamentalist Protestant churches, with some 45 percent men and children and perhaps fifty African-Americans among them. At Schlafly's rally, women and men shook Bibles and denounced the ERA "as an all-out assault on the American family." The National Council of Catholic Women, the Mormon Church, the Daughters of the American Revolution, the John Birch Society, and leaders of the "pro-life" movement were all represented.

Just as the IWY was the first experience of the women's movement for many of the delegates, this counterrally was a political baptism for Schlafly's new recruits. Like those of us at the coliseum, they too would remember those days in November in the years to come, as they worked for Ronald Reagan in 1980 and 1984, fueled the engines of Pat Robertson's 1988 drive for the Republican presidential nomination, kept watch over George Bush in 1988 and 1992 to see that he didn't waver in his support for their cause, and in 1996 threw their zeal behind Pat Buchanan's crusade.

New Right Republicans made the same kinds of attacks they had been making before the conference. Extreme-right California congressmember Robert Dornan called the delegates "sick, anti-God, pro-lesbian and unpatriotic." Speaking as the keynoter at Schlafly's rally, he said that "the great tragedy . . . was to see two former first ladies and the wife of the president stand by Bella Abzug and by their presence approving sexual perversion and the murder of unborn babies." When Gloria Steinem was told that Schlafly's group believed all the women at the conference were lesbians, she laughed. "If we're all lesbians," she asked, "where are we getting all these unborn babies to kill?"

The Texas Democrats supported the conference or kept their mouths shut, but the leader of the Houston Republicans, Harris County GOP chairman Jerry Smith, was not so hospitable. He called the delegates "a gaggle of outcasts, misfits and rejects." Speaking for the Republican women delegates, Mary Louise Smith invited Smith and Dornan to meet with the Republican women attending the conference. Somehow they never found the time.

Years later, when I returned to Houston for another convention—utterly different in tone and promise from this one—I would remember the torch. As I watched the ugliness of the 1992 Republican convention and the rancor spewed out against women and others who did not fit the mold that most of the Republicans there wanted, that sprawling Texas city became a microcosm of all the tensions ravaging America. Leaving Houston in 1977, I was filled with the optimism that America gives its citizens when its politics work and no good goal seems unattainable. Leaving in 1992, I was filled with a numbing despair. I felt hate —hate of a kind I had not experienced before. In 1977 I would have tried to convince those who disagreed with me to change. In 1992 I wanted to destroy them.

In assessing the conference, *Washington Post* political reporter David Broder wrote prophetically that "women's rights may prove as divisive an issue inside the GOP in the 1970s as civil rights was in the 1960s." Elly Peterson was a former chairman of the Michigan GOP and national RNC officer and one of the most highly respected women in the party. She was in Houston with us and when we left she said, "We're coming out of this with a whole new breed of women" who are potential recruits for the Republican party "if we just don't label them as misfits and oddballs." But as Peterson and the rest of the Republican feminists knew, that's what was already happening. "Women's rights are as American as apple pie," read a banner waving over the IWY delegation of Bill Steiger's Wisconsin, but the old guard and moderate Republicans were already shying away from these rights, capitulating to the New Right agenda.

American women were participating in a revolution in Houston, but for the revolutionaries in the Republican party—both women and men—the counterrevolution had already begun. We were its first targets.

7

The Successful Trial Run

"Moral decay thrives in America," proclaimed the New Right's mail. Crafted mainly by Richard Viguerie's direct-mail company, these missives fairly screamed that Americans were angry about school busing, gun control, the ERA, quotas, high taxes, sex education, the Panama Canal treaty "giveaway," abortion, and family decline. As usual, "women's libbers" were blamed for many of the nation's problems—they were destroying morality and family life, taking jobs away from men, and turning their backs on the home. Those problems that couldn't be laid to women Viguerie's mail blamed on that other most popular of American scapegoats, big government.

These were the major themes of the 1978 campaign, the first act in the 1980 presidential nominating follies. The more attention the women's movement drew from the press, the harsher and louder grew the New Right's invective against it. By cloaking their attacks in a mantle of religiosity and morality, they discovered they could gain respectability both for themselves and for their argument. Their detractors called them deliberate exploiters of social discontent. No, they insisted, they were holy warriors, white knights, tough but honorable John Waynes out to battle those who sanctioned the killing of babies and enticed women away from their God-given destiny as wives and mothers. They were acting for the good of the country. But the New Right also knew something was missing: They needed the credibility and additional resources that a religious connection could give them. They needed a formal link with the nation's right-wing evangelical ministers.

These ministers, many of them southern, opposed the social changes that had begun more than a decade before. They railed against the Supreme Court's decisions on abortion, pornography, school prayer, busing, and aid to parochial schools. Through the late sixties and early seventies they had preached their opposition, but while they all had similar messages, they were not organized as a group. In 1976 many of them had backed their fellow born-again Christian Jimmy Carter, a Baptist, pleased that one of their own was going to the White House. But this "new Southern Democrat" disappointed them. Carter believed in equal rights for women and separation of church and state, and he opposed a constitutional amendment sanctioning prayer in the schools. He supported *Roe v. Wade,* even though he opposed Medicaid funding for abortions.

Thus, by late 1977, two major forces were each seeking a partner that would enhance their strength and empower their message. The New Right was in search of religious legitimacy; the preachers were looking for a political leader and a political movement more compatible with their beliefs. Phyllis Schlafly, who had built a Religious Right constituency of fundamentalist and evangelical women in the South over the previous five years, had already introduced the ministers to the New Right politics of the Republican party, but it would be another year before the New Right and the Religious Right would actually team up.

What Jerry Falwell and the other evangelical preachers of the right, like Pat Robertson of the Christian Voice and James Robison of the Religious Roundtable, needed in order to further their social agenda was to learn how the political game was played. They knew how to register their parishioners, lobby, and work on campaigns, but these were routine skills. What they did not have was the political acumen and inside know-how that would give them control of party committees, caucuses, and conventions—the steps necessary to gain national political power.

The New Right professionals had that know-how, and they needed the preachers as much as the preachers needed them. Nineteen seventy-eight would be the year of their trial run. They would work together in loose coalitions, albeit wary of each other, often bickering, yet clear about their target: feminists, liberal Democrats, moderate Republicans, and at times the old guard of the Republican party. On women and their issues, Schlafly was the New Right's guide. In the Republican party, the Young Republican and NCPAC leaders showed the way.

While Weyrich and Viguerie were part of the group that would fashion the entrance of the preachers into the New Right revolution, it was the young men who had learned their politics in the Young Republican National Federation (YRNF)—Howard Phillips, Charlie Black, and Roger Stone—who taught them about the insider world of the party. Stone, as knowledgeable as Black, played a major role in linking the Republican party with the New Right and then the Religious Right. Elected YRNF chairman in 1977, he used the organization to build the New Right's power at the same time that his compatriots were using NCPAC, which he had co-founded with Black, Terry Dolan, and Arthur Finkelstein, to stir up discontent among Democrats and independents.

This linking was shrewdly planned. New Right leader "[Paul] Weyrich disguised the fact that his attraction to Jerry Falwell was initially based on calculation and strategy," E. J. Dionne, Jr., writes in *Why Americans Hate Politics.* "Though Weyrich himself was a devout Christian, he viewed Falwell more in Machiavellian than Christian terms. 'The New Right is looking for issues that people care about,' Weyrich said. 'Social issues, at least for the present, fit the bill.'" According to Dionne, Weyrich created the name Moral Majority because he believed the majority of Americans were in agreement over the basic social issues, and that "somebody's got to get that moral majority together."

Falwell didn't announce the official founding of the Moral Majority until 1979. By then, the three major elements of the New Right revolution had joined forces in the 1978 campaigns. They were already a formidable national political machine: the evangelical churches with their ministers preaching misogynist messages on television and raking in large sums of money to further their cause; Schlafly's masses of Religious Right women; and the New Right political professionals with their insider expertise, direct-mail apparatus, and YRNF network.

As this new force gathered momentum and attention, the supply-siders and the neoconservatives took note and hopped aboard. Economic issues were the supply-siders' priority. People like Jack Kemp, who was an original member of the New Right team, saw an opportunity to add their radical economic ideas to this steamroller that seemed destined to reach the White House. Other than Kemp, who was outspoken against racial discrimination, they claimed no burning interest in racial and gender problems.

On the other hand, the neoconservatives cared deeply about such problems. Disturbed by the disorder that the demands for equity were bringing, the neoconservatives were former liberal Democrats, many of them academics—Jeane Kirkpatrick, Irving Kristol, Midge Decter, and Norman Podhoretz—who abhorred quotas and most affirmative action. But unlike the New Right, their weapons were not the bayonets and shotguns of bias. Rather, they used intellectual stilettos to oppose the civil rights and women's movements. They were also foreign policy hard-liners, concerned with what they believed were America's weakened defenses and its inability to outmatch the Soviet Union. They felt a kinship with the ideas expressed in Helms's 1976 "morality in foreign policy" plank in the Republican platform.

The old guard and moderates were all that stood in the way of this encroaching political machine, yet too often in 1978 they went along with the bigoted messages of the New Right's Republican candidates. As they had done since 1964, they turned a blind eye to the southern strategy, seldom protesting against the racism that spewed forth from these candidates as long as it was effective. Breaking the hold of the Democrats on the South had been what mattered. And when Schlafly came along and proved that misogyny could also win elections, few objected.

Until Ford's 1976 defeat, campaign tactics like these had not been advisable outside the South. In other parts of the country, the civil rights and women's movements had effective institutions to challenge such bigotry. The culture in these states was more amenable to calls for justice and equality, and a state political party there was opening itself up to press opprobrium and electoral defeat if it attempted an openly racist and misogynist strategy of the sort Helms and Schlafly pushed.

Obviously racism and sexism were to be found all over the nation, and local and congressional district political party organizations could and did run successful candidates who pushed subtle messages of bigotry. But through the mid-seventies, as a rule, most state candidates weren't ready to stake their political futures on playing to the backlash. While politicians of both parties and the citizens they represented often practiced a double standard, they did not flaunt their biases.

After Ford's defeat, this situation changed. The southernization of the party's politics toward minorities and women got under way in earnest in the 1978 elections, when some Republicans outside the South became the beneficiaries of the New Right's largess.

The New Right men set out to nationalize the southern strategy by stirring up male Democrats and independents outside the South over "social issues," just as they had been stirred up in the South. As Howard Phillips declared, "Organize discontent—that is our strategy." Men were the target because the New Right assumed that women would go along with whatever their men did. That assumption turned out to be wrong. When it came to women's issues, in particular the ERA, the New Right approach worked only in the southern states, as Schlafly's own failed efforts elsewhere demonstrated. (Her home state of Illinois was the only exception.) Her messages alienated many people, particularly moderate Republican women who were often the leaders of the state ERA campaigns. This effect was something Schlafly never seemed to grasp—as late as 1984, according to an anti-ERA leader in Maine, her blunt New Right messages during Maine's anti-ERA recall campaign "stopped our momentum dead." The recall campaign lost, and Maine's state ERA remained in place.

But in 1978, all across the South, where our side had lost ERA fights (only Texas and Tennessee had ratified the amendment), anti-ERA Republicans won office with the help of Schlafly's forces. The New Right achieved their greatest gains in these former Confederate states, where defeat of the ERA was a subtext in their campaigns. New Right populism replaced traditional Democratic party–line voting for state and local offices. It was a warning to Jimmy Carter that his southern roots might not guarantee him an election victory in 1980.

The rise of the southern New Right to major power in the national Republican party was especially helped by victories in Texas, the region's most heavily populated state and one of the nation's richest. Bill Clements won a close election for the governorship, to become the state's first Republican governor since Reconstruction, and John Tower was narrowly returned to the Senate. The twenty-four-member Texas delegation in the House now included four Republicans. The grip of Lyndon Johnson and Sam Rayburn had been broken.

Nineteen seventy-eight was also the year that brought Texas Democrat Phil Gramm to the House; in 1983 he would bolt his party and become a New Right Republican and in 1995 would run for president.

In Georgia, Newt Gingrich was elected from a mainly suburban Atlanta district comprising newly minted Republicans and Wallace Democrats who feared the gradual move of blacks into their neighborhoods and "women's lib" influence.

Gingrich ran what has since become the typical New Right populist campaign, full of mean attacks on the rich interwoven with subtle but clearly understood misogynist and racist messages. Campaigning as "the candidate of middle-class people who push a grocery cart," he attacked his opponent, State Senator Virginia Shapard, for financing her campaign with her own money and for crusading for the ERA. His advertising message in rural areas used the antifeminist family values theme: "Newt will take his family to Washington and keep them together; Virginia will go to Washington and leave her husband and children in the care of a nanny." A Gingrich campaign official described the strategy thus: "We went after every rural southern prejudice we could think of. . . . [W]e were appealing to the prejudice against working women, against their not being home." Gingrich won 54 to 46 percent and has never since lost an election.

Jesse Helms took North Carolina like one of the hurricanes that sweep through his state—powerful, destructive, and deadly serious— winning 53 to 43 percent in this former southern Democratic fortress. Raising $6.7 million, he set a new national record for spending in a U.S. Senate campaign. Schlafly's army worked hard for him. NCPAC provided money and campaign assistance. The preachers proselytized for his brand of morality. It was an impressive show of political power for the new partnership of racism and sexism in pursuit of Republican victory.

Down in Mississippi, Thad Cochran became the state's first Republican elected to the U.S. Senate since Reconstruction. Cochran agreed with the New Right, although his campaign style was more moderate than the shrill aggressiveness of his New Right Republican House colleague, Trent Lott. (Lott would be elected to the Senate in 1988.) And in South Carolina a new New Right player appeared: Lee Atwater, who as Strom Thurmond's campaign manager used racist ploys to reelect his seventy-five-year-old boss to the Senate.

Tennessee was the only state in which the New Right's efforts fell flat. There, ERA backer Howard Baker withstood their attempts to drag him down for backing the Panama Canal treaty. With a 58-to-42-percent margin, as befitted a senator of national stature, Baker's victory boosted his presidential ambitions.

Throughout the election campaigns of 1978, the ERA was a major concern for women. When it became clear that ratification would not be achieved by the March 22, 1979 deadline, the women's movement asked Congress to extend the deadline. Republican women joined their Democratic allies in Washington and in local congressional district offices to lobby for the extension. Congress obliged, and in late summer of 1978, it extended the deadline to June 30, 1982.

The battle went on. Of the nonsouthern states that didn't ratify the ERA—Illinois, Arizona, Missouri, Nevada, Oklahoma, and Utah—all had an active church presence opposing it. Some of Schlafly's most passionate workers came from Illinois, Missouri, and Oklahoma, where Christian fundamentalist women and their preachers believed in a literal interpretation of the Bible that held that women should submit silently to male authority. The Mormon Church held a similar but less harsh view of a woman's role and its members were influential in defeating the ERA in Utah, Nevada, and Arizona. Downplaying an anti-Catholicism that dated back more than a century, fundamentalist Protestant ministers and Mormon bishops joined with Catholic priests and laity in preaching against the amendment.

Intraparty Republican politics played a role in these ratification fights. In the 1978 elections, the New Right used the ERA as a wedge issue to defeat pro-ERA GOP officeholders. During the exhaustingly long battle in Illinois, many of the leaders of the bipartisan ERA–Illinois, which led the pro-ERA side, were Republican women. Republican men were much less forceful and committed, as exemplified by Governor James Thompson, whose degree of active support for the ERA was tied directly to the constantly changing attitudes of others in his party.

He was not the only Illinois moderate who wavered. Senator Charles Percy's backing for the goals of the women's movement diminished in direct proportion to the rise of the New Right and the Religious Right. By 1978, he had adopted a low-key approach to the ERA—not opposing it but doing little to help it. While he faced scant opposition in his 1978 primary, the general election was different: There he was a target of old guard and New Right animosity. During the campaign, the New Right verbally roughed him up, and the influential M. Stanton Evans, one of the original Draft Goldwater men and six-year chairman of the American Conservative Union, made a radio ad for Percy's Democratic opponent. Helped by an eight-point margin and the endorsement of Ronald Reagan, Percy won, but it had been a bruising fight.

The New Right also went after Illinois congressmember John Anderson, who was the only Republican on NCPAC's 1978 hit list of forty-four House members. Anderson was deeply religious. As a young man, he had wanted to be a minister and often said the Bible was the most influential book in his life. In his congressional office hung a picture of Christ. But despite Anderson's religious convictions and his membership in the First Evangelical Church, his right-wing-evangelist primary opponent attacked him viciously for backing the ERA and for not supporting constitutional amendments to ban abortion and sanction school prayer. Schlafly and her STOP ERA women campaigned against him. Although Anderson won in the general election, he remained unhappy with the changing direction of his party and recognized that someone needed to fight the New Right influence. He began edging toward a race for the presidency, although it was policy issues affecting the nation, rather than the health of the party, that were his chief motivations.

In many states, Republican women provided a bridge for the ERA forces to the more moderate Republican legislators and governors and made the final arguments that often clinched a victory. But this was often not the case during the ten-year ERA battle (1972–1982) in Illinois. There the ERA went down to defeat eight times, facilitated by a parliamentary move engineered by Schlafly requiring the state legislature to ratify it by a three-fifths rather than a simple majority.

Like any large and diverse group, feminists are sometimes united, as they were in Houston, and are sometimes riven by disagreements. During the Illinois ERA fight, conflicts between feminists were especially charged. Many NOW members came from out of state to work for the ERA, and the differences in style and approach between them and the ERA–Illinois advocates were as wide as the differences in style between Democratic and Republican feminists. Wavering among the moderate Republican leadership was not confined to the on-again-off-again Senator Percy and Governor Thompson, but our feminist allies among the Democrats often attacked us for coming to accommodation with such leaders. It was a problem that grew over the years. As Schlafly's Religious Right allies became more influential in the party and demanded a more religious tenor in party statements, Republican women found that the New Right was picking off many of their traditional partners within the party or crippling them into ambivalence.

A great many of the New Right's moves during 1978 were about presidential politics; 1980 was on their mind. It was the reason that, in early 1978, the Reagan and New Right forces tried to convince the RNC to dump its co-chairman Mary Crisp, charging that she was a leftist and "radical libber" because she had worked for the ERA and the IWY, and because she had criticized the formation of Reagan's political action committee (PAC). But something else was at work here. The men who had selected Crisp had underestimated her—she had proved to be more than an amiable conservative Goldwater woman from Arizona. She was an ardent believer in women's equality, and her presence as the national party's highest female officer flew in the face of the New Right's misogynist strategy.

Their attempt to unseat Crisp failed. She had many friends on the RNC, and Chairman Bill Brock stood by her; but she would remain a target until the 1980 convention.

That July, in yet another step toward consolidating New Right power in the party, Stone and Black asked Utah senator Orrin Hatch to replace Robert Packwood as chairman of the National Republican Senatorial Committee. Packwood, an outspoken ERA defender, had led the pro-choice fight in the Senate, and the New Right hoped to soften him up for a defeat in 1980. Ostensibly, Packwood left the committee to seek a higher position as head of the Senate Republican Conference, but this was not the whole story. Here too, presidential politics was on the New Right's mind.

Even though Packwood would gain stature as leader of the GOP conference, that position was principally about Senate policy issues, not about senatorial election campaigns. The senatorial committee raised money and resources for the party's senatorial candidates; and its chairmanship was a springboard for presidential aspirations. Even if he or she wasn't interested in running, a chairman could influence the party's choice for president because the committee held sway over a national network of contributors who not only gave money but influenced state as well as national politics.

In recent years senators had become as important a source for presidential candidates as governors had been. Goldwater had been the committee's chairman when he was nominated in 1964. In 1978 Packwood opposed Hatch for the chairmanship because he feared Hatch "would give preferential treatment to right-wing candidates" and would use it to gain a top position in the Senate GOP leadership.

The struggle between the New Right and the moderate and old guard senators for the committee chairmanship was spirited, and when the dust finally settled on January 15, 1979, Pennsylvania senator John Heinz, a moderate and as strong an advocate for women's rights as Packwood, had won by a single vote. It was one of the few times after 1976 that moderates won an insider battle against the New Right.

The press described the outcome of the 1978 elections as "normal," meaning the Democrats kept the Congress while Republicans and Democrats both won significant state races. On the surface it seemed that way. Democrats won the governorships in California, New York, Florida, and Massachusetts, while Republicans won Pennsylvania, Michigan, Ohio, and Illinois. Two Republican women who would play major roles in the Republican party in the early nineties won seats in congress: Nancy Landon Kassebaum was elected to the Senate from Kansas and Olympia Snowe to the House from Maine. Brock hailed Republican gains in the Midwest as "a return to the Republican dominance in the nation's heartland"—that is, a victory of the old guard in its traditional base.

That assessment was somewhat more optimistic than the outcome warranted. The New Right had continued to build its growing electoral strength through both the Republican primary and the general election campaigns. They had attacked Republican moderate incumbents in the primaries. Either they had defeated them—as in the case of New Jersey senator Clifford Case, who lost to New Right analyst Jeffrey Bell—or they had so damaged the moderates' credibility, as when New Rightist Avi Nelson slashed at Massachusetts senator Edward Brooke's pro-choice record, that even when the moderates won a primary, they were mortally wounded for the general election.

Several New Right warriors were elected to the Senate from states that figure prominently in presidential politics. New Hampshire sent former airline pilot Gordon Humphrey to Washington. Out in Iowa, Roger Jepsen, "whom the *Des Moines Register* termed an apologist for apartheid," waged a dirty campaign, attacking Democratic incumbent Dick Clarke for backing the Panama Canal treaty, for his vote for Medicaid abortions for poor women, and for his opposition to the South African government. Anti-choice groups worked fervently for Jepsen, winning votes in Catholic, Democratic blue-collar communities. It was a typical New Majoritarian campaign. The Iowa old guard and moderate Republicans didn't seem sufficiently repulsed by Jepsen's bigotry to vote for Clarke and balance out the Jepsen Democratic crossovers.

The point was not lost on candidates planning to run for president. If solidly old guard Iowa—home of moderate Governor Robert Ray, who had been reelected in 1978—could elect the likes of Jepsen, what did that say about the potential direction of the 1980 Iowa presidential caucuses? Iowa wasn't the South. And the new strategy had also worked in Massachusetts, where Democrat Edward King, running a Wallace-style campaign, attacked forced busing, abortion, welfare, and high taxes. He narrowly defeated old guard legislator Francis W. Hatch, Jr., to become governor.

The women's political movement made gains as well. Although New Right pressures had diminished the ability of Republican women to win nominations, once they were nominated and had a unified party behind them, they did well. Sixty-three of the sixty-six women newly elected to the nation's state legislatures were Republicans. Mary Crisp and the heads of the Republican Women's Task Force and the National Federation of Republican Women had led this effort, and as Crisp said, "It was no accident. I pushed and pushed and pushed." It was in fact an extraordinary record, which came about principally because of the ERA battles and IWY state conferences that had stimulated Republican women to political action.

The percentage of women state legislators rose from 9.3 to 10.2 percent; but reflecting the more welcoming atmosphere for women in the Democratic party, 57.6 percent of them were Democrats, compared with 41.9 percent Republicans. Showing clearly the impact of the misogynist strategy, anti-ERA states—Mississippi, Louisiana, Alabama, Arkansas, Tennessee, and Utah—had the nation's lowest percentage of women legislators. ERA states—New Hampshire, Colorado, Connecticut, Washington, and Vermont—had the highest.

The anti-choice movement also flexed its political muscle in 1978. In New York, the Right-to-Life party became the state's fifth official political party when it won 130,193 votes, outpolling the Liberal party and securing for the next four years a fourth-place ballot line above the Liberals. In close elections, minor-party endorsements can determine the winner. (This is what happened in New York's 1994 gubernatorial election. Another third party, the Conservative party, provided Republican George Pataki with his winning margin over Democrat Mario Cuomo.) In other states, the New Right tried this approach but found more success in directly taking over a state's Republican party machinery than in using a third-party front.

The Right-to-Life party's rise marked the beginning of the New Right's drive to unseat New York's liberal Republican senator Jacob Javits, who faced reelection in 1980. They were to succeed. Alfonse D'Amato, a little-known Long Island Republican officeholder, would start his national career that year, becoming first the Right-to-Life candidate for U.S. Senate, then gaining the Conservative party designation. Arthur Finkelstein ran a New Right campaign of innuendo for D'Amato, depriving Javits of the Republican nomination. Then Javits ran on the Liberal line, in a three-way race against Republican/Conservative/Right-to-Life candidate D'Amato and Democrat Elizabeth Holtzman. D'Amato squeaked by with a plurality of 81,304 votes out of some six million cast. It was a clever way to take over the nation's second most populous state, and D'Amato's victory insured that the New Right would have extra political leverage at presidential nominating conventions.

CBS News/*New York Times* exit polls taken on Election Day confirmed what many moderates working in the campaigns had thought: The voters of both parties were much more moderate on social issues than the congressional and senatorial candidates. Only some 16 percent of the Republican candidates said they approved of federal funding for poor women's abortions, while 37 percent of GOP voters approved.

Only 10 percent of these candidates endorsed national health insurance, compared with one-third of Republican voters.

In just two years, Brock had rebuilt the party financially and organizationally. He had opened it up to new members and issues, forming policy councils and insisting they include women and minorities. He tried—not boldly but carefully. There were no daring actions to elect women or audacious moves to bring them into the Republican congressional and senatorial leadership.

As we turned our attention to the upcoming Republican presidential nomination season, feminist Republicans kept hoping that the signals we'd seen—the losses for abortion rights in the Congress, the stalemate over the ERA, the New Right's success in defeating or silencing our Republican allies, the unwillingness of party leaders to run and promote Republican women to higher office—were an aberration. As the exit polls showed, the Republican rank and file were not anti-women; they weren't members of Schlafly's constituency, supporters of the Religious Right, or followers of NCPAC's misogynists. We tried to persuade ourselves that once a moderate man was nominated in 1980—like George Bush, John Anderson, Lowell Weicker, Howard Baker, or maybe even Gerald Ford—the bigots in the party would again be a vocal minority with minimal influence.

Task force resources were divided between the potential budding candidacies of Bush and Anderson. Some members hoped that Ford would run. Weicker decided not to, and Senate minority leader Baker became too consumed by the Panama Canal treaty battle to campaign for the nomination.

In 1978 the theme coming out of RNC headquarters was party unity, yet these words rang hollow given the New Right's attacks against moderate Republicans. When Brock secured the selection of Detroit, Michigan—a ratified ERA state—for the site of the 1980 GOP convention, the New Right howled. In a most uncharacteristically crude public remark, Bill Rusher said, "The Republican party . . . will lift its skirts and show its ankle to Detroit inner-city blacks," and again called for Brock's resignation. Weyrich angrily attacked Brock for not encouraging "right-to-life people, gun people, pro-energy people" to get involved. No Republican leader of any stature answered in kind.

The failure of the old guard and moderates to launch their own aggressive salvos in return underscored their weakness. Few of them criticized the New Right. Now and then Brock responded; in June 1978 he had warned conservatives not to place so much reliance on the Viguerie groups and called their social issues strategy, emphasizing abortion, "hazardous for the political system." But in general, he acted in a gentlemanly manner, befitting a man trying to keep his warring family together. His public allies were few, and their defense of him tepid. What was even more remarkable—and unsettling—was that those who attacked him were not even GOP leaders. Except for their activities in the Young Republicans and some previous second-level staff posts on the Hill, Rusher, Viguerie, Weyrich, Phillips (who had become a Democrat to build New Right bridges across party lines), and their ilk had never held positions of authority within the party. They were renegades, outsiders, sometimes former Democrats, yet they and their colleagues behaved like the arbiters of correctness for the Republican party—while its real leaders, the governors, the senators, the House members, let them get away with it.

And the New Right intimidators, with their newfound religious friends and their solid southern electoral core, knew it. They were ready to take over the national GOP. Racism and misogyny had paved their road to power. Nineteen seventy-eight had been a good year for them; 1980 could be even better.

8

WINNING THE BRASS RING

George Bush and Ronald Reagan had both been seeking the presidency since the early seventies and seriously campaigning for it ever since Ford's defeat in 1976. Bush formally announced his candidacy on May 1, 1979, and Reagan on the following November 13. There were other Republican hopefuls—Bob Dole, John Anderson, Viguerie and Weyrich's favorite congressmember, Phil Crane, and Clarke Reed's choice, John Connally, plus the perennials who turned up on the pundits' lists but never seemed to get their act together—Jack Kemp and Howard Baker. But only Anderson was ever a potentially serious challenge to Reagan and Bush, and he was hampered by the typical problems of a candidate who starts too late with too little money and organization, so few took him seriously.

When several hundred Republican Women's Task Force members met in Washington in late January 1979 to plan for the 1980 campaign, it was still early in the game. The jockeying for positions on the delegate slates of the presidential primaries, state conventions, and caucuses that would take place between February and June 1980 had just begun. The task force, hoping to place as many women as possible on all the slates, endorsed no candidate.

Susan McLane, now the task force chair, urged the members to raise the consciousness of all the candidates: "Feed them spaghetti and the feminist line, no matter who they are or what their positions." The ERA was the priority; the ratification deadline was June 30, 1982. Three years was not much time to convince three more state legislatures to

ratify. If anti-ERA Reagan won the nomination, Republican officeholders in the states would be lukewarm. We'd already learned in Illinois
about fair-weather friends who varied their level of commitment according to the political winds. An anti-ERA wind blowing out of Detroit would be disastrous.

So we were all anxious to see what would happen when ninety-six
prominent Republicans met at the Tidewater II Conference a week after
the task force meeting. The brainchild of Bob Packwood, this annual
conference had been organized to give party leaders a place to sort out
party policies in a congenial setting. The attendees were chiefly moderate and old guard governors, state and federal legislators, and seven task
force members: Crisp, Kassebaum, Heckler, Fenwick, and Secretaries of
State Norma Paulus of Oregon, Thyra Thompson of Wyoming, and
Mary Estill Buchanan of Colorado. The conference issued a strong public statement favoring women's economic equity that had been developed by Mimi Weyforth, Packwood's legislative aide, and other task
force members; but when it came to the ERA, a cautious hybrid
emerged.

Kassebaum and Heckler shepherded through a unanimous resolution commending the RNC under Brock and Crisp's leadership for
helping women candidates and for exerting "its leadership in achieving
equal rights for all individuals." The resolution said the party had a
"long and proud tradition of support for women as full partners in
American society and has consistently endorsed equal rights for women
. . . including the Equal Rights Amendment." To the unsuspecting,
this sounded terrific. It wasn't. The statement was the most Kassebaum
and Heckler could get the conference to agree to. Nowhere did the
resolution urge the party to continue backing the ERA.

It was a warning bell: The ERA was in trouble in the Republican
party. If even our pro-ERA leaders were unwilling to spell out their
support at this relatively collegial issues meeting a year and a half before
the convention, what chance did we have to retain the ERA in the
Republican platform? It was obvious to all of us that our only chance
for success lay in electing enough delegates who would stand up for the
ERA in Detroit. As for abortion, it was not officially mentioned at
Tidewater.

Despite McLane's call for the task force to remain neutral on the
candidates throughout 1979, we knew that if our women were to suc-

ceed in becoming delegates, they would have to run pledged to a candidate except in those states where the party leadership planned to go to Detroit uncommitted. The activists took sides early. Some pro-ERA women became Reagan delegates but found it hard going. Deloris Newell, a Michigan Reagan delegate, was ostracized by the state's twenty-eight other Reagan delegates. Neither Reagan's daughter Maureen nor Carla Hills—both ERA supporters—were trusted enough to be made delegates. They were alternates in the 168-member California delegation, which had 25 percent female membership. In fact, so distrusted was Maureen Reagan that Charlie Black, now working on the Reagan campaign, kept her from going to Iowa to campaign for her father because he feared all she'd do was talk about the ERA.

Overall, the task force members backed Bush; as the "moderate" candidate, they expected him to be as supportive of women as Ford had been. Mary Louise Smith, who had known him and been aware of his presidential ambitions since 1970, went to work for him in Iowa in the winter of 1978 without qualms. "We saw him as a moderate. He seemed to be on our wavelength," she remembers. Bobbie Kilberg, who had worked with him during the Nixon administration, felt much the same and also joined up in 1978.

Bush had solid political relationships with activist Republican women going back to the sixties, when he had first entered national politics. Many were ready to work for him now because he was an old friend. They didn't question his stand on the issues, believing him when he wrote to the task force that his "commitment to equal rights for women is unequivocal" and that he believed "the Equal Rights Amendment will assure the rights of both men and women to equal treatment under the law." Further, he wrote, he was "committed to equal treatment, equal pay, equal education, and equal responsibility for all Americans."

Barbara Bush had long been a Planned Parenthood backer, and many of Bush's friends were contributors. As a freshman member of the House Ways and Means Committee between 1967 and 1970, Bush himself had been so tenacious in arguing for family planning that the committee's chairman nicknamed him "Rubbers." Once he left Congress in 1970, he did not help the family-planning movement in any significant way. But he did nothing in those years to dispel the perception that he was strongly pro-choice either, so it had come as a surprise to the pro-choice community when, in announcing his candidacy, Bush opposed Medicaid funding for abortions except in cases of rape or incest or to save the life of the mother. Sometime during his nine-year odyssey for the presidency, he had turned anti-choice.

Responding to a task force presidential questionnaire, Bush wrote that while he opposed a constitutional amendment to override *Roe v. Wade,* he "could support a constitutional amendment to give the states authority to regulate abortions within these boundaries." In other words, he backed the elimination of *Roe* through states' rights action. Some Republican feminists excused his anti-abortion, anti-*Roe* stand: Bush was their friend, they liked him, and that seemed enough. After all, they said, he did support the ERA, and he had a better chance of winning the nomination than pro-ERA John Anderson.

McLane and her husband, Malcolm, had entertained the Bushes when they campaigned in New Hampshire, and they had been taken aback by Bush's comments on women's issues at one of his local campaign stops. In a letter she sent him in July 1979, McLane mentioned his response to a reporter's question on abortion. "What I feel I can comment upon," she wrote, "is your unfeeling, cavalier and untrue side comments which you throw into your answer such as your coy '. . . abortion, I was afraid you said that.' It is a tough issue. . . . [D]on't make jokes." She was particularly upset by Bush's remarks about women using abortion as birth control.

> This statement . . . shows a complete lack of understanding of the seriousness and pain of this operation and the difficulty women must face in making this decision. It smacks of upper-class notions that pro-choice women don't "care to be tied down to babies" and disregards the major reasons for abortions—sickness, including mental illness, poverty, young teenage pregnancies, and amniocentesis-proven birth defects.

Susan McLane, a mother of five, had caught the essence of George Bush on feminist issues. He never seemed to understand what women were saying or give an indication he tried to understand. Still, like so many others, McLane stuck with him because she thought a Bush administration would help women more than Reagan's would. As she told me, "He was better than Reagan."

So many task force members joined the Bush campaign, in fact, that their principal political activity became winning the nomination for him. The goal of finding women delegate candidates was subsumed under finding delegate candidates regardless of gender who could win support in the primaries, caucuses, or state conventions. As always, the campaign favored placing well-known Republicans on its slates—which almost invariably meant men—who could take votes away from Reagan. Not a single task force woman was able to convince the Bush hierarchy that a women's strategy aimed at electing women delegates for Bush, and attracting women voters, was worth trying. All issues are women's issues, we were told yet again. There's no need to separate them from the general strategy.

According to several women who worked for Bush, James Baker, Bush's campaign manager, was anti-choice and not sympathetic to the "goals" of the women's movement. But Baker's personal attitudes weren't the prime reason that the campaign rejected a women's strategy. First, the men in the campaign didn't believe the majority of women voters had a political identity separate from men's. National polls in 1979 indicated that men and women of similar social, economic, and educational backgrounds tended to vote similarly, although women tended to show a slight preference for Republicans. A gender gap had begun to appear in local races in states where the women's political movement was active, but it hadn't shown up yet on the national scene.

Second, the Bush campaign had bought into the misogyny strategy. An analysis of the campaign staff, Bush's own policy statements, and his leading supporters indicates that the campaign executed a clever dual-ideology stratagem. Some of the staffers had been part of the 1964 Draft Goldwater group; one was liberal GOP New York senator Jacob Javits's former press secretary, Pete Teeley; and another, Susan Morrison, had been a communications expert for the Democratic National Committee. Many of the Ford crowd were now members of Bush's campaign committee, as were Reagan's 1976 New Hampshire leader and Texas finance chairman. This collage of ideologies camouflaged the fifth-column tactic that the campaign was fashioning with the New Right. It played on Bush's New England background and Ivy League style and convinced the majority of the press, the moderate and old guard Republicans, and the pro-Bush task force women that he was one of them. Veteran *Wall Street Journal* political reporter Jim Perry saw the Bush strategy for what it was, but he was an exception. Bush is "no liberal, not even a moderate," he wrote. "He is running pretty much as a standard conservative, which is one reason his staff thinks he has a shot at the nomination."

A closer look at Bush's stated positions on the New Right's social issues confirms Perry's assessment: The differences between him and Reagan were inconsequential. In February 1979, three months before Bush announced, the archconservative newsweekly *Human Events* had signaled to the faithful that Bush was ideologically acceptable. Describing him "as a possible back-up on a Reagan ticket," it quoted a newsman who had heard Bush speak at the new conservative American Enterprise Institute as saying, "on foreign policy, he certainly seems to be all the conservatives could want." It also quoted top Bush aide Tom Lias, who said Bush planned to speak "as a conservative on both foreign and domestic policy." *Human Events* added that Bush "says he's 'very uncomfortable when he's labeled a moderate Republican,' stressing that he considers himself a conservative."

A month later, the Bush campaign picked David Keene to be its number-two man. Keene's conservative credentials were impeccable; he was a former chairman of the Young Americans for Freedom and an organizer of Reagan's 1976 southern delegate operation, had worked for Spiro Agnew and James Buckley, and was a business partner of Roger Stone. Both his leadership of Bush's political staff and his words were reassuring to those conservatives who might otherwise doubt that Bush fit the mold. "I think Bush is pretty conservative," Keene said, ". . . and after checking with conservatives around the country for the past three weeks, I learned that although Reagan is their first choice, there was some feeling that Reagan may not make it—and that Bush is considered by them a good second choice."

And so it went. Six weeks later, the campaign hired George Wallace's 1972 and 1976 presidential campaign manager, Charles Snider, and Wallace's brother-in-law, Alton Dauphin. Snider liked "the way he talks." "We wanted to be sure he was someone we could be comfortable with and that we could be effective," he added. "We checked around and found the people we've always worked with were very impressed with George Bush. I think you're going to find some other Wallace state chairmen who will get involved with Bush."

The other shoe dropped the same week that Bush announced. New Right leader Paul Weyrich had been looking around for a new horse to ride, after the campaign of his candidate, Phil Crane, disintegrated. Bush was his man: "George Bush has become a harder-line candidate than he [Crane] has."

Meanwhile John Anderson's campaign was gearing up. Its personnel came almost entirely from his House staff and the Ripon Society. Anderson's behavior in Congress on women's issues had been typical of most of the task force's so-called Republican congressional friends: flawless on paper, minimal when it came to taking action in the House that might move a bill toward becoming law. He said what we wanted to hear; he voted for the legislation we backed; but he initiated little action and built little political support.

The Anderson campaign was no more geared conceptually toward recruiting women delegates and women staff than the Bush operation. When asked whether the campaign had considered a women's strategy, Anderson's campaign manager said that "it hadn't occurred to us." Yet in response to a task force presidential questionnaire sent to candidates in the fall of 1979, Anderson wrote, "the battle plans for all of my priority states include provisions for actively recruiting women delegates and assuring that 50 percent of each slate are women. Because of my legislative record, I expect that in some cases the percentage will be significantly higher than half—and I welcome it."

As in Bush's organization, no women sat in the inner Anderson circle in these early days, although women volunteers ran the campaigns at the grassroots level: Elizabeth Hager in New Hampshire, Ann Gannett in Massachusetts, and Ann Peckham in Wisconsin. Anderson had little money and few paid staff. On the other hand, Bush's campaign was well financed and did hire several midlevel staff women, including Margaret Tutwiler, who acted as Bush's campaign scheduler and was a trusted confidante to James Baker.

By June, the misogynists and the feminists were lining up their troops for the big battles of 1980. The New Right and the Schlafly crowd were fighting passionate battles against the pro-ERA forces in Illinois, North Carolina, and Florida, and all were organizing delegate-selection campaigns. The right-to-life movement was pressuring Congress to prohibit the military from paying for abortions for its personnel and their families, even in cases where a woman was carrying a grossly defective fetus, while pro-choice Senate Republicans led the fight to continue these payments. Jerry Falwell proclaimed the formation of the Moral Majority the same week that Anderson announced his candidacy.

A month later, the National Women's Political Caucus met in Cincinnati, and representatives for Bush, Anderson, Baker, and Connally came seeking recruits. No one appeared for Reagan, Dole, or Crane. At the RNC, Mary Crisp urged Republican women to remain uncommitted until 1980 in order to assess the candidates' viability and positions on women's issues. She was fulfilling her proper role—maintaining a neutral position on presidential nominees as befitted a national party leader—but it was bad advice. If women were to have any chance of influencing the 1980 nominations, they needed to be lining up behind candidates at that point.

Throughout the summer and fall of 1979, task force women tried to get themselves and other women onto presidential delegate slates in the ERA-ratified states of California, Iowa, Michigan, Colorado, and New York, but they had little success. New York would return to its preseventies record of only 17 percent women delegates. I, who had twenty-two years of service to the New York Republican party and had been an alternate to the 1972 and 1976 conventions, couldn't convince my state's male leaders to support a Republican feminist to be a delegate. I was again only an alternate. My story was similar to those in other states. You either had to be an elected official, be related to one, or be very rich, to be a delegate to the Detroit convention. None of the presidential campaigns, including Anderson's, initiated a full-fledged drive to include significant numbers of women on their slates. When the convention opened in Detroit, 29 percent of the delegates were women and 38 percent of the alternates. Interestingly, Minnesota, which had a strong Reagan delegation, topped the list with 53 percent. This astounding success had come about because the delegates had been selected at a convention where politicians could more evenly balance slates, and because the highly effective Minnesota women's movement had made its politicians aware of the necessity and benefit of recruiting women. The Reagan women delegates were beneficiaries of the feminist movement.

·   ·   ·

On November 4, 1979, exactly one year before Americans would vote for president, a mob of Iranian students stormed the American embassy in Teheran and took more than fifty Americans hostage. The Shah of Iran had fled his country the previous January, and the Ayatollah Khomeini had established an Islamic republic in Iran. The attack on the embassy came after the United States allowed the former shah to enter the country for medical treatment on October 22. This action not only changed U.S. foreign policy in the region but influenced the direction of the 1980 campaign. The hostage crisis was to dominate the country's attention and focus awareness on the nation's foreign policy for the entire year to come. Analysts thought it might give Bush the advantage because, of all the Republican hopefuls, he had the most actual foreign policy experience (although Anderson had served three years as a foreign service officer). But in the first few months after the attack, all the campaigns said little on the issue, watching as the nation closed ranks behind its commander-in-chief and the Carter adminstration attempted to deal with the crisis.

Soon after the attack, Reagan announced his candidacy in New York City. In seeking the nomination, his campaign adopted a dual strategy: to win over the old guard and moderates while consolidating control over the New Right. They couldn't have a repeat of 1964, when moderates hadn't worked for Goldwater, or 1976, when the Reaganites hadn't worked for Ford. To defeat a sitting president, even one as unpopular as Jimmy Carter had become, required the commitment of all Republicans.

To moderates and some of the old guard, Reagan seemed out of touch with the realities of ordinary citizens' lives, lacking the judgment and the intellectual qualities necessary in a president. Serious concern had arisen around the country, as well as within the party, about his lack of foreign policy experience. There had been ample disarray in the Carter adminstration's handling of foreign policy before the hostage crisis in Iran—it had faced problems in the Middle East and in Pakistan, Cuba, and elsewhere; relations with the Soviet Union were deteriorating. Many people found it unsettling to contemplate what Ronald Reagan might do under such stresses. Those who knew him conceded that he was a likable fellow, but outside his immediate circle of political supporters, few Republicans believed he had the capacity to win a national election, let alone be president.

The task of his campaign was to disentangle Reagan the man from Reagan the hard-line ideologue. It was Reagan the man they believed they could sell to the American public. They had to build on his reputation for decency, and to convince old guard and moderate Republicans that he wasn't a radical, that he had the combination of strength and common sense needed to lead America's defense and foreign policy—so lacking, they pointed out, in Jimmy Carter. They also had to prove to the nation that Reagan was compassionate—that his plans to cut taxes and government programs Americans liked were in their best interests.

In addition, the team had to persuade the party that he was not going to destroy it by insisting on ideological purity. Their job was to prove that he was electable, that he wouldn't be a Goldwater scaring the country by calling for the dismantling of Social Security, that he wouldn't consider nuclear war to get back the hostages in Iran. By winning the early primaries and state conventions and caucuses, the campaign hoped to show that he was a unifier, that he wasn't "unstable," as some Democrats were saying, and that his policies were based on the truest Republican traditions of Lincoln, Teddy Roosevelt, and Ike.

They also had to convince voters that Reagan wasn't a bigot. The policies he was to champion had the effect of perpetuating bigotry and stirring up those constituencies that were truly sexist, racist, homophobic, and religiously intolerant. He opposed abortion and "forced" busing for school integration, and he supported a constitutional amendment allowing prayer in the schools. To more centrist Republicans, these stands were as important in determining his qualifications for president as were his foreign policy, defense, and fiscal positions. To win their loyalty, he had to sound more moderate than his policies would later prove. The team's strategy was to hold to the New Right's policies but to talk another game, one that was more conciliatory and gentler, that fit more with the warm, casual nature of Reagan's personality.

The campaign downplayed social issues. It was clear that the Reaganites expected the New Right to support them in exchange for Reagan's backing their social agenda, but before the election they minimized its importance. The campaign intentionally ignored women's issues, never mentioning them unless publicly asked. It "forgot" the task force's questionnaire until we had announced the results from other candidates to the press and reported that Reagan, Crane, and Dole hadn't answered. Within a day, we had answers from Crane and Reagan. Reagan didn't state his position on the ERA, protecting equity for college sports programs, federal family-planning programs, or drafting women. But he and Crane distinguished themselves by being the only candidates to tell us they backed a constitutional ban on abortion.

The Reagan camp had to contend with some contradictory history on this issue. Back in 1967, during his first year as California's governor, Reagan had signed one of the nation's first laws liberalizing the conditions under which women could obtain abortions. (One result of this law was to decrease the number of children on California's welfare rolls during his administration. He was to boast about this during the campaign but chose not to acknowledge the reason it came about— fewer unwanted babies had been born to poor women because the state had paid for their abortions.)

During the campaign, in what proved to be a typical pattern in his treatment of feminist policies, he said he hadn't "thought much about the issue" of abortion at the time he signed the law; he had let his father-in-law, Dr. Loyal Davis, who favored it, persuade him. Thereafter he had been lobbied by Catholic leader Francis Cardinal McIntyre and had announced he regretted signing the bill. He had changed his mind, he now said, and that was that. Early in 1979, the Reagan campaign stated that there would be no compromise on abortion.

All those years of winning what seemed to nonpolitical people to be inconsequential fights, such as the "positive action" struggle, were finally paying off for the New Majoritarian strategists. The constant maneuvering for control of the senatorial campaign committee, the staffing of the RNC with New Right partisans, the incessant attacks on Crisp and Brock, and the election of New Right leaders like Hatch and Gingrich had given Reagan an advantage in the nomination sweepstakes. In fact, in the late fall of 1979, the New Right was so convinced that the GOP brass ring would be theirs that Bill Rusher, never one to mince words about remaining true to the New Right ideology, wrote that "in order to win the GOP presidential nomination, a conservative candidate must trim toward the center," and "the rightward swing of the national mood in recent years ought to make it easier for Reagan to inch a bit toward the nation's floating 'center' without overdoing it."

Then Bush beat Reagan in the January 26 Iowa caucuses, 31.5 to 29.4 percent. The New Hampshire primary was to come on February 26. For one month, the right had to face the possibility that its man might lose. But Reagan rose to the challenge. Just before Election Day, his campaign rented a hall for a debate with Bush, and then, without telling him, invited all the other candidates to participate. The moderator, the executive editor of the *Nashua Telegram,* refused to let the others participate because the ground rules the newspaper had set were for a Bush–Reagan confrontation. Reagan grabbed the microphone, declared that he was paying for it, and insisted that all the candidates be allowed to speak. Bush stood to the side, ineffectually protesting that the rules provided for a two-man debate. Reagan had proved he could take charge of a difficult situation. It was the turning point of the campaign. He won big in New Hampshire, and his victory train never stopped again until it delivered him to the White House.

The incident was a vivid delineation of the two candidates' characters. Reagan was clearly a man who knew how to manipulate the rules to his advantage, and who understood what any good actor knows to do when the lines no longer fit: Ad-lib, and do it with style and aplomb.

In Nashua, Bush revealed his Ivy League WASP upbringing. With his ingrained sense of propriety, he could fight just as hard as the next man, but he could not shift to street fighting when the rules were changed—he was unable to ad-lib. In this sense, he exemplified what was happening to the moderate wing of the Republican party: The rules had changed. The New Right was using gutter techniques to win, and it was succeeding. This is not to say that the old guard and moderates had not used unprincipled tactics over the years to win elections; they certainly had. But it was always with the veneer of an unspoken code of civility; unsavory actions, by contrast, were usually planned and implemented quietly. Now a new game of politics was being played in the Republican party—out in the open, in your face. Reagan knew what to do. Bush didn't.

Not that Bush and his team weren't masters at the old behind-the-scenes game. They had cultivated the New Right at the same time as they had gone after Reagan. They had seduced moderates and the press into believing Bush was a moderate while he backed the New Right's social agenda. But it was over for him after New Hampshire. Twenty-five primaries remained, but the race was finished. The states that had not yet selected delegates all had large Reagan constituencies. Bush would hold on until late May, winning Connecticut, Pennsylvania, Michigan, and the District of Columbia, thereby maneuvering himself into vice-presidential contention.

Only John Anderson stood in Reagan's way. But less than a month later, it was all over for him in the Republican party as well. In the Illinois open primary on March 18, Reagan beat Anderson 48.4 to 36.7 percent, and the press declared him the unofficial nominee of the party.

On April 24, Jimmy Carter ordered a secret military mission into Teheran to save the hostages. It was a disaster. Eight Americans died, five were wounded, and the avenue of negotiation for the release of the hostages was lost for the near future. Secretary of State Cyrus Vance resigned over the failed mission, and the abortive attempt embarrassed Americans, making them feel ashamed of a commander-in-chief who seemed not up to the job. Reagan, whose military service in World War II had been confined to making training films for the army, began to look better than U.S. Naval Academy graduate Carter, who had spent eleven years in the navy and been an officer on a nuclear submarine.

Carter was in trouble. He had presided over one of the highest inflation rates in modern U.S. history—18.2 percent that February—and a U.S. foreign policy humiliation that some felt was equal to Vietnam. The Republicans had their issue—Carter's failed leadership now evident to many Americans—and they had their candidate, Ronald Reagan.

The campaign wasn't yet over. Americans didn't like Carter, but many were still uncertain about how extreme Reagan might be. Enter John Anderson, who the day before the hostage-rescue fiasco left the Republican party and declared himself an independent candidate for president, offering the American people the "Anderson difference." It was a crucial blow to party moderates and to Republican feminism; but in his quixotic venture, Anderson did prove that many Americans were looking for an alternative to the Republicans and Democrats.

From its very beginning, while he was running as a Republican, Anderson's candidacy had been a prime example of how not to handle a campaign. What made his failure especially poignant—both as a Republican and then an independent—was that Anderson himself was a notably forthright, intelligent, and capable man who genuinely had his nation's best interests at heart and put them above personal ambition. But despite his extensive experience as a member of Congress, he and his campaign had little grasp of political realities. It is no exaggeration to compare the events in this campaign to the distorting mirrors in an amusement park funhouse. Everything the Anderson team did bore some connection to the matter at hand but was invariably just a little skewed.

A successful presidential candidate must be in touch with the politics of his party and must cultivate its most influential members. Reagan and Bush did. Anderson never appeared even to want to. He didn't do the painstaking glad-handing so necessary to build a national party following. He had even lost touch with his own district. As his campaign manager Mike MacLeod said, "We got sidetracked in our presidential plans because we had to spend so much time protecting Anderson's congressional seat." The New Right took full advantage of this disarray. Anderson had been a New Right target for a long time, and when he ran for president, the Illinois Republican establishment— including Charles Percy—endorsed not Anderson, the man who'd spent his political life working for the voters of Illinois, but Reagan, whose only connection was that he had been born in the state.

Anderson's problems were not unique to him. Ever since 1960, Republican moderates have not paid serious attention to grassroots recruiting. In the beginning, his campaign seemed to believe it could win the Republican nomination with little money, few Republican supporters among party officials, and an issues strategy based on the assumption that the party still had enough moderates to defeat the Reaganites and others. In late 1979 and early 1980, the Anderson people kept arguing that the Reagan conservatives and New Right would split their vote in the primaries, and that there would be enough old guard and moderate Republicans unified by their fear of the New Right to elect Anderson. This assumption had no basis either in the polls or in the numbers; there weren't that many in these constituencies to go around if Bush, Baker, and Dole were added to the equation.

Anderson's real strength was with non-Republicans. Massachusetts, New Hampshire, Vermont, Illinois, and Wisconsin, where he would do well, did not have closed primaries. All were either open to all voters regardless of party affiliation, or allowed independents to vote along with registered Republicans. Most of the rest of the primaries crucial for the nomination were in states with closed primaries. Reagan was consistently the favorite among Republican officials in these states and among activists who voted in these primaries. The Anderson analysis was predicated on a Republican infrastructure that had fallen apart after Ford's defeat.

Nonetheless, before he left the party, Anderson's base of supporters was stronger than the Republican delegate count had indicated. He nearly won the Massachusetts primary; Bush beat him by only three-tenths of a percent, and in Vermont he had lost to Reagan by only one percent. But Illinois dealt him a serious blow; the anticipated crossover votes of Democrats and independents never materialized. Campaign Manager MacLeod said they knew it was all over two weeks later, when Anderson came in third in Wisconsin.

Anderson was known as one of the best orators in the House, and he could have electrified the nation at the GOP convention. He opposed all of the New Right's social agenda: He was against prayer in the schools and discrimination against homosexuals; he supported the ERA and women's right to abortion; and his commitment to civil rights was unwavering, although he recognized the strains that school desegregation had cost localities and favored school districts devising their own methods to comply with the law, with busing as a last resort. He was a balanced-budget fiscal conservative appalled at Reagan's supply-side plans, and an internationalist who backed the SALT II treaty between the United States and the Soviet Union.

Anderson had attracted Republicans who assumed that even if he didn't win the nomination, he would lead the moderate cause in Detroit and use his delegates to leverage moderate ideas into the Republican platform. That ended, of course, when he left the party. His independent bid for the nomination had enduring repercussions: It struck a death knell for any leverage that moderate Republicans would have in the national party throughout the Reagan–Bush years.

When Anderson announced his independent candidacy, his Republican supporters were forced to choose between him and their party. Forecasting a typical pattern for us in the Bush–Reagan years, moderates split into two opposing camps, further weakening our capacity to be an effective force. Ripon men had formed the core of Anderson's GOP nomination effort. Now, wrote *Ripon Forum* editor John Topping, "Riponites are hardly of a single mind as to the current political situation. Many individual Ripon members will work actively for the election of John Anderson, others will work for the regular Republican ticket, including Ronald Reagan. The Ripon Society will focus its efforts on the strengthening of the structural and idea base for the Republican party." The only progressive organization in the Republican party had retreated back to think-tank status.

Guided by Democratic political consultant David Garth, other moderates followed pied piper Anderson into the waters of independence, never to return to the GOP. The New Right and the Reaganites couldn't have asked for a more useful ally. The New Right had no use for Anderson Republicans, since they sullied the purity of its ideological agenda, while the nonideological Reaganites, those old guard Republicans, wanted unity. Let Anderson go. Eventually, they knew, Bush would join Reagan, and he'd bring back many moderates.

The Anderson decision unsettled us women. We weren't leaving the Republican party, but we had lost a potential leader for Detroit. Despite his withdrawal, thirty-seven delegates voted for him at the convention. If he'd stayed with the Republicans, he would undoubtedly have had more. Given Bush's solid credentials with the conservatives, Anderson was the only candidate who could have been a serious threat to Reagan's unity campaign.

All revolutions have their heroines and heroes whose heresies lead them to be burned at the stake. Mary Crisp was ours. During her three years as RNC co-chair, hounded by the New Right for her beliefs, she had nonetheless traveled more than 300,000 miles to raise money for the party and recruit new members, had honorably represented Republicans at the IWY conferences, had worked for the ERA—which was still GOP policy—had brought women into the party, and had helped raise the number of Republican women officeholders to its highest level in history. She had admirably fulfilled her duties as the highest-ranking woman in the national GOP.

But now Crisp's enemies increased the pressure on Bill Brock to remove her from the RNC, saying she was simply too liberal to head the party of Ronald Reagan. While she had stayed scrupulously neutral on the candidates, her positions on the New Right social issues were the same as Anderson's, and her opponents used that old trick of guilt by association to get her. All they needed was proof that she was disloyal, and they would be able to convince Brock and her other RNC friends to drop their protection.

The ERA battle was just coming to another crucial vote in the Illinois state legislature. Tensions were running high. One month before the Detroit convention, Crisp was in Illinois speaking for the ERA, and she told the press that Anderson was a creditable presidential candidate because of his ERA support. The *Chicago Sun-Times* then ran an inaccurate headline saying she would be endorsing Anderson. Crisp protested vigorously. "I never endorsed Anderson," she said. "That is so inconsistent and incompatible with how hard I worked for the party! I have been a team player all along."

But she *had* imprudently said that Anderson was the answer to the "big dilemma" facing Republicans who supported the ERA and that an Anderson victory was not "so farfetched." That did it. All hell broke loose at the RNC. The New Right called not only for her resignation but for Brock's, because he had ostensibly tolerated Crisp's "questionable loyalty." Crisp told the press that she was being harassed by her political enemies and that her office phones were tapped. "I hired a professional security consultant, who'd been an intelligence officer in Vietnam, to sweep my office," Crisp says. "He found an electromagnetic field around my deck emanating from another building which was 150 yards across a parking lot. He also found an unexplained wire in the ceiling of my office which he claimed could have been used for eavesdropping. Brock said the inspection by the security person I'd hired was inconclusive."

Brock then hired Terry Dolan's brother-in-law to sweep Crisp's office. He said he found no magnetic field or anything indicating a tap. It was never clear what had happened. To this day Crisp believes that her offices were tapped because the New Right was looking for proof she was helping Anderson—and that she was set up.

After the sweep, it was all over for her. Brock stripped her of all official duties in Detroit, canceled her RNC schedule, and made it clear she would be out when her term ended at the convention. As in a Communist purge, Crisp's name was excised from all official RNC convention documents. A review of the official convention papers shows not a trace of Mary Crisp. She is not included in the preconvention or convention literature. A stranger unfamiliar with the folkways of the national GOP would have thought she never existed. Only in press clippings do you find her mentioned.

The New Right had succeeded in insuring that no top-ranking Republican woman would spoil the purity of the Reagan coronation. The Reagan campaign concurred. Crisp standing before the delegates might well have generated the same kind of booing, shouting, rage, and abuse that Nelson Rockefeller had received at the 1964 GOP convention. A watching nation might have seen played out before its eyes the intensity of New Right hatred in some of the Reagan delegations.

The task force women were split. Former chair Susan McLane, who'd resigned for what was to be an ill-fated run for Congress, Bobbie Kilberg, Jill Ruckelshaus, Millicent Fenwick, and Mary Louise Smith were for Bush. The rest of us were trying to decide what to do. Bush had endorsed Reagan in late May and was maintaining a low profile while his New Right staff worked to gain him the second slot.

Six weeks before the platform hearings opened in Detroit, we tried to craft a strategy that would make Reagan keep the ERA in the platform. *Washington Post* columnist Judy Mann caught our group's frustration in the words of one task force woman: "If he [Reagan] chooses to send a signal that the party is going to reverse a historic trend, that will be truly upsetting. . . . It will be putting moderates and women into a real tailspin as to what they should do. . . . If he wants to keep it [the ERA plank] in, it would be in his interest to send a back channel signal soon before the visibility of the issue is raised." Mouthing the Bush line, another said to Mann, "I think there's a lot of feeling among a number of Republican women that they would like to see some signal from Reagan; some reason why they might be able to support him, such as a moderate as his running mate."

No signal was forthcoming. Instead, the news got worse. The Illinois legislature had defeated the ERA again, and the Illinois Republican state convention had urged that it be removed from the national platform. For the first time in its history, the Southern Baptist Convention formally entered abortion politics and endorsed the Human Life Amendment. On the last day of June came *Harris v. McRae*, the Supreme Court case that reversed the Dooling decision in New York that had found the Hyde Amendment unconstitutional. The Court ruled that the federal government wasn't required to provide Medicaid funds for abortions.

Surveys were confirming what the Reaganites had been hoping for years: The American people were receptive to the New Right's social agenda that Reagan was now stressing. Falwell's Moral Majority and his fellow evangelists were having a publicity field day with their quotes about family values and the moral decay brought on by "women's libbers."

We had experienced the New Right's hatred ourselves at various regional platform committee hearings, after Bill Brock interceded to see that we were allowed to speak. That hatred was palpable. When Susan McLane spoke at a Florida hearing, she was ridiculed and booed. Roger Semerad, who was supervising the platform hearings, said he had gotten a lot of criticism from women opposing the ERA for letting McLane speak. When task force women tried to testify in other places, he told McLane that no more women would testify. Reagan would be the candidate and the ERA would be dropped. He added that Platform Committee chair John Tower didn't want another scene between women as had happened during McLane's testimony.

Bush had received the dedication, time, money, and energy of many Republican feminists during his campaign for the nomination. Now that Reagan was the candidate, would he keep his pledge to back the ERA? Would he be Reagan's link to those American women who backed the ERA? Would he fight with us in Detroit, or would he cave to the Reagan revolution?

In retrospect, the answers seem obvious, but in the summer of 1980, we were not alone in regarding Bush as a moderate man not in sympathy with the misogynists of his party. We wanted to hope.

PART TWO

THE MISOGYNIST
ERA OF
REAGAN–BUSH,
1980–1992

9

REAGAN'S NEW REPUBLICAN BEGINNING

I'd been in Detroit once before, in the early seventies. Its landscape had shocked and depressed me then, but it was worse now. Time and politics hadn't been kind to Detroit.

On that first visit, I'd come to help the Ripon Society launch a new urban policy for the Republican party. Detroit had seemed the perfect place for such an undertaking when we planned it on the telephone, but the immensity of the city's decay dampened our youthful optimism. Perhaps it was too late for Detroit.

We stayed in a once-grand hotel that was now disintegrating like the sidewalks surrounding it. The hotel's beautifully designed art deco lobby showed the signs of slapdash upkeep. The wrought-iron light fixtures in the halls were missing half their bulbs, the oriental carpets were frayed, the elevators erratic. Like the surroundings outside, the place reeked of resignation and despair. I'd seen other American inner-city hotels and their neighborhoods past their prime, but this was the worst. For me, it exemplified Detroit itself; it had so little hope.

We spoke bravely, but our grand Ripon plans came to naught. As we were to discover, the Republican party had given up on city dwellers and was aggressively courting the less despairing, more prosperous suburbanites of the South and West. I remember leaving Detroit angry, sad, and convinced that America was headed for disaster if the cities weren't helped.

By 1980, the cracks in the sidewalks were so large, it was easier to walk in the streets. They encircled blocks pockmarked with vacant lots, luncheonettes, mom-and-pop motels, liquor stores, shabby little shops selling five-and-dime merchandise, and an occasional Howard Johnson. No trees, no charm, no beauty greeted the eye—just urban desolation. A few blocks away lay the "safety perimeter," so designated by the Republican convention staff, who had quietly warned us not to venture beyond it on foot. Within the perimeter stood the Renaissance Center with its elegant Pontchartrain and Detroit Plaza hotels, developed by private contractors with federal money to give downtown Detroit a boost. Close by were Cobo Hall and the Joe Louis Arena, scenes of the convention's formal proceedings.

As the airport bus dropped me off at a Howard Johnson motel on the perimeter, I felt the same sense of impending doom as before—only this time it would be women, not the cities, the Republicans would desert.

I'd come for Platform Committee week to fight for the inclusion of women's issues in the platform. My delegation was overwhelmingly for Reagan. Long Islander William Casey was Reagan's national campaign manager and wasn't about to let his home state embarrass his candidate's nomination. The New York Republicans who championed women's rights were gone or had little power now. Nelson Rockefeller was dead. Senator Jacob Javits was being challenged for his seat by Reagan supporter Alfonse D'Amato, and our allies, State Senator Roy Goodman and Congressmember Bill Green, although staunchly for women's rights, didn't think the fight was worth coming to Detroit eight days early. None of the New York moderates wanted to end up on Casey's bad side. Many knew him as a stalwart Republican who'd been a major party contributor and would likely continue to be. If by some chance Reagan won, they would have a New York connection to the White House. And so they did—Casey ended up as an important member of Reagan's inner circle and the controversial director of the CIA.

Ironically, this Republican convention would embrace the misogynist southern strategy in a northern urban state that had been known as the nation's trade union capital, and in a city that had been home to members of the once-powerful United Auto Workers. Detroit had lost 20.5 percent of its population in the last ten years, and of the one to two million people who remained, 63 percent were black, most with incomes below the national average. The Republicans had come to Detroit not to court its residents but to woo those who no longer lived there. It was unlikely that the racist messages the party now espoused would persuade the black autoworkers who remained in Detroit to take seriously the Republicans' other message of lower taxes and less government.

In fact, the new strategy ignored the blacks entirely. Its target was the blue-collar ethnic Democrats—the white union men and women who had fled to the suburbs in great numbers after September 1971, when a federal judge had ordered that their children be bused to integrate Detroit metropolitan area schools. Indeed, so little attention did the convention organizers pay to race that just before the convention, the Reaganites found themselves blindsided when NAACP leader Benjamin Hooks complained to the press that no prominent black man was addressing the convention. Task force member Connie Newman, a leading player in our 1972 feminist group and an assistant HUD secretary in the Ford administration, was the only black slated to give an address.

Hooks's pique was motivated by Reagan's having rejected an invitation to speak to the NAACP's annual meeting two months before Detroit. The Reagan team's excuse was that its candidate had already planned a Mexican vacation on that date. As a scheduler in numerous campaigns, I can attest to the fact that any candidate who wishes to attend an event can make the time. The point is that the black vote was not an essential part of the Reagan strategy. It was more important that Reagan, now sixty-nine years old, rest in preparation for Detroit. But Hooks won. He himself delivered an impassioned plea at the convention for the GOP to work with blacks. It brought no action.

Several statistics underscored what had happened to Detroit. Unemployment in the auto industry had risen to 30 percent. If economic disaster was striking the male autoworkers, then what was happening to the women employed in the industry? More often than not the last hired, they were usually the first let go. An American car manufacturer spent $17 per man-hour to produce a car that a Japanese manufacturer could produce for $9 per man-hour. America could no longer compete, and the American autoworker was getting the boot. The auto manufacturers said the problem was the high cost of labor. Not surprisingly, the waste and inefficiency of the industry's management wasn't a hot topic of conversation within the safety perimeter of the convention that July.

The glitz and ostentation displayed at the Renaissance Center and the Pontchartrain and Detroit Plaza, where the most favored of the

Reagan delegates, staff, and party VIPs were staying, mocked the party's claims to populism. It made me very uncomfortable. I live in Manhattan, which has its share of such displays, yet there was something different about this Reagan crowd—an arrogance that rarely surfaced in New York GOP circles. The last time I had seen this kind of self-importance at a Republican convention was in Miami Beach in 1972. Many of these delegates believed they had a special right to flaunt their wealth. After all, they'd earned it. Those autoworkers, they said, don't understand that in order for them to hold on to their jobs, they've got to stop asking for so much. If American business is going to compete with Japan, it must have lower taxes, less government regulation, and lower labor costs.

These pronouncements were the supply-siders' mantra. Supply-side economics was a rehash of the free-market economic theory that had been dropped in the 1930s, when it proved unresponsive to ending the Depression. As Sidney Blumenthal, who perceptively chronicled the rise of the right to power, wrote: "It was a revival of the oldest chestnut in classical economics, Say's Law, once the Alpha and Omega, but refuted by John Maynard Keynes." Say's Law posited that "those who supplied goods and services generated their own demand. Some succeeded and others failed, proving the market's neutral genius." It was the invisible hand postulated by Adam Smith that would bring new investment and eventual full employment, if one just had faith and waited. But Keynes's theory said that supply did not create demand; rather, it was the fine-tuning and pump-priming of the economy by the government that kept free-enterprise systems in equilibrium, stimulating demand for goods and bringing robust economic activity.

When stagflation hit America in the late 1970s, however, supply-siders Jude Wanniski, Arthur Laffer, Jack Kemp, and others convinced Reagan that by following Say's Law and giving free rein to the market through drastic tax cuts and minimal government regulation, great wealth could be created. Capitalism would blossom in a way not known before. It was the perfect economic doctrine for Reagan, demanding "from its believers" what Blumenthal calls half knowledge and half faith, promising "hope and opportunity" but discounting "sacrifice and complexity." But it would be disastrous for America because this Reaganomics, as it would soon be called, did not include increasing taxes to ease budget deficits. Supply-side doctrine preached that economic growth would bring about deficit reduction; increased taxes were not necessary.

Women as a group stood to lose from a supply-side thrust. Since women on the whole are poorer than men, a policy aimed at enhancing wealth by cutting taxes that paid for programs that helped the poor and middle class would disproportionately hurt them. We had reason to oppose the supply-siders on this alone, but we did not pay much attention to what they were proposing. We stayed away from economic policy fights because we considered our fiscal conservatism to be no different from that of the party, meaning old-style balanced-budget economics—cutting of inefficient government programs, taxes to pay for necessary programs, and deficit reduction.

Economic theories had not heretofore been an issue for most feminists; nor had supply-siders been pressing their theories back in 1972 and 1976. During platform week at those conventions, women's issues had been a pawn in the platform struggles over economic and foreign policy. They had been trading cards that elected officials who were our reputed friends swapped with our opponents to win the right's agreement to more moderate foreign and economic policies. This time around, foreign policy was not as contentious an issue for the New Right, since Reagan appeared to agree with them.

Economic policy was a different matter. As the Platform Committee maneuvering began, the supply-siders weren't sure they would be able to convince the moderates and old guard to turn their backs on Keynesian economics. For them, the controversy over the ERA was a tactical gift. It diverted the attention of the moderates and old guard away from an economic policy that more of them would surely have opposed if they had been paying attention. Also, those who hoped Reagan would pick Bush to be his running mate didn't want to antagonize him. Women's issues thus provided cover for the supply-siders' chicanery.

The Detroit convention was a mass of contradictions. The wealthy called for workers to support their candidate even though his policies would cut their pay, diminish their benefits, and even lose them their jobs; libertarian Republicans advocated government policies that would place the harshest of constraints on women's freedom; fiscal conservatives supported the manipulation of government budgets that would bring about gargantuan deficits.

Few delegates paid attention to this lunacy. The only issues that generated passionate debate during platform week were women's concerns and the fifty-five-mile-an-hour speed limit. During the convention itself, most of the energy was expended on presenting Reagan the man and winning the White House. Yet despite the apparent lack of interest in its content, the Detroit platform was important. Its neatly compiled lists of the rights and wrongs of party philosophy, embellished with grandiose past and future claims of Republican contributions to the nation, laid out quite accurately what were to become the policies of the Reagan–Bush years. It wasn't a document of empty promises. It was a road map of the supply-siders' plans and the New Right's anti-women agenda.

The Reagan electoral strategy aimed to expand some of the base Ford had won in 1976, which was 117 electoral votes from the sixteen western states and an additional 40 from New Hampshire, Vermont, Indiana, Oklahoma, and Virginia. The team planned to invade Carter's southern base to win Texas, Mississippi, Louisiana, and Florida for another 60 votes. That would leave them 53 shy of the 270 needed to win the White House. Their dilemma was whether to try to win more southern states or to go after Illinois, Ohio, Pennsylvania, New Jersey, and Michigan, with their 116 votes. These states were the home of old guard and moderate Republicans and the targeted Reagan Democrats— blue-collar ethnic Catholics. The Reagan team decided the payoff would probably be greater in the North; they feared that Republicans wouldn't be able to wrest any more of the South away from Carter.

That was the electoral strategy. But before it could be addressed, another problem had to be tackled in Detroit. Despite its boasts about the success of the conservative revolution and the southern strategy, the Reagan high command knew it had to keep the moderates from deserting the party. Although the Reaganites controlled the GOP's national machinery, they controlled few of the northern state organizations. They needed not only the votes of the moderates of these states but their organizational skill, money, and time. The challenge in Detroit was to make the moderates feel wanted.

The convention program was organized to foster unity. To prove they welcomed all Republicans, unlike 1964 when most moderates were left out, Reagan operatives gave the moderates, and women in particular, prime speaking slots. The coveted first-night keynote speech went to

Ford, with less important slots to his former secretary of defense, Donald Rumsfeld, and his former treasury secretary, William Simon. The opening night was an ironic olive branch to the Ford administration, whose hopes for a second term they had dashed.

The Reagan organizers recognized that their biggest problem in achieving unity would be women, and while battles with us would go on during platform week, they hoped all would be peaceful by July 14, the day the convention itself opened. They lined up Nancy Kassebaum, Margaret Heckler, Carla Hills, Mary Louise Smith, Anne Armstrong, and Connie Newman—all either task force members or its friends—as featured speakers. They were the organizers' insurance policy, in case the New Right's misogynist planks angered the convention. If there was trouble, they now had these loyal moderate women to soothe the unhappy feminists. In contrast, the only New Right men to address the delegates would be Jack Kemp, Louisiana governor David Treen, and a little-known first-term Congressmember from Indiana named J. Danforth Quayle. The New Rightists would get what they wanted in the platform; they didn't need prime speaking slots.

But that was the convention. Platform week would be a different story, and Reagan's team knew it. There is nothing more unpredictable or less controllable than delegates who feel cornered, which is exactly how the pro-choice and pro-ERA women and their male allies felt as the Platform Committee first met on Sunday, July 6, to get organized.

Just because the committee had been stacked and the majority was anti-ERA and anti-choice didn't mean there couldn't be trouble, so the New Right Reaganites had taken protective steps. There were twenty members of Congress on the committee, none of whom supported both the ERA and choice. On the anti-choice side were many of the New Right's big Senate guns—Helms, Dole, Jepsen, William Roth, and James McClure, and to keep everyone in line, Platform Chairman John Tower of Texas. With the exception of Dole, all opposed the ERA as well. Malcolm Wallop of Wyoming broke the mold by supporting abortion rights and opposing the ERA, but he wasn't about to deviate from the Reagan convention script to battle actively for choice.

Our pleas to our friends in the Senate and House—forty-four of them—to come and help us fight for our two chief issues had produced only one brave soul, Margaret Heckler. What these friends had done instead was to send a public appeal to Tower in Washington to retain the 1976 ERA plank. It was a woeful response. Politics by long-distance press release is no match for hardball politics on the scene, and of the forty-four, only Heckler came for platform week. Anti-choice Heckler would lead the ERA charge without benefit of any House colleagues. Millicent Fenwick, her comrade-in-arms in Kansas City, wasn't a delegate. The other pro-ERA congressmember on the committee, David Stockman of Michigan, who would become Reagan's director of the Office of Management and Budget, had other priorities. He was there to ensure that the supply-side agenda went into the platform. The lineup of congressmembers on the committee read like a NCPAC roster. Only old guard Robert Michel of Illinois could be considered as not New Right, but he too opposed the ERA. It was the largest number of anti-ERA members of Congress to serve on a Platform Committee since the modern women's movement had begun.

To the uninitiated, 20 members of Congress out of the 106 delegates on the committee might not seem like a lot, but they were the ones who knew how to manipulate the process. Moreover, they had had the advantage of having worked out their strategy in Washington with Reagan's convention political people. Of the delegates who came from outside the Beltway, few had had experience in this kind of national politicking, and none could have been a match for the twenty even if they had wanted to be. They knew little about the parliamentary rules of the House or even realized that these rules—not the customary Robert's Rules of Order—would govern the convention. To make matters worse, no governors or other prominent elected officials were on the committee to challenge the New Right congressional heavies.

Out of the total committee roster, 68 members were opposed to the ERA, 14 had no opinion, and only 24 were in favor—and of those, only 16 liked the 1976 ERA plank.

We had to challenge the Reaganites. We couldn't let them and the nation think women's rights weren't worth fighting for. Knowing we had little chance to get twenty-seven signatures for a minority report forcing a debate on the convention floor, the task force, again led by Pamela Curtis, decided on a guerrilla press strategy. We would let the nation know the party was turning its back on women. The press would learn in great detail that Republicans had passed an ERA plank in 1940 and that its rejection now was truly a step backward. We also thought that such stories might force the Reagan strategists to loosen up their hard line. We might be able to negotiate a concession.

And we succeeded. Along with the handicapping over Reagan's choice of running mate, the loss of the ERA was the convention's other big story. It was featured in all the nation's major news outlets and around the world. As Alice Tetelman remembers, "We didn't think we had a chance, but we put that sucker on the front pages of the national papers for thirteen days and it was worth it."

Anticipating that we would cause just the kind of public relations trouble we did, Reagan's team had tried to head off our fire by floating a pseudocompromise. Two days before we task force women arrived in Detroit, a *Washington Post* headline announced its Trojan horse: "Reagan at Odds with Conservatives on ERA Platform Plank." Reagan's chief of staff, Ed Meese, said in the article that Reagan "would accept a pro-ERA platform plank even though he personally opposes it."

A draft plank Meese had organized was circulating among staff and the press. It included almost word for word the statement agreed to at the Tidewater conference back in February, reaffirming "the party's historical commitment to equal rights and equal opportunity for women, a commitment which made us the first national party to endorse the Equal Rights Amendment," and it included a statement that hadn't been in Tidewater: "We are proud of our pioneering role and do not renounce our stand."

Meese was clever. At the same time that he floated the trial balloon, he signaled to Schlafly and company that the ball was in their court by saying in the *Washington Post* article, "Obviously, the Governor accepts what comes out of the Platform Committee even if that conflicts with his personal view." And just in case the anti-ERA people missed the point, Meese spelled it out further: "Reagan would prefer a platform plank which opposed sexual discrimination without specifically mentioning the amendment."

It was a brilliant maneuver and predictably did just what the Reagan team wanted. On cue, the anti-ERA forces burst into action. Schlafly announced that she was "shocked" that "anyone would submit a draft plank with ERA in it. . . . They must know we've got the votes to beat it." Roy Brun, the Louisiana Platform Committee delegate, sent a telegram to the committee threatening to introduce language stating the

"U.S. Constitution is too sacred a document to be changed." In this carefully orchestrated ado, Reagan looked like the reasonable man trying to be the bridge between his ardent followers and the moderates.

It may have fooled the press, but it didn't fool us. Nonetheless, we knew that unless Reagan released a few delegates, we didn't have the votes to pass even the Tidewater-style draft language. The Platform Committee would do just what Reagan wanted and what Schlafly had carefully programmed—get rid of the ERA plank but not have it be his fault.

On opening day of the committee deliberations, July 7, Reagan's team was quoted as describing the Meese draft as a "compromise plank." It was step one in the kind of strategy that would guide the Reagan–Bush campaign—and their administrations—whenever women's issues arose. First, say you're for women. Second, oppose any move that will give them real power but propose a measure or slogan that gives the appearance of doing so. Third, get some visible moderate women to agree publicly with your approach, but also ensure that they say the issue affecting women, whatever it is, is of lesser priority to the nation than other issues championed by the candidate, such as lower taxes and a strong defense. Fourth, firmly implement the antifeminist policy.

The Platform Committee hearings on the ERA loosely followed this script. The phony pro-ERA draft plank reaffirmed the party's commitment to equal rights for women but then attacked the ERA for becoming mired in "legal tangles, dubious precedent . . . and divisive political struggles." It pledged to "rise above the present unproductive stalemate . . . to make equal rights for women a full reality in our society." Then it honed in neatly on Schlafly and Ervin's states' rights and excessive-government arguments, criticizing the Carter administration for placing "pressure against states which refused to ratify the ERA."

Pro-ERA Michigan governor William Milliken was the only governor willing to speak up for the amendment at the hearings. He was testifying in a wilderness. To drop the ERA plank, he told the committee, "would be a public demonstration that this party has abandoned its goal of equal rights for women." Milliken had done what he felt he could; the two Michigan Platform Committee delegates would vote for an ERA plank, and that was it. Presumably all the other pro-ERA governors had opted out because to take a stand might jeopardize their candidate Bush's chance to be Reagan's running mate. They feared that the Reagan campaign would assume that by such a stand they were following Bush's wishes, and thus undermining Reagan. They would be confirming what some New Rightists said: Bush could not be trusted with the Reagan Revolution.

Detroit wasn't Kansas City. That first day, we came face-to-face with the Reagan forces' tight control over their delegates. Our task force members had a difficult time lobbying Platform Committee members. Many of the committee members were actually afraid to be seen talking to us. We resorted to following women members into the ladies' room to speak to them. We also had our first direct contact with the Religious Right. Kathy Wilson couldn't get Moral Majority Alaska delegate Don White to talk to her until she answered his question about whether she'd been "saved for Christ."

The day after the hearings, the Human Resources Subcommittee took up the Meese draft plank. A worried chairman Tower tried to close the meeting to the public and press. For our part, we needed public scrutiny for our press strategy and to force a change in the Reagan script, so we lobbied the subcommittee to oppose Tower's ruling. In the only time that day that the delegates showed any independence from the script, the subcommittee voted him down, but it made little difference in what then happened.

The tactics were ones we had encountered in the past. State legislator John Leopold, a newfound friend of the task force's from Hawaii, moved that the subcommittee replace Meese's draft with the 1976 pro-ERA platform plank because, he said, to drop the 1976 plank would be a "retreat from principle." Trent Lott, the subcommittee chairman, allowed no debate on the motion, and it was defeated 11 to 4. Schlafly's forces then amended Meese's "compromise" draft to take out all language that might indicate that Republicans supported the ERA, and this time Lott allowed a long debate. At one point he also revealed his considerable contempt for the goals of the women's movement. As Rebecca Leet remembers, Lott corrected a confused delegate by saying, "You're on the wrong section. . . . [W]e're not talking about equal rights . . . we're talking about women's rights." This outright chauvinism startled the task force women, but none of the subcommittee members even reacted. Schlafly's no-ERA plank, without Meese's "compromise," passed easily. The first step toward ending forty years of official Republican championing for women's rights had been taken.

Reagan's people were still worried about what we might do, however, and near the end of the subcommittee debate, Californians Nancy Chotiner and Lorelei Kinder, who worked on women's issues for Reagan and had been huddling sporadically with Schlafly all day, approached Tetelman and Curtis to tell them that Reagan was personally in favor of women's rights. The goal for all was to win the election, they said, and we mustn't split the party over the ERA. (I've always found it interesting how often the men who oppose women's rights use women to negotiate for them.) They discussed a series of compromises with our two members, including a meeting with Reagan and a "unity" statement.

Our ERA team was responsive to this plea and worked throughout the next day to come up with platform language that would "recognize" the efforts of ERA proponents but would accept the dropping of the party's ERA support. I thought our willingness to compromise was a strategic mistake, but Curtis and Mary Louise Smith finally accepted this "recognition" language for the plank, arguing that we had to do it if we were to keep communication open between the task force and the Reagan campaign and national party. After all, they said, we were still Republicans.

A few hours later, the subcommittee took up the abortion issue. A CBS survey of the convention delegates taken just before platform week had shown some encouraging results. Fifty-one percent *opposed* a constitutional ban on abortion, 34 percent favored it, and 14 percent gave no answer. In spite of the influence of the New Right and the Religious Right, the majority of the convention did not agree with the anti-choice movement. But if we knew this, so did the Reagan strategists; and we all knew as well that if the choice issue got to the convention floor, some delegates might abandon the script.

Choice was the women's issue in which the Reagan campaign had the most at stake. It was part of their wedge into the neighborhoods of the Reagan Democrats, and they weren't going to let it get compromised away just because more than half the delegates didn't believe in banning abortion. Choice was also the issue where we could marshal genuine delegate sympathy—assuming we could find a way to release it from the Reagan team's Platform Committee fortress.

John Leopold accepted the challenge. The fight over the ERA had whetted his appetite. The anti-choice advocates were ready for him. Their strategy replicated the one played out a couple of hours earlier with the ERA. Reagan had said he'd accept the 1976 abortion plank, but the subcommittee "revolted," ostensibly against his wishes. Leopold moved for the party to support the expansion of family-planning programs as an alternative to abortion, while keeping the language of the 1976 plank. With no debate, his motion was defeated. The anti-choice steamroller rolled on. The 1976 conciliatory language, what little there'd been, was thrown out, and in its place came an abortion plank unequivocally affirming a constitutional amendment banning abortion and opposing the use of taxpayers' dollars for abortion (as in Medicaid funding). The plank also charged the Supreme Court with "intrusion into the family structure through its denial of the parents' obligation and right to guide their minor children." The last phrase astounded us; we couldn't understand what relevance the drafters' view of parents' rights had to do with abortion rights. If logic prevailed, as it didn't, these same people should also have been against government "intrusion" into women's lives. The gap between our view of individual rights and theirs was indeed large.

Nor was that the end of it. Virginia delegate and Moral Majority adherent Guy Farley, Jr., proposer of all harsh anti-abortion language that day, set off a bombshell. He asked that the party pledge to appoint Supreme Court justices who believed in "traditional family values and the sanctity of human life." Lott, visibly annoyed, ruled that Farley's amendment wasn't germane, but he couldn't kill the idea. The subcommittee asked that the proposal be sent down the hall to the subcommittee dealing with judiciary issues.

A little later someone handed me a piece of paper. The judiciary subcommittee was considering the following plank: "We applaud our presidential candidate's pledge to appoint justices to the Supreme Court who respect the sanctity of innocent human life." "Our presidential candidate's *pledge*?" Either the anti-choice people were out of control, or Reagan really wanted to pack the Supreme Court. No doubt Farley was a revolutionary and he and his New Right compatriots wanted their candidate to subvert the judicial system, but if Farley was accurate, Reagan had agreed to it.

We congregated in the hall and agreed on a strategy. Some of us headed off to alert the press, who weren't even following what was happening—all the attention was on the Human Resources Subcommittee—and the rest went off to see how we could take advantage of the gift that had been given to us. Maybe it could unlock the fortress. Promising to select judges according to an anti-choice litmus test flew in the face of the nation's tradition of judicial impartiality. Were Meese and Casey, both lawyers, so afraid of the political power of the right-to-life movement, or perhaps so strongly in agreement with it, that they would undermine that tradition? Had the Moral Majority pulled a fast one on the Reagan high command? We now had an issue that affected all Americans, not only women. The integrity of the judiciary was at stake. Surely the legal profession would be outraged.

The press barely reacted. It seemed to view Farley's audaciousness as the work of some oddball that would go nowhere. One reporter I told shouted, "I'm not in the advocacy business," and stormed back into the Human Resources Subcommittee.

The other subcommittee passed Farley's proposal and adjourned for the day. But Reagan's people were as alarmed as we were. Whatever they had thought about Farley's idea, it was too provocative for them now. When the full Platform Committee met the next day, Reagan's "pledge" had disappeared. In its place the full committee had voted a plank that said, "We will work for the appointment of judges at all levels of the judiciary who respect traditional family values and the sanctity of innocent human life." They had extricated Reagan from his purported pledge to undermine the judicial system, but it was also clear they had no intention of letting the party back down on the court-packing plank. When our Platform Committee delegates raised questions about the ethics of the plank, the anti-choice members pointed out that certainly everyone favored the sanctity of innocent human life. Finkelstein's law was working: The words masked the intent. Both sides knew the Republican party was pledging itself to the appointment of anti-abortion judges.

With like-minded subcommittee members, lawyer Michael Brewer, Chris Milliken, and I drafted a minority report that said a plank on abortion "is not in the best interests of the Republican party, its members, its officeholders and candidates, and should not be included in a political party's platform." It was the same argument we'd used for years: Abortion doesn't belong in politics because it's a private matter.

It didn't work. Many committee members agreed but were afraid to act against what Reagan's operatives said were his wishes.

We also wrote a minority report on the judiciary plank, using these same arguments but adding that "judges should be appointed on the basis of their judicial experience, background, and general ability, not on the basis of single issue politics—whether they support or oppose any single issue." With this addition, we hoped we could find twenty-seven people so outraged by the judiciary plank that we could get to the floor.

I remember waking up on July 9, the day the full Platform Committee would first consider the platform, thinking, "Today is my son's ninth birthday, and today I'm about to witness the trampling of my beliefs by this party I've worked for all my life. Why do I bother?" But the question was a momentary mind game—I knew why I was there. My son and daughter's future depended upon stopping these zealots. Maybe, I thought, the lawyers on the committee will care enough about the integrity of America's judicial system to at least delete the judiciary plank. Maybe some members will even care about the freedom of women.

The Equal Rights Amendment was the first women's issue on the full committee's agenda. The committee executed the ERA with the efficiency of a guillotine. Reagan insiders Martin Anderson, James Brady, and Richard Allen sat near the front like three watchful Madame Defarges, taking notes and making sure all went well. Their vigilance wasn't necessary. Like Trent Lott in the previous day's subcommittee session, Chairman John Tower allowed no direct vote on the ERA; the killing was done by sleight of hand. The only vote was on an amendment offered by the court-packing virtuoso, Guy Farley, Jr., who moved that the party recognize "the legitimate efforts of those who support or oppose the Equal Rights Amendment." It was the Kinder–Chotiner "compromise." The blade fell. By a vote of 90 to 9, the Republican party ended its long formal commitment to women's equality with an innocuous amendment that skirted the issue.

Why had the killing been done so backhandedly? They didn't want us or the Democrats to be able to say during the fall campaign that the Republican party had voted in such-and-such numbers against women. Of course they "recognized our efforts"; they had to. Republican women were the only ones seriously challenging their bigotry. But it was meaningless. The deed was done, and the press reported it accurately in great detail.

On the abortion plank, the maneuvering followed the same pattern. No vote was taken directly on the plank; instead, the Platform Committee voted 75 to 18 against softening the call for a constitutional amendment banning abortions. With the hope we might not have to go the signature route, District of Columbia delegate Jan Evans asked for a vote on our minority report, which included dropping the court-packing plank and repeating the message that abortion is "a personal issue inappropriate to a political document." She was shouted down in a voice vote. The blade fell again, and the court-packing plank stood unchallenged. Afterward, for public relations reasons, the Reagan team told the press that its candidate would have been willing to accept wording "that leaned somewhat further toward a fuzzy middle-of-the-road position."

Moreover, the team's game wasn't over. High drama at conventions usually comes in waves, one incident after another, building toward the big ninth. July 9, 1980, was one of those big-wave days. The Republican party both rejected women's rights and a woman who had devoted more than sixteen years to its welfare. While we were struggling with the ERA and legal abortion planks, the RNC was meeting to publicly accept Mary Crisp's forced resignation. It was no routine conclusion to her term of office, which formally ended at the party's convention. It was an ousting that the New Right had orchestrated and to which Brock had acceded after the Anderson debacle. The RNC members were tense and the members uncomfortable as Crisp bade them farewell:

> Although our party has presented the outward appearance of vibrant health, I'm afraid we are suffering from serious internal sickness. . . . Our party has endorsed and worked for the ERA for forty years. Now we are reversing our position and are about to bury the rights of over 100 million American women under a heap of platitudes. Even worse is the fact that our party is asking for a constitutional amendment to ban abortions.

When she finished, several women in the audience applauded, a few old friends from the Goldwater days embraced her, and a pro forma resolution of appreciation was passed. But for most of the Republicans at the convention, her speech fueled resentment, not agreement or sympathy. The press picked up the tension, placing her attack on "GOP sickness" next to headlines crying "Republican Right Crushes Backers of ERA, Abortion" and "GOP Scuttles Four Decades of ERA Support."

The Republican delegates we spoke to were almost universally outraged. Inaccurate reporting fueled the flames. As the *Chicago Sun-Times* had done a little earlier, *The New York Times* reported incorrectly that she had endorsed Anderson. Reagan attacked her personally, a tactic he rarely used, saying unjustly that "Mary Crisp should look to herself and find out how loyal she's been to the Republican party for quite some time." All this dampened whatever chance we had to get twenty-seven signatures to bring the court-packing and anti-choice minority reports to the convention floor. Because we were identified with Crisp on these issues, the few delegates who held independent views and weren't controlled by the Reagan juggernaut suspected our motives and wouldn't sign for fear of appearing disloyal.

Outside Detroit's safety perimeter, however, the reaction was different. To many Republicans across the nation, to the delegates who would be arriving for the convention itself in four days, and to most of those Americans who had heard or read about Crisp, as well as to us, she was a brave, honorable woman who had stood up for women's rights. The Reagan campaign realized she had created substantial sympathy for herself and our cause, so it moved immediately to limit it.

The campaign's carrot was the "legitimate efforts" pseudocompromise language of Farley's amendment. Heckler agreed to accept the 90–9 committee vote and not organize a floor fight. Mary Louise Smith said, "Yes, the ball game's over," but by acknowledging the "legitimate efforts" of both sides of the controversy, the Reagan convention leaders "had picked up the votes of some ERA supporters on the Platform Committee."

The Reagan team knew, however, that the Farley language was not enough to counteract our accusations that Reagan opposed women, so the platform also included a women's section that attempted to compensate for dropping the ERA and denying women reproductive choice. It stressed the same list of economic concerns for women as the 1972 and 1976 platforms did, but there the similarity ended. The Detroit platform shifted subtly but significantly away from the party's traditional championing of help for all women to singling out special treatment for homemakers and mothers and downplaying those women who worked outside the home.

The Religious Right's "family values" message had become part of Republican philosophy. Past platforms had always praised strong families, but now a woman's identity separate from her role as a mother and homemaker was diminished. Applauding the contribution of homemakers to the economy, the platform pledged to expand individual retirement account (IRA) eligibility for them. It offered little for the working woman and/or mother. Taking a swipe at the ERA, it pledged "equal rights and equal opportunities for women, without taking away traditional rights of women such as exemption from the military draft." Child care was now solely the responsibility of the private sector. In 1972 the party had supported "publicly or privately run, voluntary, comprehensive, quality day care services locally controlled but federally assisted." In 1976 this support had been watered down but the concept remained. Now it was gone.

It was important that mothers and homemakers be supported, the platform stated, because of their role "in maintaining the values of this country." The patriarchal viewpoint that women were the fount of morality was explicit. The Moral Majority reigned: Women should stay home, obey their husbands, and raise the children. Gone was the party's view, laid out in the 1972 platform, that "while every woman may not want a career outside the home, every woman should have the freedom to choose whatever career she wishes—and an equal chance to pursue it."

We refused to concede. Despite Heckler and Smith's acquiescence to Farley's "legitimate efforts" amendment, we decided to call Reagan's bluff. He said he wanted to help women? Well, we'd ask him to pledge some specific action to prove it. Eight of the nine Platform Committee members who had voted against Farley's amendment sent Reagan a letter asking to meet with him "to present our point of view and . . . to clarify your views. . . . [Thus] you will signal your openness . . . to those who feel strongly about equal rights for women." The letter added, "The perception of the public and the press is that Republicans have repudiated the ERA. Despite the sections of the platform which sensitively address other important 'women's issues,' we are accused of abandoning equal rights for women." And then we waited.

Revisionism created by Reagan campaign rhetoric quickly set in.

NFRW chair Betty Heitman, his handpicked successor to Crisp at the RNC, declared that the platform went "far beyond the ERA" and addressed the major problems facing today's women. Republicans weren't against women being protected by the Constitution, she maintained; we just thought the states should decide what should be done, and until they did, the party had passed a women's rights plank that was the most comprehensive in GOP history.

Maybe the Platform Committee delegates believed Heitman's line that the ERA wasn't necessary, but the country didn't, as a CBS News/ *New York Times* poll taken in early July documented. Since the poll showed that 54 percent of Americans supported it, the claim by Brock and others that it wouldn't cost the party votes was questionable at best. But as Martin Anderson said, the Reagan camp didn't want a "divisive, angry battle, perhaps on the convention floor, that would alienate people watching on television." Caution was needed, so the Reagan team accepted our request to meet with him. He'd meet on Tuesday, the second day of the convention, but only with women. The three men who had also signed the letter weren't welcome. (We never found out what this nugget of sexism was about.)

On Monday, July 14, the convention's opening day, an estimated twelve thousand ERA advocates marched past Cobo Hall, where the Platform Committee had passed the platform, and the Joe Louis Arena, where the delegates would vote on it. At the rally that followed the march, only Margaret Heckler and Connie Newman of the pro-ERA women who were scheduled to speak at the convention had the courage to stand with us. Noticeably absent were the others—Armstrong, Kassebaum, Hills, and Smith. Betty and Gerald Ford were nowhere to be seen. Five male congressmembers—Bill Green of New York, Jim Leach of Iowa, Pete McCloskey of California, James Jeffords of Vermont, and Carl Purcell of Michigan—and Senators Jacob Javits, Charles Mathias, and Ted Stevens stood up for their principles and marched with us, but their colleague Charles Percy didn't show.

The rally's speeches were suitably fierce and matched the heat of that Bastille Day. Jill Ruckelshaus caught our spirit: "My party has endorsed the Equal Rights Amendment for 40 years. . . . Dwight Eisenhower endorsed ERA. Richard Nixon endorsed ERA. Gerald Ford endorsed ERA. But something happened in Detroit last week," she cried out. "Give me back my party."

We were defiantly exuberant as we walked back to the Renaissance Center, hoping the meeting with Reagan would change his mind. Flush from the rally's excitement, I entered the Pontchartrain and saw Bill Casey waiting for an elevator. I'd known him for fourteen years; we'd talked about women's rights many times. He'd always seemed bemused by my words, but he had never argued with me. "Reagan's going to have trouble with women, Bill," I said. "Do something. Give us a break." The elevator opened, and he mumbled, "I'll see what I can do." Years later I saw him again, and he reminded me they had done something. And they did.

It was Monday afternoon, and Tuesday was traditionally the day the convention passed the platform. We had been unable to get the necessary signatures for either minority report. This year was not 1976. There must be no debate on abortion on national television. Reagan's image mustn't be sullied with the shrillness of right-to-life speakers. The official line was that extremists had taken over the Platform Committee on social issues, and some of the press bought it. In fact, the Reaganites had worked closely with Schlafly and the various right-to-life groups, and the committee did just what the Reagan campaign expected it to do. It wasn't out of control. They were all part of the same team.

Although Charles Percy had chosen not to stand up for the ERA at the rally, that Monday he harshly criticized the judiciary plank as

[the] most outrageous I have ever seen in a Republican platform. Its design is the worst sort of extremism of the 1964 convention reincarnated. If you say every judge you pick has to be against abortion, what's to stop [you] from putting in a litmus test on ERA, gun control, or anything else? . . . If moderate Republicans go home and feel they have been totally rebuffed I hate to think what's going to happen to the party.

But his words were ineffectual—and too late. He hadn't even been able to get his own state's Platform Committee members, Rose Veith and Congressmember Bob Michel, to sign our court-packing minority report.

·   ·   ·

On Tuesday morning, before the convention was to vote on the platform, sixteen Republican women sat around a table with Ronald Reagan in his sixty-ninth-floor hotel suite. They were charmed by the man but disconcerted by the experience. Smith and Heckler were the chief spokeswomen. Helen Milliken, wife of the Michigan governor and co-chair of ERA America—whom the Reagan operatives had originally not wanted to have attend—was there. The Platform Committee women who'd signed the letter—task force leaders Alice Tetelman and Pamela Curtis, Senator Kassebaum, Betty Murphy, Carla Hills, and Reagan's feminist daughter Maureen Reagan, who had eloquently testified for the ERA during platform week—completed the group.

Responding to a question implicitly referring to Bush, Reagan said that being for the ERA wouldn't be a barrier in a running mate. He also said that while he opposed the ERA, he'd establish a White House liaison to review state laws that discriminated against women, and that he would enforce federal sex-discrimination laws. The women asked him to make a strong statement on women's rights at the convention. He didn't answer. No one brought up abortion.

Tetelman remembers, "As the discussion started, I'm looking at this man and watching him as Peggy [Heckler] explains our concern that Americans, especially women, will think he's against women. He smiles blankly, and I'm saying to myself he doesn't get it." Smith recalls that "our hopes were very high that we could make a difference. . . . [A]fterwards, I came out feeling we hadn't gotten very far. It just wasn't concrete." Tetelman agrees. "I felt lousy when I left," she says. "What had we really gotten?"

It was a pure Reagan performance, shiny like mercury and hard to get your hands on. But the women did get more than they realized at the time. Casey had kept his word: We had lost the ERA, reproductive choice, affirmative action, and nearly the entire feminist agenda; but to demonstrate his commitment to women's rights, Reagan pledged to appoint a woman to the Supreme Court and others to top positions in his administration.

After the meeting, Reagan issued a statement promising to "do a number of things to advance, guarantee, and promote equal rights" for women. And then in a Kafkaesque description of the reality the campaign team wished to convey to the world, he added, "While individual Republicans will continue to advocate different methods for achieving the goal of equal rights for women, our party has written the most comprehensive plank on equal rights it has ever had, and we are united as a party in our goal." Mission accomplished. For public consumption, the Reagan team got what it wanted—unity. Afterward, Smith told the press, "We came away feeling good. . . . It was productive. It was open. It was not harsh." Heckler was also diplomatic, though with a somewhat sharper edge to her voice: "The meeting was very important symbolically and it went well. . . . He will have to address women's issues during the campaign and this was a good start." Only task force chair Curtis was blunt: "A lot of consciousness-raising still needs to be done with the candidate and his staff."

With no minority reports, only one avenue was left at the convention to show the nation that not all Republicans agreed with Reagan's agendas for women and for the nation's judicial system: We would try to convince six states to call for a suspension of the rules in order to have a debate. This would substitute for a direct vote on the platform and could open up the possibility of amending it. As the Tuesday night session began, Javits, Green, Mathias, Leopold, Ann Peckham of Wisconsin, Susan Catania of Chicago, and others fanned out on the floor to find six courageous states.

The Michigan delegation, although led by ERA supporter Milliken, wouldn't be one of the six. Once aggressively progressive New York was controlled by Casey and his band of Reaganites. Javits and Green couldn't even deliver for the rules suspension. Others, like New York congressmember Barber Conable, who agreed with us, were working hard to convince the Reagan operatives that Bush should be Reagan's running mate, and they wanted no unpleasantness on the floor to mar Bush's chances. The last nail had been driven in on Monday, when Javits and D'Amato, although locked in a bitter primary fight for U.S. senator, agreed in back-to-back news conferences that they too were for Bush. Led by Leopold, Hawaii would support the motion to suspend the rules. Massachusetts was supposed to agree too, but when time came to move for the suspension, there was only confusion. Massachusetts congressmember Silvio Conte, who was pro-ERA, announced that his state wanted a roll call on the platform as a whole, not suspension of the rules for a debate. It wouldn't back Hawaii's call. No other state came to Leopold's side. The challenge was stillborn.

With that, the New Right's social agenda became the official policy of the party of Lincoln. No debate, no roll call, no heated exchanges heralded the demise of a historic tradition. A few loud noes echoed through the Joe Louis Arena as Congressmember John Rhodes, who was presiding, declared the ayes had it. The 1980 Republican party platform was approved.

The pro-choice forces didn't stage a floor fight because prominent pro-choice Republicans wouldn't stand up. The pro-ERA forces didn't stage a knock-down battle in front of the nation's television audience because they hoped that George Bush, the "moderate" candidate, would be Reagan's running mate. Heckler expressed the sentiments of people like Milliken and the party leaders who'd marched with us before the rally. "George Bush was pretty much out of it when I arrived here last week for the platform committee," she said. "But the ERA issue has cut so deeply, I now think they are looking at George in a different light." They expected Bush to bring moderation to the Reagan campaign.

Moderate men were unwilling to believe the New Right truly threatened women's rights. Pennsylvania's young lieutenant governor, William Scranton III, said publicly what many allegedly moderate delegates had been saying around the bars and restaurants the night before the Tuesday platform vote. He talked about the 1964 convention compared with this one.

> I mean, the Equal Rights Amendment is an interesting issue, but it's not really going to cut a lot in the election in the fall. In 1964—I'll never forget it—there was bitter hatred from the conservatives. But now conservatism has gained intellectual legitimacy. Ronald Reagan can be flexible. The ERA argument is not an argument about whether there should be equal rights— only whether we need an amendment. In 1964, those people were dead set against civil rights, period.

Scranton and his friends hadn't been on the front lines for choice and ERA in recent weeks. They had no idea that "those people" were as dead set against civil rights as ever—only now they had added women to the list of those they were targeting. Bill Milliken, intellectually honest and fair-minded, refused to believe the boast of Jesse Helms, after the Platform Committee had voted unanimously to send the platform to the floor with no minority reports, that he had achieved 99 percent of what he wanted. Said Milliken: "The day will never come when the Jesse Helmses of this world dominate the party."

On Wednesday night the convention nominated Ronald Reagan by a vote of 1,939; there were 37 votes for John Anderson and 13 for George Bush. Bush, the man who was most delegates' second choice, finally got Reagan's call at 11:37 P.M. Of course he was delighted to be his running mate. Of course he would accept the party's platform. Of course he would do what needed to be done to win in November.

"More than anything else he [Bush] wanted to be president, and he did what he had to do to become it," one of his close political friends, who had been with him in the long trek to the nomination, said in a recent interview. "In the beginning, I don't think he was anti-choice, but then he came to believe the pro-life people. He changed. As for the ERA, it wasn't important to him if it stopped him from getting the vice presidency."

Bush was like most of the party men with whom Republican feminists had worked. They simply hadn't thought much about women's rights—these Ripon Society members, graduates of Ivy League schools, and moderate legislators and party officials. Scranton's remarks weren't too far removed from those that Bush had often expressed: Bush wasn't against women's rights, but why all this fuss, given the overall picture of presidential politics, the *big* issues—international affairs and U.S. economic policy?

Yes, Bush had called Reagan's supply-side theories "voodoo economics" and his abortion stand "unwise" and his opposition to the ERA "backward thinking," but all that was over. At his first joint news conference with Reagan the next morning, Bush said he'd emphasize "the common ground" and was "not going to get nickel-and-dimed to death with detail." He refused to acknowledge support for the ERA.

All those Bush ERA supporters like Smith, Heckler, and the Millikens who had already said they would back Reagan had paved the way for Bush. It was easy for him to drop his ERA support. He was the rooster, the bait to bring the ERA chicks into the coop. He had delivered the moderates of the party. He got his reward. Now he'd go out and deliver Michigan, Pennsylvania, and New Jersey for the Reagan–Bush revolution.

Bush did exactly what he had planned to do if given the opportunity. He knew the odds on how many modern vice presidents had become president, but his dream was nearer. All he had to do was wait the eight years. Besides, Reagan would be seventy years old in the second month of his presidency. Bush might be president before the eight years were up.

Helms and his cohorts complained that Bush was too moderate, but the complaints were modest for Helms. The Religious Right Pro-Life Impact Committee, headed by Marlene Elwell, a woman who eight years later would run presidential candidate Pat Robertson's Midwest field operations, laid out their real expectations:

> Reagan stated his assurance that Ambassador Bush "can enthusiastically support the platform across the Board." The Pro-Life Impact Committee enthusiastically supports the Republican platform plank which gives unequivocal endorsement to a human life amendment to the Constitution. Accordingly, we take Governor Reagan's statement of Ambassador Bush's position literally. . . . We are overjoyed with the unity of purpose expressed by the Republican platform and the commitment of Governor Reagan on the issue of abortion. . . . Reagan reiterated that this unity of platform and policy will be maintained. We expect no less. We are committed to turn the words of the Republican Platform into the law of the land. We welcome any candidate's change of view, tested and reinforced by time, which will bring this result to pass.

Reagan kept his promise to the women he met that Tuesday morning. Four paragraphs into his acceptance speech, he singled out our issue, joining his style to the sensitivity of young Bill Scranton and the philosophy of Schlafly:

> Now I know that we have had a quarrel or two, but only as to the method of attaining a goal. There was no argument here about the goal. As president, I will establish a liaison with the

fifty governors to encourage them to eliminate, wherever it exists, discrimination against women. I will monitor federal laws to ensure their implementation and to add statutes if they are needed.

And that was it. No sweeping colorful language. No oratory. Just two policy pronouncements. We shouldn't have been surprised. Stan Evans, who'd been with Bill Rusher and Clif White at the beginning of the new conservative movement, summed it up best: "The forces that started working in our politics in the 60s have now become predominant in the GOP. Barring unforeseen disasters, it seems likely they will soon become equally dominant in the nation."

10

THE "WOMEN'S PROBLEM"

The 1980 presidential campaign was more complicated than most, and by the time it was over, the Republican party had been transformed. No longer dominated by the eastern establishment and midwesterners in the mold of Taft and Ford, it was now a radical institution, southern and western in outlook, filled with former Democrats, and set on discarding for good the old-time party policies of balanced budgets and respect for women's rights.

After Detroit the message of the Reagan revolution was spelled out for anyone who bothered to read the platform, but Reagan the man was still an unknown to most. His inner circle: Casey, Meese, Michael Deaver, Nofziger, Richard Wirthlin, and James Baker—newly on board after the Bush nomination—fashioned a remarkable campaign facade of hope for America centered on Reagan's personal charm. Reagan the amiable actor would transcend the meanness of the Detroit agenda.

This selling of the candidate was a tapestry of myths—some of them so deeply embedded in America's psyche that it was hard to realize that they had little connection to the late twentieth century. Reagan turned perceptions upside down and made up his own description of the nation's reality. He pretended we could return to small-town life. He glorified the moral character of entrepreneurs. He attacked government as corrosive and charged that it was the greatest threat to America's liberty. He championed the nuclear family, ignoring the fact that for many Americans the nuclear family was not attainable even when desired. (He also ignored the reality of his own dysfunctional family.) He never said so directly, but the sotto voce campaign message was that the nation's moral disintegration (presuming this really existed) was the fault of the women who weren't taking care of their children. It was not the fault of societal forces and global economic changes but of women who worked outside the home.

The weaving of this tapestry of hypocrisy and myth had begun in earnest after the 1978 elections. The warp and woof were already there in the record of Reagan's years as California's governor, in his numerous speeches for GOP officeholders, and in his 1976 run for president. Yet until the pressure of the 1980 campaign forced action, they hadn't been woven into a comprehensive agenda for the nation. The man and his message were a blur to all except his most avid followers.

Reagan's unauthorized biographer, Lou Cannon, wrote, "The source of Reagan's inspiration was less the Constitution than the movies. His mind was filled with movie scenes more vivid to him than many actual events." In the world of movies from which he took his cues, on which he built his political philosophy, there was no women's movement, no women's liberation; but there were competent, powerful women like Joan Crawford in *Mildred Pierce* and Katharine Hepburn in all those movies with Spencer Tracy. Reagan himself wasn't anti-women. He was no more a misogynist than he was a racist or a homophobe. He appreciated strong women; his closest friend, his wife, Nancy, personified the strong woman that those of us in the women's movement understood. She was smart, and she'd sought out her opportunities within the confines of the sexist society she had grown up in, finally succeeding in her goal of becoming first lady. So how did this man who didn't dislike women come to lead a political movement whose capacity to win power rested in part on a strategy of keeping women down?

The challenge of the Reagan campaign team, the men who scripted the scenario that Reagan and the Republicans were to follow first in the campaign and then in the White House, was to make Americans believe that the candidate and his party were interested in opportunity for all. The campaign's task was to deliver what the angry sexists, racists, and homophobes wanted without revealing this ugly agenda. The New Right had already perfected such techniques in their recent successful forays into electoral politics, and now it was up to the Reaganites, such as Ed Meese and pollster Richard Wirthlin, to make use of them. The tactical problems were enormous, but the team was blessed because it had Ronald Reagan—the perfect man to represent something that wasn't.

Jimmy Carter and Walter Mondale were renominated at the Democratic convention on August 4, with a platform supporting the ERA, federal funding of abortions, and a $12 billion jobs program. But voters were weary of Carter and his lack of leadership, and the ignominious Iran hostage situation remained unresolved. Reagan made it his business to appear decisive and pleasant, a style that befitted the man himself. The New Right messages he espoused were toned down. Listening to Reagan and Bush's campaign rhetoric in the fall, a voter might have missed them. Their words sounded similar to those of Nixon, Ford, and Ike, but they weren't. These were different Republicans, these New Right Reaganites.

Among the issues the campaign knew it had to face were the anger many women harbored toward the Republican party because of its rejection of the ERA and their fear of Reagan's anti-Soviet belligerence. A partnership with the moderate women was essential. Since the themes enunciated in Detroit would be continued into the fall campaign— Reagan was for women but against the women's movement—it was important to co-opt the moderates right away.

The team turned again to Mary Louise Smith and Bobbie Kilberg. Within a month after Detroit, at the same time the Democrats were nominating Carter and showcasing their women on national television, Smith and Kilberg organized a Reagan–Bush Women's Policy Board, comprising an impressive number of Republican feminists like Audrey Rowe, former chair of the National Women's Political Caucus, and Major General Jeanne Holm, who had been President Ford's special assistant for women's affairs. Trying to prove Reagan was a champion for women was a daunting task, so as has often happened when the party tries to justify actions that contradict its principles, the Reagan women turned to party history for plausible arguments. The board sent women voters a pamphlet lauding a hundred years of Republican leadership for women and citing the Ford administration's record for "breaking down barriers against women," as if to imply this would be the party's continuing commitment. Saying that Reagan too "cares about women," it listed legislation he'd signed as governor of California that prohibited sex discrimination in employment, equalized community property, established credit rights for married women, and extended disability benefits to pregnant employees. What the pamphlet didn't note was that Reagan had spearheaded none of these laws; he had followed the lead of the California legislature.

The rest of the pamphlet was equally duplicitous. It repeated the GOP platform's support for "total integration of the work force to bring women equality in pay" but then argued, "What good are equal rights and opportunities if there are no jobs?" Attacking the Carter administration's stagflation record, it insisted that the best way to help women was to revitalize the nation's economy. It was a familiar tactic to keep women in line—if you trust us and sacrifice your personal interest to the greater good, we'll see that the economy gets better and you'll share in the improvement. The problem was that there was no guarantee, no ERA, no way to ensure that if the economy did improve, women would share fairly in this outcome.

In 1980 the Reagan–Bush feminists sold out for a hope that Reagan wouldn't ignore women. They turned their backs on the women's movement, believing they would be the conscience for women within the party. They knew they were in the minority, but they hoped to turn things around. As Smith said, the party came first.

At first, hoping that the pamphlet would do the job, the campaign tried to downplay women's issues, but Carter and Anderson forced it to confront the "women's problem." Carter kept implying Reagan was hostile to women. Having finally awakened to the potential of the women's vote, independent candidate Anderson was ardently courting this vote and having some success. Crisp, who had become co-chair of his National Unity campaign in August, crossed the country speaking out for Anderson and was often joined by Democratic, Republican, and independent women. Helped by a first-class women's staff, including longtime Republican feminist pioneer Catherine East, Anderson's campaign developed a women's issues statement that was the best of all three candidates. It made a genuine commitment to women's rights, and many Democratic women signed on. Prominent Democratic feminists like Sissy Farenthold, founding chair of the National Women's Political Caucus, urged American women to support the "unabashed feminist" John Anderson. Although the Democratic platform had endorsed the ERA, Carter was now equivocating, and Farenthold urged feminists to "abandon party ranks and traditional party loyalties" and to stop being "mired in our traditions of timidity. We will only be a constituency and be recognized as one when we vote as one."

Alarmed by Anderson's popularity among women, the Reagan team picked up on the same arguments Carter was using in his campaign. Anderson might have some worthwhile ideas, but "how much good are they with no party to support those ideas and . . . no legislative or political base to enact his proposals?" The team was out to prove to doubting moderate women that a third-party candidate could not govern in a two-party system—that a vote for Anderson was a wasted vote, since he couldn't win. Because women were also alarmed by Reagan's hard anti-Soviet line, the Reagan team also worked to reassure them that they need not fear he would lead the country into war against the USSR.

Reagan and Anderson got the chance to test their strength with women voters in a debate on September 21. (Carter refused to participate.) Its overstructured format dampened any lively give-and-take, but as would happen in later presidential debates in the eighties and nineties, a question on abortion did elicit a passionate response. Anderson emotionally defended women's freedom of choice, and Reagan defended the fetus. Although pundits gave Anderson a slight edge in the debate, it was not a major breakthrough for him. It was for Reagan, however. He came across as a decent man who wasn't mean-spirited toward women. He played down social issues, offering the familiar argument that the economy and a stronger defense were the nation's "real" concerns.

Polls showed Anderson's appeal to women shrinking after the debate, principally because they felt he didn't have a chance. Before September 21 Carter had been leading among women by 40 to 32 percent, but for a while afterward Reagan overtook him. The lead didn't hold: Carter went on the offensive, implying that Reagan's election would bring war and racial and religious strife. It worked. By mid-October, he had regained his margin with women.

The Reagan campaign decided it needed to take stronger action to resolve its "women's problem." Reagan issued a statement saying that "false and misleading accusations have been made" that he was "opposed to full and equal opportunities for women." He regretted having to raise the issue "for fear that discussing it might lend even a scintilla of credence to such a charge." His "entire life—public and private—has been devoted to the dignity of all people," he proclaimed. "I could never personally tolerate any kind of discrimination." He then reiterated his promise to appoint a woman to the Supreme Court and to appoint "intelligent, committed, qualified, and responsible women" to his administration.

There were no women of any stature in the campaign, however. Reagan insider Lyn Nofziger said later, "I haven't figured out yet why there were no women. Except that there never had been, and Reagan probably figured, if he bothered to figure at all, that that's the way it was supposed to be."

At the same time that Reagan was defending his record on women, a Gallup survey showed that "36 percent of the voters were not strongly committed to any candidate and could change their minds." The campaign desperately needed a jolt. Reagan's statement hadn't made much difference. After weeks of avoiding a debate, the Reagan team decided a debate was their best hope. With Anderson no longer a factor, Carter and Reagan went at it alone.

The debate marked the beginning of the end for Carter. While there was disagreement afterward as to who actually won, Reagan definitely succeeded in convincing enough voters, especially women, that despite his militant talk about standing up to the Soviets, he wouldn't plunge America into a nuclear war, and that he was a capable man who could be entrusted with the presidency. The nation seemed ready to give him a chance to straighten out Carter's economic mess, although the majority of American women weren't still quite sure about him, as the election results would prove.

When, shortly before Election Day, rumors of an imminent release of the American hostages in Teheran turned out to be untrue, America's frustration with Carter's confused foreign policy and his stagflation economics pushed undecided voters toward Reagan. The doubts about him weren't gone, but fence-sitters threw up their hands and decided to take a chance on him. Reagan won big—50.8 percent for him, 41 percent for Carter, and 6.6 percent for the prodigal Republican-turned-independent John Anderson—achieving an electoral vote landslide, winning forty-three states. On January 20, 1981, Inauguration Day, the Iranian hostage crisis ended. Just as Reagan was finishing his inaugural address, the hostages boarded aircraft for the flight from Teheran.

The strategy of bigotry had helped win Reagan the nomination, and voter disgust with Carter's ineptitude, plus Reagan's congeniality, had elected him president.

Most of those who voted for him, however, were not endorsing the New Right's program; in fact, many were not even aware of it. This did not stop the New Right and the Religious Right from taking credit for his victory. They heralded Reagan's 489–49 electoral vote, the third largest in the twentieth century, as a mandate for their social agenda. Proclaiming his movement a "sleeping giant," Jerry Falwell said it had registered four million new voters and "influenced another 10 million who had stayed away from the polls out of frustration" in the past. In the future, he predicted, the Christian right would unseat liberal candidates who supported abortion and homosexuality and rejected the Moral Majority's interpretation of family values. By threat and innuendo, he told the nation—and more specifically, the Republican leadership—that attention must be paid. His revolution was on the move.

After the polling data had been sifted and analyzed, however, all but a few hard-line ideologues agreed that the conservative agenda of the GOP platform hadn't been the cause of Reagan's victory. The voters had provided no mandate for New Right conservatism. They were simply weary of Carter's lack of leadership. Reagan had offered them hope. As political analyst William Schneider wrote:

> the voters were voting for a change, and they were certainly aware that the type of change Reagan was offering was going to take the country in a more conservative direction. They were willing to go along with that, not because they were convinced of the essential merits of the conservative program, but because they were willing to give conservatism a chance.

It was not a broad-brush conservatism that they endorsed, however. Polls consistently found the public moving to the right on economic issues but not on the social agenda. Election analyst John Robinson of Cleveland State University reported in 1980 that "there was no evidence of a shift since 1973 on issues like abortion, pornography, extramarital sex, the 'family constellation' of issues. . . . There was quite a shift prior to 1973, but toward a more liberal stance, and opinion has stayed there."

The 1980 election was significant for another reason. While Reagan had transcended the Republican anti-women message, his party had not fared so well. For the first time since analysts began keeping track of women's voting patterns in the early fifties, more American women voted Democratic than men. It was a change of major proportions. The gender gap had arrived, although its scope was debated. Most surveys reported that men had given Reagan about 55 percent and Carter 36 percent of their vote, while among women Reagan beat Carter by a close margin of 47 to 45 percent—or 48 to 43 percent, depending upon how the exit poll questions were phrased. All agreed that Anderson's vote had been evenly divided between men and women.

From that year on, gender politics changed. Differences between women and men began to show up not only in voting but in party identification, evaluation of presidential performance, and public policy attitudes. Not surprisingly, women tended to side more with the Democratic candidates and their policies. For eight years, the women of America had been struggling with the issues raised by the women's movement. Few were untouched by its message. The constant battles within the Republican party between feminists and misogynists had made them acutely aware that the Republican party opposed women's rights. For those women—such as Schlafly's followers—who found the increasing opportunities for women frightening, or who believed traditional values offered more to women, the Republicans' opposition to such rights was welcome. For women who had joined the work force full-time—over 43 percent by 1980—the Republicans' narrow-mindedness made many of them distrust the party.

In the 1980 election sweep, the party wrested thirty-three House seats and twelve Senate seats from the Democrats, thereby gaining control of the Senate. Four of these House seats went to pro-ERA women. New Right Republican Paula Hawkins was elected to the Senate from Florida, joining Nancy Kassebaum, the only other woman in the Senate. She was swept in with the Reagan tide and with the help of women from all parties. They were stimulated by her aggressive style and populist record as a consumer advocate, even though a majority of Florida women rejected her anti-ERA, anti-choice views.

The New Right and the Religious Right had also worked hard for Hawkins. But that was not the case with the Republican senatorial candidate from Colorado. There the New Right went after feminist Mary Estill Buchanan, a forty-five-year-old mother of six and a long-standing Republican activist who had served the party and Coloradans honorably as their secretary of state. When the right prevented her from winning the Republican nomination at her state party convention, she painstakingly collected signatures statewide to get on the primary ballot, where she beat the New Right's candidate and became the party's nominee.

But the Moral Majority refused to endorse Buchanan, and Weyrich's Committee for the Survival of a Free Congress endorsed her Democratic opponent, Senator Gary Hart. Buchanan's race exemplified the lengths to which the antifeminist right would go to defeat feminist Republicans. Like Reagan, Buchanan was a defense hard-liner and a fiscal conservative—stands that Falwell's and Weyrich's organizations supposedly backed. On social issues, she and Hart held similar positions, although Hart was unquestionably the more liberal candidate overall. Yet the New Right called Buchanan a "traitor to the family" and likened her to a representative of Satan. Buchanan was not afraid of such accusations and gave as good as she got, calling the Moral Majority "a haven of hypocrisy" and standing her ground on her feminist positions. She lost by only one percentage point, 50 to 49 percent, although Colorado voted overwhelmingly for Reagan. It was one more proof that for the right, party loyalty was a one-way street.

For those of us in the women's political movement, the 1980 election was bittersweet. The misogynist New Right had gotten their candidate into the White House. On the other hand, the long-awaited women's vote had finally surfaced. Women were no longer consistently voting like their husbands and other male relatives; they had become a distinct political constituency. The world of politics had changed. While the Reagan White House might try to ignore us, we knew the tables had been turned. A new political dynamic now existed that would be as influential as when women had won the vote.

The national Republican feminist effort was subsumed under the leadership of Kathy Wilson, who became chair of the National Women's Political Caucus, and my sister-in-law Gayle Melich, NWPC executive director. Wilson spent her four-year term bravely slashing out at the administration's policies against women, while Melich developed programs to increase the number of women candidates from both parties. The original task force group broke up. Some became Democrats, like Chris Milliken, who preferred to put her energy behind politicians who didn't think feminists were the devil's handmaidens. Others dropped out to pursue personal careers. Smith and Kilberg sought a future in national GOP politics, hoping through their friendship with Bush to "sensitize" (their word) the party's and administration's policies to women's issues.

We others went into exile from national politics. We tried to build feminism within local and state Republican parties by running candidates and cajoling and shaming Democratic feminists into helping us. We saw our exile as only temporary, however. We were not giving up, even though Buchanan's campaign in Colorado had taught us what would happen to any Republican feminist who dared challenge the right. We were simply waiting it out. In time, we believed, we would "take back our party."

When the Reagan administration took over, with the exception of Meese and William French Smith, the New Right was not in the governing inner circle, but they held important second-level leveraging positions within the administration. Gary Bauer, one of the New Right's most vocal ideologues, started in the White House's Office of Policy Development and rose to become Reagan's domestic policy chief in his second term. Reagan appointed Donald Devine, campaign coordinator for right-to-life policies (and Clarke Reed's buddy during the RNC "positive action" fights of the mid-seventies), to head the Office of Personnel Management (OPM). This was like putting the fox in charge of the henhouse, since the OPM manages the personnel system of the federal civil service. Devine didn't disappoint us: He immediately moved to eliminate reimbursement for abortions from the health insurance plans of federal employees and to strike the Planned Parenthood Federation of America from the list of charities that federal employees could voluntarily check off their paychecks.

The administration created a new position specifically for the agenda of the Religious Right. The former Moral Majority executive director, the Reverend Robert Billings, was appointed assistant secretary of education for nonpublic education "as a sop to conservative private school groups." Columnists Rowland Evans and Robert Novak described Billings as a "militant backer of private church education." His position wouldn't need Senate confirmation, thereby limiting the ability of public school advocates to express their outrage at the establishment of a government post to help religious schools.

Charlie Black, Roger Stone, and Paul Manafort, their business partner, didn't join the administration. Instead, they established a highly successful consulting and lobbying business, parlaying their insider influence into making money while pushing New Right legislation and policies. The leaders of the Religious Right also stayed on the outside but used their newfound status as friends of the White House to lobby against family planning and abortion, for prayer in the schools, and for federal assistance to religious schools. They also appointed themselves keepers of the administration's social policy and howled whenever they felt it strayed from the Detroit platform.

In the early days of the Reagan revolution, the White House reverted to type and pretended the "women's problem" didn't exist. Among the men it was business as usual, which meant not sharing power with women. The only woman besides Nancy Reagan with any significant influence in the White House was Helene von Damm, Reagan's personal secretary when he'd been governor. Von Damm became a major player in the personnel transition office, where she furthered the New Right's goals. Anne Armstrong participated in some of the preliminary discussions about cabinet appointments, and Elizabeth Dole prepared papers on health and human services, although during the transition Dole, who had served Reagan's campaign so loyally, was considered suspect. According to von Damm, New Right money man Joseph Coors vetoed her name for possible secretary of commerce because "she would be seen as too liberal."

There was only one woman in the first Reagan cabinet, Jeane Kirkpatrick, whom Reagan appointed ambassador to the United Nations. It was an important role but was widely considered to be a cut below the prestige of other cabinet positions. Kirkpatrick was an academic and a neoconservative who would stay clear of women's issues during the Reagan years. She supported the ERA. She was thought to be unsure about abortion, but it was a subject she didn't raise.

In 1974 Kirkpatrick had published *Political Woman,* a groundbreaking book on women in politics at a time when few in her profession, political science, even considered there was much to say about the subject. Kirkpatrick must have decided that analyzing women's role in the world wasn't as challenging as analyzing foreign affairs, and after her book was published, she shifted specialties. She is supposed to have first caught Reagan's attention with a *Commentary* article about President Carter's foreign policy, in which she noted the differences between revolutionary Communist totalitarian governments and authoritarian dictatorships. She was eminently qualified to represent the Reagan government at the United Nations, but her appointment clearly served a second purpose as well. The Reaganites knew they needed a token woman appointment, but they didn't want to have to tangle with the right over their selections. Kirkpatrick was acceptable to Joseph Coors, and her appointment was a cosmetic solution to the women's appointment "problem."

The pattern of appointing women who were married to insider men, which had begun with Nixon, was continued. In 1981, despite the right's opposition, Elizabeth Dole became the only woman on the White House staff in an executive position. As the head of the Office of Public Liaison, she was the White House contact for minorities, business, labor, the arts, consumers, the disabled, and any other group to which the White House thought attention should be paid. Interestingly, the press announcements about this new office mentioned no liaison for women. Nevertheless, Dole worked with Washington's women's organizations, which gave her high marks for trying to raise the White House's consciousness about the inequities women suffered in pensions and insurance.

This particular effort of Dole's, however, would end in September 1982, when the president appointed Dee Jepsen, an anti-ERA, anti-abortion Christian fundamentalist, to be the White House's liaison to women's groups. Jepsen was the wife of Roger Jepsen, the senator who had slashed and burned his way across Iowa in his 1978 New Right campaign, and her appointment showed the subtle but steady strides the right was making toward taking over women's policy in the administration.

Four months after Jepsen's appointment, Dole became secretary of transportation, and Faith Whittlesey, a New Right Pennsylvanian who had risen through the national Republican ranks, replaced her as head of the Office of Public Liaison. Whittlesey, a bright self-made lawyer, was aggressively committed to the right's social agenda and had proved to be a tough negotiator for its platform planks in Detroit. The New Right men felt she could be trusted.

As a member of the original California Reagan team, von Damm knew how to find the truly loyal Reaganites. She was the New Right's bird dog, pointing out to the inner circle those who would foment the Reagan revolution. Acting as an ideological gatekeeper, she protected the truly pure revolutionaries. Eventually she became assistant to Pendleton James, the chief of presidential personnel, and when he left in the fall of 1982, she took over his job. Von Damm was Reagan's true patronage boss. While she could be and occasionally was overruled by the inner circle, she wielded great power. She made it clear that only those with New Right credentials should receive appointments. She claimed she wanted to put women into the administration but that it was difficult to find conservative women who would serve. She established a task force to find qualified women, but

> there were obstacles. One of the biggest was that women who are politically active and interested tend to be disproportionately on the left end of the spectrum. Even within the Republican Party, most of the women were moderates or liberals. That left us with a very constricted pool from which to recruit.

Von Damm's single-focus perspective infuriated less ideological Republicans, and women's groups pointed to the small number of women appointed to high-level jobs in the early years of the administration. Kassebaum publicly criticized the White House's attitude that there weren't any qualified women: "I really get very tired of hearing, as I did one day from the Cabinet Secretary, that we just haven't had any names sent over to us. I resent it when I hear there aren't any women with the qualifications."

And yet von Damm proudly argued that even though it was hard to find women whose ideology was correct, the administration had placed more than seven hundred women in "important positions." Even setting aside what "important" signified, this was still several hundred fewer than Carter's record.

Mary Louise Smith was one of those who didn't pass the von Damm ideological test. Her friends floated her name for U.S. treasurer, but the New Right quickly quashed that idea and turned on her, criticizing her for being a Bush supporter first and coming late to Reagan.

They claimed she had used her "Republican leadership positions as a base from which to promote causes that are anathema not only to conservatives but to most mainstream Republicans." They ridiculed her for organizing a women's advisory board during the campaign "that was stacked with supporters of ERA and abortion—issues that Reagan himself was clearly on record against. Creation of this board upset many of Reagan's strongest backers in the pro-family movement and was considered a major campaign blunder." Her friend George Bush didn't come to her aid. Bay Buchanan, sister of Pat Buchanan, became the U.S. treasurer instead.

As Mary Crisp had been the martyr for feminist Republicans in 1980, Mary Louise Smith was our martyr in the early Reagan years.

The U.S. Commission on Civil Rights was one of the administration's first targets in its drive to undo the gains made by the civil rights and women's movements. The commission had been established by Congress in 1957 to measure the progress of integration and the nation's compliance with civil rights laws. By the late sixties, it had become a symbol of the national consensus on the need for civil rights for all Americans. Although its powers were limited to education and moral suasion, its record was distinguished, if largely unnoticed by the public.

From Eisenhower on, all administrations had put the full force of governmental authority behind measures that would bring about equality of opportunity. The Reagan administration intended to narrow this historically broad focus by dismantling established methods of fighting discrimination, and to limit the government's role to enforcing antidiscrimination laws solely in cases of individual grievances. It was an approach, with modifications, that Clarence Thomas would follow when he became chairman of the Equal Employment Opportunity Commission in May 1982.

The administration fired the Civil Rights Commission's chairman, Arthur S. Flemming, a distinguished former member of Eisenhower's cabinet, and the vice-chairman, California Republican Stephen Horn, and replaced them with black conservative Clarence Pendleton, Jr., and Mary Louise Smith. It was the first time in the commission's twenty-four-year history that any of its commissioners had been fired.

As in Detroit, the Reagan team hoped to use Smith as a credible feminist woman to approve antifeminist policy.

They had underestimated her, misjudging her deep commitment to civil rights. When Pendleton moved promptly to implement the White House's instructions and narrow the commission's focus, Smith voted with the commission members who wished to preserve its broad focus. The administration then tried to force out Jill Ruckelshaus, who had been appointed to the commission by President Carter. Its black male appointee to replace Ruckelshaus was so lacking in credentials and created such an outcry among civil rights groups and Congress, however, that his name was withdrawn. Under a so-called compromise between Congress and the White House, Ruckelshaus was to be retained, but when it came time to reappoint her, the White House denied there was such an understanding and instead replaced her with Robert Destro, former general counsel of Milwaukee's Catholic League for Religious and Civil Rights. Smith stayed until December 1983, but under great duress and constant attack from the New Right. Afterward, the White House refused to appoint her to another position compatible with the devoted service she had given the party.

In June 1983 the commission took the Reagan administration to task for its poor appointments record on women and minorities, saying that it was "disappointed and concerned that overall representation of women and minority men among top Reagan administration appointees thus far is below the levels achieved during the Carter administration," and that

the Reagan administration's appointments record had reversed a trend of ever more women and minorities appointed to high-level positions by succeeding presidents, both Democratic and Republican, in recent years.

Occasionally, however, the administration did show it could rise above its ideological commitments and act in the finest traditions of the presidency. Early in Reagan's first year, when Justice Potter Stewart resigned from the Supreme Court, women waited to see whether Reagan would keep his promise to appoint a woman justice. There had been so many disappointments over the years—why should this time be any different?

It was different. The president named Sandra Day O'Connor to be the first woman justice on the Court, generating genuine excitement nationwide. As the public learned more about this Stanford Law School honors graduate, mother of three sons, wife, judge, and former Arizona state senator, its support for her appointment was enthusiastic and bipartisan. Only three major political groups opposed her nomination —the New Right, the National Right to Life Committee, and the Moral Majority. As a state legislator in 1970, three years before *Roe v. Wade*, O'Connor had supported legislation to repeal Arizona's abortion prohibition, and in 1973 she had co-sponsored family-planning legislation. Falwell attacked, saying "good Christians" should be worried about O'Connor, to which Episcopalian Barry Goldwater angrily responded, "Every good Christian ought to kick Falwell right in the ass."

Pat Buchanan demeaned Reagan's campaign promise as "frivolous," and charged he had committed "political adultery." As usual, Buchanan issued a threat:

In nominating Ms. O'Connor, the White House has left the right-to-life movement no choice but to oppose her with all its resources, no choice but to depart, temporarily and perhaps permanently, from the President's coalition, no choice but to put the heat on Senators like Orrin Hatch—up for reelection in 1982. . . . [T]he abortion issue is not just a social issue; it is the overriding social issue that split the FDR coalition and sent millions of Southern evangelical Christians and Northern Catholics into the camp of a Republican President with whom they may disagree on a dozen other issues. Their demoralization is a political tragedy of the first order—and so damned unnecessary.

Reagan liked O'Connor, and after meeting her he never interviewed anyone else for the position. She refused to get into the abortion issue at her Judiciary Committee hearings and acquitted herself honorably as a person who would uphold the highest standards of judicial impartiality. When Orrin Hatch endorsed her because he believed her to be "conservative but not inflexibly so" and said that "she would try to strictly interpret the Constitution," the fight was over. The Senate confirmed her nomination unanimously.

O'Connor's appointment was a milestone in America's slow journey toward fulfilling its promise to all its citizens. Republican feminists took special pleasure in knowing that we had played a role in her nomination. If we hadn't sought the meeting in Detroit and asked for the Court appointment, it might never have happened. What if Reagan had not been pushed to make a public pledge in the campaign? With his right flank pressuring him so hard, would he have acted? Given the virulence of O'Connor's opponents, it seemed questionable.

Traditionally, the paperwork for judicial appointees is a shared responsibility between the White House and the Justice Department, and in O'Connor's case, Reagan's attorney general, William French Smith, worked with Meese and Michael Deaver to prepare the background on O'Connor. After that, however, the tradition changed for a while. According to von Damm, "For the first time, an administration moved the decision-making process [for judicial selection] directly into the White House and away from the Justice Department." As she noted, "there was a strong institutional pride among the lawyers at the Justice Department, and therefore strong resistance to political appointments."

Von Damm interceded to see that "the Reagan Revolution was being waged by true Reaganites," taking particular pride in ensuring that only true Reagan conservatives were selected for federal judgeships. She insisted her office did make "an effort to find women judges, but that turned out to be difficult," because even though there were qualified women jurists, "it was awfully difficult to find qualified women jurists who were also conservative in outlook." In the end, though, von Damm believed that one of the "greatest accomplishments" of the Reagan legacy would be its nomination of conservative judges. There is no question she was right. The Reagan judges would become the cutting edge of the Reagan legacy, enduring long after he left the White House. By Meese's count, Reagan appointed "almost half of the federal judiciary—371 judges out of a total of 761. Of these, three appointees were Supreme Court Justices, eighty-three were appellate court judges."

The policy onslaught on women began with the first Reagan budget in 1981. This "family values" administration proposed major tax cuts and budget reductions of $44 billion, of which one-third would directly hurt poor women and children. Particularly hard hit were the Aid to

Families with Dependent Children programs (AFDC), 93 percent of whose recipients were children and women with few job-related skills. Cuts were proposed for Medicaid, food stamps, child nutrition, school lunches, child care, civil rights enforcement, the WIC program (which provided food for low-income pregnant women, infants, and children), fuel assistance, housing, student loans, education, employment and training, and Social Security benefits for student dependents of retired, disabled, or deceased workers. Programs would be eliminated, reduced, or shifted to the states through block grants. (If this list sounds familiar, it is because it would return in a slightly harsher form in Newt Gingrich's 1994 revolution.) Every major national women's organization attacked the Reagan budget for endangering the "rights for which women have struggled over the last several years." They predicted accurately that "the net effect of the Reagan proposal is a redistribution of income, widening the income gap between the rich and lower classes."

Also in early 1981, several "human life" constitutional amendments were introduced in Congress. The one attracting the most initial attention came from the junior senator from North Carolina, John East, known as "Helms on wheels" for his devotion to his mentor's policies and because he was confined to a wheelchair. East's amendment championed the words of the Republican platform that gave a fertilized egg more rights than a woman. It didn't simply abrogate *Roe v. Wade* by making abortion a crime; it made the fetus superior to the woman. The amendment's strict principle of fetal personhood permitted no exceptions, not even for the life of the mother. Abortion would be murder and a woman who underwent it would be a "sinner"—the religious component was clear. She could be charged with murder, either directly or as an accessory, as could all others involved—including doctors and other health professionals. Constitutional attorney Rhonda Copelon wrote that "if the fertilized egg were constitutionally a person, anything with even a risk of fetal destruction could be criminal. The IUD and some forms of the pill could be outlawed as deadly weapons." The world that Margaret Atwood was to depict so vividly in *The Handmaid's Tale* in 1986 seemed closer than any of us could have imagined possible.

In an effort to find language acceptable to more members of Congress, Jesse Helms and Henry Hyde scuttled East's bill and enlisted Reagan's help to pass legislation declaring that the "life of the fetus" was entitled to protection under the Fourteenth Amendment. In March the president told the press he thought this Hyde–Helms bill would make a Human Life Amendment unnecessary because "the Constitution already protects the right of human life." It was a promising endorsement for the anti-choice forces, who were ready to do battle for the legislation.

But on March 30 came John Hinckley's attempt to assassinate Reagan. Americans were horrified. Their enormous outpouring of sympathy and warmth for the wounded president not only reflected admiration for his courage but lengthened the new administration's honeymoon with Congress and the American people. The White House decided to take advantage of Congress's goodwill and focus its energies on passing its first priority, the tax-cut package, rather than incite further controversy over outlawing abortion.

With the plans of Helms, Hyde, and East sidetracked, the anti-abortion advocates were split over how to proceed. Late that fall, Hatch tried another tack: He introduced an amendment that would give Congress and the states equal power to restrict or ban abortion. The White House offered no help, however, and he failed. The fight for a constitutional amendment to ban abortion would continue for a while, but by the mid-eighties it was dead. The White House and the right-to-life movement had discovered other, less complicated ways to end legal abortion.

At the end of Reagan's first year in office, economic worries were the dominant concern of much of the nation. The country was entering its worst recession since the Depression, thanks to the tight money policies of the Federal Reserve and the White House's inept failure to take advantage of an incipient recovery in 1981. The nation's unemployment rate rose from 7.4 to 10.8 percent, the highest since 1940. Women and minorities had been hit particularly hard by the drop in employment. As national women's groups fought arduous battles in Washington to beat back the worst of the New Right–Reagan policy agenda, political women began organizing for the 1982 midterm elections.

Reagan and the national Republican party tried to pin the recession on Jimmy Carter and past spending by the Democrats. This was not the judgment of the Federal Reserve or many economists, who blamed the problems on the mounting deficit that was constricting investment capital. But the voters didn't care whose fault it was. They wanted relief.

When 1981 gubernatorial races in New Jersey and Virginia confirmed what the 1980 elections had shown—more women were voting Democratic than men—the Republicans who'd pretended there wasn't a women's problem began to worry about 1982. A women's backlash against Republican candidates was under way. A CBS News/*New York Times* poll had confirmed what we all knew, that while 61 percent of men approved of Reagan's presidency, only 46 percent of women did. State and local Republicans discovered that the administration's New Majoritarian strategy was hurting their campaigns. The national Republican campaign committees for the Senate and House warned their candidates to develop their own approach to women and to separate themselves from the Reagan record on women. In July 1981 pollster Louis Harris reported that "for President Reagan and the Republicans, the single most formidable obstacle to their becoming a majority party in the 1980s is the vote of women."

What was jarring to us was the Washington Republican establishment's surprise at this "news." Where had they been for the last six years? A variety of reasons were given to explain women's anger, from Reagan's opposition to the ERA and abortion to the poor economy and the administration's social agenda. But no one said publicly what we feminists knew—that the Republican party's misogyny was registering on women, that six years of constant Republican hostility were having an effect. By pursuing their regressive social and economic policy even as the recession deepened, none of the Reagan circle seemed to understand what was happening to many women. Public policy analyst Linda Tarr-Whelan spelled it out:

Women make less than men in every job at every educational level. The median wage for all women workers in 1980 was $11,220; for men it was $18,006. . . . One half of all poor American families are headed by women, sixty percent of all unmarried women over 65 depend solely on Social Security and have an annual income of $2,500, compared to $3,400 for unmarried men on Social Security. . . . Only 1 percent of American women earn more than $25,000 per year, . . . 93 percent of all welfare recipients are women and their children,

nearly two-thirds of Medicaid recipients are women . . .
nearly 70 percent of all food stamp recipients are women.

On June 30, 1982, the ERA died. Its demise was barely noticed in the press. The majority of Americans still favored it, but in smaller numbers than in 1972, when Congress had sent it to the states for ratification. But the battles in unratified states like North Carolina, Illinois, and Florida in the previous year had proved that a majority of male legislators didn't want to share power with women, considered the ERA an unwelcome intrusion of federal power, and thought it would be too expensive to implement.

The ten-year battle was not a complete loss, for it had focused public attention on inequities toward women and become the symbol of demands for change in women's lives in the workplace and at home. Many women became feminists because of their work for the ERA. The struggle had raised public officials' consciousness of women's problems, it energized women to run for office, it brought other issues on the feminist agenda to the public's attention, and it forced state governments and courts to correct gender bias in state law. To the millions of women and men who had worked so hard for the ERA, its death was a catalyst for even greater political activity. They threw themselves into electing feminists and their allies in the 1982 elections, using the rallying cry that the Republicans were responsible for the ERA's death.

The gender gap dominated the election results. What was most evident throughout the nation was women's anger at the deteriorating economy, which they took out on Reagan and the Republican party. Proving that women would vote issues and party over gender, they voted against even Republican feminists. When it was over, the women's vote had given Democratic congressional candidates a significant edge over their Republican opponents. While the GOP held on to the Senate, it lost twenty-six House seats. ABC News/*Washington Post* exit polls reported that 53 percent of women voted for Democrats, compared with 47 percent for Republicans. In exit polls for House races, women favored Democrats by 59 to 38 percent. As Ruth Mandel, an authority on the women's political movement, analyzed the outcome, "women's votes elected the Democratic governors of New York, Connecticut and Texas. NBC News also credit[ed] women's votes with deciding the gubernatorial race in Michigan." A majority of women voters had not bought the Republicans' argument that they would do the most for women by cutting taxes and budgets. But it was more than anger that brought these striking results: For the first time since the birth of the women's political movement, effective machinery had been in place to harness this anger. It was the greatest coalescing of women's organizations for an election since the suffrage campaign.

More women had run for office in 1982 than ever before: 3 for the U.S. Senate, 55 for Congress, and 1,643 for state legislative seats. National women's organizations united in a bipartisan drive to get out the women's vote, although partisanship did enter into some campaigns. NOW, by far the best funded of the feminist political groups, sought to elect Democrats to Congress and refused to support Republican feminists Nancy Johnson in Connecticut, Millicent Fenwick in her bid to become New Jersey's first woman U.S. senator, and Congressmember Margaret Heckler in her bid for reelection in Massachusetts. Fenwick and Heckler lost; Johnson, whose district was traditionally Republican, won.

Would the White House change its policies toward women after this wake-up call? I remember attending a postmortem session where Reagan's pollster Richard Wirthlin—whom I'd known since 1964, when he'd been my father's pollster in his run for governor of Utah—complained that Republicans had lost because of poor party organization and wasteful television commercials. He never mentioned the gender gap until I raised it during the question period. Yes, he agreed, the party is in trouble with women, but that will change as soon as the economy improves. He rejected the notion that women were angry at Reagan and the Republican party for policies that prevented women from improving their lot. He denied that the Reagan team had made a systematic effort to win votes through a backlash strategy in 1980 and 1982. Yet he couldn't explain why American women were moving away from our party. After the election the White House made a few cosmetic changes directed toward women voters, while Wirthlin turned to his polls and focus groups to find the "angle" to win back the women for the 1984 campaign.

A Justice Department memo to the White House's Legislative Affairs Division in December 1982 summed up the situation: "If the administration has any hope of reversing feminist momentum away from the administration, we must recognize that women's concerns are not generally so parochial as 'women this and women that' but arise from perceptions of the economy, military matters and other major national issues." A month later, Reagan's popularity dropped to 35 percent, an all-time low. More than 11.5 million Americans were out of work. Many were women, and many were wives of blue-collar men—Reagan Democrats—who were experiencing the disintegration of the nation's industrial base as manufacturers either closed down or moved their plants to countries with cheaper labor.

But the Reagan inner circle didn't seem to want to recognize the direct connection between its policies of dismantling programs that helped women and their children and of stopping the ERA, and the hostility women harbored toward the president and the party. To have done so would have meant refuting the political strategy through which Reagan had won the presidency, and this his political advisers would not let him do, even if he had been inclined to. The White House stayed true to its misogynist policies, and rather than addressing the causes of women's anger—lack of economic opportunity and equitable treatment —it relied yet again on public relations and image repair.

The White House pragmatists—Deaver, Baker, and Nancy Reagan —organized the appointments of "safe" women, special commissions, publicity gimmicks about women's concerns, awards for prominent women, and an occasional speech by the president about women's contributions to the nation. They even recruited Maureen Reagan, hoping filial devotion from a feminist daughter might help.

In January 1983 Elizabeth Dole, having sufficiently proved to her White House colleagues that she could represent the administration's antifeminist line, was appointed secretary of transportation. She had demonstrated to the Reagan team that she was disciplined and would keep her attitudes about women to herself. She had even said publicly that she no longer backed the ERA and that she supported Reagan's position on eliminating discrimination against women through reviewing state and federal law. During the fall campaign, she had been the White House's principal messenger to women, arguing that the gap between men's and women's economic conditions wasn't the fault of the party, and that "the president's policies were designed to deal with the 'real gap' between the sexes in their financial and legal status." She had convinced Reagan to form a White House Coordinating Council on Women to investigate how the government could help women with child care, child-support enforcement, pensions, and insurance policies. But after she went to Transportation, nothing significant came of these projects. The council proved to be a campaign tool, not a commitment to further policies for women.

The White House also assessed the possibility of appointing Margaret Heckler to a prominent position. Overall, she had been loyal in the previous two years, using her position as co-chair of the bipartisan Congresswomen's Caucus to veto most caucus criticism of Reagan's policies. Reagan owed her. She was less trusted than Dole, but the president took a chance and appointed her secretary of health and human services. As expected, her nomination angered the *Human Events* people, while feminists were cautiously hopeful. Heckler had represented a two-to-one Democratic district, and her votes for Reagan's budget had been the principal reason she lost her House seat in November. But even as she had championed Reaganomics, she had opposed the president's proposal to slash Social Security benefits, which would have weighed most heavily on women and children. She had also protected the Women's Educational Equity Act from the administration's knife. Women in Washington knew that except for her opposition to abortion, Heckler had excellent feminist credentials. Possessed of a first-class mind, she knew Washington and could be an advocate for women in cabinet meetings. She could argue against the administration's misogynist policies. We were pleased.

Yet the cards were stacked against Heckler from the beginning. She passed appointments muster only because the administration intended to treat her in the customary manner with which it dealt with feminist Republicans—by surrounding her with New Right "protectors" once she took office. She would become a prisoner in her own agency.

When Heckler became HHS secretary, Reagan appointed John Svahn—the previous chief of his California administration's welfare system and then U.S. Social Security administrator—her undersecretary. He came as part of the Heckler appointment package, meaning she lacked the cabinet secretary's usual power to appoint her own deputies. Moreover, the day after her selection, she made a tactical mistake in acknowledging to the press that she didn't have sufficient administrative

experience and thus welcomed Svahn. The admission weakened her
before she had even begun.

Nor was Svahn her only watchdog. To ensure that Heckler didn't
stray on reproductive health issues, even though she was anti-choice,
the administration kept on Marjorie Mecklenburg, who had been appointed deputy assistant secretary for population affairs in the department by Heckler's predecessor, Richard Schweiker—a sponsor of a
constitutional amendment banning abortion during his days in the
Senate. Mecklenburg was a founder of the National Right to Life Committee and past president of the Minnesota Citizens Concerned for Life.
There was no ambiguity about her agenda.

Two weeks after Heckler's and Dole's appointments, Reagan made
another stab at correcting his "women's problem." In his 1983 State of
the Union speech in January, he attacked pension discrimination
against women and asked for tougher laws to enforce child-support
payments and for private-sector help for child care. In March some
Republican women congressmembers, including Olympia Snowe, now
co-chair of the Congressional Caucus on Women's Issues, followed up
with a letter to Reagan complaining that he had not so far fulfilled his
pledges. It got them a meeting with the president.

Reagan promised to lay out how he would implement the points in
his State of the Union speech; some administration proposals would be
forthcoming. None were. Instead, Faith Whittlesey, who would be expected to be responsible for such implementation at the White House
Office of Public Liaison, did nothing. As Snowe noted, "Six months
after this speech, they [the White House] failed to recommend one
proposal." Whittlesey even opposed Reagan's pension reform idea.

A top White House aide told Peg Simpson, a political reporter who
had been closely following the growing conflict over women's issues at
the White House, that Whittlesey politically marched to her own drum-
mer: "She's the only person here who says there isn't a gender gap.
Every conservative Reaganite agrees there is one."

Whittlesey's women's portfolio was taken away from her thereafter,
and Michael Deaver took over the task of translating Reagan's pledges
to women into policy. Now Deaver, the White House's public relations
man par excellence, not a policy implementer, was in charge of the
"women's problem." Nothing changed.

Meanwhile, the misogynists were busy cutting opportunities for women by slicing budgets and abandoning the enforcement of discrimination laws. In every government department that dealt with specific women's programs, rollback was the watchword.

The most torturous battles came over education, where the administration tried to reverse the civil rights policies of Nixon, Ford, and Carter. When Congress refused to cooperate in eliminating federal funding for college and school programs aimed at ending sex discrimination, the White House turned to judicial action. In August 1983 the Justice Department filed a brief in a pending Supreme Court case brought by Grove City College in Pennsylvania against the U.S. government. The college had argued that it was exempt from Title IX of the 1972 Education Act, which banned sex discrimination by educational institutions that received federal financing, because *it* didn't accept direct government aid; only its students were the recipients of federal grants and loans. The Justice Department's brief argued that the ban applied only to specific educational programs or departments that received federal money, not to the college as a whole. This argument was contrary to the way Title IX had been interpreted and enforced ever since its enactment. If the Justice Department's interpretation were accepted by the Court, it would mean that a college could not discriminate in any department that got federal funds, but was free to discriminate anywhere else in the institution. What the Justice Department was doing was narrowing the scope of civil rights law.

Title IX had been highly successful in opening up educational opportunities to women, doubling the number of doctoral degrees and tripling the number of women entering medical school. It had strengthened women's sports in the country by doubling the number of sports open to college women. Sports writers would praise Title IX programs the following year as a crucial contributor to the impressive showing of America's women athletes at the 1984 Olympic Games in Los Angeles.

On February 28, 1984, the day after the Iowa presidential caucuses, the Supreme Court ruled in favor of the administration's position in the *Grove City* case, enraging women's and civil rights groups who believed the decision could cut the heart out of civil rights law. *Grove City* was a body blow to the very foundation of the civil rights philosophy that had governed the nation since the first federal civil rights laws were passed in the early sixties. It would affect not only women but minorities, the disabled, and the elderly. For the next four years, Congress and the White House warred over *Grove City*. In 1988 Congress finally passed the Civil Rights Restoration Act overturning the law laid out in the *Grove City* decision. Reagan vetoed it, but with the help of twenty-one Senate and fifty-two House Republicans, the veto was overridden. Civil rights law was returned more or less to where it had been when Reagan's men set out to emasculate it.

For the rest of Reagan's first term, the administration pressed on with its social agenda. The tension between the White House and women's groups—feminist and not-so-feminist—was electric, and the slightest misstep away from civilized discourse set off angry sparks that in less contentious times would have been shrugged off by both sides as not worth a response. One of the worst offenders was the president himself, who seemed to bumble into one off-putting statement after another. We didn't know whether to laugh or cry when twelve hundred members of the International Business and Professional Women's Club were turned away by mistake at the White House gates for a tour that had been scheduled for a year; and in an attempt to apologize for the mix-up, Reagan said, "I happen to be one who believes that if it wasn't for women, us men would still be walking around in skin suits carrying clubs." Any number of similarly unthinking and demeaning words— and actions—came from the men in the administration. As 1984 dawned, many Republican activist women, including myself, began to think seriously for the first time about abandoning the Republican party.

11

"TEACH THEM A LESSON"

The White House's principal objective in 1984 was to reelect Reagan. It was not interested in women's sensibilities except as they might affect his electability. As the year began, the White House was encouraged. The women's problem might not be the reelection hurdle it once feared. Although women were still less enthusiastic than men, polls showed that at least 57 percent of Americans approved of the president's performance, even as they were unhappy with his failure to cut unemployment and reduce the federal deficit, now projected to reach an all-time high of $200 billion before year's end.

The recession was over, and in fact economic growth was reaching boom proportions. Inflation had dropped dramatically and was at an annual rate of 4 percent. This spectacular change in the nation's economic life had come about chiefly because Federal Reserve chairman Paul Volcker had changed course in the late fall of 1982. During most of the first two years of the administration, the Fed had imposed harsh tight-money policies on the country. Forced by a crisis in the U.S. banking community after the Federal Deposit Insurance Corporation had closed down the Penn Square Bank in Oklahoma City in July, and by Mexico's default on loans, most of which were held by U.S. banks, Volcker had loosened the money supply. This brought an immediate increase in business activity. By the spring of 1983, the recovery had begun.

Admittedly, those enjoying this new prosperity were mainly upper-income people, but there was a general feeling of optimism and the

White House seemed unconcerned that many women and children, especially those in single-parent families, were not sharing in the recovery.

The 1984 Reagan campaign would again adopt the New Majoritarian strategy, this time with particular emphasis on winning all the southern, border, and western states, which held 266 of the 270 electoral votes needed for victory. James Baker was the campaign's political leader. Other insiders included Michael Deaver, Bob Teeter, and Californian Stu Spencer, whose political judgment Nancy Reagan most trusted. Teeter, a well-known, highly respected pollster from Michigan whom I had known since Ripon Society days, would be a nonideological voice in Reagan's inner circle. Spencer was the granddaddy of political consultants, who knew Republican politics better than almost anyone in America. In 1976 he had been the one urging Ford to pick Anne Armstrong as his running mate. New Right men Ed Rollins, late of the White House political office, and Lee Atwater, his deputy, were assigned to flesh out the strategy; two other New Rightists, Jim Lake and Charlie Black, joined Dick Wirthlin, who continued as Reagan's pollster; and by early January, the team was in place.

Later Baker's assistant Margaret Tutwiler, who had become the White House political affairs officer, joined the circle as White House liaison with the campaign. She was the only woman other than Nancy Reagan to have any substantial say in the campaign strategy.

The team viewed the gender gap as an irritant, but being thorough professionals, they set up a project to counteract it. It would be focused principally on the national convention in Dallas in late August, but the serious early work was done by Wirthlin. Ever since the 1982 midterm elections, he had been analyzing the women's vote, polling and holding focus groups to identify women who would vote for Reagan. Not surprisingly, he discovered that married women with children who didn't work outside the home were the president's strongest backers, but this was 1984, and they now constituted a minority of America's women. Using Wirthlin's data, the campaign eventually crafted an approach to target the majority, and found that the old campaign saws of peace and prosperity were still the most persuasive message for attracting women to Reagan.

As was standard for a Republican campaign, the message focused on economic issues. This time it was targeted in particular on working women and the elderly or widowed. And also true to form, the campaign had the national co-chairman of the party—now Betty Heitman—organize a women's outreach effort to stress Reagan's economic successes. Heitman's National Women's Coalition of professional women and Washington activists were mainly pro-choice, but most of them agreed with the campaign's emphasis on "cutting government spending" and "curbing creeping socialism." Coalition member Marianthi Lansdale, vice-president of a family-owned investment firm and pro-choice, was typical of how many felt. While considering abortion a key issue, Lansdale said Reagan's opposition to abortion didn't bother her. "I don't think [reversals] are going to occur. We've made too much progress ever to go back," she said. "The economy is too important; if we go down the tubes economically, we've had it. If abortion is that important to you, then you're really not a Republican."

At first, there was little action on the women's front. The polls consistently showed Reagan doing well, and the inner circle thought it prudent not to tangle with the misogynists on Reagan's right flank. Seeking the women's vote too assiduously would awaken a controversial giant that they preferred to leave asleep. It was better not to arouse the bigots in Reagan's electoral coalition.

But feminist Maureen Reagan took exception to this wariness. When her father told her that he was worried about his image with women, she leaped at the opening he had given her. With Wirthlin's help and with guidance from Republican consultant Wilma Goldstein, Maureen Reagan developed a plan to counteract women's anger toward her father and the Republican party. Becoming a part-time consultant to the Republican National Committee, she recruited Republican women officeholders essentially to be cheerleaders for the Reagan record. At first the inner circle ignored her efforts, but she persevered and finally convinced them to agree to a series of White House briefings for elected Republican women. It was a first for the Reagan administration—a systematic effort to reach out to political women who weren't part of the National Federation of Republican Women. Maureen believed the briefings helped her father. She wrote:

> We heard from many women office holders afterward who reported that for the first time they had been able to reveal in their respective caucuses some inside information from the

highest levels of government; for the first time, they said, the men had listened.

Maureen Reagan and her small staff held fund-raisers for Republican women candidates. They pumped out press releases and gave speeches about what the party and the administration were doing for women. They were effective with Republican audiences, but once they ventured beyond them, they often met with hostility and incredulity. Reagan's appointments record could be defended somewhat, but his policy record could not. As Louis Harris reported in a study on women's attitudes in late 1983:

> You will see more women convinced that they are still coming up short in the pay scale and in equality of pension benefits . . . the gender gap is going to widen. Younger women overwhelmingly feel that they're treated inequitably. Corporate wives are becoming more militant. As long as Ronald Reagan is around, the problem will only be exacerbated. Women feel that he is just not with it. The battle is joined and though it's not quite the point reached in "Lysistrata," a whole new generation of women feels keenly about these issues.

Nevertheless, in March, while Gary Hart and Jesse Jackson were making life uncomfortable for Walter Mondale in the Democratic primaries, almost half of American voters had already decided to vote for Reagan, and as the months passed, the number increased. To political professionals, his reelection was certain. In June the Gallup poll showed him beating Mondale, who had finally wrapped up the Democratic nomination earlier that month, by 19 percentage points. The question became not who would win, but how big would be Reagan's victory. Nixon's 1972 campaign became the model for the Reagan strategists, and as in 1972, they devised a way to attract women's attention. Maureen Reagan's work and Heitman's coalition were the most visible of these efforts, but there were others as well.

The campaign notified state Republican parties that the White House wanted women delegates sent to the national convention to guarantee that the television images coming from the convention floor would be filled with women's faces. Party officials were told to tell prominent Republican men officeholders to let their wives, mothers, sisters, and daughters be delegates in their stead. This was affirmative action the Republican way, not by quotas or rules mandates but by old-fashioned patriarchy. It was the party's answer to the Democrats' fifty-fifty delegate-selection rule. The campaign also encouraged Republican women officeholders to become delegates, but in many states the party leadership preferred to send female relatives of the more important party members rather than Republican women who had gained prominence in their own right. There were exceptions in states where women had broken into the party leadership on their own, but many of the women delegates at the 1984 GOP convention were there because of blood ties. Except tangentially, merit and party loyalty were not the main criteria for the Republican party's affirmative action in Dallas.

This patriarchy may have had traditional roots in the party, but it was also necessary. Nineteen eighty-four wasn't 1972. A well-organized elite out to systematically destroy the women's movement now held veto power in the party. Even if Reagan's team had wished to implement a rule to balance the delegations more equitably, it could not have succeeded. Reagan may have been more popular than Nixon, but he owed his nomination to people who opposed women's rights. The Religious Right and the New Right were too powerful to challenge in Dallas without incurring a nasty fight. So Reagan's inner circle faced women's issues, not as in 1972, when there'd been sincere support for women, but like 1980, when illusion and deception governed. Their plans were upset, however, by a development that stunningly transformed American politics.

For us, she was hope. She affirmed—just by being there on that podium before all those cheering women with their flowers and flags and joyousness—what we had wanted to believe since we were little girls: that America's blessings could be ours if we worked hard and played by the rules. It wasn't only men but women too who'd have a chance to follow their dreams.

That night of July 19 in San Francisco, when she accepted the Democratic party's nomination for Vice President of the United States, Geraldine Ferraro gave us back those dreams that had been so brutally assaulted by the Reagan years. "Occasionally in life there are moments which cannot be completely explained by words. Their meaning can only be articulated by the inaudible language of the heart," she said, quoting Martin Luther King, Jr. And as she stood there before her party and the world's television audience, a new resolve swept through many of us who'd been depressed, frustrated, and beaten down by a political movement that saw women as tools, objects, and second-class human beings.

Ferraro won our hearts that night, and none of the ugly campaign that followed ever took us far from her. Not even in November, when the majority of American women joined American men in deciding that Reagan deserved a second term, did the optimism and promise that her candidacy gave us dim. A respectable part of America's male-dominated establishment now believed a woman could be president. The taboo had been broken, and although it was the Democrats who had taken this bold step, they had cleared the way for all women. As one woman wrote Ferraro, "I'm thirty-six years old. I'm a Republican. For years something's burned inside me. Resentment about the way women are perceived in the world. Shame in halfway believing it. And now you've come along to say—never again do I have to feel this way. I am free. Thank you for my liberation. You have changed my life."

For feminists, Ferraro's candidacy was proof that our work was producing results. The pace was still too slow, the triumphs still few. Yet the overall direction *was* forward. We were on the right track. Ferraro would never have been nominated without the women's movement. Its thirteen years of organizing for the ERA, choice, economic equity, child care, and the other women's issues had raised the consciousness of all American women regardless of their race, religion, or where they came from. The movement's political groups, which had taken that consciousness and translated it into an effective political infrastructure, were finally bringing political power to women.

What was remarkable was that a movement still so young should substantially influence the nation's politics so soon. Ferraro was nominated because women voters had demonstrated that they would support candidates, in particular women, who were sensitive to their needs. There was a tactical political reason now to give a woman an opportunity to be president. Women were more forcefully displaying that long-hoped-for public consciousness that was separate from male voters—an "issue sensibility different from men," as gender gap authority Ethel

Klein called it in her book *Gender Politics*. Publicly, feminists said women voters would vote for Ferraro and thus for Mondale, but they also knew that study after study showed that vice-presidential candidates have little effect on voters' presidential decisions. Even so, they hoped 1984 would be different. They dreamed.

Ferraro's nomination was a far-out gamble for Mondale, who knew that the polls consistently showed him losing to Reagan. If he were to have a chance, his campaign had to bring back the Reagan Democrats, and Ferraro seemed to epitomize where they had come from, except that she was a success story, and for many Reagan Democrats times had become hard. Born of poor Italian-immigrant parents, she had put herself through college and law school and become a crime-fighting prosecutor, then a member of Congress. Her district, which she described as "Archie Bunker territory," was full of Reagan Democrats who in 1980 had given Reagan a 13 percent victory margin while reelecting her by 17 percent. In a time when the Reaganites constantly trumpeted the need for "family values," Ferraro was dedicated to her husband of many years, her three children, and her Catholic faith. As Mondale said, "She was tough . . . she stood for a compassionate approach by government. It was a sign of respect for ethnic America."

Mondale and his campaign were fully aware that if enough Americans were still too frightened by the prospect of a woman president, Ferraro might make his margins worse. Yet he took the chance, and in doing so, he confirmed the remarkable qualities of the American political system: its flexibility, its openness, its capacity to adjust to the ever-changing demands of its citizens—qualities that have made America the world's longest-running democracy.

Democrats who wanted Mondale to pick Gary Hart or Lloyd Bentsen thought Ferraro's selection was misguided. For Republican feminists, her nomination was a fortunate choice, not only on its merits but for the tactical advantage it gave us. In early 1984, after the White House had unceremoniously dumped Mary Louise Smith from the U.S. Civil Rights Commission, we had determined that no feminist, not even one as honorable and loyal to the party as Smith, could survive the administration's harassment of women. The New Right and the Religious Right controlled the party's social agenda. We could have little influence over Reagan's campaign. We wouldn't be able to change the platform. Bush wouldn't lift a finger to help us. The few delegates we could elect wouldn't be able to alter the convention script.

But we no longer embraced a kamikaze mentality. Until Ferraro's nomination, we'd decided to organize locally and bide our time nationally. After it, we used her nomination as a wedge to get attention and resources from Republican leaders for our women candidates. Some Republican women activists even threatened to back Ferraro, although few actually did: The exceptions were Mary Crisp, Kathy Wilson, Californian Mary Stanley, who'd been a Reagan supporter until 1980, and Betsy Griffith, who had written a *Newsweek* op-ed column, which appeared early in the week of the Republican convention, in which she said the national party had given Republican feminists a choice either to "keep quiet or to keep out." Griffith switched. Along with the rest, I didn't go to Dallas but I didn't switch. I thought I could do more for my beliefs by working within the party.

Ferraro's candidacy galvanized the opponents of the women's movement within the New Majoritarian coalition. Much of the ferocity of the fall campaign against her can be traced to the inner circle's willingness to turn over the party's positions on social issues to the Religious and New Right. The Republican National Convention came a month after Ferraro's nomination, giving the misogynists enough time to hone and polish their attack on her and the women's movement alike. The Reagan team wanted nothing to spoil the grand Texas nominating party for Reagan. It canceled the traditional regional platform hearings, instead holding hearings only during platform week, and it turned the Platform Committee over to the women's backlash advocates. A few Don Quixotes, like Congressmember Jim Leach, Senator Lowell Weicker, and Mary Louise Smith tilted at windmills that week, arguing they wanted to lay the groundwork for a return of moderates' influence at the 1988 convention. But there would be no minority reports, lacking twenty-seven people on the Platform Committee who would publicly challenge the right-wing line. And even if there had been, a *Los Angeles Times* survey of the delegates showed that three-quarters considered themselves "fairly or very conservative." There'd be no floor action. The convention belonged to the Religious Right and the New Right. As Pamela Curtis told the press, "I don't have a place there. . . . This is going to be very much Ronald Reagan's convention." Republican feminists stayed home. Our money and time could be more profitably spent electing Republican women.

In Dallas the Reagan campaign set out to show that women supported the party. The bulls "graciously" stepped aside so Americans would know that Republicans were as fair-minded as Democrats. The convention program was liberally sprinkled with women in prime-time speaking slots. In other, less enlightened years, the ambitious males wouldn't have allowed themselves to be pushed aside for such image-making; tokenism would have prevailed. But Ferraro's nomination had given the Mondale campaign real zip and excitement. A party usually gets a boost in the polls from its convention but this time was exceptional. The Democrats had gotten extensive press coverage, and one "special Gallup poll done for *Newsweek* immediately after" had actually shown Mondale catching up with Reagan.

Some public relations genius on the convention organizing team had labeled the first evening's proceedings Ladies Night. The most coveted slot of that night, the keynote speech, went to Katherine Ortega, the thirty-six-year-old U.S. treasurer who had replaced Bay Buchanan. Ortega dutifully told the delegates that she believed in Reagan not because she was a woman or a Hispanic but because she was an American. It was a worthy try, but the evening's emotional highlight came from Jeane Kirkpatrick, who brought the convention to its feet with her indictment of the foreign policies of what she called "the San Francisco Democrats." (She was referring to the site of that party's recent convention, but the subtle message was that something was not quite right with people from San Francisco.)

Kirkpatrick should in fact have been the keynoter, but she had had too many conflicts with the Reagan State Department and White House insiders. From the beginning of Reagan's first administration, there had been a split in the White House between the pragmatists and the hardliners. Along with Bill Casey, William Clark, and Caspar Weinberger, Kirkpatrick was a cold-war ideologue, and she found herself in constant conflict with pragmatists Secretary of State Al Haig and his successor, George Shultz. The Baker-led team's refusal to give Kirkpatrick the keynote slot was strictly tied to campaign strategy. It was not that Reagan didn't agree with Kirkpatrick's ideology—he did. But Wirthlin's polls showed that hard-line rhetoric might frighten women into thinking Reagan would get America into a war with the Soviets. Kirkpatrick's politics had better be downplayed.

The organizers' most cynical choice of speakers was Nancy Hogshead, a three-time gold-medal winner in the recent 1984 Olympic Games in Los Angeles. It was not lost on the feminists watching this first-night extravaganza that Hogshead had been the beneficiary of a women's sports program of the sort that the Reagan administration hoped to overturn as a result of the *Grove City* decision.

Maureen Reagan did not address the convention. The organizers were afraid of what she might say and how she might say it. Yes, she had been campaigning hard to get her father elected, but in her own way she had also been preaching a message of feminism. She could be a dynamic speaker, and her words to the convention about women's equality would surely have upset the preachers of the Religious Right. And even if she had accepted careful scripting, the organizers were concerned her appearance at the podium might be interpreted as a subtle acceptance of her brand of Republicanism.

Perhaps the most interesting indicator that times were changing even inside the Reagan circle was the reintroduction of the first lady's speech, a "women's" pitch approach used at the 1976 convention by Betty Ford. Nancy Reagan hadn't addressed the convention in 1980, but this year, while she made no pitch for women as Ford had done, she showed she was aware that she had to be more than a behind-the-scenes backup for her husband. By standing before the convention and thanking the delegates and the American people, she took on a public surrogate's role that had been privately hers from the beginning of Reagan's political career. It was intriguing to watch her unfold her public political wings.

As the Reagan team pragmatists choreographed an illusion of GOP concern for women, they did not forget the New Right, the Religious Right, or their friends in the National Conference of Catholic Bishops. Former Democrat, now newly minted New Right Republican Phil Gramm spoke just before Kirkpatrick, guaranteeing him a sizable audience, since hers was the most awaited speech that first night. Moral Majority founder James Robison gave the convention's opening prayer, and his colleague Jerry Falwell also got prime-time placement, giving the formal blessing after the roll call nominating Reagan and Bush. The belligerent anti-choice Reverend Rene Gracida of Corpus Christi, Texas, who would later become a fixture in denying women family-planning information, also got a chance to lead the delegates in prayer.

During platform week, the misogynists had written a mean-spirited platform limiting women's opportunities. Mississippi congressmember Trent Lott was the Platform Committee chairman. His committee included his New Right co-revolutionaries: Newt Gingrich, Henry Hyde, Phyllis Schlafly, Roger Jepsen, Vin Weber, Jack Kemp, Jim Courter, Bill McCollum, Marilyn Thayer, Holly Coors, and Robert Kasten. There was no real contest during the committee sessions. On women's issues, the platform was revisionist. It offered the same old saws about Sandra Day O'Connor and Reagan's appointments of women as proof of a commitment to equal rights, and it again reminded Americans of the party's illustrious past, "the first major party to advocate equal pay for equal work, regardless of sex." And again its plans for the future were not so illustrious. The party still supported "equal pay for equal work" but said Reagan's economic policies had "produced a record number of jobs so that women who want to work have an unmatched opportunity." And as in 1980, it promised to "further reduce the 'marriage penalty,' " which had been reduced but not eliminated.

Gone were the other 1980 pledges to help women. The party took credit for winning enactment of the Retirement Equity Act, which reformed private pension plans to help women. This legislation had passed because moderate Republicans and Democrats had joined together and the White House had gone along.

A special section on women's rights had been replaced by a special section on "family protection." As expected, it was the Moral Majority's agenda. The platform commended Reagan for appointing federal judges committed to "traditional family values," and just in case someone might not get the point, it added: "We reaffirm our support for the appointment of judges at all levels of the judiciary who respect traditional family values and the sanctity of innocent human life."

Words respecting the views of pro-choice Republicans, so hard fought in 1976 and watered down in 1980, were now gone. The new language was uncompromisingly anti-choice and included a new sentence: "The unborn child has a fundamental individual right to life which cannot be infringed." It reaffirmed support for a Human Life Amendment and, hearkening to the Hyde–Helms effort in 1981, added backing for legislation that would say the "Fourteenth Amendment's protections apply to unborn children." To its continued opposition to public funding of abortions, the platform added eliminating funds for organizations that advocated or supported abortion. (This was the administration's infamous 1984 Mexico City policy, which aimed to stop the American government from backing international family-planning organizations that didn't perform abortions themselves but aided organizations and governments which did. The policy would become a major battleground in the abortion fight over the next eight years.)

As usual, the platform's preamble lauded freedom:

> From freedom comes opportunity; from opportunity comes growth; from growth comes progress. . . . No matter how complex our problems, no matter how difficult our tasks, it is freedom that inspires and guides the American Dream. If everything depends on freedom—and it does—then securing freedom, at home and around the world, is one of the most important endeavors a free people can undertake.

And then, with only a few noes scattered among the tumult of yeses, the Republicans of 1984 adopted a platform that sanctioned the Religious Right and the New Right to go forth and slay the women warriors of the women's movement and all those others who stood in the way of their freedom to impose their will on others.

There was no backing down for unity's sake, as at the 1980 convention. Reagan made no pledges to appoint women to high positions. His fifty-five-minute acceptance speech mentioned not a single specific women's issue, but he did let the nation know that Republicans "believe in the sacredness of human life."

Ferraro's nomination unnerved some in the Reagan campaign. His team would take "all necessary steps" to see that the shifts in women's vote didn't undercut the president's victory margin. They would take no chances. But more than political caution was involved in the attack of bigotry to which they subjected Ferraro, of a kind never before experienced by a vice-presidential candidate. In our politics this kind of treatment is usually visited on the candidate for president.

The campaign's attack against Ferraro was full scale, complete with an exhaustive investigation of every facet of her personal life. It was as though Reagan's victory depended on destroying her. It didn't seem to matter that two weeks after her nomination, various polls showed that nearly 55 percent of those likely to vote were for Reagan, or that throughout the fall he remained comfortably ahead. Their assault on Ferraro was gratuitous as well as cruel. They didn't need it to beat Mondale.

A team had been dispatched to New York to track down dirt on Ferraro and to leak it to the press. The charges came quickly thereafter. Within a week of the San Francisco convention, Ferraro found herself immersed in questions about her husband's finances and her financial-disclosure filings to the Federal Elections Commission from previous campaigns. True, she brought some of this intense scrutiny upon herself by making a flip remark about her husband's reluctance to release their tax returns to the public. Eventually, the returns were released. Then for ninety minutes she explained to the press about the couple's finances and everything the reporters could think to ask her. Thereafter, Ferraro wrote, the national press "stopped harassing me and started taking my candidacy more seriously." The suspicions about her husband continued, but most of the public seemed satisfied that Ferraro was honest and deserved to hold America's second-highest office.

Nevertheless, the harassment did not stop. Allies of the Reagan team went after Ferraro with the same ferocity exhibited three hundred years ago by the "good Puritans" of Salem. From the very first day of her campaign, she was dogged by pickets whose shouting often drowned out her speeches. They pushed and shoved and yelled anti-abortion and ethnic epithets. They waved signs similar to the kind all pro-choice candidates had gotten used to encountering, but these were consistently a little crueler—pictures of tombstones labeled "For Gerry's Kids: Rest in Peace," "Ferraro: Vice-President for Death," "Ferraro, A Disgrace to Motherhood."

Initially the Reagan–Bush campaign denied having any connection to the attacks, but they were lying. The press found them out. The National Right to Life Committee admitted it "was in constant contact with the Reagan–Bush people." An audiotape from a New Right leadership institute training session for picketers told them: "When the press starts asking around who's holding up the signs, about what group you are with, just say, 'I'm a concerned citizen.' Don't say, 'I'm with Students for Reagan.' " An NBC News report conclusively tied the trouble-makers to the Reagan–Bush campaign.

None of this was surprising. Since the days of CREEP and NCPAC and the rise of other New Right groups in the seventies, Republican presidential campaigns had always had a guerrilla unit assigned to damage the opposition. The dirty-tricks brigades hadn't shut down just because the Watergate Committee uncovered them. Young Republican men who had performed many of the Watergate era dirty tricks became the leaders of NCPAC and the operatives of Reagan's campaigns—men like Roger Stone, who was the campaign's northeast and mid-Atlantic coordinator in 1984.

The cruelest attacks came, though, from another part of the New Majoritarian coalition: the leaders of Ferraro's own church. Archbishop John O'Connor, who had been a Republican before he changed his registration to independent when he moved from Pennsylvania to New York that fall, led the Catholic Church's charge. On September 8 O'Connor criticized Ferraro publicly for signing a 1982 letter, together with two other Catholic members of Congress, that invited Catholic legislators to attend a meeting where abortion and the Church's position would be discussed. O'Connor denounced her because the letter also noted that not all Catholics agreed with the Church's position on abortion. "I can only say that Geraldine Ferraro has said some things about abortion relevant to Catholic teachings which are not true," he said. "What has been said is wrong—it's wrong."

After O'Connor's denunciation, the number of anti-abortion harassers at Ferraro's campaign rallies swelled. The ugliness reached its climax in Scranton, Pennsylvania, four days later. Facing an estimated crowd of 25,000 noisy pro-choice and right-to-life demonstrators, Ferraro laid out her position on how candidates should deal with their religious beliefs relative to the general public.

> Religious leaders and other citizens should speak out forcefully on matters that they feel are important. I respect their point of view. I encourage open debate and I question no person's sincerity.
>
> But I also have my duty as a public official. When I take my oath of office, I accept the charge of serving all the people

of every faith. I also swear to uphold the Constitution of the United States, which guarantees freedom of religion. These are my public duties, and in carrying them out, I cannot, and I will not, seek to impose my own religious views on others. If ever my conscience or my religious views prevented me from carrying out those duties to the best of my ability, then I would resign my office before I'd betray the public trust.

Scranton's Catholic bishop attacked her, charging her views were "absurd" and "dangerous," and said that for Ferraro to be acceptable to the Catholic Church, she would have to do all she "could within the law 'to stop the slaughter of innocent human beings.'" She was being asked, not very subtly, to leave her church if she continued to respect the nation's tradition of separating church doctrine from state law. To her church, she was an apostate.

Religious controversy isn't new to American politics, but for most of their history, Americans have risen above it. The new influence of the women's backlash strategy brought religion into American politics in an unwelcome and distasteful way. Religious doctrine was being exploited to limit all women's opportunities, not simply those who believed in that doctrine. The 1984 presidential campaign brimmed with a religious bigotry not seen since 1928, when Protestants had pilloried Catholic New Yorker Al Smith in his race for president. But the bigotry of 1984 was of a different kind—its basis was misogyny. Ferraro was hated because she symbolized all the things the Religious Right detested. She was attacked not only by the Moral Majority and other right-wing Protestant groups but by her own kind—both her church and her ethnic family.

Ferraro canceled marching in Philadelphia's Columbus Day parade because the city's Catholic leader, John Cardinal Krol, who had been given the honor of presenting an invocation at a high-viewing television time at the Republican National Convention, threatened "to pull all the Catholic kids from the parade" because she was a disgrace who didn't represent the Catholic or Italian community. The New York Republican Italian community, led by Senator D'Amato, refused to let her march at the front of her hometown's Columbus Day parade. The *New York Post,* a newpaper known to be sympathetic to D'Amato, linked her by innuendo to the Mafia. Unlike previous instances when Italian-American men had been unfairly linked to organized crime, no Italian-American organization came to her defense, although an ad hoc group of Italian Women for Democrats protested.

Throughout all this brutality, the Reagan camp kept quiet. Not a word came from the men who knew better—Ronald Reagan, George Bush, James Baker, Bill Casey, Mike Deaver, Bob Teeter, and the rest—as if this outpouring of hate were political business as usual: just another campaign. It wasn't. This was a new, malignant corruption of America's political system, willfully accepted by cynical men and their willing female allies.

In the campaign's last weeks, the press woke up at last. Columnist Richard Reeves described what was happening:

> The stoning of Geraldine Ferraro in the public square goes on and on, and no one steps forward to help or protest—not even one of her kind . . . the sons of Italy and fathers of the Roman Catholic Church are silent or are too busy reaching for bigger rocks. Other women seem awed and intimidated by the charges and innuendo: Heresy! Mafia! Men are putting women in their place.

The public hate campaign against Ferraro ended when the campaign ended. But the nation's political landscape was not so easily repaired. The so-called pragmatists of the Reagan team had allowed a cancer to be unleashed in the land by their willingness to make common cause with the misogynists and ethnic and religious zealots. They had let themselves be manipulated by the New Right and the Religious Right's earlier threats to desert Reagan. The inner circle's reaction was cowardly as well as unnecessary, since Reagan hadn't needed the bigots in order to be reelected. Some indication of concern for protecting America's domestic tranquillity would have been more honorable. As Reeves so aptly wrote, "If Geraldine Ferraro is stoned without defenders, she will be only the first to fall. The stones will always be there, piled high, ready for the next Italian, the next Catholic, the next woman."

On Election Day Reagan won 59 percent of the popular vote and a record 525 electoral votes. Only the District of Columbia, and Minnesota by just 3,761 votes, went to Mondale. With almost 55 million votes,

Reagan won "more votes for his Republican candidacy than had ever been cast for a U.S. politician." So what if a little hardball had been played? The nation obviously didn't mind, the winners claimed.

It was another major win for Reagan the man, the morale booster, the anesthetizer of America's fears. It was not a victory for his deficit-producing economic policies, or for the Moral Majority's social agenda, or for Catholic doctrine toward women, or for misogyny and bigotry. On those issues, the polls showed the majority of voters agreed with Mondale and Ferraro.

As for women, they followed the same pattern as in 1980: A majority voted for Reagan, but in smaller numbers than men. The gender gap "ranged from four to nine percentage points depending upon the poll." NBC News found that 64 percent of men had supported Reagan, compared with 55 percent of women; the CBS News/*New York Times* statistics were 61 and 57 percent.

Even in a year when the top of the ticket had been so popular, women proved their vote had to be taken seriously. They provided Democrats with the margin of victory in the Illinois, Michigan, Massachusetts, and Iowa Senate races, and they elected Vermont's first woman governor, Democrat Madeleine Kunin, and the nation's first elected woman state attorney general, ex-nun and Rhode Island Republican Arlene Violet. There was some poetic justice in the defeats of New Right Iowa senator Roger Jepsen and Illinois senator Charles Percy; women's votes had made the difference. One senator had been too extreme, the other too equivocal. Both had felt women's anger. In House races a majority of women supported Democratic candidates, and a majority of men voted for Republicans.

Incumbency and regional bias still helped elect candidates who were opposed to the women's agenda. Incumbent senators Rudy Boschwitz and Jesse Helms retained their seats, and Texans elected New Right Phil Gramm to the Senate.

Several analysts commented on the mystery of sexual politics and their inability to understand why women voted as they did. But the vote was no mystery. A majority of women had believed Reagan was a more effective leader than Mondale would be, and their fears of four years before had been assuaged: Reagan hadn't gotten America into a nuclear war, let alone a nonnuclear war, and Grenada and Lebanon didn't count. They saw no reason not to stay the course. The economy was booming, even if many weren't sharing in its bounty. Those who weren't hoped they soon would. Women were touched by the same encompassing issues as in 1980, peace and the economy; but in the end, as in most presidential races, most had made up their minds based on the candidate's personality.

Ferraro's candidacy was another step forward for the women's political movement. She politicized more women—a coalition of women's groups, the national Women's Vote Project, registered 1.8 million new women voters. The trend begun in 1980 continued. The proportion of women voters exceeded that of men, jumping from a margin of 0.3 percent in 1980 to 1.8 percent in 1984. Democratic pollster Dotty Lynch reported that two million more people voted for Mondale because of Ferraro. As Rosalie Whelan of the National Women's Education Fund added, "You do not make serious social change in one election. . . . We [the women's movement] have been at this for about a decade. The white male establishment has had control for 200 years."

One other wrinkle to Ferraro's candidacy makes it difficult to assess her impact as the first woman vice-presidential nominee. She had handed the Republicans a gift with her offhand remark about her husband not wanting to release his tax returns: "You people who are married to Italian men, you know what it's like." That did it. She had made herself a target. It was a handy way for her opponents to paint her as in some way a Mafia tool. Respectable Ferraro was pictured as perhaps not so respectable, and besides, she was a New York City liberal at a time when ethnic Democrats were being seduced away from the party by antiliberal rhetoric. As Thomas Mann, executive director of the American Political Science Association, said, "I think too much was expected of a Ferraro vice-presidential bid. . . . Her candidacy did nothing to slow down the defection among white Southerners and urban ethnics [from the Democratic party] but there is not much evidence that it accelerated it."

Mann had gotten it only half right. The other half of the story was that Ferraro hastened the slow but perceptible alienation of independent and Republican women from the party of Reagan. Some who finally voted for him did so unenthusiastically. Even the married women who were home full-time with their youngsters weren't necessarily enamored of a party that was telling them how many children they could have. Reagan, yes; the Republican party, no.

In the winter of 1985, at our first meeting of Republican women activists after the election, many wanted to quit. Leave the party to the Falwells, the Reagans, the Helmses, and the Hydes. Others argued about the importance of hanging in, of maintaining a feminist voice in the Republican party. But another factor held great weight in our decision to stay and fight: Bush's old friends—and he had many among Republican feminists—argued that we couldn't desert him. Certainly, he now opposes the ERA and choice and is silent on other women's issues, they said, but that's only because he has to be loyal to Reagan. Once he's president, he'll be with us. We'll get our party back. And so for the second time in five years, Republican feminists sublimated their goals for Bush's political future.

In Reagan's second term we struggled over how much time should be spent fighting the Religious and New Right and how much finding Bush supporters. Was it better to work within the party for our goals or outside? Over the next four years, as the administration's assault on women became worse and the anti-abortion movement moved closer to banning legal abortion, our dilemma worsened. We wandered in a schizophrenic political land—one day hating our party and the administration for their misogyny and the next day believing that with Bush or Howard Baker or one of the "good moderate men" as president, the party would shed its sickness. The harder we tried to hope, the more difficult it became to sustain it.

12

THE COALITION CRACKS

From the day Reagan won his second term, the New Majoritarian coalition began to fall apart. For four years, the different factions in the Republican party had pretended they could get along with one another. For four years, in the name of loyalty to Ronald Reagan, those who wanted to be president put their own ambitions on hold. Yet within a year after the greatest electoral college victory in modern American history, the coalition's key players were all plotting how to outflank one another in their pursuit of the White House in 1988.

Reagan may still have been president, but his ability to unify his party had ended. Just as voters viewed him independently of the party he headed, so the leaders of the coalition's factions—those who had engineered his nomination and worked for his election—saw him as separate from the party's nominating machinery. They expected Reagan to anoint Bush as his successor, so they set out to circumvent his influence and build their own political machines. Each hoped to make his choice the next leader of the New Right revolution.

The coalition disintegrated on three fronts—at the Reagan White House, elsewhere in Washington, and around the country. Several founding pillars of the New Right faced financial and credibility problems. In 1985 Richard Viguerie's business fell apart because his company extended "too much credit to conservative groups" and because of "his expensive, unsuccessful run for the Republican nomination for lieutenant governor of Virginia, competition from direct mailers, and a bad investment." Eventually he became solvent again. NCPAC went into debt. Another NCPAC founder, its executive director, Terry Dolan, died of AIDS. His homosexuality, known to political insiders but never publicly acknowledged until the cause of his illness could no longer be hidden, undercut NCPAC's moral authority with the Religious Right, creating still more tension between two groups that had never been comfortable with each other. The more religious New Right leaders like Paul Weyrich shed few tears when, after Dolan's death, internal dissension in NCPAC ended its political clout.

The Religious Right also faced problems. In 1986 its moral self-righteousness was compromised when Pat Robertson's protégés, television evangelists Jim and Tammy Bakker, were caught up in financial scandals regarding their PTL religious empire and Jim Bakker was found to be involved in an extramarital affair with the church secretary, Jessica Hahn. With the PTL's riches up for grabs, two of Reagan's strongest Religious Right backers, Jerry Falwell and Jimmy Swaggart, fought publicly over who would control the PTL. As each day's headlines and television screens made obvious, the leaders of the Moral Majority were far from the paragons of virtue they had claimed to be. Two years later, during the heat of the 1988 primary season, Swaggart would again demonstrate the quality of his morality when he was caught with a prostitute.

At the White House, the pragmatists who had kept the disparate Republicans marching together behind Reagan were gone, and with them the influential centrist view that had kept them functioning together on an even keel. James Baker had become secretary of the treasury, and Michael Deaver started his own public relations firm. The new chief of staff, Donald Regan, a Wall Street executive who didn't understand the collegial nature of politics, exacerbated tensions. Other than Nancy Reagan, there was no one in the inner circle to keep the rightist ideologues from taking over. Bush might have exerted a moderating influence, but he had 1988 on his mind and was busy forging a partnership with those very ideologues.

A major accomplishment of the pragmatists in the first term had been to keep Reagan and his administration from appearing extreme. That veneer was disappearing now. Reagan appointed Pat Buchanan to be White House communications director, overseeing the preparation of the president's speeches. Buchanan was not only one of the most vocal, articulate, and extreme of the New Right warriors, he was also the most antifeminist. He was soon working his various hostilities into White House statements and Reagan's speeches with the same skill and acerbity he had demonstrated as Spiro Agnew's wordsmith during the Nixon years.

Buchanan's presence was a cause for alarm. As Deaver said of his arrival, "Reagan does not need anyone to the right of him." Much of the president's hold on the American people rested on his remarkable ability to connect with them personally through his speeches. Buchanan was now shaping the substance of those speeches. It was a significant boost for the New Right cause.

The antifeminist team was scattered throughout the government. Gary Bauer, who would become the architect of some of the administration's cruelest policies against women, moved from his post as chief deputy to Secretary of Education William Bennett to director of the White House's Office of Policy Development. There he implemented the New Right's agenda on abortion, child care, AIDS, and welfare issues.

Ed Meese, who left the White House to become attorney general, continued the Justice Department's policies of narrowing civil rights law and ending abortion rights. Indicating that the administration meant to step up its attacks on women's rights, Solicitor General Charles Fried filed a brief asking the Supreme Court to overturn *Roe v. Wade*. It was the first time the U.S. government had fully thrown itself against *Roe*. Some observers of the solicitor's office found the brief the most strident that that office had ever filed.

It was the opening salvo in a sustained effort to erode reproductive rights. During Reagan's first term, the anti-choice forces had repeatedly complained that the administration wasn't doing enough for their cause. While he faithfully delivered a message to the annual Right-to-Life March on Washington on each anniversary of *Roe v. Wade,* they claimed he had not put the full weight of the presidency behind eliminating abortion and cutting family-planning programs. In the Bush era in the late eighties, when the assault on choice became still worse, the myth arose that Reagan hadn't been so bad on choice after all. But he had. The actions of the Reagan administration and its anti-choice allies on the Hill dealt a serious blow to women's freedom, especially during his second term.

During his first four years, the political infrastructure of the anti-choice movement was strengthened within the executive branch. Movement leaders administered the programs touching on women's health, including family planning and contraceptive education. The pro-choice Republicans in the administration were unable to counteract these actions without losing their jobs. Ever since *Roe,* the abortion issue had been so touchy that the majority of the old guard and some moderate Republican leaders had tried to ignore it; silence was their way of coping. The White House pragmatists during Reagan's first term had adopted the same approach. The president and the national party were acknowledgedly anti-choice, but it was better to follow the line aptly described by Bob Teeter at a June 1984 campaign strategy session: "It's one issue we ought not to talk about. . . . They [anti-abortion groups] know where we stand, and we've got a lot of people on the other side."

But in Reagan's second term, the silence ended. The rallying cry of the Religious Right openly became the administration's: Abortion should be illegal. Government must impose whatever laws and regulations were necessary to protect motherhood. It was the "new morality."

This assault touched everyone in the field of women's health. The First Amendment rights of doctors and nurses were to be encumbered with gag rules that required them to tell their patients what right-wing ideology determined was moral, not what was correct medical practice. The government would require family-planning clinics to notify parents of teenagers when their daughters received contraceptives, reversing the long-held principle of confidential access for all women of childbearing age. Years of research had shown that parental notification on sexual matters has no effect on curtailing teenage pregnancy; girls who are unable to talk to their parents usually have good reason for their reluctance. This research was ignored.

Neither intellectual inquiry nor foreign policy was immune to the "new morality" strictures. The administration ended research on the comparative health risks of childbirth and abortion, on the efficacy of family planning programs, and on contraceptives. It sanctioned the unreliable and discredited rhythm method of birth control, which the Catholic Church endorsed. It applied the Mexico City policy to U.S. foreign policy, cutting family-planning funding to countries that gave financial support to women who sought abortions.

As the right-to-life movement grew stronger in the middle of Reagan's first term, pro-choice Republicans sought to counter its influence, and those who were active in the national Planned Parenthood Federation of America formed Republicans for Choice (RFC), a 501(c)(4) tax-exempt organization. This national grassroots Republican network set out to lobby legislators against the Reagan anti-choice agenda.

The RFC worked through Planned Parenthood's offices, its members drawn principally from the organization's state and local boards and from the Republican Women's Task Force. However, some women felt that a group attached to Planned Parenthood could not adequately represent the views of all pro-choice Republicans because out of necessity, it would have to put Planned Parenthood policy first. They also felt that direct political action was needed, but as an educational and lobbying organization, RFC was prohibited by law from actively participating in political campaigns.

It was because of these constraints that Republicans organized outside Planned Parenthood in California and New York. In early 1984 I joined with Barbara Mosbacher, Pauline Harrison, Barbara Gimbel, Frances Reese, and Mary Curley to form the New York State Republican Family Committee. We would lobby and speak out against the anti-choice agenda and build a cadre of pro-choice Republicans. We would build a third force. We chose the name Family Committee because we believed that the key to strong families rested on individuals having the right to choose. We also believed that our tolerant view of the world more accurately reflected the family values of the majority of Americans.

The committee grew quickly to several hundred members. Mosbacher and Curley were New York delegates at the 1984 convention and took conventioners aback with their vigorous criticisms of the Reagan anti-choice record. Even their pro-choice buttons made the Reaganites uncomfortable. Several Religious Right advocates questioned their right even to call themselves Republicans. The experience whetted their appetite for more open combat, and they came back fired up to take on New York's anti-choice Republican establishment.

The committee joined the state's pro-choice coalition, Family Planning Advocates (FPA). It was the first Republican organization to join this coalition, and FPA welcomed an active pro-choice presence in both parties. The issue transcended party politics. For the New York State Republican party, the committee filled a void that had existed since the end of Nelson Rockefeller's governorship in 1974.

Under the guidance of Harriett Stinson, California Republicans for Choice was organized, also filling a Republican gap within that state's pro-choice coalition. Like the New Yorkers, the Californians lobbied for pro-choice legislation and looked for ways to counteract the influence of the anti-choice right within the party. Although no other formal groups of Republicans were formed at that time, individual pro-choice Republicans across the country increased their backing for pro-choice candidates, and in Reagan's second term, when administration pressure to destroy *Roe* increased, legislators like Weicker, Packwood, and Green received welcome political help from the grassroots.

There was, of course, no dissension about choice within the Religious Right, but by 1986, outside Washington the Religious Right was severely factionalized. Pat Robertson had left the Reagan–Bush fold to organize a run for the presidency. (His soul mate Jerry Falwell, less adventurous, endorsed Bush.) Robertson was convinced he had the troops and money to challenge the Reagan establishment. His electronic church broadcasts drew sixteen million television viewers every month, more than any of the other evangelical preachers, and he had a strong infrastructure of churches and schools to support him. In spite of the scandals that were embarrassing the Religious Right, Robertson believed he was powerful enough to win the Republican nomination.

In September, carefully timed for the beginning of the fall midterm election campaign, Robertson announced that if within a year three million people signed a petition supporting his run for the presidency, he would be a candidate. This ploy allowed him to activate his followers in a political cause that would "test their devotion to Christian principles." Once they had sworn their allegiance by signing, they would be ready to storm the local citadels of the GOP—the county committees, the precinct organizations, the state committees.

The three million signatures came in quickly, and Robertson was off. His supporters openly moved in on the Republican party, financed by Robertson's own religious empire and by the activists who had joined his crusade. Nearly half of the contributors were women, many of them veterans of Schlafly's battles. The Robertson army joined the party's county, city, and state committees that had traditionally been the sole province of the old guard and moderates, and more recently—in some places—the New Right. Before his campaign, Robertson's Religious Right cadres had simply voted Republican. Now they became officers in the party itself.

When Robertson's people took over their territory, the old-timers were furious. It was one thing to have the electoral support of the Religious Right. It was a very different matter to have them trying to run the party. The prospect of a religious zealot like Robertson as the GOP's presidential nominee was deeply disturbing.

Robertson's aggressiveness, plus the stepped-up activity of the anti-choice movement, convinced Republican feminists that we had to take action beyond the pro-choice GOP groups we'd formed. But we had a serious strategic problem. Many of our supporters, including governors like Tom Kean of New Jersey and John McKernan of Maine, were Bush people. However much they abhorred Robertson and the prospect of his candidacy, the Bush political command was determined to keep the New Majoritarian coalition together. That included all factions of the Religious Right. Bush valued his endorsement from Falwell and was not about to alienate the element of the Religious Right that wasn't helping Robertson. Our insistence that women would be a potent factor in the forthcoming election because issues that most intimately concerned them were under attack did not sway the Bush insiders.

Many Republican operatives saw Ferraro's failure to attract enough women to elect herself and Mondale as proof that women were not politically conscious enough to prefer candidates who championed women's issues. In spite of evidence from the gender gap, they kept repeating that broadly defined economic issues could almost always convince women to vote Republican. Reagan's victories and popularity among both sexes were a case in point. What these operatives failed to understand was that the misogynist message of the New Right and Religious Right was scaring women away from the Republican party. The Great Communicator was on his way out. After 1988 he would no longer be around to calm the country into thinking he was keeping the "crazies" in his party in line. Just as women had been frightened by Reagan's cold-war rhetoric during the 1980 election, they now feared that the Republican party was not only uncaring but turning extreme.

The 1986 elections gave feminists their opportunity. Long gone was the misguided notion that women vote for women candidates on the basis of gender; rather, they make their choices—sometimes regardless of party—for those candidates who best represent their special concerns. More and more women were making the link between women's professional success and the power of women's issue politics. The bipartisan Women's Campaign Fund raised half a million dollars for feminist candidates. Democratic women funneled money into their EMILY'S List PAC. (EMILY's List had been organized by Ellen Malcolm in 1985. EMILY was an acronym for Early Money Is Like Yeast, and it was to stimulate the formation in 1992 of a similar national effort, WISH List, by Republican women. Until then, they formed local and state PACs.) Republican feminists gave directly to candidates through an informal network of old task force members and the newly organized local pro-choice PACs.

The 1986 election results documented our belief that women were beginning to use the candidates' positions on feminist issues as a guide on how to vote. Republican feminists Connie Morella of Maryland and Pat Saiki of Hawaii were elected because Democratic women voted for them. Democrat Barbara Mikulski won reelection to the Senate with a huge 61 percent victory over Linda Chavez, who had presided over the dismantling of the civil rights policies of the U.S. Civil Rights Commission. Chavez's New Right tactics and policies had unsettled Republican and independent women voters. Paula Hawkins also went down to defeat in Florida; women voted for her male Democratic opponent because she represented the anti-women policies of the GOP.

But feminists certainly did not win them all. The avenging Religious Right caused the defeat of two pro-choice moderate Republican gubernatorial candidates: Norma Paulus in Oregon and Arliss Sturgulewski in Alaska, using tactics like those that had defeated Mary Estill Buchanan in 1980. Fired up by Robertson's candidacy, the Religious Right saw the defeat of these two women as a calling from God. Turned off by this extremism, Democratic women stayed with the Democratic male candidate. The defeat of Paulus and Sturgulewski was ominous because it opened up the Republican party machinery in both states to the Religious Right just in time for 1988.

Overall, the midterm elections turned out to be a fiasco for a Republican party, which had too long depended upon the image of Ronald Reagan for voter appeal. Reagan's popularity hovered around 67 percent in the polls during the fall campaign, but it didn't carry over to the elections. At the insistence of his wife and staff, he'd campaigned extensively for Republican candidates, making fifty-four appearances in twenty-two states. Yet although he campaigned for thirteen Republican senatorial candidates, nine were defeated. Even allowing for the idiosyncratic nature of state elections, where presidential power is often not transferable, the Reagan effort was a failure. The November elections proved that the Reagan political era had come to an end.

The Democrats won a fifty-five-member majority in the Senate and increased their margins in the House directly because of the women's vote. For the past six years, an informal collaboration in Congress between Reagan Republicans and conservative Democrats had allowed the passage of Reagan's economic policies. The collaboration was now over.

As John Dillin of *The Christian Science Monitor* reported, "Without the women's vote, Republicans would have probably hung on to Senate seats in Georgia, North Carolina, and North Dakota, and the GOP would have probably picked up seats in Colorado, Louisiana, and possibly California. In other words, the Senate would still be Republican by a comfortable margin."

In her book *Abortion Politics*, an analyst of the right and the abortion issue, Michele McKeegan, notes that "of the twenty-three Christian Right candidates for the House, none of the seventeen challengers won, four incumbents were re-elected, and two were replaced. Only four of the fourteen Senate candidates who had scored 90–100 percent on the Christian Voice's biblical scorecard won, while a half dozen right-wing senators . . . were turned out of office." Paul Weyrich bluntly called the elections "a disaster for our side." No pro-choice incumbents in the Senate or House were defeated. The women's mainstream political movement, in particular the pro-choice coalitions, were proving they had political power. Anti-abortion initiatives were defeated in Massachusetts, Rhode Island, Oregon, and Arkansas. Viguerie's monthly New Right propaganda magazine, *Conservative Digest,* still operating despite his financial problems, admitted that the elections "suggested for the first time that the infusion of voter support to the GOP from the white Christian community carries with it some major liabilities."

The 1986 election proved that the women's political movement was slowly gathering strength on the state level as well. The number of women state legislators increased from 13.4 to 14.8 percent. Twenty-five women won statewide office, compared with seven in 1984. Madeleine Kunin was reelected governor of Vermont with the women's vote. In

Nebraska, for the first time in U.S. history, two women from the major parties competed for the governorship. Republican Kay Orr beat Democrat Helen Boosalis with a campaign that principally focused on taxes. While Boosalis won the majority of the women's votes, reflecting the alienation of even centrist women from the Republican agenda in this conservative state, Orr won with the votes of crossover Democratic men. Her victory reflected a trend that was to show up more frequently in the years to come.

Most of the time, foreign policy had little influence on the New Majoritarian coalition. It did make a difference, though, in the case of the Iran–Contra scandal. One day before the 1986 election, the news broke that the Reagan administration had secretly sold weapons and spare parts to Iran in violation of the law that prohibited the sale of arms to nations that sponsored terrorism. As the months passed there were further revelations: This operation, run principally by Oliver North, had gone on for more than a year, from late summer of 1985 until mid-October 1986, and some of the proceeds of these sales had been diverted to fund the Nicaraguan Contras.

It was a major scandal, and two days before Thanksgiving, Attorney General Meese went before the nation and tried to explain what happened. The revelations had an immediate effect on Reagan's popularity, which dropped from 67 percent in November to 46 percent in December. Under pressure from Reagan's inner circle, Don Regan was forced to resign and the president brought in Howard Baker to be chief of staff to deal with the uproar.

In February 1987 the Tower commission issued a report that found Reagan "confused and uninformed" on Iran–Contra activities and that charged other administration officials with responsibility for them. Congressional hearings on Iran–Contra played on national television throughout the spring and summer before a riveted nation, its cast of characters led by a skillful Oliver North, while the president denied he had known of the diversion of money to the Contras.

At the White House's domestic policy development office, Gary Bauer revved up the attack on abortion, teen pregnancy, and welfare women, as if the best defense for Reagan's Iran–Contra troubles were a strong offense on social issues. Reversing the traditional argument that federal assistance to the poor is of help to them, he issued a report blaming welfare for the disintegration of the family. Poor women shouldn't receive government aid, he said, but should be set free from welfare dependency to find their own way. What struck many of us at the time was that Bauer had singled out women and children as his linchpin to welfare reform.

Simultaneously, the White House offensive against women's reproductive health continued. The polarization over choice built as Robertson organized his presidential campaign. For several months, New Right senators Orrin Hatch and Gordon Humphrey tied up reauthorization of the nation's Title X family-planning programs, which had enjoyed bipartisan support since their creation during the Eisenhower era. Federal funding of abortions came under attack. The *Grove City* battle dragged on, and the atmosphere in Washington on issues affecting women grew even nastier. Tension within the party and in the country over the New Right's social agenda was reaching the breaking point. It finally exploded on June 26, when Supreme Court Justice Lewis Powell resigned from the Court and five days later Reagan named Judge Robert Bork to replace him. All the frustration that had built up over seven years of attempts to weaken civil rights law and restrict opportunities for women and minorities finally boiled over.

In September 1986, when Chief Justice Warren Burger resigned, Reagan had elevated Justice William Rehnquist to Burger's position and appointed conservative Antonin Scalia to the Court. Some feminists had lobbied against Rehnquist and Scalia, but in general women had been focused on winning the 1986 election and did not take an active role.

Bork's nomination, however, set the alarm bells ringing. Bork was a brilliant intellectual with a wit that delighted his peers; he was also arrogant and aloof. A White House briefing book described him as a man who "has never wavered in his consistent and principled protection of civil rights, civil liberties, and other values that can actually be derived from the Constitution and federal law." Bork had never stated whether he would vote to overrule *Roe v. Wade,* it said, although he had questions as to "whether there is a right to abortion in the Constitution." Yet a report by the Senate Judiciary Committee contradicted the White House, finding that Bork had "opposed virtually every major civil rights advance on which he has taken a position," disapproved of the ERA, and had considered *Roe v. Wade* unconstitutional.

Feminists were very much aware that the Court was now divided 4–4 between Reagan appointees and those who had voted for *Roe*. The time had come to mobilize. There was no ambiguity about the import Bork could have as a Supreme Court justice. As *Human Events* had said of his nomination, "the president could advance his entire social agenda—from tougher criminal penalties to curbing abortion-on-demand to sustaining religious values in the schools, etc.—far beyond his term." Pro-choice and anti-choice partisans both believed legal abortion would be overthrown.

Those of us in the pro-choice Republican movement pored over the Bork record and found it wanting. By the time the Judiciary Committee hearings opened on September 15, we had joined the Coalition Against Bork. The New York State Republican Family Committee, its counterpart in California, and Planned Parenthood's Republicans for Choice lobbied senators and drummed up Republican opposition. We recruited former task force members and exhumed our old lists of ERA supporters. On this issue at least, the moderates were leaving the New Majoritarian coalition.

Fifty-one votes were needed in the Senate to confirm Bork's appointment. The battle centered on moderate northern Republican and New South Democratic senators. They had won their elections by backing social centrist policies and did not wish to be identified with racist and sexist agendas. But before the nomination was sent to the Senate, the Judiciary Committee of eight Democrats and six Republicans would hold hearings. The committee was split: five for Bork, five against, and four undecided. Of the undecided, only one was a Republican, Arlen Specter of Pennsylvania.

The Judiciary Committee met in the same Senate caucus room that had hosted the Watergate hearings and, ending only two months before, the Iran–Contra hearings. By now the setting was very familiar to a public that had spent months watching Oliver North exert his boyish charm to great effect. Bork was a very different witness. His answers to the senators' questions tended to be long esoteric treatises on the law. Rather than showing himself to be a New Right exemplar of definite opinion and great passion, he came across as a man who equivocated.

He was on record as criticizing the 1965 *Griswold v. Connecticut* decision that overthrew state bans on the sales of contraceptives and established a constitutional right to personal privacy, which was the basis on which *Roe* had been decided. Yet when several senators quizzed Bork, he did not restate his position of record. He still opposed *Griswold,* he said, but he never directly gave his opinion on the privacy construct of *Roe.*

Bork was expected to be the symbolic defender of the New Right's ideas, yet all he did was alienate. Throughout the hearings he did not give straightforward answers to straightforward questions. His approach to the law seemed cold, bereft of any awareness of the human impact his decisions would have. The more he talked, the more he frightened people. And he frightened women in particular when he gave a microscopic analysis of whether they have a right to equal protection under the Fourteenth Amendment, and whether he still thought *Roe* should be overturned.

It was Specter who finally made the difference. A moderate Republican who had been an aggressive public prosecutor in Philadelphia, Specter knew his law, and he questioned Bork with an intellectual zeal that brought out the core differences between the fundamental views under debate. Like most students of the law, Specter believed the framers had considered the Constitution not as an absolutist tract but as an ever-changing document that would adjust to the changing needs of the people. This meant an evolving concept of liberty, including privacy rights. Bork did not share this respect for what Specter termed "the conscience of tradition." According to *Boston Globe* reporter Ethan Bronner, whose book, *Battle for Justice,* chronicled the hearings, Specter was bothered "that Bork seemed selective in choosing which principles could grow and evolve and which were bound by original intent. It appeared as if Bork's selection were based on his prejudices."

On October 1, while the hearings were still under way, Specter announced he would vote against Bork's confirmation. When he called Bork to tell him, Bork said, "I thought I addressed your concerns." Specter replied, "You did address my concerns, but you didn't resolve the doubts that I had."

Within a few hours, three southern Democrats on the Judiciary Committee followed Specter's lead. It was all over. The full Senate rejected Bork's nomination, 58 to 42. A moderate Republican standing against a Republican president had made it easier for others to follow suit. For the moment, *Roe* was safe.

Later, when the firestorm over the rejection had died down, some said the independence of the nation's judiciary had been damaged in the process, that hysteria had taken over. Bork's confirmation hearing had been less civilized than many in the past, but the principal blame for this politicization of the judiciary didn't rest with those who voted against Bork. It rested with the leaders of the New Majoritarian coalition who had decided in the mid-seventies that the face of America's judicial system must be changed to reflect their view of justice. It rested with those Republicans who had accepted the theory behind the 1980 court-packing plank, and who had given the New Right's legal agenda the respectability it didn't deserve. Bork and his followers were wrong to charge later that those who had defeated him "stood outside the American mainstream" with "their radical ideas" and were "not liberals but nihilists." On the contrary, opposition to him was broad-based and came from all sectors of the nation.

At the time the Bork hearings were going on, the presidential nominating game got seriously under way. The Bush campaign adopted a strategy similar to the one it had used so effectively in 1980. His highly competent staff, most of them nonideological, set out to energize his vast political network, putting it to work raising money and proselytizing for recruits. As always, the network included the old guard and moderates that had been its core in 1980; but during his years as vice president, he had deliberately expanded his relationship with the New Right, and many more of them felt comfortable with Bush than the general public knew. Californian Robert Dornan, known as one of the most garrulous New Right members of Congress, exemplified the goodwill that many longtime Reagan revolutionaries felt for Bush. In an article entitled "Why My Choice Is George Bush," Dornan wrote:

> George Bush has become a Reagan Republican. . . . The vast majority of people who have made these recent years the greatest of George Bush's 20-year public career are conservatives. They cannot, and will not, be forgotten. . . . Under Ronald

Reagan we have not won all the time, but in the final analysis we—and the country—have won. So we conservatives should feel secure about our dominant role in the Republican Party; it is one of the reasons so many of us are supporting the Vice-President. He needs us as much as we want him.

The press often said that the New Right distrusted Bush, coming to this conclusion because men like Viguerie and Weyrich were always accusing the vice president of trying to destroy the Reagan revolution. It was not true. In fact, Bush had been more loyal to the Reagan revolution than had his detractors, who were constantly taking Reagan to task for not being ideologically pure. What the Reagan revolutionaries feared was not Bush's ideology but his lack of fire for their cause.

Bush's loyalty extended to the New Right's social agenda. He never wavered. His staff kept a tight rein over his positions on women's issues, particularly abortion and family planning. So paranoiac were they on the matter, in fact, that an anti-choice filter was applied even when it was not relevant. In the fall of 1985, Mary Curley, one of the Republican Family Committee's founders—and the wife of one of Bush's principal fund-raisers—wrote Jim Pinkerton, research director of Bush's PAC, the Fund for America's Future, asking for Bush's position on family planning. What she received instead was a statement on Bush's position on abortion, which included opposition to federal money for abortions except for danger to the life of the mother, support for a constitutional amendment to overturn *Roe,* and support for the Human Life Amendment with exceptions for life endangerment, "assault rape," and incest. Nowhere in this array was there a mention of family planning.

The committee already knew Bush's position on abortion. Pinkerton's answer confirmed what we had already suspected: In the minds of the Reagan administration and its designated presidential successor, family planning and abortion were the same thing. Earlier that fall, we had stumbled on this strange mind-set by accident when Barbara Mosbacher, another committee founder, wrote RNC chairman Frank Fahrenkopf, Jr., that she was resigning from the Eagles, an organization of big-contributor Republicans, because of the administration's hostility to family-planning programs. Mosbacher scrupulously avoided mentioning abortion. She had hoped to convince the party and the administration to modify their hostility to family planning by documenting its importance. As she wrote, "with an annual increase in world population of 85 million people and the U.S. teenage pregnancy rate rising precipitously," there was no rationale for "curtailing U.S. government efforts to help third world nations contain their populations" or for "crippling Title X, the nation's mainstay law aimed at reducing . . . unintended pregnancy."

But Fahrenkopf, ignoring what Mosbacher actually wrote, interpreted her resignation as anger over abortion. In the minds of the Bush staff, pregnancy prevention and making a choice to abort after becoming pregnant were the same thing. Opposition to both were part of the right-to-life movement's agenda, and Bush wasn't about to allow any questions to be raised about his anti-choice commitment.

But his stance greatly disturbed pro-choice Republicans, many of them prominent contributors and longtime friends, and they let it be known through a continuing stream of protests. By March 1987, when the problem could no longer be ignored, Bush took a superficial step in their direction by announcing he had shifted his abortion position away from Reagan's. From now on, he would accept abortion in cases of rape and incest as well as danger to the life of the mother. The maneuver did not persuade anyone involved in the abortion battle, since Bush still advocated outlawing *Roe v. Wade*.

The New Right couldn't make up their minds whom to back. Back in February 1986, at the annual Conservative Political Action Conference, where the movement often tried out its ideas and tested candidacies, a preference poll of conservative organizations had found that Bush was the favorite with 36 percent, followed by Kemp with 17. Robertson got only 4 percent. But a straw poll of the conference participants showed Kemp winning with 71 percent, and only 11 percent for Bush. Kemp's New Right supporters weren't going to give up easily; they had packed the conference.

Bush's machine hired South Carolinian Lee Atwater, a deputy political director at the White House and briefly a political consulting partner with Black, Manafort, and Stone, to consolidate his lead among grassroots conservatives, especially in the South. Atwater was a perfect complement to Bush's establishment inner circle, and he set about raiding Kemp's New Right base and undercutting Robertson. In his speeches, Bush increased his emphasis on the New Majoritarian agenda and his backing for Bauer's domestic juggernaut. It was Bush, of all in the administration, who now became the strongest defender of the anti-choice mantra, "stop killing the babies," and of the New Right's programs on women, children, and the poor.

War within the New Majoritarian coalition broke out in Michigan in 1985 and continued for two years, as Robertson's forces infiltrated the Republican party. In a technique startlingly reminiscent of tactics used by the Soviets to take over democratic socialist governments in Eastern Europe after World War II, Robertson's team "created political cells masquerading as mere voter-education brigades that would have been the envy of the godless communists he so conspicuously despised." These cells were made up chiefly of evangelical Christians, many of them women who had first been recruited into politics by Schlafly's crusades. Women were the mainstay of Robertson's organization and voting support. Catholic Marlene Elwell was his prime organizer and a whiz at recruiting new members. She was the one who had issued the glowing endorsement of Bush on behalf of the Pro-Life Impact Committee after he was nominated in Detroit. Ironically, Robertson would owe the success of his grassroots victories in Michigan and later in Iowa to women like Elwell.

Not only were Robertson's recruiters' methods atypical; the recruiters themselves were more dedicated and tenacious than Michigan's party regulars. Working through large church networks, the organizers registered conservative Christians, who became precinct captains and filed for other party offices. They passed around petitions to become delegates to the party's county and district conventions. Training videos were shown to newly enrolled voters, who then went out and registered more "Christians." Robertson encouraged his new followers with television sermons about "a new vision of America in which citizens ask God to guide their government"; and when he won what he thought was control of the Michigan Republican state party, he said, "We saw the hand of God going before us in Michigan affirm our every step." It was old-style political organizing, with evangelical television rather than torchlight parades providing the pizazz.

The Kemp and Robertson leaders in Michigan had formed a marriage of convenience to stop Bush. But the Kemp campaign soon discovered that the Robertson ground troops were more interested in proselytizing God's word than in promoting the Republican party. As the months passed, some of Kemp's New Right Michigan operatives grew uncomfortable with the zealotry of Robertson and his followers, fearing they were ruining the party. They also began to believe that Robertson might renege on his promise to throw enough delegates to Kemp to enable him to come in second in Michigan, after Robertson. The marriage fell apart. In the end, a new Bush–Kemp alliance formed and won Bush 37 delegates and Kemp 32. Unhappy with his winning only 8, Robertson promptly held a rump convention and claimed a decisive victory over the other two.

Robertson's Michigan women organizers then moved on to Iowa, where thousands of new Republicans were recruited for him. Here a well-established cadre of Religious Right people had worked hard to elect Roger Jepsen and beat back the ERA. Dole won the Iowa caucuses with 37 percent of the vote, but Robertson surprised everyone by getting 25 percent. Bush and Kemp trailed badly.

But Robertson couldn't keep up on the issues. Bush, Dole, and Kemp ran circles around him. He said he would abolish Social Security. He called the Civil Rights Restoration Act "one of the most frightening pieces of legislation that has been brought up." He said abortion opponents should look to "the wonderful process of mortality tables" to change the Supreme Court and overturn *Roe*. He scared New Hampshire voters when he claimed the Soviets had placed missiles in Cuba, and when his claim was shown to be nonsense, he further damaged his credibility by claiming he had been "misunderstood."

Ultimately, professionalism prevailed. Bush had been working for the nomination with single-minded intensity for a long time. His organization was simply too good, and he beat them all in New Hampshire. Three weeks later he won sixteen of the seventeen Super Tuesday contests—fourteen of them in southern or border states. He lost only Washington State, which went to Robertson. But with the victories in the South, the race was over. He would be the Republican nominee in August.

He won also because he embraced the tenets and the style of the Religious Right in his campaign. At Atwater's behest, Bush the Episcopalian had campaigned across the South, appearing before church groups and mouthing their agenda. In Atwater's home state, where half the voters claimed to be born-again Christians, "Bush . . . appeared before two dozen evangelical preachers in Greenville and assured them: 'Jesus Christ is my personal savior.' "

Bush may have won the nomination, but the brand of Reagan Republicanism he represented lost control of the Republican party machinery in more than one-third of the states. Robertson was more successful than anyone realized at the time. His organizational base had been the network of charismatic superchurches with memberships as large as twenty thousand. Once he had built cadres in these churches and convinced the ministers of the importance of his "political work for God," it was easy to hold political meetings in the church buildings and to use church bulletins for his messages. Robertson had awakened the political consciousness of these enormous congregations just as Falwell and his Moral Majority had done in the early eighties.

The Religious Right Christians had veto power or took over control of the Republican party in Hawaii, Alaska, Nevada, Minnesota, Iowa, Arizona, Georgia, Louisiana, North Carolina, Oklahoma, Oregon, South Carolina, Texas, and Virginia. They became party officers to advance their religious vision, which went beyond an attachment to Robertson. As one supporter said, "We are bigger than Robertson though . . . we have issues versus just party loyalty," and another prophesied, "I notice that everyone tries to make the movement very personal to Mr. Robertson, but I think that's a mistake. The issues will remain long after the candidate has stepped away from politics entirely."

Atwater found this to be the case, as Bush tapped into the Religious Right constituency. He had a special liaison to these religious groups not only during the nomination period but during the general election campaign. As political religious expert Allen Hertzke describes it, the Bush campaign discovered it could neutralize Robertson's influence in the superchurches by having a Bush backer request the same kind of help with church bulletins and meeting space. Moreover, Robertson's charismatic branch of evangelism wasn't appreciated by the larger Southern Baptist Convention, which found Bush more appealing once he had proved to it that he was as correct on the social issues as Robertson. Bush and his campaign co-opted both Robertson evangelicals and Southern Baptists. In exchange, he relinquished to them effective control over those issues the religionists cared about.

.   .   .

Bush's teams set about repairing the New Majoritarian coalition in anticipation of the election, but in their zeal they ignored the moderate women of the party and the nation until polls in the late spring showed the vice president with an 18 percent gender gap. With action imperative, they turned to one of their most valuable weapons—the Bush political women—to help repair the damage.

13

VALUABLE WEAPONS:
BUSH'S POLITICAL WOMEN

The "women's problem" proved to be more difficult for the Bush campaign than it had been for the Reaganites because Bush and his friends had perpetuated a myth that when he became president, he would be "good" for women; that unlike Reagan, he would act forcefully for women's equality.

But the record was otherwise, and throughout the months before the New Orleans convention, polls indicated women were skeptical of Bush. The White House was still implementing policies that impacted harshly on women and children, and Bush had embraced the misogynist strategy long before; it was part of what he believed would give him his ticket to the White House. Still, as in the past, he continued to receive help from large numbers of political women who confirmed by their enthusiasm that the myth might be working. The campaign encouraged the myth even as it shaped its policies toward women to please the Religious Right. Crucial to the success of this strategy was the continued loyalty of the Bush political women—all of us, whether it was those who embraced his candidacy with great enthusiasm or women like myself who stayed with him because he was the best of those candidates who stood a chance of winning the nomination. Bush at his worst was preferable to the others: Dole, Kemp, Robertson, Haig, and Pete Du Pont.

The women leaders who backed Bush were an impressive lot. Well educated and politically savvy, they were much more competent in the world of politics and government than the political women leaders of the right, other than Phyllis Schlafly, Linda Chavez, and Marlene Elwell.

There were his female supporters in Congress—Lynn Martin, Marge Roukema, Olympia Snowe, Connie Morella, Nancy Johnson, Claudine Schneider, and Pat Saiki, all pro-choice and dedicated workers for women's legislation.

There were his highly competent and experienced personal and campaign staff in Washington: Margaret Tutwiler, Janet Mullins, Connie Newman, Sheila Tate, Peggy Noonan, and Theresa Behrendt, and new arrivals like Mary Matalin, Deborah Steelman, and Lindsay Johnson. Out in the field, women political operatives like Eileen Padberg and Colleen McAndrews in California and Barbara Zartman in New York put together efficient campaign organizations. Longtime political loyalists Mary Louise Smith, Bobbie Kilberg, Nancy Thompson, Susan McLane, Elsie Hillman, Sally Pillsbury, Mary Curley, and Barbara Mosbacher raised money, recruited supporters, and were ardent cheerleaders for their friend the vice president. The vaunted thoroughness of the Bush campaign and its capacity to anticipate all possibilities, well documented by veteran reporters Jack Germond and Jules Witcover, were due in no small measure to the talents of these women.

The majority of them supported at least some part of the feminist agenda. They certainly didn't agree with the right's medieval view of women. Yet all threw themselves into electing a man who had done little in the last seven years to indicate he would support what they believed. For the longtime staffers and friends, it didn't matter. For the rest of us, faith and hope substituted for rationality. We'd do what we could to get Bush to come around.

For the feminists among us, our target was the August GOP convention in New Orleans, and while we would seek to strike the 1984 misogynist language from the platform, the platform was only part of a larger goal. We wanted the Bush team to put forth a strong women's agenda for the campaign that would blow the misogynists and the Democrats out of the water. We wanted him to present his vision of what could be done for American women.

The Republican Women's Task Force was actively back in national GOP politics, having decided after a seven-year hiatus to try again. Organizers of the August 1987 NWPC convention, held in Portland,

Oregon, had invited the officially announced presidential candidates of both parties to speak, but none of the Republicans showed up. It was disheartening, but it did not really surprise us.

In Portland, Linda DiVall, who was just coming into her own as a prominent Republican pollster, tried to stem some of the anger aimed at the GOP but did admit that "it would be less than credible to say the Republican party doesn't have a problem with women. But," she gamely added, "the party has recognized the problem and has a unique opportunity in 1988 to demonstrate its appeal to women." DiVall's brave words belied the truth. Maureen Reagan, now RNC co-chairman, hadn't come to Portland to defend the GOP's women's record, nor had Elizabeth Dole, Mary Louise Smith, or newly elected Nebraska governor Kay Orr. At the time, I said what a lot of Republican women were feeling: that after years with a split personality, I'd decided the stress and strain of being effective both as a Republican and as a feminist were too difficult. Instead, I would "subordinate my feminism and support the nominee, be a good loser, and then move in."

So we set about working for Bush from within and outside the campaign. The first sign that the inside women and their male allies might be having some success came a month later, when Bush declared before a "safe" NFRW crowd that "we should not be satisfied until women earn not just 70 percent of what men do, but 100 percent." Pay equity, he promised, would be a key plank in his campaign platform.

On Columbus Day, Bush's speech in Houston formally announcing his candidacy embodied a softer, kinder language that we'd seldom heard since he became vice president. He said:

> We don't need to remake society—we just need to remember who we are. . . . [W]here is it written that Republicans must act as if they do not care, as if they are not moved? . . . We are the party of Lincoln. Our whole history was protecting those who needed our protection and making this a kinder nation. We were also formed to stand for justice, and personal decency. . . . We need a new harmony, too, among the races. . . . The sadness of racial tensions in America should have ended completely by now. . . . we must, finally, leave the tired old baggage of bigotry behind us.

It was George Bush at his best. On this day, the nineteenth-century liberal philosophy of his Protestant forebears won out over the mean-spirited twentieth-century cant of the right-wingers he'd espoused. There was, however, one glaring omission in his speech: Where were women? His statements about opposing bigotry and seeking harmony were pointedly limited to racism.

One week later, the stock market crashed. It was the greatest fall since 1914, but most compared it to the crash of 1929 that had heralded the Great Depression. This 1987 crash did not bring on a depression, but it ended the Reagan boom and eventually threw the nation into a recession. The question now became whether Reaganomics, with its emphasis on tax cuts, needed to be reexamined; and if so, whether Bush as the heir apparent would do the reassessing, or whether he would stay the course. After Bush came in third in the Iowa caucuses with 19 percent of the vote, behind Dole (37 percent) and Robertson (25 percent), the answer came quickly. The supply-siders' slogan—no tax increases, only tax cuts—became Bush's message in the New Hampshire primary. When Dole refused to sign a pledge not to raise taxes, it was all over for him in tax-fearing New Hampshire. Bush beat him 38 to 29 percent.

But while Bush had reinforced his credentials as a supply-side warrior, his campaign knew the Democrats would question Reaganomics. With economic policy now a potentially damaging campaign issue, Bush's team realized it had to come to terms with the GOP gender gap problem. A first-rate collection of women staffers and volunteers and an occasional statement on women would not be enough to solve it. The campaign decided to build its own women's campaign organization rather than work with the existing national women's organizations. When forty-two of the existing organizations met in Iowa a few weeks before the Iowa caucuses to formulate a women's agenda for the presidential election, all the candidates from both parties were invited. Again, none of the Republicans showed up. The Bush campaign had different fish to fry.

Spurred on by Maureen Reagan and led by Julie Belaga, who had lost her Connecticut gubernatorial race in 1986, the RNC encouraged the formation of a political action committee, GOPAL (GOP Women's Political Action League), to elect women Republicans. GOPAL was solely a creature of the party. (It differed from WISH, a PAC for Republican women that was independent of the party structure and more able to relate to independent and Republican women angered by the national party's official anti-women policies.)

The campaign also formed economic policy groups to hold and attract women. It was what Republicans had been doing ever since the rise of the backlash strategy. Organized outside the NFRW, the groups' formation would always be announced with great fanfare, proclaiming that "American women must be the leaders" to stop the Democrats from increasing taxes, deficits, and regulations. Their honorary advisory boards included the administration's women stars of the moment, and Elizabeth Dole was always a member. These groups would come and go, serving their purpose of bringing women into the campaign. The women would get an opportunity to hear about the administration's policies, perhaps meet the president or vice president, and see the glamorous side of Washington life. There would inevitably be a conference where the administration and outside experts would brief them on the campaign line. The women would then be asked to raise money and recruit for the party and the campaign. There was nothing wrong with this approach, and many women found their way into governmental appointments through participating in it.

But these ad hoc groups never sought any long-term improvements for women. They were vehicles to further a short-term goal: the election of a Republican president. They were captive to the strategic aim of the campaign team, whose sole interest was to ensure that women didn't cause the defeat of their candidate. They were puppet organizations.

The groups followed the script exactly: The campaign team coopted women. Nowhere was this more evident than with the pro-choice women who joined the groups, thus tacitly giving their approval to an administration and candidate who worked against their rights.

By the time Bush had secured the presidential nomination on Super Tuesday 1988, his campaign, pressured by Bush's political women, recognized that these fronts weren't going to be enough to protect him from the very real wrath of America's women. Massachusetts governor Michael Dukakis had clinched the Democratic nomination after the April 23 New York primary, and with some minor variations, polls that spring consistently showed men split about evenly between Bush and Dukakis and women overwhelmingly preferring Dukakis. In early May, Dukakis enjoyed an 18 percent advantage over

Bush with women. A *Los Angeles Times-Mirror* in-depth survey of America's electorate indicated that women were more likely to be sympathetic to peace, civil rights, and environmental movements, and less likely to be pro-business enterprisers in tune with Reagan–Bush economic policies. To some degree, the economic-front groups had been preaching to the converted. The Bush campaign had been wary of reaching out beyond economic issues to women for fear of antagonizing the Religious Right and some of the New Right.

In 1980 Bush's campaign team had successfully kept his moderate supporters with him while he convinced the right that he was an acceptable choice to be Reagan's vice president. The same technique was once again in operation. To solidify his relations with the Religious Right, Bush met with them throughout the spring. He asked Robertson for his support, which Robertson gave. Lee Atwater and Robertson's campaign manager, R. Marc Nuttle, mapped out ways that the Religious Right could help elect Bush. Nuttle was satisfied, explaining that the Bush campaign had "done a miraculous job of trying to bring everybody in."

Dealing with the New Right was more difficult. They were beginning to split into factions, some pressing the misogynist message, and others—mainly libertarian Kemp supporters—deciding it was time to stop attacking women. Gingrich's and Kemp's people, including Black (who had run Kemp's failed campaign), helped Bush. Viguerie and Phillips were again threatening to form a third party and criticizing Bush for not being sufficiently wedded to "conservative" ideas. By now, however, their wailing had become so tiresome and predictable that few in the party's leadership took them seriously. Their day in the sun had passed. The action on the right was now with Robertson. This shift in power toward the Religious Right would make the position of women even more perilous. For all their bombast and rhetoric against feminists, Viguerie and Phillips didn't bring with their messages the mystical overlay of religious certitude of Robertson and his compatriots.

As for Kemp's team, Black, Manafort, and Stone, they'd shown themselves to be entrepreneurs first, accommodationists second, and ideologues seldom. They had fashioned a lucrative consulting business that included some of the world's premier third-world dictators. They were making money because of their inside track during the Reagan years and now with the Bush campaign. They were fixers in the grand tradition. Governing wasn't their interest; they didn't seek government appointments except for their clients. Their former business partner and colleague in the political wars, Lee Atwater, was running the Bush campaign, and their hope was that Bush would make Kemp his running mate. They fitted right into its organization, with Black getting the job of managing the platform at the national convention along with Bush's newfound friend, right-wing ideologue John Sununu, the governor of New Hampshire, whom Bush considered primarily responsible for his victory in that state.

Over on the women's front, the insider Bush women kept pushing the campaign to make a gesture toward women that would have policy ramifications, rather than another public relations maneuver. A guerrilla war started up in earnest. They had a difficult time because Gary Bauer had no intention of changing the Reagan administration's policy toward women. Just to prove who was in charge, his office produced a new series of anti-women policies. Jo Ann Gasper, a convert to Roman Catholicism who "opposed most methods of birth control," replaced Marjorie Mecklenburg as director of the nation's family-planning program. Gag rules, restrictions on birth control information, audits, defunding—all were tools Gasper and her male anti-choice assistants used to cripple family-planning programs. Simultaneously (and ironically), they continually decried the rise in teenage pregnancies.

Bush issued another allegedly strong "women's statement" proclaiming that "we've had enough excuses. It is time we had equal pay for equal work. . . . I will not be satisfied until men and women earn the same wage for the same job." It was difficult to believe he meant it. In mid-April, I'd heard him speak at an Association for a Better New York (ABNY) breakfast, and along with other women that day, I'd been disturbed by his response to a question on child care and the ERA. He told the ABNY crowd that the ERA had not been the answer to women's problems, but he offered no ideas on how better to bring about rights for women, while on child care he stated his opposition to federal control and then quickly segued into his equal pay statement.

What disturbed me most about the Bush reply was not his throwaway line on child care but the entire tone of his answer. After reflecting on it—and confirming my sense with others at the breakfast—I decided that the problem was less in the substance of what he said (although that was not very clear either) than in the seemingly flippant and irritable manner in which he responded. It was as though he was saying to himself, Do I really have to answer that again?

Part of his response obviously derived from his age, his class, his upbringing, and the conventional patronizing of women that most men of his generation grew up with. Intellectually, he appeared to believe that women are equal to men in brains and ability and deserve the same opportunities and respect as men with similar attributes, but that was not what he was communicating. He came across as a man who wished he didn't have to be bothered with inconsequential issues like these when the "real" issues were war and peace and jobs. His manner reinforced the condescending image that many women—including many who had voted for Reagan—saw in his 1984 debate with Geraldine Ferraro, when he insulted her with a comment implying she didn't understand foreign policy. They also remembered that the next morning, he had offhandedly said at a campaign rally about the debate, "We tried to kick a little ass."

The modern women's movement had been in operation for eighteen years. Its message had spread throughout the nation. It touched all women, whether or not they agreed with it, and it had affected their lives. While Bush appeared to grasp the roots and the impact of the civil rights movement, I didn't think he understood—in his gut—the sensitized environment that surrounded discussions of women's issues in public forums. I suggested to a friend in the campaign that he be taught to be more perceptive—and if that wasn't possible, that he be given words and phrases to help him sound as though he were.

I urged Bush to participate in sessions with the women in his campaign to raise his consciousness and to develop some succinct programmatic approaches to women's problems. Other Bush advocates were trying to convince the campaign to connect with women's organizations too. Pamela Curtis challenged him to reach out beyond his safe constituency and attend the Business and Professional Women's annual convention in July. The BPW had 653,000 members (53 percent of them Republican), and Curtis said many of those Republican members wanted to help. She even suggested gamely that Bush reach out to groups with a majority of Democrat and independent members, although she was fully aware the Bush camp would not go that far.

Thereafter we waited for the repackaging of Bush on women's issues. The Reagan administration had had no child care policy. Nancy

Johnson had taken the lead on this issue in the party and introduced the Child Care Services Act in the House. Among its provisions to expand child care, the legislation proposed giving grants to start child care facilities, eliminating unfair liability insurance and tax codes for them, and allowing states to provide sliding-fee-scale child care certificates for low-income working families. While her bill was in no way as comprehensive as what the Democrats were proposing in their Act for Better Child Care Services (ABC), it was a step toward solving a serious problem. Since Hatch had agreed to back it in the Senate, Johnson thought her legislation might have a chance with the White House.

The women in the Washington campaign office let those of us outside the Beltway know that the Bush campaign was planning a child care pitch, coupled with a public relations blitz to show off Bush's attractive family of children and grandchildren—something that he had never done during his vice presidency. But to get the Reagan–Bush administration to accept a child care policy turned out to be a nightmare. Both Bauer and Education Secretary Bennett opposed child care. Even Bennett's wife participated, lobbying with a *Policy Review* clipping that said "day care harms children." Bauer characterized "day-care centers as about as beneficial to children as heavy drug use." When she became secretary of labor in late 1987, Ann McLaughlin had announced that child care would be a top priority for her department, and then several months later she had surprised Washington by issuing a report that concluded there was no child care crisis in America, only "spot shortages" and "shortages of options." Her bureaucratic report, shaved at the edges to make it politically acceptable to Bauer and other Religious Right leaders, contradicted the voluminous data gathered by child care experts that substantiated the depth of this crisis.

The campaign's child care announcement didn't get off the ground before the convention. By late April, it still had made no substantive advances on the women's front. Infighting over control of the platform and the selection of the vice-presidential nominee consumed the party's insiders. *The New York Times* reported that Bush was "prepared to let the 1988 Republican platform be an updated version of the 1984 platform." Don Devine, now director of the American Conservative Union, organized the Committee to Save the Reagan Platform to block any leftward movement by Bush, making some believe that the right was fearful Bush would drop the Reagan agenda and that it was exerting public pressure on the vice president to ensure he maintained his cooperation. On the other hand, we weren't sure what Bush would do.

Rather than form a countercommittee to Devine's, which was our first impulse, those of us outside the Beltway accepted the advice of our Bush campaign friends, who said we could get a fairer platform for women by not disrupting their efforts to unify the party. They told us we were reasonable people. We could surely understand how crucial it was to have the conservatives completely behind Bush. It was the standard unity line, but we bought it. We didn't have much choice, and besides we were encouraged by some polls in late May that indicated that the gender gap had risen to 24 percent in Dukakis's favor. Surely those figures would hasten the repackaging effort.

Kemp's men had launched a full-scale drive to make him Bush's running mate. Delegates were encouraged to lobby Bush operatives for Kemp, whose friend Black saw to it that he got a prime-time speaking slot on the opening night of the convention, where he would be a warm-up cheerleader for the night's big event: an address by Ronald Reagan. Some task force members toyed with starting a Draft Kassebaum for Vice President group, but intermediaries let us know that the senator wasn't interested. She hoped Bush would pick Dole.

During the first week in June, the ABC News/*Washington Post* poll reported that the gender gap had hit 28 percent. The backlash strategy was backfiring. Republicans out in the states began to speculate openly that Bush would lose the election. His friends in Washington felt the same way but were more discreet in their comments. It was time to speak out. I told Walter Robinson of *The Boston Globe* that "the Reagan–Bush team has not paid much attention to women over the last seven years. . . . The tone and the attitude have been, If you're a working woman or a single parent, they don't care." I added, as did other Republican feminists around the country to their local press, that while we were not happy with Bush's policies toward women, he would be a vast improvement for women, and he cared.

The Bush camp reacted at last. In early June prominent women from all wings of the party were invited to Washington to participate in focus groups to tell the Bush campaign what women wanted. Connie Newman and Lindsay Johnson, Nancy Johnson's daughter, led some of the groups, and their presence encouraged us to think that the long-promised women's issues project was at last getting off the ground.

The campaign was organized into two sectors: those that focused on people, and those that focused on issues coalitions. Women were the priority target of the people groups. In the issues groups, women's concerns were separated into the Family Issues Coalition and Workforce 2000, a reflection of the schizoid nature of Bush's own political strategy. The rationale for this division was that career women might not be "easily appealed to through [the] Family Issues Coalition," which would stress child and elder care, adoption, drugs, education—subjects the campaign said were primarily of interest to evangelicals, conservatives, and Catholics. (What a curious and arbitrary judgment, I thought. *I* was interested in all those "family issues"—as were many women, with or without careers, who were not Catholic, evangelical, or conservative.) Workforce 2000 would also cover child care, elder care, and drugs, but it would omit the other family-issue areas and concentrate instead on jobs, the economy, and entrepreneurship.

Even though across the country the battle over women's reproductive rights had heated up, reproductive health issues were not on either group's agenda.

The organizers explicitly ruled out the label Women for Bush for the groups. While their purpose was to attract women voters, the campaign's aim, as it had been in 1980 and 1984, was to bring women into issue-oriented constituencies rather than organize them by gender, thereby limiting their ability to speak as a "women's voice." This is not to say that some women didn't prefer this approach, but it undercut the political power of the women's movement.

Three weeks before the Democrats met in Atlanta—a site deliberately chosen to prove they were still a force in the South—to nominate Dukakis and Texas senator Lloyd Bentsen as his running mate, the women's project finally took off. It was late in the game, considering the gender gap and the possibility that women voters could deny Bush a November victory. A politically savvy outsider surveying the polling data since the 1986 elections would have assumed that Bush's team would gear up no later than early spring of 1987. But campaigns are difficult to organize even in the best of circumstances. In the case of this campaign, the bias against women's opportunity in the Republican constituencies Bush believed he needed to win was probably the reason for the late start. As had happened over and over again since 1980, those in the party in Washington who didn't agree with the misogynist messages did not want to get into a knock-down public fight over women's issues. During the Reagan years, they had learned they could achieve their economic and foreign policy goals by letting the right do as it wished on social issues, especially those directly affecting women. They had also learned that numerous highly skilled and loyal women would help them with their "women's problem," despite their backlash politics.

Lindsay Johnson and Connie Newman were among those women, and in a memo they wrote with Ceci Cole McInturff to George Bush, they outlined the results of the focus-group meetings. They gave Bush fair, honest information about women. Now he could never claim he hadn't heard Republican women's points of view. Nor was their advice cluttered with backlash-strategy bias—something the men of the Reagan–Bush camp usually got into in questions related to women's issues. Even Reagan–Bush pollsters as honorable and professional as Wirthlin and Teeter didn't escape this bias because their contact with the now broadly based women's movement was minimal. Their political experience didn't include much exposure to feminist thought and action, except from those feminists who criticized Republicans and Reagan. The few times they had bothered to consult with Republican feminists, such as Mary Louise Smith, their suggestions were discounted as radical, inappropriate, or anathema to the Reagan revolution. Yet just as James Baker hired women for high-level jobs, so did Wirthlin and Teeter. Personnel were one thing; the political agenda another.

The women in the focus groups said they had "tremendous affection for Bush" and thought it ironic that someone who was perceived as "respectful, open-minded, and caring" had such a large gender gap problem. Yet they doubted that the Bush campaign would do anything because "they'd been to this kind of meeting before" with no results.

They were also critical of the media's "simplistic approach to covering women and the gender-gap." If the campaign had the will, they said, "a combination of substantive policy references that are relevant to women, as well as symbolic gestures of inclusion" might help. Their suggestions for action could have come from a feminist manual: Integrate women into the campaign at all levels; have Bush hold at least two public meetings a week with women; provide press opportunities for women at the New Orleans convention with Bush stating he looked forward to the day "when all the faces seated on the floor are more evenly divided by gender, or when women make up a *majority* of delegates"; put women's perspective in all campaign rhetoric; drop the phrase "traditional family" and replace it with a description that more accurately reflects America's diverse family structures; and emphasize a belief in equality when asked about the ERA.

Responding to a longtime complaint of Republican women of all ideological stripes, they strongly urged that women of the stature of Carla Hills and Lynn Martin be added to G6, the label attached to the all-male Bush campaign inner circle. They also wanted the campaign to adopt a rule that Bush "should *always* be introduced by a woman, and should never appear on any dais that is not equally divided between women and men," and that Barbara Bush should campaign more "as a walking positive advertisement" for her husband.

Then we waited for G6 to move.

The gender gap struggle heated up inside the Washington campaign and in the state Republican party organizations. Asked about a report released by the organizers of the Iowa Women's Agenda Conference showing Dukakis holding a 28 percent lead over Bush among women, Bush's press secretary, Sheila Tate, laid out the Bush campaign line. Brushing off the significance of the polling numbers, she said, "It's our view that it's more of a traditional Republican polling problem than it is a George Bush problem." In other words, the Republican party had trouble with women, but Bush didn't. As a result, said Tate, "we're not running around and dealing with a lot of so-called 'women's issues.'"

The leaders of the campaign believed Reagan had survived the gender gap by building up his support among men, and so would Bush. But unlike Reagan, who had always maintained a comfortable following with men, Bush and Dukakis were running at about the same level. The Bush strategy aimed to regain the GOP lead among men and to simultaneously win over the women's vote as long as these efforts did not jeopardize Bush's positive ratings with men. The uneasy truce between those who were following the backlash strategy and those who wished to win by convincing women to vote for Bush continued until Election Day.

Ethel Klein, who had prepared the report on the Iowa Women's Agenda Conference, wrote that the gender gap was about women's economic vulnerability, not the personalities of Bush and Dukakis. "There are very few differences between men and women in their evaluations of the two nominees. . . . Rather, women have a more pessimistic view of the future of the nation's economy and their own financial situation than men." Consequently, said Klein, more women believed they were being hurt by the economy and wanted a change. Women were earning less than men, and elderly women, who survive longer than men, had less to live on. A slowed-down economy, the hardships imposed on women by the Reagan budget cuts, and the administration's anti-choice policies were all hurting women. Klein found that the polls at the time showed the gender gap was strongest among women earning less than $25,000 and those making more than $50,000 a year, but was not significant among middle-income women. Thus the challenge for those in the Bush campaign who favored a comprehensive pro-women strategy was to increase Bush's appeal among the middle class and to bring back those in the higher income category. The campaign didn't feel the Reagan–Bush policies gave them much pull with women earning $25,000 or less.

Reproductive rights was the Achilles' heel of this grand strategy. As the Republican convention approached, Reagan's policies continued to wreak havoc on these issues. Middle-class women, especially those in the suburbs, were particularly aware of the brutal battle going on over family-planning programs and abortion. Armed with data on the gender gap, Barbara Mosbacher, Pauline Harrison, and I went to Washington to plead the case for eliminating all 1984 right-to-life language from the 1988 platform and replacing it with a statement on families that urged family-planning education and the development of a private-public partnership for "quality, affordable child care." We urged an abortion-neutral platform.

When we entered a shabby room at the Bush headquarters on Fifteenth Street, we found a roomful of men seated around an oblong table. After all the obviously unsuccessful sensitivity training of the last two months, the campaign included only one Bush staff woman at the meeting, and she turned out to be a secretary who never opened her mouth and sat in the corner. No women from the campaign were present. Their absence told all and set the tone before a word was said. It was insulting. The three of us sat next to one another at one end of the table, facing the men.

The leader of this male assemblage was Hal DeMoss, a Bush friend from Houston responsible for seeing that the 106-member Platform Committee didn't step out of line. Ten days before, DeMoss had told *Newsday* reporter Saul Friedman that the Bush campaign would "adopt the 1984 platform as the basis for this year's document to avoid 'spilling blood on the floor' of the convention in a fight with angry conservatives." DeMoss had added, "We're sending a two-pronged message—comforting the movement conservatives by not pulling away from the positions of four years ago and telling the other side that we're not going to be more explicit or go even further" on conservative issues. This last statement referred to an attempt by Robertson to get a plank endorsing creationism.

The nine men seated around the table identified themselves, and except for DeMoss, C. Boyden Gray, the vice president's counsel, and Woody Kingman, a former New York colleague of mine who I hadn't known would be there, everyone appeared to be between twenty and thirty-five years old. I thought how easy it would have been to include some of the young Bush women.

"Extreme positions don't win elections," I told the group. "How can women take seriously a party that champions a woman's economic freedom while devaluing her personal freedom? Drop the anti-abortion plank. Bush can be anti-choice, but he should respect how the rest of us feel by not shoving another right-to-life plank at us. You are asking us to vote against our own personal self-interest."

They sat stone-faced. Only my old friend Kingman was animated and interested. We were making little connection, as if they thought we were pariahs. My arguments about winning the election by moving to the center and developing a strategy that included a special appeal to women elicited a few polite coughs.

But I could see they were ill at ease when I finished. When Harrison and Mosbacher made their pitch for dropping the anti-abortion plank, it set off hostile questions from the younger men. When we suggested they needed to integrate women into their campaign and increase the visibility of Barbara Bush and the Bush children, one man suggested that such an emphasis on the wonderful Bush family would cause resentment among widows and divorced women. So far afield and unperceptive was the comment that later we decided the questioner must have had some truly weird experiences with women.

Then they asked us what we planned to do. Their questions were too inquisitive, too specific about the tactics we planned to use. I became wary, suddenly realizing this little give-and-take was a fishing expedition; they were gathering intelligence for New Orleans. The three of us had worked together for years. We'd faced the politicians of Albany, the anti-choice zealots, and the equivocators, and these Bush men were no match for those people. I was not impressed by the attempt of the men around the table. Realizing what was happening, we told them nothing of value. They asked me to send them specific suggestions on what to do about the abortion plank. The meeting accomplished nothing except to underscore just how far apart we were. They killed the spirit of goodwill—the desire to help Bush—that had motivated our journey.

As we left the room, we met Newman and Johnson, who invited us to talk about what had happened. Fearing unfriendly staff intrusions, we went out of the headquarters building. Safely settled in a basement bar café down the street, we told them about our unhappiness with the meeting and wondered where they'd been. They implied that the men hadn't wanted them there. They were pro-choice. It would have been difficult, they said, in a roomful of right-to-lifers. They urged us to write the Platform Committee chairman, Kay Orr, and her two cochairmen, Wisconsin senator Robert Kasten and California congressmember Jerry Lewis. All were on record as anti-choice, although Lewis had made commendable moves toward including women and their issues in the House GOP agenda.

I wrote all three on behalf of the Republican Family Committee, asking that the platform not mention abortion. I argued that it would "send a signal to the nation that the Republican party is not dominated by one interpretation of morality and that its umbrella is broad enough to include people with differing views on such matters." Other pro-choice GOP groups wrote similar letters. We talked to those members of the Platform Committee who might be sympathetic to our approach. We called every Republican leader we knew. We burned up the telephone lines.

The silence from the three was unnerving. Even letters from major pro-choice contributors who had raised hundreds of thousands of dollars for Bush had no effect. None of the letters were even acknowledged. Pro-choice Republicans were obviously on some special blacklist.

Three weeks before the Platform Committee hearing in New Orleans, George Bush surprised us by speaking to the Business and Professional Women convention. It was one of the few suggestions in the Newman–Johnson memo, along with more public appearances by the Bush family, that the campaign implemented. Elizabeth Dole came with him, heightening rumors he might choose her as his running mate. Bush proposed a thousand-dollar tax refund to help parents care for children four years of age and under. Deborah Steelman, who had been hired only six weeks before as Bush's first full-time adviser on domestic policy, developed the proposal, working with, among others, Nancy Johnson. Bush's four-point program "would cost $2.2 billion," which included $1.5 billion for a tax credit for poor parents, but it was "close to the $2.5 billion called for in the Democrats' proposed ABC bill, which placed the emphasis on helping states provide child care for lower-income working families." Bush's proposal didn't begin to deal with the numerous facets of the nation's child care needs, but it was a start—after all, for eight years the Reagan administration had had no policy. It was a recognition that more than ten million preschool children had mothers in the work force. We gave a cheer for the women inside the Bush campaign.

We didn't know it then, but Bush's child care plan had the blessing of Phyllis Schlafly, who had derided the ABC bill and "instead proposed a toddler tax credit that would give money directly to families whether the mother worked or not." Bush's child care proposal was an attempt to accommodate the two views of "family values," and both would end up in the 1988 platform.

The women in the campaign told us there would be a full-fledged women's agenda in the fall. I wasn't convinced; the meeting with DeMoss had made me suspicious. Nevertheless, all the Bush political women would be in New Orleans. We'd have a chance to find out just what our candidate for president planned to do with his "women's problem." In the meantime, we were all working hard to diminish his gender gap.

14

VICTORY WITHOUT HONOR

"That's enough. Thank you."

Marilyn Thayer gaveled down my allotted five-minute testimony at the two-minute mark. She lost her cool. She cut me off in midsentence when I asked that there be no abortion language in the Republican platform.

Marilyn Thayer, chairman of the Family and Community Subcommittee of the Republican Platform Committee and Reagan delegate to the last three GOP conventions, was having a hard time. I didn't fit her script. I'd been given prime time to testify as the executive director of the New York State Republican Family Committee, and I had had the nerve to urge a neutral position on abortion. The name of our committee must have confused them: They must have thought that an organization with *family* in the title would surely be anti-choice. Just before the gavel dropped, I'd suggested that we could "each hold our own strongly felt views and still be tolerant of others, particularly on matters of deeply felt private and religious beliefs." A call for tolerance seemed more than anti-choice Thayer could stomach.

None of the other subcommittee members said a word. No one challenged her, even though it was evident by the way they shifted in their seats that some were uncomfortable with her dismissal of me.

I didn't argue. I didn't make a scene, although in retrospect I should have. I thought we were going to make some progress in the platform, that our friends inside the Bush camp were going to deliver something for our side. I would have done more for our cause if I'd embarrassed the convention managers right then and there—demanded my right to finish speaking and when Thayer refused, given the press their first story of the first day of George Bush's troubles with women at the Republican convention in New Orleans.

As I got up from the table facing Thayer and walked back to the fold-up chairs set aside for the public, the print press rushed me with questions: Does this mean Bush is going to have trouble here at his own convention? What are you pro-choice people going to do?

The first shot in the Bush convention team's war against pro-choice Republicans had been fired. Phyllis Schlafly, who was in the room monitoring the hearings and getting ready to testify, saw immediately what was happening. Before C-SPAN—the only television operation covering the hearings—could disengage and come over to interview me, she sat down at the table and started reading her statement. Thayer looked relieved. C-SPAN turned its cameras on Schlafly, who testified for more than fifteen minutes. I talked briefly to the press about my hope that this was an isolated case of an overzealous anti-choice person unable to listen to those who disagreed with her. If Thayer should bottle up discussion during the subcommittee's deliberations, I said, we'd get our chance when the full Platform Committee met.

The pattern was the same as in 1980. The fifteen-member subcommittee was again stacked with people who were pushing the Religious Right's social agenda. Several had been Pat Robertson delegates and were now pledged to Bush. The ubiquitous Charlie Black was in charge of implementing the campaign's platform strategy and had this subcommittee locked up tight. I'd identified only two moderate subcommittee members: John Easton, defeated for the governorship of Vermont in 1984 by Madeleine Kunin, and Connecticut senator Lowell Weicker.

At the last minute, Lynn Glaze of Delaware showed up, substituting on the subcommittee for her state's senator, William Roth. None of us had ever met her. As she said to me later, "I was a ringer." To my delight, she was more than willing to make the other proposal in my written testimony: that the party back alternatives to unwanted pregnancies such as family-planning programs. Schlafly's operative on the subcommittee, former Democrat Bunny Chambers, who had fought the good fight against the ERA in Oklahoma, swiftly moved to table Glaze's motion without discussion. Thayer was happy to comply. Two more attempts to change the anti-abortion language met with the same fate. Glaze finally got Thayer to approve a roll call without debate, and our side lost 11 to 3, picking up a surprise vote from the Virgin Islands delegate, Edgar Ross.

The outcome of these quadrennial exercises was by now so predictable that I had to agree with columnist Richard Reeves: "One of the ironies of American politics is that our conservative party, the Republicans, is a mirror image, structurally, of Western Europe's Socialist and Communist parties." The Republican party mirrored the hard-edged discipline of highly ideological parties in which committee "deliberations" are not forums for open give-and-take debate but show procedures to prove the depth of party unity.

Several weeks before the convention, I had spoken to Platform Committee members Weicker, Nancy Johnson, and Claudine Schneider about our platform strategy. Schneider never showed up in New Orleans for platform week. Her vacant seat in the first row of the committee was a constant reminder to us that for whatever reason, she hadn't been able to fight. Weicker's staff was there to help while he commuted back and forth from Washington, where crucial appropriations battles were being fought. Only Johnson was fully present and ready.

I asked Bush staffer Deborah Steelman to convince the campaign to give some signal that the candidate wasn't totally in agreement with the misogynist line on reproductive rights. She told me the campaign would not make any changes, no matter how modest. The trade-off on women's issues would be Bush's child care proposal, which would be used to placate unhappiness over the anti-choice position. Schlafly was on board for it, calling the proposal the most respectable option around for helping mothers in the workplace. There would be unity among the women at the convention on at least one women's issue.

The right's antagonism toward federal child care policy during the Nixon administration had essentially vanished, dissipated by changing conditions. The data indicated that by now, more than 74 percent of employed women were full-time workers, while 56.7 percent of married women living with their husbands were in the labor force. The great majority of these women had children under the age of six. It was impossible to ignore this reality. While Schlafly and the "family values" lobby preferred to find ways to keep mothers at home, they agreed with us that keeping families together should be a priority—and that meant helping working mothers. Later that week, the child care plank sailed easily through the Platform Committee.

Even without encouragement from our allies inside the campaign, we decided to try for a change in the anti-choice plank anyway. The evening before the full committee deliberations, along with Johnson, Glaze, Easton, Marjorie Bell Chambers, Nancy Thompson, and a few others, we met to map out a strategy. A count showed we had between thirty and thirty-five of the ninety-nine members expected to vote, enough for the twenty-seven required signatures for a minority report that would get us to the convention floor the following week.

But Black and his staff wanted no debates on the floor, let alone within the Platform Committee. We were under constant surveillance, as well as pressure not to rock the boat. As we had learned so bitterly in 1980 and to a lesser degree back in 1972 and 1976, the committee leadership would discover any plan we made. Our best approach was to leave our plan of action loosely structured. We knew who our potential friends were, and we'd try a series of challenges and amendments—which the Bush team would try to defeat—to win them over.

After years of convention battles, we had learned how Black operated. He used fear to keep recalcitrant committee members in line—fear that they wouldn't get the appointment they wanted, fear that someone might tell on them for some indiscretion, fear of being ostracized, fear of damaging the president or hurting the nominee's election chances. Any leverage would do, short of physical abuse.

We knew we'd never win over the right-wing ideologues nor did we try, but we also knew there were many reasonable people on the convention committees who would listen to appeals for fairness. Many of them were outside-the-Beltway party officials. From many years of lobbying, these Republicans had learned to recognize the pressures put on them by Washington political consultants who seemed to care little about their state and local interests. They had worked in the party for years and had a sturdy grasp of political maneuvering. They recognized when the maneuvering went beyond civil conduct and fair play, and a few always rose to challenge the New Right consultants. They might not agree with us on all the issues, but as we had found over the years in presenting our women's agenda, many more were open to our appeals

than one would have thought from watching the committee's deliberations. They weren't necessarily swayed by the ubiquitous unity argument. Even party harmony and loyalty to the nominee had their limits.

Using a looser strategy that played to the issue of the moment,
rather than focusing on a fixed short-term goal, allowed us more flexibility in identifying those one or two places where Black and his aides
had pushed too hard. Richard Reeves's description of the party, while
apt, wasn't a hard-and-fast rule. The American system of selecting delegates was still too open for total control, and there were always people
of goodwill on the Platform Committee who would let no one dictate
to them. Their conscience ruled their decisions. They could throw a
monkey wrench into even the best-laid plans of the New Right operatives—and sometimes into ours. Now we strove for open debate, hoping that this would give our arguments a full airing and persuade the
independent thinkers to back us. At a minimum, a few would speak out
—if the committee leaders gave them the chance. We'd been successful
in 1976. We hoped that Bush would now relent a little. He wasn't
Reagan, we kept telling ourselves. It was important that he seek his own
vision, his own way of leading. He had to get out from under Reagan's
shadow, out from under the grip of the New Right and the Religious
Right.

When the Platform Committee began discussing the draft platform
drawn up by the Bush campaign, we didn't know where the fireworks
would erupt, but we knew they would. Just as our opponents watched
Schlafly for instructions, I stood where Nancy Johnson and others could
see me if something required immediate coordination. Johnson moved
to strike language supporting the Mexico City policy, and we got our
first vote when Marilyn Shannon of Oregon tried to table it without
discussion. Johnson lost by 36 to 30. Considering that the misogynists
were supposed to be in control, we were elated by these numbers. A full
third of the committee wasn't voting. The vote confirmed the accuracy
of our count the previous night.

The infamous abortion plank came upon us again. Over in the
center of the visitors' section, in front of the risers where the committee
members sat, I saw John Wilke, president of the National Right to Life
Committee, flash a signal to New Hampshire governor Sununu. Bush's
point man on the committee, Sununu had been keeping it in line with

gestures and nods and occasional notes to the delegates. The hour of confrontation had come.

Marjorie Bell Chambers set off the spark. A former president of the American Association of University Women and chair of the U.S. National Advisory Committee on Women during the late seventies, Chambers challenged the language of the 1984 abortion plank that said, "We believe the unborn child has a fundamental individual right to life which cannot be infringed." She moved that the words "which cannot be infringed" be dropped, and she told the committee:

> What I object to is the implication of these words, that in the conflict over which of two lives has the greater right to life, this statement implies the fetus will always have the greater right. . . . [T]here are circumstances when the mother should have that right. . . .
>
> I ask with this phrase . . . where is the mother's inalienable right to life, liberty and the pursuit of happiness in rearing the children she already has? "Cannot be infringed" says to me that men and fetuses have a right to life at all times but women lost that right when they become pregnant. . . .
>
> I consider [that] this implied government-forced sacrificing, in all cases, of the mother for the fetus, especially a woman with other children, expresses religious intolerance for my beliefs and those of many who share my beliefs. . . .
>
> How can a woman fulfill her full potential if the federal government can deny her the right of control over her own life? If she chooses to sacrifice her life, fine; but the federal government should not make that choice for her.

Chambers had dropped a bombshell. The members started talking loudly among themselves, as did the audience. Wilke gesticulated at an alarmed Sununu, who quickly gave directions to Black's staff. Schlafly's women, Bunny Chambers and Marilyn Shannon, tried to cut off debate by repeatedly moving to table. Committee chairman Orr, who had been previously chastised—appropriately—by nonright-wing committee members for letting the tabling gimmick get out of hand, finally let a debate begin. The arguments were heated and terrific. For a few minutes in New Orleans, democratic give-and-take broke free of Charlie Black's vise. When the roll-call vote came, the noise made it hard to get a true count. Orr announced that the Marjorie Bell Chambers amendment had been defeated 55 to 32. My count was 55 against, 33 for, and 11 not voting. It was a victory for us. The vaunted machine contained a sizable crack. We had enough votes for a minority report, plus some to spare. We promptly got a minority petition printed, and within half an hour it was being circulated for the twenty-seven signatures.

Then we got stopped cold: The eloquent and fearless Marjorie Bell Chambers, who had spoken up as though she were Susan B. Anthony, suddenly folded. She wouldn't sign the petition. When we entreated her to tell us why she wouldn't back up her passionate words with action, she answered lamely that she didn't want to do anything to hurt Bush's chances. She had simply wanted to make her point about the plank's unfairness.

It made no sense. To this day, I have never had a satisfactory answer to the mystery of Marjorie Bell Chambers's skittishness.

Chambers's unwillingness to champion her own cause undid us. There were no fair-play or moral arguments we could use if the proposer wouldn't back her own cause. Weicker and Johnson proposed a few more amendments. Then Johnson made an impassioned plea: "Have you ever faced a teenage kid who is the victim of incest for two or three years and then finally finds herself pregnant?" she asked. "You are not doing that infant a favor to have it birthed nine months later, carried in a host body that is filled with anger, fear, and terror of what created this." A few more minutes of debate followed, but Johnson's eloquence changed no one's vote. The fight was over.

The anti-abortion plank in Bush's platform was more vicious than the one in Reagan's in 1980, which did not include the phrase "cannot be infringed" and which had thrown a meaningless crumb to pro-choicers by recognizing "differing views on the question." This 1988 Bush plank was the identical twin of the 1984 plank written by the Religious Right, only now it praised religious and private organizations for offering alternatives to abortion.

Robertson had gotten his pound of flesh, and Black had done what he'd been hired to do: He delivered for his boss. There could be no doubt that on women's reproductive issues, Bush was going to prove that he was tougher than Reagan.

·   ·   ·

Our focus shifted to other women's issues, such as parity. D.C. Platform Committee member Nancy Thompson, who had been with me at the 1977 IWY convention, had been concentrating her energies on a statement that the party supports women "seeking an equal role in the governing of our country and is committed to the vigorous recruitment, training, and campaign support of women candidates at all levels."

The Women's Campaign Fund had proposed the text for this parity statement to Nancy Johnson's congressional office. But Johnson's plate was already full with the family and children amendments, so she had asked Thompson to shepherd the statement through the Platform Committee. The parity idea wasn't new: Since the 1920s, helping women candidates had been part of the Republican party's rhetorical tradition, and it had become policy with the NFRW founding in 1938. But policy wasn't reality, and as we knew all too well, the party's systematic recruitment and election of women had for years been honored more in the breach than in the observance.

What was new this time was that all the women on the Platform Committee—Religious and New Right, old guard and moderate—agreed that electing women in equal numbers was a good idea. The closest to any real disagreement came when Thayer objected to calling on the party to "fund" women candidates—even though it had been doing so for years. The committee obliged her and changed "fund" to "campaign support." Lost in all the discussion was the fact that this modest plank was proof that the women's movement was positively influencing even antifeminist women, even as they opposed it.

Bush's child care proposal was a poor carbon copy of the Democrats' Act for Better Child Care Services bill, but a step had been taken in a feminist direction. We Republican feminists welcomed this new flexibility. Who cared if political pragmatism, rather than conviction, had motivated the Bush campaign's decision to back child care? At least they had recognized that the majority of American families no longer consisted of Mom, Dad, and two kids nestled in Dick-and-Jane domesticity. Even Schlafly's women were pleased by the "toddler tax credit" for families of modest means. It would help their constituency, Robertson advocates and blue-collar Reagan Democrats. A *Los Angeles Times* survey of the convention delegates showed that they opposed federally funded child care by a four-to-one margin but liked this proposal. It was the all-too-familiar Republican way of dealing with a social problem: Give people tax credits and incentives, and they'll buy in. But the fact remained that the Bush campaign had recast a feminist idea and were using it to hold together the New Majoritarian coalition. The great equalizer of political change—the American voter—was altering some elements of the right's misogynist strategy. In this platform, the retrenchment persisted only with reproductive rights.

Another change taking place within the New Majoritarian coalition was brought on by the onslaught of AIDS in the eighties but had first been anticipated with the arrest of House member Bob Bauman in the fall of 1980. The New Right and the old Goldwater Young Republican leadership had always had gay men in their midst. Most of them had stayed in the closet, never indicating their sexual orientation. Now Bauman, who had been part of the YR team that Rusher and White had built to take over the Republican party in 1964, was charged with sexually soliciting a sixteen-year-old boy in downtown Washington. He was then serving his seventh year representing Maryland's Eastern Shore congressional district. Tactician of the Goldwater Young Republicans and a founder of the militantly conservative Young Americans for Freedom whose first executive director was Viguerie, Bauman had long been an important far-right leader. At the time of his arrest, he was chairman of the American Conservative Union, one of the mainstay organizations founded after 1964 to provide an ideological home for Goldwater's followers.

With the New Right's rise in the mid-seventies, the ACU's policy pronouncements became laced with misogynist invective, and Bauman, a married Catholic with four children, became one of the New Right's most virulent attackers of the women's movement. He fashioned the legislative strategy for the anti-choice movement and was credited with writing the Hyde Amendment. Such a loyal advocate for the movement was he that even after his arrest, the Maryland Right to Life Committee endorsed him for reelection. The committee's PAC chairman, Gerald Meyer, had said: "You're talking here about a personal act. . . . For me personally, the sexual orientation perhaps is a little disturbing. But this action certainly has no bearing on his office." It was a while before those in the anti-choice movement would distance themselves from Meyer's line.

But Bauman's homosexuality was much more complicated for the Protestant Christian Right than for the anti-choice movement as such. His difficulties underscored just how fragile was the alliance between the Religious Right and the New Right. Bauman had been a major force in linking the New Right with the Moral Majority and the Christian Voice. It was Bauman's strategic political acumen that had helped the Moral Majority defeat Alabama Republican John Buchanan, a sixteen-year House veteran, in the 1980 Republican primary.

The campaign against Buchanan was unusually dirty by any standards. Buchanan's opponent, a former member of the John Birch Society, claimed to be the only true Christian candidate. Buchanan, a former Baptist preacher, was outraged that anyone would claim that there was only one acceptable Christian position on political issues. He warned at the time of his defeat, "We need to be very careful about this confusing of political issues with what is moral and Christian." This was precisely Bauman's problem with his Protestant Right friends. One of their most successful fund-raising appeals had been built around making crude attacks on homosexuals. For them, homosexuality was against God's will and the Bible. Religious Rightists could not be as forgiving as could those New Rightists whose political venom was generally directed at feminists rather than gays.

The charges against Bauman were dropped after he pleaded acute alcoholism and agreed to enter a court-supervised alcoholism rehabilitation program. Bauman lost his seat in Congress, eventually came to terms with his homosexuality, was divorced from his wife; and along with other New Right gay friends, he started the gay Republican movement. Now his candor unnerved many of his old political allies. Under pressure, he resigned the ACU chairmanship. Falwell and Weyrich deserted him as "no longer a credible spokesman" for conservative causes. His sexual unmasking initiated a split within the New Right that would have ramifications beyond Bauman's own personal difficulties.

Some of the closet gays within the New Majoritarian coalition began to have second thoughts about their attacks on the pro-choice movement and its belief in a woman's right to privacy, realizing that their attacks against a woman's freedom were fueling attacks against gays and lesbians. Although their goals were very different, the feminist and gay movements both sought individual freedom for all people. Just as a misogynist policy that turned over reproductive rights decisions to the government was anathema to traditional Republican beliefs, so was a homophobic policy that encouraged the government to punish people for their sexual orientation.

AIDS was the catalyst that finally opened the split within the New Right between the libertarians and the more authoritarian moralists like Weyrich and Schlafly. It was AIDS that brought about a more tolerant policy toward gays within the party. When Kemp's campaign collapsed, many of the libertarians on his team shifted to Bush. In late June Bush embraced some of the recommendations of a presidential advisory commission for legislation and other federal measures to help AIDS victims. As he had done with child care, Bush carved out a policy different from that of Reagan, who had taken no official stand on either issue at that time.

Bush said "he supported the issuing of a presidential order to put in place voluntary guidelines barring discrimination against AIDS victims." Discrimination against carriers of AIDS "should not be seen as a gay rights issue," but the disease must be understood in terms of its effects. He was not worried that antidiscrimination legislation would be the first step toward a national gay rights bill, he said, adding, "I don't think that's what is intended here at all; therefore it doesn't concern me. . . . We have a national health problem" and thus "a Federal responsibility." Pro-choice women and men were delighted that Bush had found a new tolerance, however limited. We couldn't help noticing that he had used the language of the women's movement—that reproductive matters should be viewed as a health matter, not a moral one—to justify his new AIDS policy. Bush took this stance, he said, because he abhorred "discrimination against innocent people." Unfortunately, his abhorrence didn't extend to discrimination against pregnant women.

It also didn't seem to cover minorities, women generally, the elderly, or the disabled, for he had already shown his willingness to accept discriminatory policies in civil rights. At first he wouldn't say how he stood, but then he backed Reagan's March 16 veto of the Civil Rights Restoration Act, which after four years of difficult negotiations in the Senate and House had finally reached the president's desk. Congress overrode the veto, but the votes necessary to override came only after a limitation on abortion rights, pushed by the National Conference of Catholic Bishops, was placed in the bill.

At the subcommittee hearings on the AIDS plank, Congressmember William Dannemeyer of California had delivered testimony excoriating AIDS victims, proposing inhumane restrictions on their liberties so they didn't "spread the disease." For several years Dannemeyer had been carrying on a crusade against homosexuals, sloganeering that "God created Adam and Eve, not Adam and Steve," and making the preposterous claim that AIDS victims release "spores" that cause birth defects.

Deborah Steelman, who was covering the AIDS plank hearings for the Bush campaign and reporting back to Charlie Black, told me that Black was particularly concerned that none of Dannemeyer's hateful language get into the platform. At the full platform hearings, working with a few New Right libertarian operatives, she succeeded in keeping ugly homophobic wording out of the platform and putting in its place a sensible plank on AIDS. It pleased all of us who sought an equitable and humane policy for every American.

But for women, that kind of policy still had a long way to go. I didn't know what history lay behind Bush's decision on AIDS policy, but its political context was a familiar one. Once again, as in 1976 and 1980, women's rights had been traded. In this case, the New Right libertarians got protection for AIDS victims, while the Religious Right got its anti-abortion and school prayer planks. Until feminist women had a more influential place within the party's inner circle or were able to build a political force that outweighed the misogynists' influence, we were not going to overcome the party's official anti-women policies. To put it bluntly, in New Orleans the New Right libertarians were more powerful than the Bush political women.

Very much aware of the importance of attracting women to Bush, and taking the spring women's focus group ideas to heart, the Bush campaign had a "counterfeminist" strategy in place during convention week. It scheduled an unusual joint press interview with George and Barbara Bush. They allowed their WASP reserve to be pierced for a moment when they briefly held hands for the cameras. But the campaign didn't have to fabricate a loving family-man image of its candidate—George Bush was the genuine article. The entire family, with all its photogenic grandchildren, were a welcome presence in New Orleans, and a dramatic contrast to the nontraditional families that now constituted the majority of the nation's domestic households. (As we looked at the assembled Bushes, it was not lost on us that the administration's policies had an especially harsh impact on families unlike theirs.)

Forty percent of the convention's speakers were women, and wherever Bush went, women accompanied him. Lynn Martin could be found telling any group of women who'd listen what a caring president he would be, and citing the child care proposal as the best proof of how he'd changed. His surrogates made no mention of the ERA or *Grove City*, or issues of pay equity, family and medical leave, and reproductive health rights. George Bush would treat women fairly once he was in the White House—that was what we heard whenever our anger over the platform threatened to get the best of us. We were all playing make-believe.

The convention program had been tightly orchestrated by South Carolinian Fred Malek, who had distinguished himself during the Nixon years by his coldly efficient technique of firing people and by his ability to construct lists of unacceptable people for the president's eyes only. At this convention Malek sought a picture-perfect performance for the television audience—no spontaneity would be allowed. Black had been specific: "We don't want any floor fights," he said. "We've asked people, regardless of how they felt on issues, not to take anything to the floor."

Now that the platform was sewn up, the only significant decision left unresolved was Bush's vice-presidential choice. Moderate pro-choice New Jersey governor Tom Kean had been given the keynote spot, but any chance that Bush would pick him faded when the New Right and Religious Right proclaimed his unsuitability to continue the Reagan revolution. When Kean's selection as keynoter was announced, New Right senator Gordon Humphrey had threatened to walk out during the speech unless convention officials offered equal time to a speaker from the anti-abortion movement. Humphrey also said he wanted "assurances from Mr. Bush that any running mate he chooses would 'enthusiastically' embrace the right-to-life plank."

Humphrey got his equal-time demand. On Monday night the delegates heard from Kay James, public affairs director of the National Right to Life Committee. They also listened to Barry Goldwater, Elizabeth Dole, Jack Kemp, and Ronald Reagan, then went to New Orleans's great restaurants and jazz bars to reminisce about the Reagan years and speculate about who Bush's running mate might be. Kemp had given a rousing speech and, except for Reagan, had received the most enthusiastic response. He had an impressive, well-managed convention operation. He might not have been able to win delegates in the field, but his team could certainly organize conventions. That night Kemp seemed to be everyone's first choice, with Dole a close second. New Right senator J. Danforth Quayle of Indiana, who had done the rounds of the caucuses on Sunday night, was the dark horse contender. He'd visited the New York delegation, but none of us had found him impressive. We called him young, weightless, and pleasant. For my part, I found him all of these things and glib as well. I hoped his visit wasn't an indication that this anti-choice baby boomer would be Bush's choice.

On Tuesday, at noon, the NWPC held a panel discussion at which I said that although many Republican women found the platform's commitment to fetal rights unacceptable, we would limit our resentment and campaign for the ticket—unless Bush chose Kemp or Quayle. One hour later, Bush announced for Quayle. After the shock wore off and our anger subsided, my feminist friends and I acknowledged what had happened: Bush had been afraid to cross the Religious Right. Quayle was one of theirs. But it was also a twofer. By choosing him, Bush had also placated the New Right authoritarians.

The press and too many of our colleagues may also have been right when they said Quayle had been chosen for his good looks; apparently that was the way to appeal to women voters, according to the Bush high command. All our consciousness-raising with these Republican men had done little to change their perception of women. We remembered a famous comment made by a Republican state chairman when handsome Phil Crane had announced his race for president in 1979: "Phil is a cinch to get nominated because every woman will want to sleep with him." Apparently, they thought women were sheep who voted on the basis of a candidate's sex appeal. An informal poll of my state's women delegates turned up none who would vote for Quayle based on looks but several who devoutly hoped that nothing would ever happen to Bush. Quayle was simply too young, too dim, and too opposed to women's equality.

The next day Barbara Mosbacher and I flew home to New York. The plane was full of tired reporters and disappointed Kemp supporters who had decided they preferred to watch Bush's nominating speech from their living rooms. Barbara and I agreed.

The Bush political women had helped him win the nomination. They had helped raise his credibility with the nation's women, and on the night he accepted his party's nomination, it was a woman, speechwriter Peggy Noonan, who gave him the words that made him eloquent and reassuring. Noonan reached deep inside Bush's soul and found the "kinder, gentler" man who would bring his own personal vision to his country. (She also gave him the "Read my lips. No new taxes" pledge that would haunt him for years.)

> I'm a quiet man, but I hear the quiet people others don't. The ones who raise the family, pay the taxes, meet the mortgage. I hear them, and I am moved. And their concerns are mine. . . . I will keep America moving forward, always forward, for a better America, for an endless, enduring dream, and a thousand points of light. This is my mission, and I will complete it.

For those minutes of his acceptance speech, Bush was no longer in Reagan's shadow. It was the pinnacle of his long pursuit of the presidency. But from that moment on, his briefly articulated vision vanished, lost in one of the dirtiest presidential campaigns in modern American history. The grand themes disappeared. The image of a kinder, gentler America was replaced with questions of who was more patriotic—who loved the American flag more and respected the pledge of allegiance—and who would be the harshest on black murderers like Willie Horton. It was a campaign that besmirched the values symbolized by the flag Bush claimed to be protecting against the Democrats, who purportedly didn't love their country well enough.

New Orleans is a city of superb food, lively music, and an exoticism that can entice even the most staid. The delegates who had enjoyed its gifts during convention week were far less diverse than those who had nominated Ronald Reagan four years before. Two-thirds were white Protestant men, and almost three-quarters had incomes over $50,000 a year. There were fewer women, fewer Jews, and fewer minorities than in 1984. They mirrored the essential elements of the New Majoritarian coalition with one important exception: The blue-collar Reagan Democrats—the populists that the New Right were always championing—were even more poorly represented than women in the party's decision-making circles. After the convention, having no natural organizational base among this group—the Teamsters were the only large blue-collar union backing the Republicans—Bush's campaign turned to social issues to attract these Democrats away from their New Deal home. Michael Dukakis had an ethnic appeal. George Bush had to rely on social issues, and the campaign knew it.

Even before Bush was nominated, the G6 decided that Bush must destroy Dukakis's credibility and cut his large lead in the polls, which in July, before the Republican convention, was 17 points. It was important to get this effort under way before the fall campaign began. With the help of Bush research director Jim Pinkerton and a series of New Jersey focus groups, they devised a negative campaign strategy centered on a Massachusetts prisoner-furlough program, one that Republicans had started, and a Dukakis veto of a mandatory pledge-of-allegiance bill. An abuse of this furlough program had led to the release of murderer Willie Horton, who on a weekend pass had brutally raped a woman and stabbed her fiancé.

Even before New Orleans, Bush went on the attack with pit-bull ferocity. He accused Dukakis of letting "murderers out on vacation to terrorize innocent people" and charged that "Democrats can't find it in their hearts to get tough on criminals." In a fatal mistake, Dukakis decided to ignore Bush's charges rather than answer them. Too many voters began to believe that Dukakis was a man who let murderers out of jail to hurt women. The Republican strategy was working. A week before the convention, Bush pulled ahead of Dukakis. Only once during the rest of the campaign did Dukakis even come near to closing the gap,

and that was after the first debate on September 25. The issue that was
to trip Bush up in that debate was the same one that continually
haunted him: Who determines when and how a woman shall have a
child?

George Bush was always awkward when it came to questions about
sex and women's reproduction, an awkwardness that was exacerbated
by his need to balance the pressures coming from various elements of
the coalition. To placate the Religious Right, for example, his Washington campaign headquarters circulated a family-planning statement using a quote from the pope. The statement said: "I am against supplying
birth control aids to minors without parental consent. As I said to Pope
John Paul II, 'Our land is built on freedom—but as you taught, freedom develops best if it keeps to the rules of morality.' We must teach
our children the difference between right and wrong, . . . in our
homes, in our churches, and in our schools."

Working at cross-purposes with his own campaign, Bush vehemently defended his opposition to legal abortion while the campaign
tried to keep the issue quiet. But even without Bush, the issue would
not have gone undiscussed. Justice Harry Blackmun, a Nixon appointee
to the Supreme Court and the author of the *Roe* decision, had warned
in a speech to law students that legal abortion "might go down the
drain." Pro-choice advocates knew that three of the four justices who
had voted for *Roe* would be over eighty by the time the next president
was sworn in; and this president's appointments to the Court would
determine the fate of women's childbearing choices.

Nothing in Bush's record indicated that he would fail to honor his
commitment in the GOP platform to appoint judges to the Supreme
Court who would follow the Religious Right's line. Equally ominous, he
could be expected to appoint young conservatives to all levels of the
federal judiciary who would be true to the Meese view of constitutional
law. Those who said Bush would be less conservative in his appointments than Reagan hadn't been watching either him or the Republican
party over the last eight years. It was a disturbing judicial legacy we
were contemplating.

Abortion was at the center of that first presidential debate on September 25, in Winston-Salem, North Carolina, at a point when the polls
were reporting that Bush had a lead of only about 5 points. Dukakis
was aggressive and focused, and Bush stumbled several times, most

egregiously over a question about abortion. If abortions were made illegal as he wished, said the questioner, did Bush "think the women who defy the law and have them anyway, as they did before it was okayed by the Supreme Court, and the doctors who perform them, should go to jail?" Bush squirmed, looked embarrassed, and sounded like a man exasperated at having to discuss a subject of such unimportance. "I haven't sorted out the penalties, but I do know—I do know—that I oppose abortion, and I favor adoption," he answered. ". . . I'm for the sanctity of life, and once that illegality is established, then we can come to grips with the penalty side, and of course there's got to be some penalties to enforce the law, whatever they may be."

He knew he had said something wrong, but he didn't seem to know what. "You deserve what you're going to get," I thought as I watched. Why was it taking him so much longer to become knowledgeable about the abortion issue than about the intricacies of the Massachusetts prisoner-furlough law? Or maybe he understood it perfectly but was too unnerved to speak coherently.

Dukakis let him have it:

> I think what the vice president is saying is that he's prepared to brand a woman a criminal for making this decision. It's as simple as that. I don't think it's enough to come before the American people . . . and say, "Well, I haven't sorted it out." This is a very, very difficult and fundamental decision that all of us have to make.

A knockout.

Next day Jim Baker tried to pick up the pieces, but he wasn't much help. Women shouldn't be punished for having illegal abortions, Baker said, but doctors should. Now the doctors had become the villains. The American Medical Association said that many years ago "it was ethically acceptable for a physician to perform an abortion as long as it conformed to medical and legal standards." Now, it said, it "wouldn't offer an opinion of what would happen if the legality changed."

The reaction to Bush's ineptness came at once. His lead in the polls dropped until he was tied with Dukakis. Most Americans the press interviewed after the debate wondered how a presidential candidate, a man who'd spent his life in the public's eye, who said he had made a "moral" decision to oppose abortion, hadn't "sorted out" the ramifications of making it illegal.

During the rest of the campaign, no matter how many times Bush and Baker professed that a woman in such a situation was "a second victim" who needed to be helped and loved and not punished, they would not concede that having an abortion was her decision to make. Bush might not have stumbled quite so badly in North Carolina if he'd known a few facts. In 1958, when abortion was illegal, "eighteen states had penalties for women who survived an illegal abortion; as late as 1972 . . . fifteen states made performing abortion a crime and eleven states made the woman a criminal. In nine, it was illegal to aid or counsel a woman to have an abortion."

I agreed with columnist Michael Kinsley, who wrote after the debate:

It's tempting to ask what it says about Bush that he has been opining about abortion all these years without having even thought of one of the central questions the issue raises. But what this says about Bush's mental capacity or reflectiveness is less important than what it says about the Reaganization of American politics: the fleeing by politicians of all stripes (Dukakis, too) from any suggestion that any policy on any subject has any undesirable consequences whatsoever. We can spend without paying, go to war without killing or dying, criminalize abortion without making women criminals.

The Dukakis spurt in the polls proved to be brief. The Republicans had succeeded in making him appear to many voters to be "soft on crime" and "uninformed and inexperienced" on national defense. But issues of security weren't of primary concern to women in 1988. Economic ones were. The Reagan boom years for the well-to-do had not brought prosperity to all. Women had been particularly hard hit. Dukakis had enjoyed an advantage with women back in the spring, based on their belief that his election would help them economically. They were working more and putting in long hours for less pay than men. "Two-thirds of women in the labor force with pre-school children" were "either the family's only wage earner" or were "contributing to a yearly family income of $15,000 or less."

But by the fall, Dukakis had failed to convince women that the economy would be better and their situation improved if he became president. His campaign had paid very little attention to such issues; not until the last two weeks before the election did it emphasize jobs and the economy. By then, it was too late. Women had already decided that matters were likely to worsen under the Democrats. They shifted to Bush. It was better to stick with what you knew than take a chance on what you didn't know.

The only other issue Democrats could use to bring women back into their fold was reproductive rights, but they failed to exploit the gift Bush had given them in North Carolina, and the subject faded from attention. Still, the Republicans sought to prove that Dukakis's professed concern for women, despite the Democratic party's more admirable record and women's issues platform, was a sham.

In a political campaign, it is always the unexpected, the incident that no one anticipated, that can make or break the election. Bush's mistake in North Carolina had been a stupid one. He could easily have anticipated a question on abortion and its ramifications. He'd been lucky that Dukakis had decided not to make abortion an issue.

In the second debate, at the UCLA campus on October 13, it was Dukakis who blew it. The first question CNN anchorman Bernard Shaw asked him was: "If Kitty Dukakis were raped and murdered, would you favor an irrevocable death penalty for the killer?" The audience gasped audibly. The question demanded an emotionally angry answer. It struck a primordial nerve—a man protects his beloved against the forces of evil. It tested the most fundamental elements of a man's role—the inviolability of his wife, the protection of his home, the declaration of his love and loyalty to his family. Dukakis failed the test. Michael Dukakis, a man deeply in love with his wife, Kitty, was emotionally inert during the debate. He showed no rage at the horror Shaw described. As though he were analyzing the finer points in a zoning law, he stated tonelessly that he had "opposed the death penalty during all my life." He said he had fought crime in Massachusetts. He never mentioned Kitty. He never acknowledged what he must have been feeling—the disgust, the revulsion—at what Shaw had said.

The nation reacted immediately and virtually unanimously. If this guy didn't have the guts to get mad over a question like that, he was just too cold to be president. The campaign was over. First there had been

Willie Horton, then the pledge of allegiance, and now this. The men had already been won over, and now those women who had still felt uneasy joined them.

Bush won 426 electoral votes to 111 for Dukakis. He won nearly 54 percent of the popular vote: 48 million votes to Dukakis's 41 million. The New Majoritarian coalition had held. Bush won all the southern and border states; the West except for Oregon, Washington, and Hawaii; and most of the Midwest and Northeast, except for Iowa, Minnesota, Wisconsin, Massachusetts, Rhode Island, and New York. The Reagan Democrats, the Religious Right, the old-line conservatives, the New Right, and the moderates had stuck together. The victory mirrored those of Reagan. Where Reagan had done well, Bush did too, though with smaller margins.

Electing Bush had been a political tour de force for Lee Atwater, Roger Ailes, Bob Teeter, Jim Baker, and the rest of the Bush high command. But it had been won at a terrible cost. The pit-bull mentality that had governed the campaign—its exploitation of bigotry, its demeaning of Dukakis's honor, its questioning of the patriotism of those who called themselves something other than conservatives, its belittling of the economic yearnings of women and minorities—had made it, most experts agreed, the most destructive presidential campaign in the twentieth century.

In mid-July Bush had been trailing by 17 points. It was the campaign's skillful playing on fear that gave him the victory. A comprehensive interpretation of the election published in 1989 noted, "The victory was broad but shallow. Almost half of the Republican ticket's electoral votes came from states in which a switch of no more than one in ten would have thrown the state into the Democratic column. In such a hypothetical change, Dukakis would have won the election with 313 electoral votes."

In conserving the Reagan Republican inheritance, Bush had gravely damaged the nation. The great issues of peace and prosperity had been shunted aside for deliberately divisive issues that separated Americans in twisted ways. Not since the days of the Vietnam War had we been more fragmented. Yet our new president and his young inexperienced vice president seemed unaware of what they had done.

Men gave Bush 56 percent to 44 percent for Dukakis. The women had come around and voted for Bush, giving him 52 percent to

Dukakis's 48 percent, but their vote had not been enthusiastic. They found neither option very satisfactory.

Throughout the campaign, women and their issues had been unwanted stepchildren that both candidates tried to ignore. In the Republican party, despite the many talented women in the campaign, women were marginalized and manipulated, and the Republican platform remained committed to policies to end affirmative action, to reject meaningful child care programs, to downplay unpaid family leave, to destroy reproductive rights, and to eliminate any effective action that expanded the party beyond its conservative base. The Democrats were only slightly better: Their leadership was also too afraid of alienating men to come forth with a campaign strategy of inclusion.

Still, we decided in the end, better Bush than Dukakis, who simply did not seem up to the task. We hoped for a kinder, gentler Bush who might steer a different course from Reagan, even though the excesses of the campaign and the convention were not encouraging. Still, I found I had no inclination to cheer. I was afraid of what Bush's victory might mean.

15

Pro-Choicers Fight Back

"I know there are people of goodwill who disagree, but after years of sober and serious reflection on the issue . . . I think the Supreme Court's decision in *Roe v. Wade* was wrong and should be overturned." So said George Bush to 65,000 right-to-life marchers on his third day as President of the United States.

This wasn't a man who was seeking to unify the country after a political campaign that had distinguished itself by its divisive tactics. This was a man who knew exactly how he'd gotten elected and was signaling to his political allies that he hadn't forgotten them. As for those others who had also helped—the pro-choice Republicans—he took them for granted. The pro-choice people, the Bush operatives acknowledged, weren't as difficult as the right. You could talk to them. You could reason with them. You could co-opt them. There was no need for Bush to go to their rallies or meet with them in private.

Well, something happened to many of those reasonable people. We'd had enough. You can argue that we should have seen it coming. In fact, in many ways we had seen it but chose not to face it. There were many signs in 1988—the party's unwillingness to give women equal protection with the fetus, the selection of Quayle, Bush's choice of Lee Atwater to be RNC chairman, Bauer's orchestrated attacks against women's rights, and the continuing process of appointing to the federal courts judges, chiefly men, who were, in the words of conservative legal scholar Bruce Fein, bringing about "a seismic change" that was "steering the courts sharply rightward." As the executive director of the National Right to Life Committee observed, "Having the chief executive of the leading nation in the world work with us to keep the federal government out of the abortion business has been very important."

The problem was that the chief executive of the leading nation in the world wasn't keeping government out of the abortion business— quite the reverse. Instead, he and his predecessor instituted policies to ensure that the government would be even more involved in women's pregnancies and private lives than before. People might have the constitutional freedoms of speech and assembly and the right to bear arms in the America of Reagan and Bush, but regardless of *Roe*, women would have no fundamental right to reproductive choice.

The election of George Bush started the process of setting free many of the women and men who had supported him, exorcising the loyalties of a lifetime. These people had paid their debt of friendship to him. They'd raised money for his campaigns and contributed their own. They'd worked the precincts, and they'd spoken up for their friend George when he had embarrassed them with his "lapses" on women's rights and his pledge of allegiance, racism, and patriotism ploys. Now he was in the White House, and on the third day of his presidency, he had delivered a wake-up call to his not-so-happy friends.

Bush's statement to the marchers on January 23, 1989, made it clear he wasn't going to change course. In fact, he was even more intent than Reagan had been to see the adoption of the right's social agenda. Bauer left the White House, but autocratic New Right ideologue John Sununu became White House chief of staff, the president having forsaken the long-loyal Craig Fuller, who had been his vice-presidential chief of staff. Bush reappointed Reagan's attorney general, Richard Thornburgh. Thornburgh, whom some considered a moderate on other issues, was strongly anti-choice and promptly enlisted the Justice Department in efforts to make abortion illegal. When the president named pro-choice Dr. Louis Sullivan to be secretary of health and human services, the right rose up and threatened to stop the appointment unless Bush guaranteed, in Heckler style, that Sullivan's aides would be anti-choice. The Bush advisers agreed, thus ensuring right-wing operating control over the department's women's health policies.

Applicants for high-level appointments were subtly subjected to a litmus test on abortion. Those who were pro-choice were placed where they couldn't affect reproductive health policy. The bright insider women from the Bush campaign were rewarded with appointments only in areas that the right found uncontroversial. Carla Hills became U.S. trade representative and Elizabeth Dole secretary of labor. The Baker women went to the State Department with him. There were some pro-choice women spread around the government departments, but none were in a position to support the efforts of pro-choice Republicans outside Washington, with the possible exception of Bobbie Kilberg. Kilberg took over the community-outreach job in the White House— the post once held by Elizabeth Dole and Faith Whittlesey—but she never did reach out to us during the siege by the anti-abortion forces during the Bush years. She too was under constant scrutiny from the right, who knew her feminist roots.

In 1988, aided by the White House, the right-to-life movement began a major assault on legal abortion. The battle was fought in Congress over court appointments, family-planning monies, and restrictions on family-planning clinics, but it extended far beyond the Hill. In late 1987 thirty-year-old Randall Terry had organized Operation Rescue, a loose network of anti-choice people to blockade clinics that provided family-planning services and abortion. Although it was not a membership organization, Terry traveled America organizing demonstrations and raising the level of acrimony and hate over abortion beyond what it had been in the previous decade. Incidents of arson, bombing, and burglary of these facilities increased so dramatically that the Bureau of Alcohol, Tobacco and Firearms was given additional money from Congress to investigate them. Terry was never charged with any of these crimes but at various times went to jail for harassing and disorderly conduct.

He had first come to national attention during the Democratic convention in Atlanta, when he and his followers were jailed for disorderly conduct in blockading clinics. He appealed for funds to pay his legal bills, and in a widely publicized gesture, Jerry Falwell gave him $10,000 to help out.

During the fall campaign, Terry and his ally, Joseph Scheidler of the much older Pro-Life Action League, had stalked the Dukakis campaign, spreading chaos wherever they went. Bush's victory energized them to still greater verbal fanaticism but Terry didn't engage in nonverbal violent acts himself. He spread his gospel through violent words. Speaking at Stanford University a week after Bush's victory, Terry announced that the election had proved that the country was opposed to abortion. He boasted about his twenty-five arrests in seven cities, and he shocked his audience by telling them that if a woman were raped, he'd have the man castrated and then shot. On a below-freezing day in December, he and his followers demonstrated outside the Planned Parenthood clinic in New York City, blocking the clinic's opening for five hours. Members of the Republican Family Committee stood in the cold with hundreds of pro-choice women and men and listened to Terry harangue them as abusers and degraders of women.

We acted. I called pro-choice Republican women around the country to urge them to begin direct political action, and they started organizing. In New York we raised money for pro-choice Republicans. We protested. We wrote the White House. We asked, fruitlessly, for a meeting with the president or high-ranking staff. We called our friends in the administration. We talked to Mary Curley, who was now in Paris where her husband was serving as U.S. ambassador to France. She introduced Barbara Gimbel and Barbara Mosbacher to Étienne Émile Beaulieu, the inventor of the abortion pill RU 486, and they brought him to New York to give a lecture to the Republican Family Committee. He attracted a large crowd and helped us draw attention to the seriousness of the situation. We were speedily building a grassroots pro-choice force in the Republican party.

Republican women and men joined more than 300,000 pro-choice demonstrators in a March for Women's Lives in Washington on April 9, 1989. It was one of the largest marches there since the Vietnam moratorium rally in November 1969, and it would be topped only by another pro-choice march in 1992, which drew the biggest protest crowd in the nation's history—estimates of its size ranged from half a million to more than a million.

Polls showed that over two-thirds of Americans believed in women's right to choose: Republicans, Democrats, and independents. The White House appeared publicly not to be noticing the marches, the polls, or the blockading and firebombing of women's health facilities, although privately Sununu's office was carefully keeping track.

On April 26, 1989, the Supreme Court heard oral arguments in *Webster v. Reproductive Health Services.* The crux of this case was the legality of a Missouri law that restricted abortion by declaring that life begins at conception; outlawed the use of public facilities, funds, or employees for performing abortions; placed a gag rule on abortion counseling; and required doctors to perform fetal viability tests on women who were more than twenty weeks pregnant.

The case had been filed well before Bush took office. The Reagan administration had been instrumental in convincing the defendant, Missouri attorney general William Webster, to include the issue of over-ruling *Roe* in his brief. By the time of oral argument, both sides had been preparing for months. Bush's Justice Department also stressed overturning *Roe* in the amicus curiae brief it filed, urging that the Supreme Court validate the challenged Missouri law. In fact, according to a detailed account of the case in *Ms.* magazine, an unprecedented seventy-eight amicus briefs were filed, forty-five in support of Missouri's restrictive law and thirty-three for the pro-choice position. The anti-choice briefs, the article noted, were submitted by a comparatively limited range of groups—primarily Catholic or fundamentalist religious and anti-abortion organizations. The pro-choice briefs came from a broad range of groups, representing every major sector of American society. One of those filing was the New York State Republican Family Committee.

More than two hundred Justice Department lawyers protested the Bush administration's brief against *Roe*. Attorney General Thornburgh ignored them. He called in Charles Fried, the solicitor general under Reagan, to finish the job of arguing the anti-choice position that Fried had developed in the waning days of Reagan's second term.

Fried claimed that the Court's 1965 *Griswold* decision was justified not on the basis of a right to privacy (as the Court had concluded when it overturned a Connecticut law banning the sale of contraceptives to married couples) but because it involved "a very violent [intrusion] . . . into the details of marital intimacy." Abortion was not covered under such a right, he argued, because it involved terminating fetal life, and the state had a primary interest in protecting life. Fried sidestepped the *Griswold* determination that a constitutional right to privacy exists and that the government should not interfere in people's most private personal decisions. Frank Susman, the lead attorney for the pro-choice side, called Fried's arguments "somewhat disingenuous" and cited the well-known due-process 1937 *Palko* decision, which found that "procreational interests are indeed implicit in the concept of ordered liberty, and neither liberty nor justice would exist without them."

On July 3 the Supreme Court ruled 5 to 4 that the Missouri law was constitutional. The decision upheld the state's right to refuse the use of public funds and facilities for abortion services, to test for fetal viability, and to impose gag rules in family-planning counseling. The justices passed on the crucial question of when life begins.

The Court had narrowed women's right to abortion. *Webster* gave individual states the right to put roadblocks and restrictions on women's choice, not in the third trimester as *Roe* had allowed, but at any time the state wished, as long as it fit within the *Webster* framework. Justice O'Connor was the crucial fifth vote. In her concurring opinion, however, she tried to balance the state's interest in the fetus with the rights of the woman. The determining factor, she posited, was whether the state's restrictions placed an "undue burden on a woman's abortion decision." Justice Scalia, who wished to throw out *Roe,* ridiculed O'Connor's "undue burden" standard and implied that in not agreeing with him, she had been irrational.

The *Webster* decision meant that women no longer had a fundamental constitutional right to an abortion protected by the federal government. The battle for choice would continue in Congress (and in the courts), but now the states had been given an opportunity to experiment with their own interpretations of the constraints imposed by *Roe.* On November 18, Pennsylvania would pass the Abortion Control Act, which mandated that a woman notify her husband before she has an abortion, ordered that she be given state-published abortion information and wait twenty-four hours between her request for an abortion and the procedure itself, and required that a parent accompany a minor to an abortion provider to give consent. Other states, among them Utah and Louisiana, were also moving toward the passage of strong anti-abortion laws.

The abortion issue preoccupied pro-choice Republicans throughout the summer and fall of 1989. Polls consistently showed that they were as strongly pro-choice as Democrats. A late July CBS News/*New York Times* poll indicated that 65 percent of Republicans and 64 percent of Democrats agreed that if a woman wanted an abortion and the doctor agreed, she should be allowed to have it. When asked what they thought about the statement, "Even when I might think abortion is wrong, the government has no business preventing a woman from having an abortion," 67 percent of Republicans and 71 percent of Democrats agreed with it. The national Republican party's stand did not reflect what the American people believed. Pro-choice Republicans started assessing candidates who would be running for state offices in November and began action to run primary challengers against anti-choice incumbents.

Two legislative races in particular drew the attention of pro-choice Republicans. We sent advice and money to both. Tricia Hunter, a registered nurse, ran in a multicandidate GOP open primary on August 9 for a seat in the California State Assembly. She was the only abortion rights advocate and won by fewer than two hundred votes. Hers was the first electoral confrontation over abortion since *Webster,* and it drew considerable press attention. We thought it fitting that the first test had come in a contest between pro- and anti-choice Republicans. Hunter went on to win in the general election in November.

In South Carolina, Holly Cork ran for an assembly seat vacated by her father's death. Running in a three-way GOP primary on August 22 as the only pro-choice candidate, she faced two male challengers. One had an "evolving" position on choice, and the other, a key Robertson follower, believed abortion should be illegal and proclaimed "it's going to take men to" deal with the abortion issue "who are willing to stand the heat in the furnace." Cork won with 40 percent of the vote, forcing a run-off, and in November she became the second pro-choice Republican woman in the country to be elected because of her stand. It did not escape us that this had taken place in the home state of RNC chairman Atwater.

In New York City, immediately after the *Webster* decision, the Republican Family Committee met with Republican mayoral candidate Rudolph Giuliani, who had spent the initial months of his campaign waffling on choice. We had had a long, sometimes strained relationship with Giuliani because we had never been able to convince him of the importance of the issue. In the past, he had told us he was pro-choice but didn't like the *Roe* decision because he believed it was poorly reasoned. On the question of public funding for abortion services, one of the central issues in *Webster,* he had equivocated.

We wanted to work for Giuliani's campaign, but we wouldn't if he didn't commit fully to choice. As we sixteen women sat around a large table in his campaign headquarters waiting for him, we pretty much decided he wasn't going to take a stand and that this would be our last meeting with him. When he finally arrived, all our pent-up frustration that had been building since the New Orleans convention burst forth. After forty-five minutes of heated give-and-take, he surprised us. He said he unequivocally supported *Roe*, although he still held to his original judgment that the case had been decided on shaky legal grounds; and that as mayor he would back funding for abortions for poor women and guarantee funding for them in the city if state and federal matching funds were dropped. He opposed the narrowing of *Roe*. He had changed. There was no vacillation. A Republican leader had finally gotten the point. From then on, he was a staunch champion of women's right to choose. His wife, Donna Hanover Giuliani, marched with us in Washington at the next March for Women's Lives, and they both became enthusiastic backers of our committee's work.

Unfortunately, Giuliani's conversion came too late to help him in this 1989 bid against Democrat David Dinkins, who was elected the city's first black mayor. The effects of Giuliani's earlier waffling persisted; too many voters didn't believe his pro-choice statement. Four years later, however, he ran for mayor again and won. Being pro-choice helped him. Polls showed that moderate and liberal women—convinced he was not going to follow the anti-choice policies of his national party —felt free to support him as a more competent alternative to Dinkins, who was widely regarded as likable but ineffectual.

Giuliani's case is an excellent example of the significance of abortion as a wedge issue. Poll after poll has consistently shown that with few exceptions abortion isn't a voter's priority issue, but that in close races it can determine the outcome. When faced with a difficult voting decision, voters often use their attitude on a wedge issue to make up their minds. That is why political analysts and politicians are wrong when they argue that women's issues are of low priority because they are seldom at the top of voters' preference lists. Few women are going to rank choice as a greater priority for the nation than peace and prosperity; but when they are uneasy about a candidate, a wedge issue like abortion rights can affect their decision.

Efforts similar to ours were taking place around the country. In Virginia pro-choice Democrat Douglas Wilder beat anti-choice Marshall Coleman by 6,741 votes—less than one percent—with the help of crossover votes from Republican suburban women, and became the first black governor since Reconstruction. In New Jersey a group of Republican women tried to convince Republican gubernatorial candidate Jim Courter to come out for choice, but he couldn't make a break from his solid anti-choice voting record. Near the end of his campaign, he issued a weak statement about being against government intrusion into individuals' personal lives, thereby implying he was pro-choice; but his straddling was transparent and did not persuade voters who were worried about the *Webster* decision and knew his history. He lost to Jim Florio with an astonishing 37 percent to Florio's 61 percent. Republican women crossed over in droves; Courter's gender gap was spectacular. Overall, Republicans across the nation did poorly on November 7, and Democrats won most of the top offices that were in contention.

The Republican party had an additional worry. The ten-year national census would take place in 1990, and new legislative lines would have to be drawn when the population figures came in. The stakes were high. To lose the midterm elections the following November would mean to lose control of the statehouses and legislatures that would draw the new lines. (A district's composition is determined by a careful balancing between Republican and Democratic legislators. The party in control will always draw the lines so that its registered party voters end up in districts that give it maximum electoral advantage. This practice of gerrymandering dates back to the beginning of American political parties. It started as soon as politicians figured out that they could use the census mandate to their advantage.)

Many Republicans who hadn't bothered to protest the gradual dominance of the right's social agenda in the national party now recognized that abortion might be the issue that could defeat them in local and state elections. For RNC Chairman Lee Atwater, a defeat for the Republicans in 1990 could spell the end of his dream to make the Republicans America's majority party.

But the president seemed oblivious to all this. Atwater described Bush's psychological problem with abortion to Michael Kramer of *Time*: "You know how he deals with it. . . . He doesn't. You mention abortion to the president and he stares at the floor, fiddles with his gloves, paces around the room, trots out some old story to change the subject. Those who need to talk to him about it check his mood closely.

If he's testy, you postpone the discussion—and since there's no surer way to make him testy than to mention abortion, most often those discussions never take place."

Eddie Mahe, the New Right Reagan strategist, predicted that "abortion will be the noisiest issue across the country in 1990" and foresaw that it would surface most frequently in Republican primaries. But in a September 1989 interview with David Frost on PBS, Bush showed either a lack of understanding or an unwillingness to acknowledge the problem, just as he had not wanted to face women's issues in the 1988 campaign. Those "women's problems," he said—in a view he shared with many men in the party's leadership—were just those of "radical feminists." Frost asked whether there was "any way to lower the temperature" on the abortion issue. Bush replied, "I don't think the temperature is any higher than it's been . . . what I have to do is speak out on the excess of demonstration, where you interfere with a person's constitutionally given rights of ingress and egress, or whatever it might be. And whatever side of the issue, these . . . the extreme demonstrations take place, certainly you try to have some respect for people that differ with me, but say what I think, and fight for what I believe. I was elected President of the United States."

While it could often be difficult to sort out Bush's ideas from his confused syntax, no one had difficulty in recognizing that he never mentioned the constitutionally protected right to abortion. He had avoided addressing abortion altogether. He was the president. He could "fight for what I believe." For him, it seemed enough.

More politically astute heads knew better. Sensing it was losing the political advantage, the National Right to Life Committee announced a plan to seek restrictive legislation in several states, centering on a measure outlawing abortion "as a means of birth control." This was not only a new tactic but a new threat. Was the state now to formulate the permissible reasons for a woman to have an abortion? Was the state to decide that a woman was using abortion for the purpose of birth control? If the anti-abortion movement had its way, the equivalent of thought police would have to be posted everywhere abortions were performed to determine whether a woman who wished to abort was breaking the law.

Bush kept right on helping the National Right to Life Committee, this latest plan apparently holding no horror for him. The anti-choice climate on the Hill had become less strident, with the House and Senate slightly easing their anti-abortion position, but the climate at the White House had just gotten worse. The man who had said that in a constitutional ban on abortions he would make an exception for rape and incest victims, then vetoed legislation that would have permitted federal funding for abortions for women who were rape or incest victims.

In the House debate to override the veto, one of the leaders of the anti-choice faction, New Jersey Republican Chris Smith, stated that Bush was afraid women might lie about being raped in order to collect the federal money. Maryland Democrat Steny Hoyer underscored the president's hypocrisy. "God was gracious and Willie Horton did not impregnate that woman he raped in Maryland," said Hoyer. ". . . But if he had, which one of us would have stood in front of her and said, 'Carry Willie Horton's baby to term'?"

In all, Bush vetoed four pro-choice bills in 1989, including one that would lift the ban on funding family-planning programs for the UN Fund for Population Activities, and another that would have allowed the District of Columbia government to spend its locally raised tax money to pay for abortions for rape and incest victims.

Twelve Republican women sat in the House; eight of them were pro-choice. For the first time on a women's issue, the eight stood together publicly against their party's president. On October 25—thirteen days before the fall election—they voted to override Bush's veto rejecting federal funding for abortions for rape and incest victims. They were incensed at the administration's heartlessness. Nancy Johnson labeled the legislation "deeply, profoundly inhumane and unjust." Marge Roukema said it was hard to "go against your president on an issue as emotional as this," but wondered how a man of "great moral character" could "make such a harsh choice." But the veto override failed.

For those of us outside Washington, their bravery was heartwarming. We vowed to see that none of them were punished at the polls for taking a stand. I particularly remember that when I thanked Bush's good friend Lynn Martin for her vote, she wrote back with great emotion, "We try—we all try."

The White House seemed surprised at their audacity. But then came the disastrous election results, and a week later, for the first time in his presidency, Bush met with Republican pro-choice advocates. The meeting was not on his published schedule and was downplayed by his staff. Nevertheless, his planned fifteen-minute drop-in turned into a half-hour dialogue with Congressmembers Johnson, Roukema, Schneider, and Martin. Bush promised Schneider and Martin he'd participate in their 1990 U.S. Senate campaigns, but the women got nothing further except vague assurances that he would consider legislation that would give poor women the same rights as those who were economically better off. Predictably, the New Right objected as soon as they heard about the meeting. Having made a modest comeback from his financial problems, Richard Viguerie was cage-rattling again and now threatened Bush and the Republican national leadership. "If they want to go back to the days of 1960's and 1970's, when they didn't have a winning coalition and they were losing a lot more elections than they are now, then let them move to the left on issues of core importance to their base."

As 1990 arrived, however, the national mood lifted, thanks to spectacular events on the international front. Radical change was in the air. On November 9, 1989, the Berlin wall had fallen. The cold war was over, and three weeks later Bush had his first meeting with Soviet president Mikhail Gorbachev to map out new strategies for world peace. On December 20, U.S. troops successfully invaded Panama, causing its autocratic leader Manuel Noriega to surrender. By January, Bush's approval rating hit 79 percent, the highest for a president since the end of World War II. National pride had soared under his vigorous leadership on the international scene and was bolstered by good economic news at home, where the unemployment rate for the last quarter of 1989 was 5.3 percent, the same as when he had been elected.

Lee Atwater did not share in the exhilaration. He knew trouble lay ahead. The projected economic signs were not good. More jobs were being lost overseas even as unemployment at home was steady. Prices were beginning to rise, and the deficit, that legacy of the Reagan–Bush years, was growing larger. It would not be long before the White House and the Republicans on the Hill would have to deal with the downturning economy. *Webster* and the administration's intransigence had mobilized many pro-choice Republicans—old guard, moderate, and New

Right libertarians. Atwater recognized that if they actively rebelled, they could bring down the entire New Majoritarian house. He had to try to deflect the pro-choicers, to keep them from leaving the coalition.

There had already been one departure. Two days after the November election, the founders of the New York State Republican Family Committee broke with the party leadership. They told the press that after years of raising hundreds of thousands of dollars for the Republican party, they would no longer raise money for candidates opposed to abortion rights. They would form a PAC to fund only pro-choice Republicans and would help those willing to challenge anti-choice Republican incumbents in primaries.

Theirs was a civil war. They weren't leaving the party. They weren't going to help Democrats. In fact, they had made their decision months before, but they waited until after the election to announce it in order not to interfere with Giuliani's mayoral campaign. They were the first, and they were very brave.

Right after the New Year, I wrote an op-ed piece, which appeared in newspapers across the country, stating why pro-choice Republicans could no longer go along with the administration. It was a declaration of independence. "How can the president claim to lead the party of less government," I asked, "while championing policies that make it the party of more government control? . . . We place freedom above party loyalty. We urge other Republicans to join us. Silence now will only help the cause we oppose."

Atwater got to work. First, he reintroduced the "big tent" concept that party leaders had been trotting out over the years whenever various factions were going at each other's throats. He told unhappy Republicans to "forget politics. Do and support what you truly, truly believe. We are an umbrella party."

But Atwater's tent was an illusion. There would be no new platform planks, we knew, and no feminists would be allowed into party decision-making posts. The leadership's only tangible gesture was a willingness to help elect pro-choice Republican women candidates when they were running against Democrats. That we saw in action in Illinois, when the indefatigable Henry Hyde endorsed Lynn Martin's candidacy for the U.S. Senate against incumbent Democrat Paul Simon. "Lynn Martin would no doubt vote for Supreme Court judges nominated by President Bush," said Hyde. "Simon has not done that . . . from that perspective, she's the better pro-life candidate." We were bemused: Lynn Martin a pro-life candidate?

Buffalo News cartoonist Tom Toles laid out the reality neatly in a cartoon showing a large, properly dressed elephant addressing a much smaller, nondescript woman. The elephant is saying, "I know you're pro-choice and our platform isn't. But you're still welcome in the GOP . . . to help us get elected and enact legislation to put an end to legal abortion in all cases without exception. We're big enough to accommodate you that way." We chose not to enter the tent.

Atwater's other tactic was ingenious and characteristic: He encouraged the formation of a pro-choice movement *within* the Republican party establishment—one that would answer to him. It would siphon money and volunteers from existing pro-choice Republican groups around the nation. Back before Labor Day in 1989, a group of pro-choice Republicans had formed the National Republican Coalition for Choice, with Mary Crisp as its head. Geared toward grassroots organizing, its official goal was a pro-choice Republican party. Its unstated goal was to break up the New Majoritarian Coalition. It was independent of Atwater and the RNC. Atwater's project, even though it would not be publicly affiliated with either him or the RNC, would have more legitimacy among New Right libertarians and the old guard than Crisp's organization, because she had opposed Reagan in 1980.

Even more important, it would be able to provide Atwater with intelligence on what the other pro-choice Republicans—and for that matter, the general pro-choice movement—were doing. If any of their activities looked as though they might interfere with his political plans, his own pro-choice group could sabotage them. Atwater's group would also undercut one of the most important tools in the pro-choice Republicans' arsenal—the running of pro-choice challengers against anti-choice incumbents in Republican primaries. Atwater and his friends did not want victories of bona fide pro-choice Republican officeholders, complete with their own independent power bases. That would loosen the New Right's control over the party. The whole approach was reminiscent of a government counterintelligence operation. Atwater would have made a first-rate CIA station chief.

He recruited Ann E. W. Stone, the soon-to-be former wife of his longtime political associate Roger Stone, to form this new pro-choice group. Atwater told her that the party would never change its anti-abortion position until a pro-choice leadership emerged out of the party's conservative wing, and that leader should be a woman. As Stone recalls, "Lee looked at me and said, 'Do we know anybody like that?' I said, 'I get the message.'"

Stone had started her political career in the Young Republicans, which was where she had first worked with Roger Stone. Viguerie had hired her away from her marketing-subscription job at *Human Events* to handle his clients, the National Rifle Association and the Gun Owners of America. In 1982 she set up her own direct-mail business. It was a lucrative arrangement, both as a venture in itself and for her husband's consulting firm. She provided his firm with names, the essential start-up fuel of political organizing, and in turn often got direct-mail fund-raising clients from the firm. In 1986 she participated in its international business—which included raising money for the Contras.

Ann Stone called her group Republicans for Choice, taking the name from the Planned Parenthood Republicans who had organized Republicans for Choice in 1982. She had not gotten permission to use the name, and the national Planned Parenthood was extremely upset by her action. After some negotiating, they worked out a compromise in which Stone placed a disclaimer on her printed material saying that her committee "is not a part of, or affiliated with, Planned Parenthood." But she was able to keep the name, which gave her an immediate advantage over Crisp's organization because Planned Parenthood's Republicans for Choice had a following and an identity. The confusion continues to this day and has caused unnecessary resentment among people who need to work together.

Just as Atwater must have anticipated, Stone's group had the effect of watering down the Republican pro-choice movement's united front. Initially we had hoped to work together despite Stone's history. Her early mailings had stated that her organization wanted to change the party platform, raise money for pro-choice candidates, and get the party to favor choice. These were our goals too. But within six weeks of her announcing her group in February, her fund-raising letters were modified in a major way. She had embraced the crucial point of not challenging anti-choice incumbents in primaries. She was obviously not interested in changing the power balance in the party. One letter said (with an overabundance of exclamation points) that "we do not intend to defeat sitting Republican incumbents! Even if they are anti-choice! It is not our desire to subtract from our great Party, but rather to add to it!" Her first priority was to identify pro-choice Republicans, build a donor base, "move the party on the issue, and then we concentrate on electing candidates."

We wanted no part of it. By the time Stone built her donor base, she'd be a little richer and there'd be fewer pro-choice Republican officeholders. This was no way to build a pro-choice movement. As Atwater must have conceived, it was a diversionary tactic directed at drawing our resources away from fighting the real enemy—the people in our party who had introduced and profited from the misogynist strategy.

In New York we decided that it was time for the state Republican party to get out from under the heavy cloud of the national party's misogyny. We knew we had a strong constituency; polls taken in December 1989 indicated that 92 percent of New Yorkers believed "a woman should decide about having an abortion in consultation with her doctor, not the government." The state party held eleven platform committee hearings across New York in the spring of 1990 in anticipation of the party's state nominating convention. Barbara Mosbacher and other members of the Republican Family Committee traveled the state, hearing testimony that indicated as much as a four-to-one preference for choice. The polls hadn't lied.

State Assemblymember George Pataki, who had volunteered to be the platform committee's chairman and had a straight anti-choice voting record, was surprised when at his committee's final meeting, fourteen of the seventeen members voted to include pro-choice language in the platform. He went along, and in late May the committee presented what it called a True Big Tent Plank to the state party convention. It was passed without debate. The right-to-life leaders in the party were asleep at the switch. Avid anti-choicer Joseph Mondello, who was leader of the state's largest Republican-voting county, Nassau, got up from his sickbed and stormed into the convention in a rage. For nearly an entire day, we argued behind closed doors over whether the passed platform should stay. When the dust settled, the plank stood, although the party's executive committee also passed a resolution stating that some Republicans had "strong and unwavering beliefs with respect to the sanctity of human life in all its stages." We considered this an acceptable compromise, since the party stood by its original vote.

It was the first time in the nation's history that a Republican party convention had approved a pro-choice plank in its platform. We were immensely proud of it and believed it could be a model for the national party. It was tolerant, respectful, and fairly represented the pro-choice position. In part, the plank said:

> Our nation and the Republican Party were founded on principles of individual liberty and religious freedoms. The Republican Party firmly believes in the concept of limited government and the right of privacy. State government must not become a "big brother," regulating people in their personal affairs and lives, and the New York State Republican Party reaffirms its historic commitment to the right of privacy and reproductive rights.
>
> We recognize that there are a variety of personal beliefs and opinions on the question of when life begins and that the United States Constitution and the Bill of Rights protect the right of Americans to hold differing views. We believe that the Republican party, like the nation, has proven strong enough to accommodate this diversity.

The passage of this plank drew national attention. Pro-choice Republicans called us for copies, and other states sought to pass similar ones. The Maine GOP quickly followed suit; so eventually did Vermont, New Hampshire, and Massachusetts. Once the national Republican leadership realized the positive impact the plank was having for the pro-choice side, however, and once the right-to-life forces made it clear they didn't want the New York phenomenon to spread, the word went out to other parts of the country that Bush did not look kindly on this kind of action. No one told the state parties not to pass such planks, even ones as mild as ours, and if anyone had, the states would have reacted angrily to being dictated to by Washington. Nevertheless, the word from the capital was: Cool it. Don't rock the boat over this abortion issue. Run pro-choice where you need to, but don't drag the state parties into these controversies.

·   ·   ·

On June 26, 1990, another crisis erupted that was as significant for the supply-siders and New Right people as *Webster* had been for those involved in the abortion fight. The predicted economic slowdown had hit; the administration's economic assumptions for its budget passed the previous year had been too optimistic, and the budget deficit was growing dangerously larger. The administration had two choices: either agree to harsh spending cuts or impose new taxes to cut the deficit. On that June day, Bush agreed with the Democratic congressional leaders to a deficit-reduction package that raised taxes.

He had done what the right had feared he would do—he'd gone back on his word on a sacred pillar of the Reagan revolution. He'd broken Peggy Noonan's "read my lips" pledge. By his action, he admitted that the debt the Reagan–Bush administration had saddled on the country was a disastrous mistake. Three days after his announcement, when asked whether he had really meant his campaign no-new-taxes pledge, he replied: "I can understand people saying that. . . . I think it's wrong. I'm presented with new facts. I'm doing like Lincoln did, think anew." (This was a reference to Lincoln's urging Congress to "think anew" about freeing the slaves.)

But Bush couldn't stand the heat that resulted from breaking his pledge. The supply-siders and the rest of the New Right wouldn't let go of the issue. Rather than stand up for his June 26 decision, he retreated; and to be certain that his right allies would not question his integrity again, he intensified his support for their social agenda. For Bush, the political damage had been done. Now not only the moderates but the New Right felt he was an opportunist who lacked a central core of beliefs.

Anger over Bush's broken tax pledge, combined with the pro-choice revolt, hurt Republicans in the 1990 midterm elections. The turnout of Republican voters for congressional races was among the lowest in history. Bush's approval rating among all voters dropped into the mid-50s. In all fourteen southern states, the Democrats won control of the governorships and both legislative houses. Across the nation, Democrats gained a slight edge in control of legislatures and state-houses. While voters kept telling pollsters how frustrated they were, they took their anger out chiefly on the governors rather than on Congress. Out of thirty-six states, fifteen governorships changed party hands.

There were three new Democratic women governors. Kansas became the only state in history to have a woman governor, senator, and congresswoman all at the same time. Ann Richards became the first woman governor of Texas elected in her own right because women gave her a 61 to 39 percent vote over her sexist Republican opponent Clayton Williams, with Republican women crossing party lines. In Massachusetts, pro-choice Republican William Weld was elected in a reverse situation, when Democratic women crossed over for him. A libertarian Republican who backed both women's rights and gay rights and was an environmentalist, Weld had won a bruising primary against a party-endorsed anti-choice candidate. It was one of the few places in the nation where the New Majoritarians were challenged in a primary and were defeated.

Immediately after the election, some analysts said the abortion issue was a wash and with a few exceptions had not had an impact on the outcomes. In a closely researched and reasoned op-ed article in *The New York Times*, Valerie Syme of the Abortion Report (a press service that provides news on abortion) and Doug Bailey of the Hotline (another press service providing political news) documented that the issue did have an impact. "Abortion decided more winners and losers than any other [issue]," they wrote. "It was not always the most debated or prominent issue . . . but it changed results by 5 percent or more, enough to decide any close race." They concluded that "the issue tends to have the greatest impact at the state level," that anti-choice voters tend to be more single-issue voters than pro-choicers, that "abortion is unlikely to be a decisive issue unless you have diametrically opposing views," and that no abortion position "is likely to matter much if the candidate is not otherwise qualified or competitive."

Pro-choice forces did even better than right-to-lifers, not only electing Ann Richards and Bill Weld with their crossover votes but defeating anti-choice Florida governor Bob Martinez, a Republican, and anti-choice Minnesota governor Rudy Perpich, a Democrat. Six gubernatorial winners, in Maine, California, Illinois, Vermont, Oregon, and Connecticut (four of whom were Republicans), would have lost their races if they had been anti-choice, Syme and Bailey determined. Pro-choice forces also defeated two anti-choice measures on Oregon's ballot and passed Nevada's pro-choice initiative.

In 1990 abortion had now become a large enough issue to pull voters, especially women, away from their focus on a candidate's economic policies. But Republican feminists had long faced the dilemma of choosing between a misogynist fiscal conservative candidate and a feminist moderate who was not fiscally conservative. Now the electorate at large was facing the same dilemma. The formula that seemed to work the best was the one adopted by Weld and by New Jersey's Christine Todd Whitman, who surprised everyone by almost defeating prominent incumbent Senator Bill Bradley by running as a pro-choice, cut-taxes conservative. These candidates had rebuffed the bigotry aspects of the New Majoritarian strategy. They wouldn't play the fear game. Their popularity was the first positive sign since 1980 that possibly—only possibly—the misogynists' hold over the party might be weakening. It didn't mean the right was weakened—far from it. But it did suggest that for the first time since the Bush capitulation in 1980, some new generals were arriving to challenge its messages of hatred and fear.

16

FAITHFUL FRIEND OF THE RIGHT

On the domestic front back in Washington, the Bush administration was pressing forward on the Religious Right agenda, orchestrated from the White House by John Sununu. It maintained administrative pressure on family-planning clinics. It refused to rescind its 1989 extension of the Reagan administration's ban on federal money for research using fetal tissue. It was still looking for ways to overturn *Roe,* although it had learned from the Bork fiasco and had decided to be cautious in its first Supreme Court nomination. In July 1990, when Justice William Brennan, who had voted for *Roe,* resigned because of illness, the White House nominated David Souter, a federal judge from New Hampshire. An intensely private man, Souter's legal reputation was known mainly to his peers, and in his hearings before the Senate Judiciary Committee, he refused to indicate where he stood on controversial issues. He was confirmed with little fanfare.

Bush also continued Reagan's policies on civil rights. On October 22, he vetoed the Civil Rights Act of 1990, which had passed Congress by comfortable margins. In the same way that the Civil Rights Restoration Act had been needed to nullify the Supreme Court's *Grove City* decision, so Congress had passed this 1990 act to correct Court decisions that undermined, among other things, the ability of women and minorities to win job-discrimination suits. It was only the third time in American history that a president had vetoed a civil rights bill. Reagan's veto in 1988 had been one of them; the other was in 1866, when Andrew Johnson vetoed legislation giving civil rights protection to the newly freed slaves. In those two instances, Congress had overridden the vetoes, but in Bush's case the Senate failed by one vote to override. Standing foursquare against what he described as the act's system of quotas, Bush had proved he had the muscle to deliver enough votes of southern conservative Democrat and moderate Republican senators to pass the right's litmus test.

For several years, women's groups had been lobbying for a Family and Medical Leave Act that would allow individuals a few months of unpaid leave from their jobs in order to take care of a new baby or sick family member. This issue had gone through many permutations since it was first discussed in the early eighties. During the campaign Bush had said he favored parental leave, but only if businesses provided it voluntarily. The bill that finally arrived on his desk affected only 5 percent of America's employers and 44 percent of employees, because it applied only to companies with fifty or more workers. Few Americans on either side of this issue were enthusiastic about this watered-down legislation. The act's main value was in establishing the principle that both parents share a responsibility for at-home care of family members.

Not surprisingly, the bill displeased the Religious Right, which did not like both parents getting equal status in the home. The Religious Right's friends in Congress said they would support it only if the provisions applied to mothers alone and not to fathers. Bush got the message. The bill that arrived on his desk provided twelve months of unpaid leave for both parents, leaving health benefits intact. In mid-June 1990, he vetoed it because it included these benefits and the dual-couple concept. Congress failed to override.

At the White House, the child care bill, heralded with such fanfare in the 1988 campaign, was finally signed into law on November 5, 1990. During the campaign, Gary Bauer and Phyllis Schlafly had weighed in in favor of Bush's "toddler tax credit" and vouchers for religious schools. Bauer, now heading a New Right group called the Family Research Council, called the plan "philosophically sound" if it would "explicitly provide funds for mothers who stayed at home." The child care bill was a hodgepodge of tax credits, vouchers, block grants to states to improve child care services, and incentive money to businesses for child care; it called for the expansion of Head Start programs into a full day. But in its final form, the bill relaxed quality standards for child care and appropriated little money for any of it. It was too little, very late.

Like the Family and Medical Leave Act, this product of excessive compromise also made no one happy. Bauer had not gotten his proviso, while his side called it "blatant discrimination against the mother who takes care of her children." Libertarians were upset because the vouchers could be used for child care in religiously sponsored child care centers, which they saw as a violation of the separation of church and state. Provisions such as this one made clear that the only social legislation a majority of Republican members of Congress would support was that which ceded something to the Religious Right.

The nation was paying comparatively little attention to such goings-on, however, because of events in the Near East. On August 2 Saddam Hussein's Iraq had invaded Kuwait, generating an international crisis. The UN imposed a ban on trade with Iraq and called for an international coalition of member nations to protect the legitimate interests of Kuwait. On August 14 Bush delivered a fiery speech demanding "the immediate, complete, and unconditional withdrawal of all Iraqi forces from Kuwait," compared Saddam Hussein to Hitler, said this stand was "to protect the freedom of nations," and proclaimed as he concluded that there was "no substitute for American leadership." It was Bush the commander-in-chief again taking charge in international events—with all the vigor that he was not asserting at home.

Throughout the fall, under Operation Desert Shield, a UN coalition of nations assembled a vast buildup of ground troops, armaments, and air forces for an invasion of Iraq, should it not meet the UN Security Council's January 15 deadline for withdrawal. By the time the six-month buildup was completed, the number of American personnel in the Persian Gulf was as many as had been sent to Vietnam at the height of the war. In the meantime, not wanting to fall into the trap of going to war without congressional approval as in Vietnam, Bush asked for an authorizing resolution from Congress under the War Powers Act. For three days the Senate and House heatedly debated the president's request, with the Senate finally approving by 5 votes, the House by 67. It was not a strong endorsement for a nation about to go to war, but this ambivalence would soon be swept away by what followed.

In the United States, Chairman of the Joint Chiefs of Staff Colin Powell coordinated every stage of the planning with the army general who would lead the UN coalition, H. Norman Schwarzkopf. On January 16, 1991, the day after the deadline expired, Desert Shield became Desert Storm with the launching of air and missile attacks on Iraq. The ground invasion began on February 23 and lasted only a hundred hours. Four days later, the Persian Gulf war was over. It was a spectacular display of international collaboration and military might and skill. It was also America's first internationally televised war and made heroes of those who led it, not least the president. At the war's end his poll rating was 87 percent, "the highest recorded since the June 1945 rating for Harry Truman at the time of the German surrender in World War II."

For Sununu, ruling imperiously and with a very heavy hand at the White House, it was a heady time. Lee Atwater had been stricken with a brain tumor a year before and lay dying. His acumen was missed. The president seemed to have no one else in his political inner circle with the skill and subtlety to keep the various parts of the coalition together —Sununu was the converse of Atwater. Atwater's loyal deputy Mary Matalin, who ran the RNC admirably during his slow, painful illness— he died in March—was especially critical of Sununu's role. As she summed it up later, "John Sununu contributed more than any other single human being to the downfall of this presidency."

Sununu's impact extended far beyond his dictatorial style of governance. Under his guidance, the administration pursued the New Right agenda with a determination that brought it into direct conflict with Congress. After ten years of Reagan–Bush morality initiatives, the figures on teenage sexual activity were growing significantly worse, yet the dismantling of programs that could be used to stop unintended pregnancies had accelerated. Invigorated by the newfound political strength of the pro-choice movement, Congress reversed the Mexico City policy, restored funding for the UN Population Fund, reversed the ban on fetal-tissue research, and again tried to restore Medicaid funding for rape and incest victims. Bush vetoed every single bill.

Then came a Supreme Court ruling that was as destructive to individual freedom as *Webster*. After the Reagan administration established gag rules forbidding doctors and other professionals in federally funded family-planning clinics from counseling patients about abortion or referring them on to other doctors, several clinics and their doctors took the administration to court. Among their charges was that their right of free speech had been infringed. On May 23, 1991, in the *Rust v. Sullivan* decision—in which Justice Souter cast his first anti-abortion vote—the Supreme Court ruled 5 to 4 that the gag rules were legal. (O'Connor voted with the minority.) The majority contended that the rules "do not significantly impinge upon the doctor-patient relationship" and that a doctor "is always free to make clear that advice regarding abortion is simply beyond the scope of the program."

Rust gave the federal government the power to decide what a doctor could tell a patient about *any* treatment for *any* medical condition in a federally funded institution. The decision went so far as to uphold the government's right to forbid doctors and others from mentioning the word *abortion* whenever government money was involved. The medical profession and its patients were aghast and warned that stopping a doctor from giving a patient adequate medical advice could provoke malpractice charges.

Equally destructive was the effect of *Rust* on civil liberties. It expanded the government's control from the issue of a woman's right to abortion to the free speech of all those helping her. There was an enormous public outcry. Cartoonists had a field day. One barbed drawing showed a family-planning clinic with a sign out front reading: "The Supreme Court has prohibited us from informing you that having an abortion is a legal alternative."

Responding to the widespread outrage, the House acted quickly, voting 353 to 74 to overturn the gag rules. It was the largest margin the House had ever given an abortion-related bill. The Senate followed suit. Would Bush sign it? All through the summer and fall of 1991, Roger Porter of the White House staff and pro-choice Republican senator John Chafee negotiated to head off a veto. Doctors protested the gag rules. Bush's old friends came out of the woodwork imploring him to approve the bill. The Religious Right, aided by Sununu, lobbied for a veto. In the end, Bush did what he always did in such situations: He succumbed to the pressure from his Religious Right–New Right base and vetoed the bill. Beaten down by the New Right and the supply-siders' assaults on him for breaking his no-tax pledge, he had no fight left for a struggle over the free-speech rights of doctors and nurses.

Worse, the great margins in the House for an override vanished. Sununu and his staff convinced the Republicans and anti-choice Democrats to back the president. The override attempt failed by twelve votes.

In early summer the White House upped the ante again. On July 1, two days before the second anniversary of *Webster,* Bush named Religious Right favorite Clarence Thomas to fill the Supreme Court vacancy created by the resignation of Justice Thurgood Marshall. Here was a man who was almost certainly in the right-to-life camp, whose sympathy with right-wing fundamentalists was widely known, and who was being appointed to sit on a Supreme Court that was teetering on the edge of overturning *Roe.* Long before Anita Hill arrived on the scene three months later, pro-choice advocates were stupefied by the White House's political arrogance. The administration was taking to heart Gary Bauer's words of warning: "If these issues [abortion] are thrown overboard, they [Reagan Democrats] will go back to their economic interests, which are decidedly not Republican. . . . If the party chooses to decide this issue on the basis of polls, it sends a very bad signal."

The Clarence Thomas hearings caused enduring repercussions for the White House and its allies in the Senate. Women were not the only ones appalled by what Anita Hill was put through in her interrogation by the Senate Judiciary Committee on October 11 and 12. As a transfixed nationwide television audience watched, Hill, a professor of law at the University of Oklahoma, described her experiences of sexual harassment by Thomas and was interrogated brutally, arrogantly, and at times mockingly by senators whose sexism and insensitivity leaped out with every sentence. There was a special irony in the harsh way in which women's rights supporter Arlen Specter used his highly honed prosecutorial talents to cross-examine Hill. Liberal Democrat Ted Kennedy, bruised by a recent scandal over his own behavior, sat virtually mute. In this setting it made no difference where the committee members stood on feminist issues. They were for all intents and purposes a hanging jury.

The White House won: The Senate voted to approve Thomas 52 to 48. He was sworn in on October 23, 1991, just after the administration filed a brief on the side of Operation Rescue in a clinic blockade case in Virginia. Sununu was on a roll.

But the costs were heavy. The hearings hit a raw nerve. Most women who had ever felt the pain and anger of being ill treated because of their gender identified with Hill. Those of us in the women's movement were beyond anger. We were determined to find candidates to run against those senators if it was the last thing we did, and we would beat them. Nonetheless, within the Republican Family Committee, among the women in California and South Dakota and the other places where pro-choice GOP grassroots groups were springing up, there was despair. Clarence Thomas had been the last straw. As I surveyed pro-choice Republicans in other states to see how many delegates we might have for the 1992 Houston GOP convention, what they told me most often was, Why bother? If we lose *Roe,* they said, they had had it with Bush and the Republican party. It was no longer worth hanging in.

And losing *Roe* looked like a real possibility. The Supreme Court had agreed to hear another abortion case, *Planned Parenthood of Southern Pennsylvania v. Casey,* and we knew it would be the big one. A Planned Parenthood clinic in Pennsylvania was challenging the state's 1989 Abortion Control Act, and the Bush Justice Department would join the state of Pennsylvania to argue for overturning *Roe.*

The messages coming to us from Washington were mixed. Our friends inside the administration kept telling us to keep fighting, that Bush would come around "a little"—although they acknowledged his abortion position would not change. Hypocrisy reigned. In his State of the Union speech in January 1992, the president said the cornerstone of his health care program would be "preserving and increasing" patient choice in picking a doctor. Bush believed in patient choice as long as that patient wasn't a woman with an unintended pregnancy.

Quayle had weighed in, trying his hand at being Atwater: "We are a party that though we have a position on abortion, that those who disagree with us should not feel excluded because of that issue. . . . People in responsible positions said there's no use having this fight; let's make sure the big tent concept issue is agreed to." They were empty words. While we were trying to get a meeting with someone in authority at the White House, Pat Robertson was negotiating his endorsement of Bush. We couldn't get an appointment. The White House didn't want to talk to pro-choicers.

At the moment, however, we were among the least of its problems. The country was in a recession. For the first quarter of 1992, national unemployment rose to 7.3 percent and Bush's approval ratings fell below 50 percent. New Hampshire was particularly hard hit, and in the February 18 primary, it had reacted more favorably than expected to Pat Buchanan, who was running for the GOP nomination and won a startling 37 percent of the vote. The president, very angry that he had not done as well as he should have, was in no mood to talk compromise with anyone. He was still angrier when two days after New Hampshire, Ross Perot told Americans that he was available to run for president.

March 10 was Super Tuesday, with eight state primaries, six of them in the South, and Bush wanted to sew up his nomination then and there. He also wanted to allay the fears of those in the New Right and Religious Right who were being seduced by Buchanan.

The Bush campaign knew Buchanan wasn't going to deny the president the nomination—no one was worried about that—but it did fear he might destroy party unity. The president moved to shore up his credentials with the Religious Right; his hard line against pro-choicers clearly wasn't enough. He fired National Endowment for the Arts chairman John Frohnmayer because NEA money had been given to an art museum that had put on a show of what Buchanan called "filthy and blasphemous art." He apologized for the 1990 budget agreement that had caused him to break his no-new-taxes pledge. It seemed to help, in that he won all eight Super Tuesday primaries, but Buchanan had damaged him nonetheless.

As the campaign focused on how to win over the Buchanan Republicans, Charlie Black played his usual role of trying to hold the right flank and keep the moderates quiet. Working with Phyllis Schlafly and her Republican National Coalition for Life (which she had founded with Bauer and Beverly La Haye of Concerned Women for America on November 1, 1990), Black was asking Republican officeholders and delegates to sign a pledge that they recognized "the Republican party was founded on the principle that no human being should be considered the property of another," that this principle was three times "ratified . . . by the American voter," and that they would "help elect qualified pro-life Republicans" and retain the party's "pro-life" plank. Signing a pledge hardened the political process because it made it more difficult for political people to negotiate out of polarizing situations. It was a technique that Newt Gingrich would use in 1994 to lock Republican members of Congress into his Contract with America. Black and Schlafly's workers would tell those they approached that the president needed their signature. The tactic worked well in the anti-choice strongholds of the South, where they found eager signers, but not as well elsewhere.

The pro-choice side took several steps of its own. First, Ken Ruberg of the Republican Mainstream Committee brought Mary Crisp and Ann Stone together and helped them discuss their disagreements, which led to their signing a memorandum of understanding on March 6. Despite Crisp's great animosity at Stone's unwillingness to take on anti-choice Republican incumbents in primaries, the two agreed to bury the hatchet for the convention. The months of battling had sharpened Stone's understanding of the issues, and she'd moved away from her earlier equivocal attitudes on choice. We were no longer hearing that she was both "pro-choice and pro-life." The memo between them was negotiated like a legal document and was unusual for politics in its specificity. The signatories agreed not to accept a "pro-life big tent" as proposed by Quayle. They agreed to oppose the 1988 anti-choice plank and to advocate a plank that endorsed "the concepts of freedom of choice, the right to privacy and reproductive rights"—meaning the *Roe* decision and the proposed Freedom of Choice Act, which was legislation to codify *Roe*. They attacked the use of abortion-related litmus tests in judicial selection and encouraged support for "family planning services, education, and contraceptive research." Stone's willingness to sign the document lessened our suspicions that she would sell out the pro-choice cause at the convention if Black asked her to. Although tensions remained over fund-raising raids and the issue of pro-choice challenges in primaries, to the world the two choice groups were partners, albeit uneasy ones.

Second, Nancy Johnson and the pro-choice Republican women in the House worked with the White House to formulate model platform language to be proposed in place of the 1988 language.

Third, we asked the pro-choice governors—John McKernan of Maine, Pete Wilson of California, Jim Edgar of Illinois, and William Weld of Massachusetts—for help at the Houston convention. In New York we had tried to put together a pro-choice delegation but had been stymied by former New Yorker Rich Bond, who was now RNC chairman. Bond let it be known he wanted no "troublemakers" in Houston. The New York GOP was now under the control of New Right anti-choice Senator D'Amato, who had selected his former staffer Bill Powers as state chairman. Powers's dream was to rebuild the New York party into the national political power it had been before 1964, when the imposition of delegate rules that favored southern and smaller western states had stripped states like New York of some of their power. He was not about to cross the Bush campaign.

There were to be no primaries in New York; it was a solid Bush state and party leaders selected delegates based on service to the party. My Republican county chairman, Roy Goodman, made me a delegate, but Bond didn't want me. Not until three weeks before the Houston convention did New York release its official list to the press. I was on the list after all and pledged to vote for Bush's nomination. I thought all the fuss about keeping me off the delegation was shortsighted. They needed women like me in Houston to prove the party was truly the big tent they claimed.

On paper, our strategy seemed a good one. The grassroots pro-choicers, in conjunction with their governors and pro-choice legislators, would constitute about a third of the convention delegates. But at best this would be enough only to leverage a minority report and perhaps make a marginal change in the plank or add a statement indicating support for the concept of separation of church and state. We were kidding ourselves.

The White House wasn't worried about pro-choice Americans, especially Republican ones. It was worried about the Religious Right, and the worry never abated. It was shared by party leaders all over the country. Governors' staffs told us their bosses couldn't do anything. No one wanted to battle the right, not even Weld, whom the press kept picturing as a man who would stand up for what he believed in.

The same thing happened on the Hill. Nancy Johnson, Susan Molinari, Olympia Snowe, and the other pro-choice women had decided to go along with the strategy of not embarrassing the president. None would be members of the Platform Committee, and in the Senate we no longer had our stalwart supporter Lowell Weicker. He had finally given up on the GOP, left the Senate, and become an independent, and he was now governor of Connecticut.

In the middle of May, Quayle launched the Bush campaign's "family values" offensive in San Francisco. Charging that a "breakdown of family structure, personal responsibility, and social order" were the cause of the Los Angeles riots after the Rodney King verdict in late April, he mocked the TV character Murphy Brown for having a child out of wedlock and called for "social sanctions" to punish women like her. The show's executive producer, Diane English, fired back: "If the vice president thinks it's disgraceful for an unmarried woman to bear a child, and if he believes that a woman cannot raise a child without a father, then he'd better make sure abortion remains safe and legal." But Quayle wasn't finished. A few days later, sounding like a protégé of Robertson and Buchanan, he launched an attack on the "cultural elites" who, he said, "respect neither tradition nor standards. . . . They seem to think . . . that fathers are dispensable and that parents need not be married or even of the opposite sexes. They are wrong."

For months, a quiet campaign to unload Quayle had been under way. Several of the New Right libertarians were again pushing Kemp; old guard types wanted Dole or Defense Secretary Dick Cheney. But Quayle's offensive made headlines everywhere, and it shut down all speculation: The Religious Right wanted him. In mid-July Bush announced that Quayle was his man. As Quayle had done ever since the 1988 New Orleans convention, he would help Bush keep the Religious Right in the Republican stable.

On June 29, amid all these disheartening events, there came at last a good day for women—for the moment, at least. The Supreme Court rendered its decision in the *Casey* case, stating in a 5-to-4 vote that "the essential holding of *Roe v. Wade* should be retained and once again reaffirmed." But it was a limited victory. *Roe* may have been sustained, but it was being chipped away. As in *Webster* and *Rust,* the Court in *Casey* placed restrictions on when and how a woman could get an abortion. Justice O'Connor's "undue burden" test was to be the primary legal criterion for determining those circumstances. O'Connor, Kennedy, and Souter wrote the majority opinion and were joined in their vote by Blackmun and Stevens.

Webster had opened the door to restrictions on abortion by letting state legislatures test the limits of *Roe.* It had allowed the states to refuse the use of public funds and facilities for abortion services, and to impose fetal-viability tests on women who were more than twenty weeks pregnant. *Rust* had restricted women's access to medical information and limited the freedom of health professionals. *Casey* allowed the state to impose waiting periods and require informed consent and counseling of women before they could obtain abortions in clinics funded by federal money. All that the Court threw out in *Casey* was Pennsylvania's spousal-notification requirement, which it said was an "undue burden" on a woman. States could still continue to place restrictions on women's choice.

Casey was certainly better than losing *Roe*, but it had not made life much better for women. Sarah Weddington, who had argued *Roe* in 1970, said of *Casey*:

In theory, *Roe v. Wade* is still on the books, but in terms of how it impacts women's lives, it is a shadow of its former self. Up to now, the Court has said, "It's a woman's decision, and you people in the legislature, leave her alone." Now they're saying, "It's still her decision, but you people in the legislature can erect hurdles and roadblocks so that only women who are the most determined, who have the most money, who are the most sophisticated make it through. . . ."

Weddington characterized the ruling as "patronizing" to women and underscored that "the only surgery that you have to, by law, wait twenty-four hours for . . . is abortion—as if women don't think about it before they get to the clinic."

Several months before, *The Wall Street Journal* had reported that "some anti-abortion leaders say that a ruling restricting abortion rights might be preferable to triggering a huge political backlash." As Burke Balch of the National Right to Life Committee had added, "The key is the framing of the issue, not just overturning *Roe*." A decision to throw out *Roe* would have intensified the anger of pro-choice Americans: The quiet, normally uninterested citizen would have been aroused. The next pro-choice march would have been even larger than the record-breaking one of April 1992. Balch knew what the pro-choicers knew: that he and his colleagues could get much further if they pursued their game of quiet, steady erosion. They did not want grandstand extremist gestures like those of Randall Terry and his Operation Rescue.

Since the threat to legal abortion no longer seemed imminent to the general public that supported choice, some in Washington thought the rebellion in the Republican party and in the nation at large might subside. Bush's campaign could woo the Religious Right without trouble from the moderates, now reassured that *Casey* made *Roe* safe. And as for his economic program, Bush staffers thought, he had promised never again to seek higher taxes. The prognosis for a smooth convention in Houston looked bright.

Glad though I was that *Roe* had at least survived, I felt *Casey* had drained us of our energy, our ammunition. As we prepared to go to the convention, we were on automatic pilot, flying through the fog with no safe place to land in Houston and no friendly force to join us. The Bush campaign had done just what it planned. It had silenced the party's influential pro-choice officeholders.

17

THE COLLAPSE OF BUSH

The Houston convention belonged to the right. It belonged to Pat Robertson and Jerry Falwell and their exclusionary vision of Christianity. It belonged to Paul Weyrich and his New Right authoritarians who wanted a Cromwellian America: narrow, puritanical, and intolerant. It belonged to the right-to-lifers and Phyllis Schlafly, and to Marilyn Quayle's petulant antifeminism.

It was not George Bush's convention. It was neither a Texas-style hometown blowout celebrating his presidency, which was what he must have wanted, nor a tribute to his plans for America for the next four years. Rather, the Houston convention was the denouement of the Faustian bargain that Bush had struck in 1980. He'd willingly let the right take over his party to win himself the White House. He'd let them institute policies that sought to relegate women to their pre-Enlightenment status. He'd let them set his domestic social agenda and bully him on economic policy so he could play the great statesman on the post–cold war stage. There was a price to pay, and in 1992 George Bush paid it: The price was the White House.

Houston was different from any Republican convention I'd ever attended. It was even worse than San Francisco in 1964, when the Goldwaterites had disliked the old guard and moderate Republicans but nonetheless had not charged they were degenerate, godless people. In Houston the sanctimonious and the sectarian dominated.

The parties were large and lush, and the Texans were their usual friendly, big-hearted selves. But just below the surface was a tightness, a pinched falsity of goodwill, coming from the Platform Committee meetings. Some Platform Committee members quickly sized you up: Were you a God-fearing Bush delegate, or one of the other kind? I learned during platform week not to say I was a pro-choice Bush delegate unless I wanted to spend the next hour justifying not the rightness of my position but my faith in God. Robertson's disciples didn't want to talk secular issues.

The New York delegates were housed in the RNC headquarters in the Hyatt Regency Hotel. Robertson's minions had also set up shop in the hotel, with their leader holding forth daily in an improvised television studio on the mezzanine, open for all to watch. I'd been greeted upon arrival at the lobby door by two women passing out paperback copies of Robertson's book on the new world order, and in my packet of welcome-to-Houston memorabilia was a tract on how to find God in my "everyday life."

Charlie Black and Rich Bond were set on insuring there would be no dissonance in Houston. No testimony was taken from interested outsiders; that had been disposed of in hearings held around the country in the spring. Back in May, Mary Crisp, Ann Stone, and other pro-choice Republicans had made enough noise at the GOP hearings in Salt Lake City to convince Bond and Black that they would ruin the unity image being constructed for the television audience during the convention.

On the first day of platform week, Barbara Mosbacher, who was not a delegate, flew down from New York to represent the Republican Family Committee. The Hyatt refused to rent us a public room for her news conference. They said we were an "issues" committee and that the RNC had prohibited the use of the hotel's facilities for "issues" events. We circumvented this out-of-character Texas hostility by renting a private suite in the hotel and inviting the press for breakfast. The story leads were as we expected: "Heavy-handed Republican managers bar Bush Chairman Robert Mosbacher's sister from renting a room." (Her brother was chairman of the Bush campaign, a member of G6, and Bush's personal friend of many years.) We'd gotten the public's attention, thanks to our adversaries. Later that week, I watched the "issues" Christian Coalition crowd hold several press conferences at the Hyatt. None were in private suites.

Mosbacher briefly laid out for the press the traditional argument that Republicans are different from Democrats because they believe "government should interfere as little as possible in an individual's life." She tweaked the opposition by adding that "some anti-choice critics claim that only they have the 'moral' ground. That same argument was used to burn witches in the seventeenth century." Excerpts from her remarks ended up on *The New York Times* op-ed page two days before the convention opened.

Bond and Black had numerous ways to make life even more difficult for pro-choice Republicans. The executive director of Mary Crisp's group, Nancy Sternoff, couldn't get rooms for its members in Houston. The convention-arrangements staff reserved motel space for them more than two hours away from the George R. Brown Convention Center. In a repeat of our hotel incident, Sternoff was told that pro-choice groups would not be allowed to display their brochures, pamphlets, and other items at the convention center, even though Robertson and Schlafly's materials were abundantly available. It was standard-issue harassment.

The rest of what we encountered wasn't standard. The convention center where the platform subcommittee met was an armed camp. Security was tighter than I'd ever seen it. There were few passes to the allegedly public platform subcommittee deliberations. An outsider would have thought from the way we were treated that we were a battalion of Clinton Democrats from Arkansas come to storm the Platform Committee, rather than a hundred or so pro-choice Republicans. Police officers and security seemed to outnumber Republicans.

Black's immediate challenge was to crush the pro-choicers and insure that the platform mirrored the social agenda of Robertson and Schlafly. Abortion was only one issue in the agenda; the Bush campaign gave the Religious Right carte blanche to fashion planks on education, the arts, environment, morality, health care, the family, and even land use. Foreign policy and the economy were reserved as the White House's province. Although the Bush team minimized the right's influence in these areas, the New Right supply-siders succeeded in pulling a fast one, passing a plank in subcommittee that said the 1990 budget agreement was "a mistake." This was a first. I didn't know of a single case in Republican history where the party's platform attacked its presidential nominee's record. When the Bush campaign woke up, the plank was rewritten to read, "Republicans believe that the taxes insisted on by the Democrats in the 1990 budget agreement were recessionary."

The campaign team had planned carefully. The platform subcommittees were named in order to confuse. The Subcommittee on Individual Rights, Good Homes, and Safe Streets was to cover abortion—not the Subcommittee on Family Values, Education, and Health Care, where it logically belonged. For the organizers, abortion was not a health issue. The other aim was to keep secret as long as possible which subcommittee would debate abortion so that pro-choicers would have a harder time laying out their lobbying strategy.

To make the platform abortion debate appear credible to the public, the planners sought to give the appearance that most Republican women were anti-choice. Mary Potter Summa of North Carolina was the subcommittee's chairman and star player. Chief legislative assistant to Jesse Helms for two years, Summa, a lawyer, had excellent right-wing credentials. The Individual Rights Subcommittee had twenty-one members—fourteen women and seven men. The Bush campaign had stacked it with seventeen right-to-lifers, the majority of them women and followers of Robertson. As in the last three conventions, Illinois congressmember Henry Hyde led the anti-choice forces. He was the only nationally elected official on the subcommittee.

The absence of prominent elected pro-choice leaders from platform week disturbed me. We had problems not only with the Religious Right but with our so-called friends who had decided not to challenge Bush. Their absence confirmed that the usual arrangement had been made with the White House "not to embarrass the president with a fight." Every attempt that nonelected pro-choice leaders made to enlist the help of pro-choice elected officials had been met with equivocation or some version of let's wait and see how it plays out. None of the prominent pro-choice governors—McKernan, Wilson, Edgar, Weld—were willing to fight. In early spring all had rejected our requests for meetings to plan tactics in Houston. As platform week dragged on, it became clear that we were being hung out to dry.

One of the worst examples of this all-talk-and-no-action approach was California senator John Seymour, who was to lose his reelection bid that fall to Dianne Feinstein. Our forces desperately needed a leader of equivalent rank to Hyde on the subcommittee. Seymour could have easily had his pro-choice governor Pete Wilson appoint him to the Platform Committee. Instead, Seymour flew into Houston during platform week and held a press conference to state his support for a pro-choice plank, then left town.

The four pro-choice members on the subcommittee were well-meaning individuals with little understanding of what they faced. To make matters worse, one of them—our potential leader, Vermont state senator John Carroll—was in Chicago at a legislative conference, so he never even got to the subcommittee's first and only meeting.

Delegates Mary Wiese of South Dakota and Bobbie Breske of Delaware were articulate but not schooled in the ways of platform politics. Barbara Bush's friend, Deborah Leighton of Massachusetts, told me she had strict instructions from her governor, Bill Weld, "not to rock the boat" or do anything that could be viewed as disloyalty to Bush. Despite his fine pro-choice record in Massachusetts, Weld had no intention of trying to change the plank. In several conversations with his staff just prior to platform week, I could get no commitment of help. Since his representative on the subcommittee was so weak, we assumed that he had decided that the way to concur in the don't-embarrass-the-president strategy was to avoid becoming a Platform Committee member himself. Politically sophisticated, Weld knew that platform fights are fought during platform week. He copped out.

Black's staff watched us like sentinels, making it difficult for us to communicate with our four pro-choicers during the proceedings. Yet I noticed that Ralph Reed, executive director of the Christian Coalition, had no problem using staff pages to get messages to Summa throughout the day. When a hearing is fairly run, the committee staff serves all. We had been obstructed by this tactic in previous conventions, but the staff seemed under even more rigorous control this time. It was a true Charlie Black special.

These elaborate precautions were scarcely necessary, however, since our opponents had the votes. The Bush team was afraid of something. It certainly shouldn't have been us. Reed ran around like Barnum on opening night of the circus. Schlafly was his Bailey, moving in and out of the room, ordering about her staff, and spinning her line to the press.

Sitting in seats provided for the public, pro-choice and anti-choice partisans eyed each other warily. The subcommittee members were in the front, the public in the middle, and the press at the back. Bush operatives were casually scattered around on all sides.

All subcommittee members had copies of the draft platform. Each line of the draft dealing with the subcommittee's area was to be read out loud. The subject matter was dizzying in its sweep—home ownership and the progrowth economy, enterprise zones and the burning of Los Angeles, the evils of the welfare system and the grave threat of violent crime, too much protection for the rights of criminals and neglect of victims' rights.

The Bush campaign had written these planks. The subcommittee members had received the eighty-five-page draft platform late the previous evening, when most of them had just arrived. Only a dogged few had had time to read it, let alone ponder the ideas being proposed. The subcommittee had just this one day to approve the sections that pertained to it. On Tuesday the Platform Committee would sit as a whole, since Black wasn't about to let the process drag on. The longer the deliberations lasted, the greater the potential for trouble.

After several interminable discussions about innocuous word changes and grammatical errors, the committee came to the individual rights section, the prelude to the abortion plank. The reader began:

> The protection of individual rights is the foundation for opportunity and security. . . . Today, as in the day of Lincoln, we insist that no American's rights are negotiable. . . . We renew the historic Republican commitment to the rights of women, from the early days of the suffragist movement to the present. . . . [W]e assert economic growth as the key to the continued progress of women in all fields of American life.

People stopped whispering and chattering; the reporters in the back, who had been moving around, actually stood still. The moment we'd all been waiting for was at hand. The reader then read the antiabortion plank from 1988. As we had been forewarned, the Bush campaign had left it intact.

A dark-haired, middle-aged woman raised her hand. It was grandmotherly Bobbie Breske. Summa looked surprised—she had not expected a revision in the script. Breske moved that Republicans make an exception to the 1988 plank's words that the fetus had inalienable rights. "Are we to neglect women?" she asked. "Are we to put them in jeopardy in back alleys because a woman has been raped and does not want to carry it? . . . How can you counsel a woman who has been horribly violated?"

As Breske's voice rose, the seat-shifting and throat-clearing were audible; then came silence. Breske, a volunteer for the Psychiatric Emergency Service and Drug Information Hot Line in her Delaware community, knew about women in trouble. "I represent the people of my district and have deep, deep feelings on this. . . . Everything is not real here. The realities of life are sometimes very ugly."

Summa stopped Breske and said her time was up.

Mary Wiese took up where Breske had left off. "I feel very strongly pro-choice, and I feel we have not had a chance to dialogue. This is an issue that can win the election. I have lots of friends who will vote pro-choice. We are here to elect Republicans."

Again Summa called a halt; Wiese's two minutes were up.

Henry Hyde saw that it was time to speak up for the fetus. Showing the experience of a man who had spent seventeen years in Congress leading the anti-choice fight, he said, "I can't think of a more egregious crime than a rape. . . . There is honor in having to carry to term, not exterminating the child." He talked a long time. Summa did not cut him off. He stopped when he was finished.

The floodgates opened in a torrent of Religious Right rhetoric. "We don't have to fix it if it ain't broke," said Cathy Mickels, repeating her friend Schlafly's constant line of the last year. Summa announced that she was four and a half months pregnant. "I can tell you what's in me is not a rock, not a Coke bottle—it's a human life, kicking me and sitting on my bladder," she said, then called for the vote.

Seventeen for the fetus, three for raped women. For a moment, the room was silent; then the reporters started leaving. Following the script, Summa-turned-diplomat wound up the session with the Atwater–Quayle big tent. "It is important for the Platform Committee to construct a document with which the president is completely comfortable," she said. ". . . [T]he Republican party is a party which includes and supports persons who hold a variety of opinions." No one reacted. The subcommittee meeting adjourned.

Pro-choice delegate Leighton, who had not been able to find her voice during the deliberations, now found it. She told the press that she hoped "there is room in the party for people of differing opinions on the subject."

For the full committee meeting the next day, Hyde had reinforcements. His New Right House colleagues Bill McCollum of Florida, Vin Weber of Minnesota, Gerald Solomon of New York, Robert Walker of Pennsylvania, and Joe Barton of Texas had joined him. The chairman and co-chairman of the committee were Religious Right supporters Oklahoma senator Don Nickles and Missouri governor John Ashcroft. The campaign had given up its previous charade of showcasing women leaders. Summa was now just another member of the Platform Committee.

No pro-choice governors, senators, or congressmembers were committee members. Our leaders on the committee were ardent but woefully inexperienced. John Carroll had finally arrived from Chicago and had been briefed about the previous day's events; he was ready to fight. Maine's governor, John McKernan, had not come but sent two pro-choice delegates, State Senator Charles Summers and Doris Russell, who had been a delegate at the last four conventions. Neither Carroll nor Summers had ever been a delegate to a Republican National Convention. Deborah Leighton was not joined by her male Massachusetts colleague, Dale Jenkins, until the end of the week—long after the Platform Committee had finished its work. Bobbie Breske had told us that she didn't want to be part of any organized pro-choice effort—she just wished to express her opinion and would continue to do so. On the other hand, Mary Wiese gladly worked with us.

A cursory count showed only a dozen people willing to oppose the plank's wording. Through the years New York's Rita di Martino had presented herself as a women's rights advocate, yet she told me emphatically that she would not vote with us on even the slightest change, not even for a big tent statement. When I asked whether she would abstain, she refused, even though she was representing a state Republican party that had a pro-choice platform. Other women delegates had said the same thing to my colleagues. They were committed to do what the Bush campaign wanted.

Every imaginable scenario pointed to a repeat of the previous day's circus. The Pro-Choicers outside the Platform Committee were a strange amalgam: Ann Stone's staff, the Mainstream and Ripon people, and Mary Crisp's earnest grassroots enthusiasts. Crisp's people had paid their own way to come to Houston to help us. Few had ever attended a national convention and were taken aback by the Religious Right's version of "free and open debate." Believers in the separation of church and state, they were shocked by the Christian Coalition's messianic messages and the Bush campaign's acquiescence to them.

We were sitting in various areas of the room as the line-by-line reading of the draft platform began. The layout and cast of characters were similar to those of the day before, only grander. The 106-member committee was seated on six rows of risers, set apart from everyone else. Unless they came down from the risers, it would be impossible to talk to them during the proceedings. The only way to reach them was through written messages delivered by Black's pages.

Bo Callaway, Black's whip, was seated in the middle of the first row. Hyde sat behind him in the second row, ready to grab the attention of the chairman and the press. The committee's officers, the parliamentarian, and the staff were stage right of the committee on separate risers. All were bathed in bright television lights.

While the reader read the platform, Reed and Schlafly were doing their in-and-out run-about dance as they had done yesterday. Considering that their platform planks were in place and they had the votes, I wondered why the performance. They were going to win, yet they acted as though they were losing, while we who knew our cause was lost were acting as though a miracle would happen. Crisp and Stone talked to the press continually: about the possibility of a neutral plank, an exception for rape victims, a true "big tent." It was a circus all right, but we were under different tents.

I knew, of course, that Robertson and the Christian Coalition were organized all over Houston and that their ally, Operation Rescue, was harassing the city's abortion clinics. I also knew that at least twenty of the fifty-five delegations were effectively under Robertson's command and that they dictated the platform's social agenda. Still, nothing had prepared me for what happened. However influential Robertson was, I assumed that the campaign wouldn't give him *all* the contents in the Republican store. I had been focused on the reproductive health sections of the platform and hadn't read all eighty-five pages of the draft.

Like my colleagues, I was waiting for line 809, the beginning of the abortion plank. As I listened to the reader, I realized I was hearing a

Religious Right document, not the usual Republican party message. The reader said: "That is why today's liberal Democrats are hostile toward any institution government cannot control, like private child-care or religious schools." I thought, What's this all about? The Democratic party doesn't oppose private child care or religious schools. A sizable number of the leaders of the Democratic party are products of parochial schools. But no one spoke up. The litany continued.

Finally, there was a stir from the committee. Religious Right delegate Michael Undseth moved that the words "mindful of our country's rich religious pluralism" be changed to read "mindful of our country's Judeo-Christian heritage." (So much for religious pluralism, and for American Buddhists, Muslims, Hindus, and others not members of this Platform Committee's approved religions.) The motion passed 51 to 37, even after the Wyoming delegate pleaded that "this doesn't belong in our platform."

The Religious Right delegates spoke up when the platform didn't suit them. Undseth, who had been arrested under the RICO law for his supposedly unlawful acts during an Operation Rescue blockade of an abortion clinic, broke from Black's script by trying to get the party to take his side in his court battle with the federal government. He proposed that the party oppose the use of RICO laws in clinic blockade cases. Callaway immediately moved to stop him. Such a statement might be used by the militant AIDS activist group, ACT-UP, Callaway argued, and the party didn't want to give it support.

Hyde said he'd "like to support but I can't, . . . RICO is abused," but this amendment involves "the policy of changing the platform." What Hyde didn't say was that Undseth's amendment was an attack on the Bush Justice Department. He and Callaway, mindful of the coming abortion plank, were obviously concerned that adopting this amendment would give our side a justification for criticizing the Justice Department for its anti-abortion policies. Undseth lost. It was the first time during this entire platform struggle that Robertson's people didn't get their way.

Finally, the reader got to line 809. Black, Schlafly, and Reed's operatives were strategically positioned to derail the slightest provocation. The press were all over themselves at the back of the room. Vivian Petura from New Mexico fired the first shot; she wanted to drop the anti-abortion plank: "A house divided cannot stand. . . . [W]e want to re-elect President Bush. . . . We must not alienate other Republicans; therefore, I move that the entire next paragraph be deleted from the platform."

Callaway stopped her cold. We "mustn't be wishy-washy," he warned. "George Bush believes in this issue. . . . [H]e ran on it. He was elected. Either pro-life or pro-choice, we should not make him run on a platform he doesn't agree with."

The committee woke up. On cue, everyone wanted to talk. The chairman seemed to know whom to recognize. Seven delegates spoke to keep the 1988 abortion plank. Chairman John Ashcroft finally recognized Eleanor Nissley of New Jersey who agreed with Petura:

> To women, the key is her family. I am incensed that these women have less rights than men. This is not the Republican woman. I feel strongly that any reference to abortion should be in the privacy category. . . . In 1968, we supported full equality of women. . . . [T]he policy of inclusion of Tom Kean is the way to go. . . . [W]e must welcome everyone.

For a moment, the anti-choice Platform Committee members didn't talk. Then they found their voice. I felt as though we were at a National Right to Life convention: "The rights of unborn children is [sic] an inalienable civil right." "The *Dred Scott* and *Roe* . . . decision[s] are the same." "A woman has the choice to have sex, but she has the right to have a child." The "state has the right to intervene to see the child lives." "America is great because she is good. We must stand for our principle and because George Bush wants it."

After Nissley, thirteen people spoke against dropping the plank. Petura tried once more. "We are not murderers. This is not a political issue. Ladies and gentlemen, please take it out of the platform." On the first roll call on the GOP's position on abortion in 1992, Petura lost, 84 to 16.

It was Carroll's turn. He introduced an amendment to strike the anti-abortion plank and in its place put "true big tent" language. "This is a conservative position," Carroll pleaded. "The government doesn't belong in this issue. . . . We must recognize the broad diversity of this party. . . . Two values [are] at stake—the value of life . . . and the right of liberty for women and their future. . . . We are simply saying that we need to hold both values. . . . Our obligation is to define the liberty of all."

Hyde promptly took Carroll on. "The government has a responsibility to protect the weak. We've been called un-American for not protecting the weak from the strong. . . . [A]ttention must be paid. Choice is a process. Life is a value."

Wiese spoke up. "Abortion is a symptom of the bigger problem of unwanted pregnancies," she said, pleading that the party "not make abortion a litmus test." That was too much for Jeff Angers of Louisiana, who angrily shouted, "What do real men do when the children of their nation are being killed? This is an issue for all people. This is for the abortion industry that has tried to infiltrate the Republican party."

Four more members spoke against Carroll, then Callaway signaled a vote. There was no roll call, just loud noes and some scattered yeses.

Breske asked the committee to make an exception. She was even more eloquent than on Monday.

> We haven't expressed concern for those who have suffered from rape and incest. These good women deserve our compassion and support. . . . They need an opportunity to make their own choice. . . . Young women have not been addressed today. Rape is a dreadful intrusion. . . . [It] even happens to twelve-year-olds. If you are carrying a person's child, that is a dreadful thing to do to an ignorant person. We have voiced . . . no compassion for these people. . . . Is there no room for exception?

And then the whole ugly business started again: "It is God's will." "We are the party who gives life." "The party of death met a few weeks ago." "We know rape and incest, but God gives life, only He can decide that."

There was no room for exception in this platform, on this committee, or in the Bush campaign strategy, no room for human kindness. Callaway reminded everyone that the "president does not want this language changed." Hyde's voice boomed: "From a great tragedy [rape], goodness can come." In this committee, more than half of whose members were from the Religious Right, Breske's plea for Christian charity was overwhelmingly rejected.

As I sat and listened, my mind wandered. I thought of Bosnia, of those raped women caught up in wars carrying the children of their rapists. I remembered the women in so many villages in the not-too-distant past who were stoned because they had been raped by men from another village. I remembered Catholic dogma of medieval times, when unmarried pregnant women were considered agents of evil, and I thought of Salem.

I was ashamed. I thought this party stood for what my forebears and the forebears of so many sitting on those risers had sought when they fled the lands of their birth. This is not my America of freedom. This is their America, the Old World of fear, of dogma, of superstition.

The great GOP abortion debate of 1992 was over. Crisp and Stone rushed for the door, insisting to the press that that wasn't the case. Pro-Choicers could still go to the floor next Monday, the opening day of the convention, if six state delegations signed a request for floor consideration. I looked up at Nissley, who was surrounded by television cameras and well-wishers. An equally large crowd stood around Hyde.

Over the weekend there was a "press buzz" flurry about whether we could find six states. Weld and McKernan had finally arrived in Houston and met to try and do something. Elsie Hilman, the pro-choice Bush chairman from Pennsylvania, and her senator, Arlen Specter, said they were willing to join with five other delegations to go to the floor. All weekend Crisp and Stone kept the buzz going, promising that "we'll get the six." According to Mary Matalin, Black grew worried that we might indeed be able to "reopen the abortion issue and raise it on the floor." But he need not have worried. Despite all our talk, the Pro-Choicers never had the six delegations, and even if a miracle had occurred and the six materialized, there was no communication system in place on the floor to fight the battle.

The president's team had won—but at a staggering cost. The strategy that the Republican party had used so successfully for twelve years to win presidential elections was about to self-destruct.

The platform was presented to the delegates at the convention's first morning session on Monday—not the second day, as had been traditional. There was no debate. It was unanimously adopted.

That Monday night, Mary Summa appeared on the podium to

introduce Pat Buchanan, whom she called a "true statesman, [with] the courage to boldly stand with the truth, no matter the consequences." Buchanan played on his familiar sexual themes, calling the recent Democratic convention that had nominated Bill Clinton and Albert Gore "the greatest single exhibition of cross-dressing in American history." He accused Bill and Hillary Clinton of not being on God's side. "There is a religious war going on in this country for the soul of America," he proclaimed. "It is a cultural war as critical to the kind of nation we shall be as the Cold War itself. And in that struggle for the soul of America, Clinton and Clinton are on the other side and George Bush is on our side." Buchanan even upstaged Ronald Reagan, who gave an eloquent speech immediately after.

The Bush team denied they had noticed Buchanan's crusader language when they'd reviewed his speech. "I trusted them [the Buchanan people] to do what they promised [give Bush an endorsement]," recalled Jim Lake, Bush's communications director. ". . . I read the speech and it had a great endorsement. . . . I really paid no attention to anything else. I was totally concerned with Is this going to be a strong endorsement of George Bush? Is it going to make our conservative base happy?"

As Buchanan's hatred settled over the convention floor like a miasma, those of us who wore pro-choice Bush buttons were accosted. One man told me I should be ashamed; I should seek God's counsel and stop helping destroy "innocent life." Everywhere I went, someone was standing ready to save my soul.

Throughout the convention, the Bush campaign was busy ridiculing Hillary Clinton. Not since the days of Eleanor Roosevelt had a candidate's wife been so abused by her husband's opposition. The attacks didn't come directly from George Bush, of course, but from his staff. Ever since Clinton won the nomination in the primaries, the campaign tried to make Hillary Clinton the "family values" equivalent of the Antichrist. The day after the Platform Committee finished its work, Rich Bond had told the Republican National Committee, "Advising Bill Clinton on every move is that champion of the family, Hillary Clinton, who believes kids should be able to sue their parents rather than helping with the chores as they were asked to do. She has likened marriage and the family to slavery."

The press wrote this hot one up immediately. The public didn't like it one bit. The polls showed they were fed up with negative campaigning. The tactic had been mean as well as stupid politics, and the campaign realized it belatedly. The frontal assaults stopped, although nuances and innuendos against Hillary Clinton continued.

On Wednesday morning, when I returned from the confrontation with Randall Terry in front of the Planned Parenthood clinic, I went to my hotel room and cried. I, who was not a hater, realized I literally hated George Bush, and I knew I could not go to the convention floor that night and vote for him. I called Roy Goodman and said I was going home. I could not in good conscience honor my pledge to cast a vote for the president. "Turn in your credentials to me," he said. "I understand."

I tried to book a plane out of Houston. None were available until the next morning. I was stuck. I thought about calling some reporters and blasting Bush and the Religious Right, but I had no more fight in me, only exhaustion and hate. I did a few previously scheduled radio-telephone interviews. Fortunately, none of the reporters asked me to judge Bush. They must have assumed I was still his loyal delegate.

When it came time for the night session, I turned on the television set in my room in the Hyatt. Roll-call night, when the presidential candidate is nominated, draws the largest television audiences of a convention. If a speaker wants wide exposure, this is the night to be scheduled. Pat Robertson had the prime-time slot.

The night was unoriginally labeled Ladies Night, but it was really the Religious Right's Night on the Family. Robertson got straight to the point. Bill Clinton, he said, wants "to destroy the traditional family and transfer many of its functions to the federal government." He questioned Clinton's faith in God for running on a platform that "never once mentioned God." Comparing the Democratic platform to the Republican, he said, "Traditional values start with faith in Almighty God. . . . [T]hat is why we did not take God out of the Republican party platform." It was indistinguishable from his Sunday television sermons. I wondered if he had ever been out on a clinic line with Randall Terry.

There was one brief respite from zealotry when Mary Fisher, the daughter of Max Fisher, a prominent fund-raiser for the party, spoke about being HIV positive. The convention hushed, and for a few minutes Robertson's "family values" were subsumed in human compassion and forgiveness of the kind Bobbie Breske had raised. But it didn't last. Marilyn Quayle came on like evangelist Aimee Semple McPherson. She was after those "liberals who believe the grandiose promises of the liberation movement. They're disappointed because most women do not wish to be liberated from their essential natures as women." This smart, aggressive lawyer told the convention, referring to her youth in the sixties, that "not everyone concluded that American society was so bad that it had to be radically remade by social revolution. Not everyone believed that the family was so oppressive that women could only thrive apart from it." I resented her sanctimoniousness, her tone of moral superiority. I loved my children, my husband; I thrived in my family and outside it. I also wanted rights for all women that would enable them to thrive.

Barbara Bush tried to bridge the gap between the Religious Right and the rest of us. She said, "However you define family, that's what we mean by family values." It was innocuous phrasing meaning all things to all people. In the charged atmosphere of the evening, she was sanity, but she wasn't enough to quiet the forces her husband's quest had unleashed.

In nominating Bush, Secretary of Labor Lynn Martin delivered an elegant, dignified tribute of the old guard conservative kind. It was a solid midwestern nomination that would have made those sturdy Republicans Robert Taft and Everett McKinley Dirksen proud. She meant it to reassure the American people that Bush hadn't gone off the deep end, that he wasn't a tool of radical religionists. Her words were eloquent, her delivery excellent, but she didn't have a chance. The Bush campaign had upstaged itself. Barbara Bush's temperance wouldn't matter. The news out of Houston wouldn't be about the triumph of the selfless fighter for America's future that Martin described. It would be about Buchanan, Robertson, Hyde, and Marilyn Quayle. When the roll call started, I turned off the television. I was glad to be rid of them.

As I walked out of the Hyatt lobby the next morning, a Robertson woman handed me another paperback by her leader. It was an oddly appropriate farewell.

Traditional "family values" was to be the Willie Horton–patriotism tactic of the Bush 1992 campaign. This time, though, the Democrats were ready. This time the negative campaigning backfired. The Religious Right's "family values" didn't carry much weight when Americans were hurting. The economy was in bad shape. This time it wasn't only the blue-collar Reagan Democrats, used to being temporarily laid off and rehired, who were in trouble. Middle-aged, middle-management people, the suburbanites who had been voting Republican for years, were losing their jobs too. The Clinton campaign kept its focus on the real fear around the country. "It's the economy, stupid" was the reminder sign in its headquarters.

Clinton was offering hope to Americans; George Bush kept hearkening back to another time. His themes were familiar: warnings about tax increases under the Democrats, waste, excessive government spending. He preached fear of family instability, but that was not what had the country so unsettled. Clinton addressed what frightened them. Bush did not. When the president raised the call of the Religious Right, of traditional "family values," it played well to his right-wing voting base. They liked him in the South. Elsewhere there were too many doubts. The religious excess of the Houston convention had scared a great many people.

In particular, moderates had been turned off. The depth of their unease, not only about the intolerance of the Republican party in Houston but about their economic security and a sense that their government had failed them, was reflected in the appeal of Ross Perot, who ran as a third-party challenger. Voters were also dissatisfied with Bush over the abortion issue. During the campaign's only vice-presidential debate, Perot's running mate James Stockdale, when asked his position on abortion, distinguished himself by his stupidity when he said, "Let's get on past this and talk about something substantive."

Stockdale was mistaken. Abortion had affected many voters' decisions. According to a study done by Emory University professor Alan Abramowitz, "party identification, ideology, and national economic conditions had the strongest effects on candidate choice," but after the economy, abortion was the policy issue of greatest importance to all voters. It outweighed the Gulf War, defense spending, affirmative action, and social welfare. And Abramowitz found that for about a quarter of the voters, who were "disproportionately white, affluent, and well-educated," abortion had been the deciding issue. Pro-choice Republicans defected in substantial numbers from Bush and Quayle,

Abramowitz found, although most voted for Perot rather than Clinton. On the other hand, most anti-choice Democrats didn't leave Clinton and Gore, because they either didn't know the candidates' positions or didn't care enough about the issue. Abramowitz predicted that "social issues are likely to remain the subjects of intense partisan conflict in the future" and that issues such as abortion and gay rights in the military "have the potential to cause widespread defections among partisans who oppose their own party's position."

After Houston, I worked for Bill Clinton. Other pro-choice Republican women did the same. Others voted for Perot. Others didn't vote. When Bush lost, I felt no remorse. He deserved to lose.

Clinton won 370 electoral votes to Bush's 168. He won 43 percent of the popular vote to Bush's 37.4 percent and Perot's 18.9 percent—an impressive number for a third-party candidate. All those efforts of Bush's strategists to hold the coveted Religious Right base succeeded—53 percent of southern, white Protestants voted for him. But he lost the western GOP stronghold—California, Oregon, Washington, Nevada, Colorado, Montana, and New Mexico—to Clinton, and he lost those moderates Abramowitz had identified. Republican women deserted Bush in significant numbers; exit polls showed that 26 percent crossed over to vote for Clinton or Perot. The economy had been the main issue, but in close states, choice had been the wedge issue that had made the difference.

According to political scientist Gerald Pomper, if Perot had not been in the race, the Perot vote would have "divided evenly, 38 percent each to Clinton and Bush, with the rest choosing minor candidates or abstaining. . . . Perot took votes from Bush in the south, but the president carried the region. The independent took votes from Clinton in the northeast, but [Clinton] still won all these states. . . . With or without the billionaire, Clinton and Gore would have won the election."

The women's vote held for the Democrats again, favoring Clinton by about 5 points. Bush lost the men, who when dissatisfied with Clinton voted for Perot in greater numbers than the women did. Perot's machismo was more than many women could take. It had been the year of the angry woman.

In the end, 1992 was a good year for women candidates, following a pattern of slow continuous progress we'd seen for twenty years. Fueled by women's anger over Anita Hill, Barbara Boxer, Dianne Feinstein, Patty Murray, and Carol Moseley-Braun joined Nancy Kassebaum and Barbara Mikulski in the Senate. The number of women in the House grew from twenty-eight to forty-seven. The Democrats retained control of both houses of Congress, and there were record numbers not only of women in the new Congress, but also of blacks and Hispanics.

The seeds of Bush's political destruction had been sown long before, and in 1989, when he was unwilling to take control of his own destiny and let Sununu and his friends take over his domestic agenda, he had shown his weakness. Bush epitomized what had happened to the nonright leaders in the national Republican party. They were so eager to please the right, to keep them from causing a ruckus that might risk losing them an election, that they stopped fighting back.

There is another theory about what happened: that Bush's strategists were incompetent and couldn't manage the convention, and that Houston so set back the campaign that it was never able to get a handle during the fall. This theory holds that with Lee Atwater's death and Jim Baker's absence from the campaign management until after Labor Day, the Bush bench was so thin as to cause Bush's defeat. This argument does not bear up under closer scrutiny. Bush's problems in winning the nomination and unifying his party were no greater than those he faced in 1988, when his team had shown impressive skill. Besides, this time he was an incumbent president, with all the advantages that flow from the office. Nineteen ninety-two should have been easier for him.

The right's dominance in Houston came about primarily because the campaign team included people who were perfectly competent but whose principal loyalty was to a particular right-wing issue, not to Bush. When those whose first loyalty was to Bush—Campaign Manager Bob Teeter is an example—were confronted with the demands of these right-wingers, they made the mistake of trying to accommodate them. The tax issue was one example; women's issues another. The president was not the only one who capitulated.

Another important factor in the 1992 campaign was an undercurrent that was never loudly articulated. Many New Right and Religious Right leaders had mixed feelings about a Republican victory. Whoever was elected president was going to have a difficult time. Given the burgeoning deficit, the decaying social infrastructure, the rise in violence, and the ongoing problems of competing in a global economy, the country itself seemed in dire straits. By 1996, they reasoned, they would have a better chance to control the White House because conditions would have become so desperate that America would be ready for revolutionary change. It didn't matter who was president at the time; the voters would want him out. When that time arrived, they would be able to take over, rid at last of the old guard and moderate types who were anathema to them.

Many times in Houston, sitting around the bars and restaurants, I heard people from the right compare 1992 with 1976 and the way that Carter's victory had paved the way for Reagan's four years later. They spoke of George Bush with contempt. It would be easier to let Clinton have the misery of the next four years. He'd mess up, they predicted, no matter how hard he tried, because the problems were too intractable without a total conservative revolution. They observed with some pleasure that Clinton was vulnerable from a moral standpoint: too many women, too many questionable deals. They'd get those stories out during his administration. By 1996, he would be as bloodied and down as Carter had been in 1980.

This talk was too pervasive to ignore. Second-level right-wing campaign operatives used psychological sabotage as well as procedural sabotage against Bush. At the top was Black who, as in so many past conventions and campaigns, was again the center of the political action. In charge of the platform, he was the campaign's liaison to the right— or as the campaign euphemistically called them, the conservatives. From the beginning, Black had argued that Bush's right-wing base must be protected, that without it he couldn't win. Buchanan's challenge reinforced Black's point of view.

Unfortunately, once Bush beat back Buchanan, the campaign continued to coddle the right. After the nomination was clinched in the spring, the traditional move to the center, or at least toward the old guard, never happened. On the first day of the convention, I learned that Black had already signed on as a consultant to Phil Gramm's 1996 presidential campaign. It was no accident that Gramm gave the convention's keynote address. When I asked why a top Bush strategist like Black would agree to be Gramm's consultant, I was told, "Just in case Bush doesn't make it."

Conspiracy theories are not only hard to prove; they are usually a convenient excuse for those who can't find a logical explanation for an outcome. There does not appear to have been a well-thought-out plan by the leaders of the right to defeat Bush. Rather, the campaign adhered to the theory that if the coalition were again to be victorious, the right flank must be protected at all costs. If that meant alienating the other parts of the coalition, so be it.

A conspiracy requires an adversary, and in this case there wasn't one. The majority of the Bush loyalists went along willingly. There was nothing surreptitious about their acquiescence, which was more in the nature of a deliberate sacrifice to placate the gods in order to ensure an abundant harvest in the fall. Whether the Bush convention managers who came out of the right wished to destroy him, or whether they honestly believed they had to let their hard-line ideological allies dominate in Houston, isn't clear. What is clear is that they had become prisoners to their narrow perspective, and that at least some of them didn't truly care what happened to Bush.

In interviews with political campaign chroniclers Jack Germond and Jules Witcover, Teeter, Black, and Lake expressed surprise at the nation's reaction to the convention. Black didn't believe there'd been anything "bad" about the convention, but he felt "we had lost control of the spin." Lake agreed with Teeter and Black that the conservative base had to be secured, adding, "I had no idea it would cause as much backlash as it did." The kindest conclusion one can draw from their assumptions is that having won in 1988 with a hard-right stance, they believed they could do it again. For George Bush, for the traditions of the Republican party, and for women, the convention was a disaster. For the Religious Right, it was a gift from God. For the New Right— well, it just depended on whom you were rooting for: Bush in the White House in 1992, or one of your own in 1996.

The Reagan–Bush era was over. The Republican party now belonged to the theocrats and the usual unprincipled power-seekers. The New Majoritarian coalition had had a good run, but its fatal flaw had been exposed. The nation had rejected, although not by much, its message of fear and bigotry. Who would pick up the pieces now? We women had been fighting for the soul of the party for years. Now, in its defeat, we had exorcised the genie. A new era was beginning.

PART THREE

Rebirth or

Extremism

18

THEOCRATS GET A PLACE AT THE TABLE

Newt Gingrich arrived at the center of the national scene after the November 1994 midterm elections like a hurricane out to blow away the already-shaky structures of the New Deal and the Great Society. To political types who had been watching him ever since he announced in the first months of his arrival in Washington in 1979 that he would make Republicans the House majority, he had been a New Right Machiavelli with charm. A supply-side right-to-lifer who fully embraced the New Majoritarian strategy, his ascent to House speaker was the result of the maturing power of the Religious and New Right authoritarians within the Republican party.

Gingrich was a truer revolutionary for the Reagan revolution than even Reagan had been. He brought an ideologue's zeal and a canny, practical sense of how to achieve power. He thought in broad strategic terms, as any smart leader of a political movement does, and he knew what needed to be done to implement the strategy—skills that Reagan never exhibited.

When Republicans gained control of the House and Senate in the 1994 elections, the Republican party finally became the party it had been moving toward since 1980. The old guard and the moderates were out. The national Republicans were now New Right revolutionaries out to eliminate big federal government, regardless of the cost to ordinary Americans—or, as Kevin Phillips indicted them, "the party of gunk, gun clubs, and granny-bashing." Phillips seemed now to have come full circle, rejecting the theory he had created.

The national GOP had also become a fundamentalist party, condemning those who didn't agree with its religious and moral values. Many Republicans, of course, didn't agree, and leaders like Bill Weld, Christine Todd Whitman, and Arlen Specter said so. But in 1995 the party's national leaders exhibited an ideological ardor akin to that of its abolitionist founders—but with the aim not of freedom, but of its restriction.

Gingrich and his colleagues claimed the November election had given them a mandate to change the way government did its business, even though only some 38.7 percent of the nation's registered voters had gone to the polls. But midterm turnouts are rarely high; and in other days and other times, great changes in American national policy have come about through a minority vote, the most notable example being the election of Lincoln in 1860 with 39.8 percent. Just because Gingrich's revolution was endorsed by only two out of five Americans and had the potential to collapse for lack of popular support before it achieved its goals didn't mean it would. Its ideas might well catch on with the majority, and the Gingrich revolutionaries knew this. They wasted no time in keeping their promise to the American people to pass the Contract with America in the House in a hundred days, and except for the approval of term limits, they succeeded.

There was no denying that the Republican earthquake of 1994 was major. It was only the third time since the advent of the New Deal, sixty-two years before, that the GOP would run the House. The party picked up fifty-four House seats, and for the first time, it held a majority of House seats from the South. It also held majorities from the Midwest and West. There were 230 Republicans, 204 Democrats, and one independent in the new House, enough to pass legislation if the Republicans stayed together. (Within nine months, three southern Democrats in the House would defect from their party and become Republicans.)

In the Senate the Republicans had an initial net gain of ten seats, nine from the election and one because Alabama Democratic senator Richard Shelby switched parties. In the spring, after the failure of the balanced budget amendment, Colorado Democratic senator Ben Nighthorse Campbell also switched, making a total of fifty-four Republicans and forty-six Democrats—not the sixty needed to break a filibuster but within negotiating distance. Of the nation's ten largest states, Republican governors would lead eight, a record the party hadn't held since 1970. Not a single incumbent Republican governor or member of Congress was defeated.

Male voters were angry at the Democrats. In the House races, as analyst Karlyn H. Bowman reported, men voted 57 percent Republican to 43 percent Democratic. Women were a virtual mirror image, 54 percent Democratic to 46 percent Republican. It was the largest vote by men for Republican House candidates since the gender gap had appeared.

The country's mood that Election Day was sullen and hostile. Confidence and trust in Bill Clinton was shaky, even among some who had been enthusiasts two years before. The economy that had played so important a role in his victory had turned around, yet despite favorable overall economic indicators, Americans weren't happy with their lot. They felt they were losing ground. Many men and women had lost their jobs in corporations that were downsizing and slashing to make them competitive in world markets. Where in the past many workers had felt a sense of commitment to the company they worked for that they thought the company reciprocated, this was no longer the case. Many years spent working for the same firm were often meaningless for continuing employment; long-term employees could find themselves out on the street just as abruptly as recent hires. People shared a widespread feeling of insecurity and resentment, as if the rug that had been pulled out from under them under the aegis of necessity and efficiency were an excuse for greed. The market's "invisible hand" was working, but these laid-off people were asking whether some old-fashioned compassion ought to be part of the mix as well.

Kevin Phillips and others described part of the problem as a process of "financialization" that was reducing "the connection between their [corporations'] profitability and the growth of middle-class jobs. . . . Firms once committed to long-term thinking now faced money managers and speculators little concerned about existence beyond the life of a futures contract. . . . For the first time in modern U.S. history, stock prices decoupled from the real economy, enabling the Dow-Jones industrial average to keep setting records even as employees' real wages kept declining." Very few knew about the nature of the process Phillips was explaining, and most would not have found it helpful even if they had. They only knew that they were feeling insecure and poorer.

In November 1994 these angry men and some women took their pain out on Democrats. They bought the old Republican line that big government with its wasteful spending and high taxes was the cause of their economic problems, and the newer line that a cultural decline, attributable to the Democrats, was making family life less secure and crime levels high. Many women expressed their unhappiness by turning off altogether and not voting. An assessment of gender-voting numbers found that the percentage turnout of women voters declined by 6 percent, while the percentage turnout of men increased by 7 percent.

Two Republicans, pro-choice Olympia Snowe from Maine and multiple-choice Kay Bailey Hutchison from Texas, were elected to the Senate in open seats. California senatorial incumbent Democrat Dianne Feinstein overcame a record-breaking challenge by Republican Michael Huffington, who spent nearly $28 million, mostly of his own money, in a bruisingly hostile campaign. Eight women now served in the Senate.

The total number of women in the House remained at forty-seven. Nine Democratic women were defeated, seven of whom had been elected from marginal Democratic districts in 1992. Their Republican opponents owed their victories to the work of the Religious Right and the term limits movement. In their place came four new Democratic and seven Republican women, of whom eight had won in open seats.

One of the most interesting developments in 1994 was the appearance of a sizable number of antifeminist women candidates for the House. I had wondered for years why more women with the political talent of conservative activists like Phyllis Schlafly and Linda Chavez hadn't run for national office. This time several did.

Six of the freshmen Republican House women who arrived in 1994, all of them anti-choice, represented a new wrinkle in women's politics. Four were active in Religious Right causes. Linda Smith of Washington headed a local Eagle Forum chapter; Californian Andrea Seastrand and Barbara Cubin of Wyoming worked in the right-to-life movement; Helen Chenoweth of Idaho founded a branch of the Focus on the Family organization, a more militant group than the Christian Coalition. Unlike her western women colleagues, Enid Greene Waldholtz of Utah, a lawyer and former head of the National Young Republican Federation, was a New Right "family values" advocate but not an activist member of the Christian Coalition or its allied groups. The only southern woman in the freshman class was former two-term mayor of Charlotte, North Carolina, Sue Myrick, a deeply religious woman who says when she makes political decisions, she listens to "the will of God first" and "the will of the people second." In 1995 Waldholtz became involved in an ugly scandal over her husband's embezzlement of her campaign funds. While she did not resign, she was disgraced and did not seek reelection.

While the Religious Right became an even more powerful force in the party than in 1992 and continued its messages against the goals of the feminist movement, some of its leaders recognized the value of running women from Religious Right groups. Gingrich stimulated this conversion.

Unlike the Bush and Reagan campaign operatives, Gingrich figured out something Republican feminists had been anticipating for years—that the time would come when some of the women who'd been doing much of the heavy lifting for the Right got tired of taking orders and preferred to give them. He anticipated the recognition by organizations like the Christian Coalition that they had some extraordinarily talented women in their midst, seeing before they did the political potential of having women officers in his revolutionary army.

Unlike the Reagan and Bush men, Gingrich and his allies have given women an opportunity for real power. He realized that this would alienate some of his male colleagues, but he knew that in exchange he not only would enhance his image outside Washington but could begin the slow process of bringing American women voters back to the Republican party.

Women have become an integral part of Gingrich's political organization. In 1994 the National Republican Congressional Committee (NRCC) was headed by upstate New Yorker Maria Cino, and her top-level team of seven included five women. These women, together with NRCC chairman Bill Paxon, an anti-choice upstate New York congressmember, and pro-choice New York City congressmember Susan Molinari, implemented much of the successful 1994 GOP strategy. In the summer of 1994 Molinari married Paxon, and they became powerful partners in the Gingrich Revolution. She has actively recruited women into the GOP leadership, while her husband unabashedly talks about electing her America's first woman president. (On August 1, 1997, thirty-nine-year-old Molinari resigned from Congress to become a CBS News television commentator. Her forthcoming high visibility on national television will enhance her star quality, and unless she stumbles, it will burnish her husband's ambitions for her. After all, Ronald Reagan's key to the White House door came from the world of broadcasting and entertainment.)

Paxon and Gingrich are a new kind of New Right politician. Maybe because they're baby boomers and grew up with the women's movement, they are more comfortable working with women in equal relationships. They aren't hung up in the ladies-and-gentlemen sexism of the Bush generation. They have recognized that women can be full-time political players and that having well-spoken women as peers is a political advantage. But unfortunately for women, Paxon's and Gingrich's political power is derived from alliances with the Religious Right. They cannot be expected to give much help to legislation supported by feminists if it in any way conflicts with the right's "family values" goals.

Maureen Reagan was never able to institutionalize a national PAC for Republican women. Phyllis Schlafly has been helping men and some women candidates for years, but until 1992, when Glenda Greenwald and Candace Straight founded the WISH List, there was no national independent fund-raising arm for Republican women candidates outside the bipartisan Women's Campaign Fund and the NWPC. WISH did well in 1994, raising $370,000 compared with $250,000 in 1992. By 1994, the Republican Network to Elect Women (RENEW) and the Susan B. Anthony's List had appeared. Dedicated to helping "women who support the right-to-life," the list raised some $70,000 for the six anti-choice Republican House freshman women.

The seventh Republican woman to win in 1994, pro-choice New Yorker Sue Kelly, a former member of the Republican Family Committee's executive committee, was helped by the women's movement's pro-choice PACs. Kelly is more an old guard traditionalist. Reelected in 1996 after a difficult primary challenge from a right-to-life candidate, her electoral base now seems assured, and she has the potential to be a leader in tempering the more antifeminist actions of the House GOP leadership.

The New Right women have begun to discover what we in the women's political movement have been gradually learning over the years: There is power for women in working together. An incident related to the election of these seven women is illustrative. For years, polling by feminist organizations has shown that independent and Democratic voters often trusted Republican women candidates more than Republican men. New on the scene, not-so-feminist RENEW rediscovered the wheel with a commissioned poll that found the same thing. RENEW's executive director, Karen Roberts, claimed her poll findings were the impetus for what happened next. In 1994 the NRCC instituted a buddy system, in which twelve incumbent Republican House women campaigned in districts where women GOP candidates were running. They offered advice and any other help they could, and it worked. It was an approach that political feminists have used for years to ease the entry of neophyte women into politics.

When the Republicans organized the House after their great victory, the incumbent GOP women were rewarded. Molinari became vice-chairman of the Republican Conference, a first for either party's conference, and Nevada congressmember Barbara Vucanovich, conference secretary. For the first time in decades, women would lead House committees. (During the years of Democratic rule, even fewer women held leadership positions.) The Small Business Committee was headed by Kansan Jan Meyers, while Nancy Johnson chaired the House Ethics Committee. Freshman Enid Waldholtz was appointed to the all-powerful Rules Committee, a first for a freshman woman.

During the first year of the revolutionary 104th Congress, Gingrich and his New Right colleagues co-opted the moderate Republican women. They were trapped in the political system, just as moderates like me were trapped by their loyalty to George Bush. They were party to a revolution that sought to undo the women's movement. Some of them argued that they could be a leavening force in toning down the worst abuses of the right's social agenda. In 1995 this was wishful thinking. The party was headed toward adopting Gingrich's Opportunity Society, which in its most basic terms would limit women's right to reproductive choice, eliminate affirmative action, punish poor women for having children, and make life more miserable for women in general. The opportunities Gingrich hoped to provide women would be limited by the mental cages in which the Religious Right philosophies would imprison them. As has so often happened in women's history, some women would again be agents for control over their gender.

In the early nineties, when Bush was president, Gingrich came to New York City to meet with some twenty-five Republican women at the apartment of Republican feminist Muriel Siebert. His ostensible reason for the meeting was to ask for help for his political action committee, GOPAC, but we went for another reason. We were enraged by the *Webster* decision and the Republican votes for all the anti-abortion legislation that was being trundled from the right-to-life organizations into the White House and over to the congressional Republican conferences. For more than two and a half hours, we told him in detailed, reasoned, and sometimes angry words how disgusted we were by the GOP leadership's actions against reproductive rights. He argued with us briefly, then stopped. He listened. He heard our frustration, our conflict with leaders who perpetuated the dominance of an authoritarian, anti-women ideology. If it hadn't been that the last shuttle back to Washington left at nine o'clock, he would have probably stayed longer. It was a genuine consciousness-raising session for him. He didn't promise he'd change, but he said that for the first time he finally understood what was upsetting pro-choice women. He said he'd think seriously about our grievances. I believe he did.

Gingrich has not stopped voting anti-choice, but he is no longer as vocal about the issue, at least in public. On May 7, 1995, he told NBC's *Meet the Press* that "if all we did tomorrow was pass an amendment, you would have millions of women going into back alleys having abortions." He still believes life begins at conception, but now he talks about the nation needing to go through a long dialogue on abortion. His *Meet the Press* statement was a trial balloon to begin defusing the abortion issue, heralding the possibility of a change in the party's hard-line position. The problem is that the contemplated change is likely to be restrictive as well. He appears to be looking toward giving the federal government's power to determine who can get abortions back to the states, in line with the framework established in the *Casey* decision. It would be tough luck for the women who have the misfortune to live in a state that prohibits most abortions.

When the Contract with America was unveiled, Gingrich emphasized that its terms excluded abortion and school prayer, and that was the line the press accepted. It was not entirely true, however. Buried in a section on welfare reform well back in the contract's text, which few reporters bothered to read, was a call for the reinstatement of a new variety of the gag rule. Pro-choice Republican congressmembers had signed the contract. When pro-choice Republicans complained to these members about the buried gag rule proposal, they assured us that Gingrich had promised they would have a chance to challenge the rule and debate it on the House floor. During the first hundred days of the new Republican Congress, anti-choice members tried to impose anti-choice amendments. With the defiant stand of House pro-choice Republicans and Democrats, the amendments were defeated.

But the pro-choice GOP defense did not hold. The right-to-life movement had a majority of votes in the House to pass all anti-choice bills, and in the Senate, all but the most extreme. Pro-choice Republicans were not able to soften the edges of the most repressive of these bills, and Gingrich was not about to prevent the right-to-lifers from passing anti-choice legislation—nor would he want to, given they had played a significant part in his becoming speaker.

The Republican House reinstated the gag rule, the Mexico City policy, and the ban on fetal-tissue research, and it cut Title X family-planning programs. (Clinton had reversed these attacks on choice when he took office.) Pro-choice Republican women in the Congress fought determinedly to stop these four pieces of legislation, but they were outnumbered. They faced other difficult decisions, in which they had to choose between loyalty to the party's agenda and their belief in helping women. And as with the anti-choice legislation, they fought and lost.

Since 1992, the greatest change in the makeup of the New Majoritarian coalition has been the ascendancy of the Religious Right as an equal partner with the national Republican leadership. While they dictated the party's 1992 platform and had veto power over the Bush campaign's social issues, they did not make major decisions at that point.

This situation changed with the 1994 elections. The Religious Right played a major role in electing the new Republican majority, not only in delivering votes but in grassroots organizing and raising campaign contributions. John Green, an academic expert on the religious conservatives, says that "the Christian Right probably mobilized 4 million activists and reached 50 million voters." With the new Republican Congress, these theocrats got the clout they had been seeking. In May 1995, when the Christian Coalition announced its Contract with the American Family, Ralph Reed noted, "As religious conservatives, we have finally gained what we have always sought, a place at the table, a sense of legitimacy, and a voice in the conversation that we call democracy." Wisconsin Republican state chairman David Opitz put it more succinctly: "The religious conservatives aren't trying to get a nose under the tent anymore. They are the tent."

He is right, and while political people argue about just how many state Republican parties are controlled by the Religious Right, all agree that at a minimum the number is twenty and that another dozen or so are influenced by it. A good way to measure the strength of the Christian Coalition was to realize that less than a year before the Republicans met in San Diego for their August 1996 national convention, more than half of the state Republican organizations were effectively in the hands of the Religious Right.

The old guard knew this; and that is why in the spring of 1995 presidential candidate Bob Dole began backing the Religious Right's red-meat issues. Although he had always been anti-choice, Dole had steered clear of the New Majoritarian social agenda, concentrating instead on economic issues. In recognition of the NRA's power, he announced that he would make repealing the assault weapons ban a legislative priority. That same week he turned his back on the federal affirmative action programs that he and his wife had helped fashion and support for many years. He also dropped his mainstream Methodist Church affiliation and said he'd attend more evangelical church services. In only one week in April Dole attacked the entertainment industry and welfare mothers and came out strongly for voluntary prayer in the schools. He sounded like Dan Quayle, Ralph Reed, and Paul Weyrich rolled into one hot-headed right-wing preacher. When asked what had happened to the old cool, pragmatic Dole, his campaign manager said: "Any survey research you or I have seen shows that these are issues that primary voters care about or are motivated by."

In the summer of 1995 all the potential Republican presidential candidates were playing to the Religious Right, with the exception of Arlen Specter. Specter represented a combination of the old guard and moderate attitudes on social issues and embraced much of the supply-side economics of the New Right, calling for consideration of a flat tax. His campaign was run by Roger Stone, who seemed intent on forging a new power in the Republican party—the social liberal and fiscal conservative. This approach wasn't really new—it was the classic Ripon Society prototype—but it had a new twist with the addition of supply-side philosophy. Most Riponers were not supply-siders but old-fashioned deficit-cutting Republicans.

As a New Right libertarian, Stone was seeking a place at the table for his client Specter, and by inference for what was left of the moderate Republicans. They had become a minority in the GOP, and only the pro-choice women remained a potential force to keep the Religious Right from making even greater gains. It is ironic that Stone, one of the architects of the New Majoritarian strategy, was now trying to represent the faction of the party he had once set out to eliminate. His colleague-in-arms Charlie Black, by contrast, was true to his 1992 plan. As Phil Gramm's chief political consultant in his drive to become the Republican nominee, Black was doing what he had done for the last twenty years: building the New Right and cutting out the center.

Abortion was still the issue that most divided Republicans. It had even caused trouble within the Religious Right. The Christian Coalition, in an attempt to be pragmatic and follow a stealth strategy, toned down its right-to-life rhetoric. Its Contract with the American Family didn't call for a ban on abortion. Instead, it backed marginally away from the Republican platform, calling for limiting late-term abortions and cutting federal funding for all of them. Ralph Reed seemed to be trying to maneuver his way out of the abortion issue in the same way that Gingrich almost kept it out of his contract.

These two proposals were relatively minor in the overall scheme of abortion politics in the fall of 1995. Forty states already prohibited late-term abortions, and *Roe* gave the government a major role in regulating them in the third trimester. As for federal funding, there hadn't been much for years. After a gargantuan battle under Democratic-led Congresses in 1993 and 1994, Congress expanded Medicaid funding from cases where the life of the mother is endangered to include victims of rape and incest—an exception that Hyde was for the first time willing to back. But while newfound "tolerance" may have eased its rhetoric, the Christian Coalition hadn't changed its stripes, and it tried to repeal that exception. That there would be yet another battle over whether a rape or incest victim should receive a couple hundred dollars of federal money for an abortion was unfortunate.

Despite all their political acumen, Gingrich and Reed had trouble toning down the issue. Pat Buchanan, once again a presidential candidate, voiced what many right-to-lifers felt about the Contract with the American Family proposal as a whole, and abortion in particular. The contract "sets the hurdles too low," he charged. "The Coalition has given away any boldness in search for popularity and consensus." He suggested that Congress hold hearings on when life begins and vote on the Human Life Amendment, and he reiterated the goals of the right-to-life movement: elimination of funding for Planned Parenthood, for fetal-tissue research, and for the UN Family Planning Association. He added what many Religious Right advocates felt: "I believe we really ought to be bold. We won both houses of Congress. Why not do it now? If not now, when? And if not us, who? I don't think we're going to be stronger than we are now."

The rest of the Religious Right also denounced the Christian Coalition's retreat from its pure right-to-life position. Focus on the Family, the Christian Defense Coalition, Gary Bauer's Family Research Council, and the American Life League said the coalition had sold out to the Republican establishment—and in a way it had.

At the Christian Coalition's press conference in May 1995, Gingrich announced that the coalition had played a "vital part" in bringing "a revolution at the polls on November 8th." He added that "we are committed to keeping faith with the people who helped with the Contract with America . . . to scheduling the hearings . . . the markups . . . the votes on the floor." Gramm attended the press conference; Dole met privately with Reed and sent a message welcoming the coalition's contract.

The other parts of this "family values" contract called for: a Religious Equality Amendment, elimination of the Department of Education and distribution of its funds to the states, school choice based on the concepts laid out in the 1992 GOP platform; a $500 per-year tax credit for each child; restriction of access to pornography on cable TV and the Internet; cancellation of federal funding for the National Endowment for the Arts, the National Endowment for the Humanities, the Corporation for Public Broadcasting, and the Legal Services Corporation; a Parental Rights Act; and a requirement for criminals to pay restitution to the families of their victims. Like any smart political strategist, Reed had included many proposals that moderates and the old guard would find attractive, like the criminals' restitution requirement, the $500 tax credit, and the restrictions on pornography.

But the Religious Equality Amendment showed the Christian Coalition's true colors. The proposed amendment, with its wording yet to be finalized, says that "nothing in this Constitution shall be interpreted to prohibit the citizens of the United States from practicing religion in public places nor to prohibit the states from facilitating the practice of religion from their citizens." On first glance, this amendment seems innocuous and in step with the majority views of Americans, who are considered to be the most religious people of all the western democracies when measured by numbers who regularly attend religious services and say they believe in God. But we are already an actively religious people. We do not need the government to ensure our practice of religion. The proposed amendment would tear down the wall separating church and state and allow state governments "to facilitate" the practice of religion. The Supreme Court rulings over the years that have so carefully kept the government out of religion would be swept away. *The New York Times* editorialized that the coalition's amendment "embodies a radical vision for regulating the private behavior of law-abiding citizens to accord with the preferences of fundamentalist and evangelical Christians. . . . Instead of remaining a nation where millions are happy to pray in private in exchange for being let alone by government, the United States could become a Babel of government-supported public piety."

The party of less government except when it comes to women was now being asked to make another exception for religion. Republicans were again organizing against individual freedom and the Bill of Rights in order to help the Religious Right promote its social agenda. Bob Dole announced that he would work for the amendment's passage. "It may not be fashionable inside the Beltway," he said, "but I believe that we must restore religious expression to its rightful place in our national conversation and our public life." Arlen Specter attacked it as an infringement of religious liberty.

·　　　·　　　·

Fanaticism has been part of the anti-abortion movement from its beginning. What too few people have been willing to recognize is that fanaticism against women can easily be turned to fanaticism in other areas. When Randall Terry called for "restructuring the [U.S.] as a Christian republic with laws drawn from the Bible," few politicians responded. When Ralph Reed repackaged these ideas and made them more palatable by saying this was "not a Christian agenda but a pro-family agenda," the Republican leaders took notice. The Christian Coalition borrowed a page from Reagan's book on how to bring about revolutionary change. Put your ideas in a simple "family values" framework, talk gently and with feeling about how you want only the best for America, recall the happy simple past, and don't threaten. As Reed said, "We issue no ultimatums." Rather, the coalition's purpose is to "help Congress as it charts a cultural agenda" to address "what we believe is the most pressing issue in American politics today, and that is the fraying of the social fabric, the coarsening of the culture, the breakdown of the family."

The Religious Right men and women have pushed their way into Americans' lives. The Republican war against women that seemed so harmless to so many of my Republican colleagues in the late seventies has now expanded into a major effort to change the way all Americans live. The Religious Right protests that they are not imposing their ideas on the rest of us, yet they demand that we accept their faith. What they fail to understand is that the rest of us are not trying to prevent them from practicing their faith.

Religious wars are a relic of the Old World past. America has been special in world history because it has refused to become involved in them. We have always had our religious controversies. Religion has been an important force in the nation's politics from the early colonial days, to the activism of the nineteenth century that stimulated the abolitionist, feminist, and temperance movements, and up to the present. While those holding deeply religious beliefs have every right in America to influence political dialogue, I believe the present Religious Right political movement has gone beyond respecting the rights of those who do not agree with them, and that it is moving toward establishing an American theocracy.

The New Majoritarian strategy has evolved into something new. The religious part of the strategy, first introduced into the GOP with misogynist messages, has now become dominant in the national party. The question was whether the American people would vote in the 1996 presidential election for a Republican party that had embraced a view of women more compatible with fourteenth-century superstition than twentieth-century egalitarianism.

19

THE CHAOS OF THE GOP

The answer was definitive. The majority of America's voting women again rejected the national Republicans' confused notion of a woman's place in the world. For the first time in the nation's history, it was women's votes that had elected the President of the United States. Without the Nineteenth Amendment, Republican Bob Dole would likely have been the new occupant of the White House. Instead, Bill Clinton became the first Democratic president since FDR to be reelected.

Clinton had overpowered Dole, winning 379 to 159 electoral votes, and, in an impressive margin for a three-way race, taken 49.2 percent of the popular vote to Dole's 40.8 and Ross Perot's 8.5. In landslide proportions, 54 percent of women voters backed Clinton, compared with 38 percent for Dole and 7 for Perot. As for the men, they barely supported Dole, with 44 percent to Clinton's 43 and Perot's 10.

For years, critics of the women's movement had argued that a broad-based women's vote was a myth. They claimed that women were no more homogeneous than men and that gender was overemphasized in determining how a woman voted. While it is obvious that women are diverse, this argument failed to recognize that women's awareness of the condition and needs of their gender could be a unifying political force.

In 1996 the argument was unmasked. A majority of women of different backgrounds came together in a voting consensus that proved there was a women's voting bloc of sufficient consequence to determine the outcome of a presidential election. And the catalyst that brought them together was not their trust of Bill Clinton but their distrust of the Republican party.

It wasn't that Clinton wasn't vulnerable. His and Hillary's Whitewater and White House travel office problems had not gone away. Paula Jones's sexual harassment lawsuit was troubling. None of this, however, was enough to make a difference in the election.

The women's-backlash element of the New Majoritarian strategy had always aimed at playing to those who distrusted the goals of the women's movement, chiefly men, while not alienating too many of those who believed in its goals, chiefly women. This strategy had worked for Bush in 1988, when he had won male voters by 16 percentage points and women by one. The majority of women who were married, white, between thirty and fifty-nine years of age, had some college education, lived in the suburbs, and identified themselves as independents had voted for Bush. In 1996 every one of those groups gave the majority of its votes to Clinton, not Dole.

The backlash strategy had been deteriorating for years. Built on a premise alien to America's ideals, the strategy had been unsound from the beginning, but most Republican leaders did not take seriously the growing number of women angered by the GOP's hypocritical and unreasonable attitude toward their gender. The strategy collapsed in 1992 with Bush's defeat. Yet Republicans, lulled by their 1994 midterm triumph, believed it was still effective. They were convinced America would embrace their full agenda—not only its call for less government and taxes but the restrictions it was imposing on women's liberty. They were wrong.

The 1996 GOP presidential campaign was dead on arrival. The majority of women had little faith in the Republicans. There had been too many times in the last sixteen years when the GOP had either ignored women or been directly hostile to them. In their eyes, the GOP had become the anti-women's party.

The road to the Republicans' defeats in 1992 and 1996 was strewn with this history: their opposition to the Family and Medical Leave Act, their assault on legal abortion and their attempts to diminish the respectability of family planning, their lack of interest in child care, their ambivalence toward the ERA and affirmative action, their antagonism to raising the minimum wage, and their dismantling of education programs that gave women equal opportunity.

After the 1994 election, RNC chairman Haley Barbour and others denied that the Republican war against women existed. Look at the GOP record, they proclaimed: two women U.S. senators, one woman governor, seventeen members of Congress, 678 state legislators, and under the Bush administration (until Clinton's election in 1992) the most women appointed to federal positions in a single term.

All this was true. But their analysis was superficial and deceptive. Both parties had responded to pressure from the women's political movement. Both were now happy to run some women for office; they realized that women made good, winning candidates. Both were also hiring women for top jobs. Sheila Burke, Bob Dole's chief of staff in the Senate, was one of his most respected advisers. The gender of choice for press secretary was female; ironically, the job was rapidly becoming a women's employment ghetto.

Nor could anyone argue that Elizabeth Dole was not the personification of a woman who had deftly seized the opportunities opened to her by the feminists. Nor that Pat Buchanan's sister Bay, the most fiery, aggressive presidential campaign manager in 1996, had not benefited from the movement she so voraciously attacked. As a single, divorced working mother, she hardly fit the idealized model of the Religious Right woman.

But this war was not about how the GOP hired staff, treated its female candidates, or regarded the female family members of its male officials. This war was about issues. It was about the party's stands on public policies that specifically affected women's lives.

After watching the 104th Congress try to shred the safety net with its Contract with America, women's alarm mounted. For many, the last straw came in late 1995. In a struggle with the White House over how to balance the federal budget, the Republican radicals refused to pass seven government funding bills unless Clinton agreed to their budget priorities: cut taxes for the well-to-do and eliminate the earned income-tax exemption for the working poor; cut student loans, Medicaid, Medicare, family planning, Aid to Families with Dependent Children, Head Start, Meals-on-Wheels, and environmental protection. Clinton refused to accede to these demands.

As a result of this stalemate, there was literally no money for federal employees' salaries and services. For six days in November and twenty-one days in December, the government closed down, furloughing

760,000 government workers. Hard hit financially, many of them scrimped on holiday gifts and borrowed money to pay the rent.

The national parks and museums closed. Federally funded medical research stopped. You couldn't get a passport except in a dire emergency. All "nonessential" government aid was suspended. The trauma was not confined to the Beltway region. The woman who owned a grocery store in West Yellowstone, Wyoming, felt as helpless as the businesswoman who couldn't travel to meet her new clients in St. Petersburg, Russia. In actions reminiscent of Dickens's *A Christmas Carol,* the 104th Scrooge Congress cut off government services for the disabled, the elderly, and the poor of all ages—including children. A temporary truce was reached at last, and the government reopened. But the shutdown had done serious damage to Gingrich and the GOP. Women in particular found their fears confirmed by these actions: The Republicans were too uncaring and incompetent to be trusted with their vote. The New Right's scorched-earth budget had become unacceptable not only to most Democrats but to Dole and many old guard conservatives and moderate Republicans.

In his State of the Union speech a few weeks later, the president declared that the "era of big government is over," effectively co-opting the Republican messages that were most attractive to centrists, especially centrist women. The one-year era of Gingrichism was coming to a close, and Clinton would become the beneficiary of its excesses.

In early 1996 the Republican presidential candidates seemed oblivious to their party's weakness among women as they slugged it out in the snows of Iowa and New Hampshire. Even though Dole was endorsed by Pat Robertson, each was trying to outmaneuver the others for the Religious Right's vote in the upcoming caucuses and primaries.

I remember watching one of the numerous television debates just before the Iowa vote in mid-February. The candidates—Robert Dole, Lamar Alexander, Alan Keyes, Pat Buchanan, Steve Forbes, Phil Gramm, Robert Dornan, Richard Lugar, and Morry Taylor—fell all over themselves trying to prove how much they opposed abortion. Except for references to their own families and Mother Teresa, none mentioned women. It was as though we didn't exist outside our role as mothers.

One might have expected three of the nine GOP candidates who had the most sympathetic public record on women's issues, Dole, Alexander, and Forbes, to be predisposed to an aggressive campaign that reached out to women as well as men. But caught up in myths that had grown up around the backlash strategy, all three proved to be too timid.

This obtuseness was all the more unnerving because Democrats on the campaign trail were constantly speaking to women about family needs, economic security, education, the Family and Medical Leave Act, child and elder care, Social Security, Medicare, and a woman's right to choose.

Dole won the Iowa caucuses, but he beat second-place winner Buchanan by only three points. Christian right women had voted overwhelmingly for Buchanan, while many moderate and old guard conservative women, who were Dole's natural base, stayed home because none of the candidates had spoken directly to their concerns. Women generally vote in higher numbers than men, yet they made up only 44 percent of the Iowa turnout.

In New Hampshire, Dole, Alexander, and Forbes made modest efforts to win the votes of centrist women. Dole's campaign was the most aggressive in this respect, but it made the mistake, common to campaigns seeking to diminish their deficit with women, of using stand-ins. In this case, Elizabeth Dole was given increased responsibility for bringing in the women's vote. But she was not the candidate. Surrogates, no matter how effective, are not the same, and voters know that.

The Dole campaign also ran ads calling Buchanan a denigrator of women. It unearthed a Buchanan quote the Bush forces had used against him in 1992: "Women are not endowed by nature with the measures of single-minded ambition and the will to succeed." While effective, these attacks were not enough to erase the campaign's fundamental deficiency; it still hadn't provided sufficient positive reasons why women should vote for Dole, other than that he had a terrific wife.

Buchanan stormed through New Hampshire attacking the Republican establishment that had given him the opportunity to become a millionaire. He portrayed himself as the put-upon little guy saving other little guys and gals from the evil forces of capitalism and international corporate greed. He was a populist rabble-rouser—a Huey Long for the 1990s.

The ironies were lost on the voter. On primary day in New Hampshire, Buchanan shook the party like an earthquake, beating Dole 28 to 27 percent. The Republican landscape hadn't experienced a tremor like this since Barry Goldwater's nomination in 1964. Just as in Iowa, Religious Right women turned out in large numbers to vote for Buchanan, while many other women did not vote and those who did tended to split their vote among the other candidates. In an astonishing upset, the man who had frightened America with his "cultural war" speech in Houston and whom many Republicans blamed for Bush's loss in 1992 was now leading the GOP presidential sweepstakes.

The country—and the majority of Republicans—considered Buchanan an extremist for his sleight-of-hand anti-Semitism, sexism, nativism, racism, and homophobia. He angrily rejected these labels. But the evidence was there for all to see. His supporters included David Duke, the former head of the Ku Klux Klan and a sympathizer of Nazi causes, and Larry Pratt, who was not only executive director of Gun Owners of America (a group that labeled the National Rifle Association too moderate and once compared the FBI to the Nazi Gestapo) but was forced to step down as co-chairman of Buchanan's campaign following reports linking him to white-supremacist and right-wing militia groups.

In fact, it was Buchanan's anticorporate and isolationist rhetoric, rather than his bigotry, that scared many of his potential supporters. Right-wing radio talk-show host Rush Limbaugh said, "Pat Buchanan is not a conservative. He's a populist," who, because of his opposition to free trade, "wants to engage in politics that expand the role of government in people's lives."

Haley Barbour refused to say he would support Buchanan if he were nominated. Buchanan had accomplished what none of us in the party's moderate wing had been able to do: He lit a fire under those quiet centrists and old guard conservatives. Some spoke out against his intolerance, and some of the turned-off Republican women volunteered at Dole headquarters.

Something more subtle was also happening. Ralph Reed and other leaders of the Religious Right recognized that Buchanan was slowing down their ascendance in the national GOP. The New Right conservatives, those who had built the Goldwater and Reagan movements, were also alarmed. American Conservative Union political director William Pascoe spoke for them when he said, "Many conservatives are worried less about the Republican party than the future of the conservative movement. They don't want him [Buchanan] to redefine the conservative movement in his image."

Most significant of all, Dole was invigorated by his loss in New Hampshire. In defeat, Bob Dole, man of Kansas who represented the last of the midwestern national Republicans in the Taft, Eisenhower, and Ford tradition, found himself. Speaking on the night he lost, Dole said something many of us disaffected Republicans had been waiting for many years to hear from the party's national leaders:

> This is now a race between the mainstream and the extreme. We know that we're now engaged in a fight for the heart and soul of the Republican party. . . . We will decide if we are the party of fear or of hope, if we are the party that keeps people out, or brings people in.

For a few days, the national Republican party faced up to the bigotry in its midst, and Bob Dole led the charge.

His next major test came in the March 2 South Carolina primary, the first in the South. South Carolina, home of the New Right, of Strom Thurmond and Lee Atwater, would make or break Dole's candidacy. Its Republican governor David Beasley and its former governor Carroll Campbell were Christian Coalition favorites, free traders, and Dole supporters. Campbell and Beasley's aggressive lobbying to attract foreign investment had transformed South Carolina into the state of choice for many overseas businesses. Buchanan assumed his message of pro-life litmus tests for Supreme Court justices and his sympathy for laid-off textile workers would compensate for his attacks against the foundation of South Carolina's new prosperity—foreign trade and the new plants built by German, French, and Japanese companies. It was a serious mistake. While some South Carolina Republicans sympathized with Buchanan's social messages, they found his xenophobic populism, nativism, and isolationism offensive.

Dole shifted focus, quit calling Buchanan an extremist, and instead derided his unrealistic view of world trade. Recognizing Buchanan's appeal to the Christian Coalition's members, Dole strongly emphasized his own support for a constitutional amendment overturning *Roe v. Wade* and for voluntary school prayer. Dole's battle for the heart and soul of the GOP had been like a Roman candle—brief, dazzling, and out.

And the tactic worked. In one of the most New Right states in America, Bob Dole, one of the least New Right candidates in his party's race for president, beat Buchanan by 15 percentage points. Moderates, old guard, and New Right conservatives gave him solid backing. Even among people who identified themselves as Christian conservatives, Dole won almost as many votes as Buchanan. Beasley, Campbell, and Ralph Reed had delivered for him. Exit polls showed that men and women of all incomes and ages voted for Dole and that half the voters believed Buchanan to be too extreme. Dole won 46 percent of the women's vote to Buchanan's 27 percent.

Three days later, Dole swept eight more primaries. The race for the nomination was over. The Republican party had decisively rejected Buchanan, aided by moderate and old guard Republican women who feared Buchanan more than Dole's alliance with Pat Robertson. The Massachusetts vote typified this pattern. There, half of the women voted for Dole. Buchanan won only one-fifth.

Dole would be the nominee, but Buchanan refused to endorse him, vowing to fight until "hell freezes over" and promising to control the platform because "we've got God on our side."

March 5, the day Dole clinched the nomination, would be the high point of his fight for the presidency. For a fleeting interval, the non-Buchanan wing of the Religious Right and old-line Republicans came together. But it was the last time the man from Kansas was to find the warring wings of his party cooperating for his election.

Senate majority leader Dole headed back to Washington to tackle the Clinton legislative agenda, try to work with the Gingrich-led House that was now exceedingly unpopular with the American people, and run for president from inside the Beltway.

The spring was cruel to him. In mid-March a private poll conducted by Arthur Finkelstein shook the Republican establishment. At least 40 percent of Republican voters were prepared to vote for Clinton because they believed Dole and the GOP had moved too far to the right on noneconomic issues. As the *Philadelphia Inquirer* reported, "Overall, the survey showed that the GOP was 'badly fractured' on social issues and that these issues—including abortion, school prayer and homosexual rights"—had become the primary categories differentiating the party from the Democrats. The GOP stands on taxes and less government, the glue that usually held the party together, were being overshadowed by disagreements over what role the government should take on moral issues. Not only was the Religious Right's agenda breaking the party apart, it was defining the party for the nation.

Dole's—and the GOP's—problem with women voters was especially serious. Several polls found they preferred Clinton by a margin three times greater than his margin among men. White married women who had been Reagan's and Bush's hedge against the misogynist messages of the New Majoritarians now identified with the Democratic party by four percentage points, and in a three-way race they supported Clinton over Dole by nine points.

The GOP split on abortion drew the most attention in the press, but many other concerns reinforced women's antagonism toward the party. While a majority of women thought the Republicans could do better on welfare reform and cutting the deficit, the Democrats were preferred on all the social issues. On the economy, government spending, and crime, where Republicans had traditionally had an advantage, women were evenly split.

Aware of these figures, Dole kept trying to distance himself from the Religious Right, but every time he signaled he was moving toward a more centrist and tolerant position, Ralph Reed, Pat Buchanan, and Gary Bauer would yank him back by threatening to desert. He had needed some of this vote to win South Carolina, yet an analysis of exit polls in the twenty-eight Republican primaries held through late March showed that the Religious Right was not as powerful as they claimed or he feared. According to *New York Times* political reporter Richard Berke:

> the nearly 12 million people who voted in Republican primaries this year are not particularly far right on major social issues like abortion. . . . most do not think the Republican party should retain a platform plank opposing abortion; they are divided on the sensitive issue of cracking down on immigration; and most do not put the nation's moral troubles at the top of their list of factors in voting.

But neither Dole nor his campaign managers were listening to these rank-and-file Republicans—or to the majority of America's men and women. They were listening to the Christian Coalition, which as usual was using the abortion issue as a litmus test for placing its seal of approval on Republican candidates. Dole had the nomination. He no longer needed its backing to defeat Buchanan. But he did not want a repeat of Houston at the August Republican National Convention in San Diego, and he believed the Coalition support would help prevent problems with other Religious Right groups.

In addition, the anti-choice movement had convinced the Dole campaign that its latest effort to ban abortion could do serious political damage to Clinton. Its tool was federal legislation to outlaw so-called "partial-birth abortions," a phrase it had made up. The American College of Obstetricians and Gynecologists (ACOG) said there was no such term in medicine. The procedure in question, called an intact dilation and extraction (D&X), is rarely performed, accounting for an estimated less than one percent of all abortions performed each year. In the majority of cases, it is done before twenty-four weeks of gestation, or before the fetus is viable. It is done under extreme circumstances: when the fetus is severely damaged, could not live outside the womb, and would endanger the mother's life or health if the pregnancy continued, or if a normal delivery might cause her uterus to perforate, making her unable to bear other children.

Anti-choice leaders had concocted this Orwellian name for political purposes, to convince the public that viable fetuses were being arbitrarily aborted. In fact, the converse is true. According to ACOG, "If a woman's health is endangered, but the physician determines that a healthy fetus can survive, the physician does not perform an abortion, but instead interrupts the pregnancy at the latest possible stage using other procedures and the infant is delivered with full medical support to maximize its chances."

Beneath the incendiary terminology and accompanying propaganda, the primary issue was the same as always: Who decides, the woman and her doctor or the politicians? The bill introduced by Republican members of Congress attempted to restructure this question by focusing on whether the government should ban one specific type of abortion. The goal was the same one that anti-choice proponents had always sought: eliminating the right to abortion itself. Ralph Reed described the legislation as "a giant leap forward in the strategic thinking of the pro-life movement" and emphasized that the aim of the ban was to "undercut the primacy of the women and make her secondary to the fetus." Because the bill provided the necessary legislative framework for a major legal challenge to *Roe*'s constitutionality, it would accomplish the first step in dismantling *Roe*.

The Republican-controlled House and Senate, led by Dole, passed the ban, which provided no exception for the mother's health. On April 10, in an emotional ceremony at the White House in which several women "tearfully described the anguish" of having undergone a D&X after doctors told them their fetuses had "fatal deformities," Clinton vetoed the bill.

The president said he would have signed it if exceptions had been made for "life and serious adverse health consequences so that we don't put these women . . . and these families in a position where they will lose all possibility of future childbearing or where the doctor can't say that they might die, but they could be substantially injured forever. And my pleas fell on deaf ears."

After the veto, the religious overtones surrounding the issue intensified. America's Catholic bishops officially urged their faithful and those they termed others of good will "to do all that they can to urge Congress to override this shameful veto." Ralph Reed threatened, "It will be very hard, if not impossible, for Bill Clinton to look Roman Catholic and evangelical voters in the eye and ask for their support in November." In a highly unusual action, the Vatican attacked the president, calling Clinton's veto an "incredibly brutal act of aggression" against human life that "endangers morally and ethically the future of the society that allows it." A journalist for the conservative *Washington Times* described this activism as "the week the Pope became Ralph Reed. He gave the green light to the clergy, saying, 'Get involved in politics.' "

These efforts of religious organizations to use legislation to impose their views on the rest of the nation crescendoed, punctuated with cries of "infanticide" against those who disagreed with them. The criers seemed immune to the grief and pain of the woman who had carried a pregnancy for six months and desperately wanted her child, and whose fetus, because it had been discovered to have only half a brain, now had to be aborted so she would be able to bear other children. And despite the president's veto, the anti-choice forces have since then accomplished at least some of their ends. Several states have passed legislation banning the procedure; and in a semantic victory, "partial-birth abortion," the emotionally charged nomenclature the anti-choicers had concocted, has entered the language. Very few Americans are even aware that an appropriate, well-established medical term for the procedure was already in place.

Meanwhile, the GOP's quadrennial struggle over its anti-abortion plank was in full swing. Calls from pro-choice Republicans to drop the plank were getting nowhere, although this time, perhaps chastened by the loss of the White House in 1992, elected pro-choice Republicans were speaking out earlier in a way not seen so many weeks before a convention. Senators Alan Simpson and Olympia Snowe, Congressmembers Nancy Johnson, Constance Morella, and Jim Greenwood, and Governors Pete Wilson and William Weld urged action and lined up delegate support.

Governors Christine Todd Whitman, George Pataki, James Rowland, and Tom Ridge said they wanted the plank out, but the behind-the-scenes pressure they actually exerted on party leaders and delegates was minimal, despite press statements to the contrary. Still, various factions of the pro-choice Republican movement were working together, if not exactly warmly, at least in a reasonable and pragmatic manner. The Republican Coalition for Choice, now headed by Susan Cullman (Mary Crisp had retired), was leading a national effort to "yank the plank." Darlee Crockett, co-chair of Planned Parenthood's Republicans for Choice, who was based in San Diego, prepared the groundwork for August. Ann Stone, chairman of Republicans for Choice situated in metropolitan Washington, drew attention to the cause with press appearances. In New York the Republican Family Committee, now under the direction of Lynn Grefe, reactivated the Republican pro-choice PAC.

For the first time since the pro-choice GOP movement began, it had money for polling and field work and would have an office at the convention, but its effort was hampered because no high-profile elected Republican with significant power had been willing to start battling early for the cause. To have any chance of success, a delegate strategy had to be under way at least a year before the convention. The presidential campaigns of pro-choice Governor Pete Wilson and Senator Arlen

Specter had never gotten off the ground, in part because many potential supporters kept waiting for Colin Powell. By the time Powell announced in early November 1995 that he would not run, no time remained to organize delegates for another moderate.

The movement was further hindered by another problem, one just as serious as not having a candidate to rally the troops. Republican moderates, men and women, had been leaving their party in droves, and old guard conservatives were now becoming disenchanted too. The 67 percent pro-choice base of the 1992 Republican rank and file had shrunk. The GOP was transforming itself into a party of the New Right and the Religious Right.

Self-identified moderates now made up less than a fifth of the total GOP membership, and old guard deficit hawks accounted for a third. Taken together, they still constituted a majority of the rank and file—but their share was diminishing. They remained unwavering supporters of keeping government and religion apart, and they were sympathetic or active backers of the pro-choice cause. But too often they were a lethargic majority, despite moments—as when faced with a threat like Buchanan—when they had proved they could act.

The first significant leave-taking had come in 1980, the second in 1992. The third began in the spring of 1996 and included many of the old guard. They were leaving because it was now clear that the party of individual liberty and fiscal responsibility was being led by a two-headed hydra: one with a religious view that limited the freedom of women, and the other a champion of tax cuts as the panacea for balancing budgets and ending deficits.

Some of the disaffected Republicans became Democrats or independents. Others remained registered Republicans but gave neither time nor money and only selectively their votes to the national party. They were birthright Republicans who had become politically homeless. I was one of them.

From January on through the San Diego convention, I spoke to forums often filled with these alienated men and women. I urged them to try once more—to lobby Dole and their state's GOP leaders to drop the abortion plank. I focused on the abortion plank because its significance extended far beyond abortion. It symbolized the Religious Right's power to dictate to the party and potentially the nation. It represented Republican backing for government-sponsored religious doctrine and directly assaulted the First Amendment's prohibition of state-sponsored religion.

Throughout these months, Clinton continued to hold his commanding lead. The continuing struggle over abortion, the unending legislative budget battles with the White House, the anger over the GOP's shutdown of the government, and the conspicuous jockeying for good press from those who wanted to be Dole's running mate caused even his most stalwart loyalists to wonder whether anything could turn his campaign around.

In early April, for the first time since 1984 when CBS News/*New York Times* polls first began asking Americans what they thought of the political parties, the Republicans' favorable rating sank to 41 percent. It was a new low. The anti-choice offensive over the D&X abortion ban had had little political effect. Indeed, Catholics preferred Clinton over Dole, 58 to 33 percent.

"[S]weeping, almost disorienting, in its breadth", wrote *Los Angeles Times* reporter Ronald Brownstein, describing Clinton's mid-April, 55 to 37 percent lead among registered voters. With the exception of white evangelical Christians, virtually all demographic groups gave Clinton the advantage; women preferred the president by an astonishing 27 percentage points. Yet the Dole campaign offered no aggressive plan to win the women. Recognizing what was happening, Republican congressmember Marge Roukema urged the campaign to make health insurance and child support priorities. Dole, Gingrich, and Barbour weren't listening. They kept talking about lower taxes, balanced budgets, smaller government, and the Religious Right's version of family values—all issues Clinton was co-opting.

The New Right and Religious Right dumped on Dole. Picking up the Rush Limbaugh theme, Bill Kristol—New Right magazine editor, former chief of staff to Vice President Quayle, and son of neoconservative Irving Kristol—wrote in late April, "The challenge for Republicans and conservatives is to prevent a Dole defeat from derailing the ongoing Republican realignment and from blocking the emergence of a new era of conservative government. . . . Conservatives must not subordinate all their efforts to the Dole campaign."

"So who's Bill Kristol?" Dole charged in response on a Sunday news show. "What has he done in the Republican party?" Actually, Dole was expressing the sentiments of many Republicans who for years had rung doorbells, staffed phone banks, and given their money and time to the GOP. But their views no longer mattered. The pundits and so-called intellectuals of the right were moving their not-so-quiet take-over of the party along too successfully to worry about the protests of "ordinary" Republicans.

Not only did the right savage Dole; it increased the heat on pro-choice Republicans. Buchanan, Schlafly, and Bauer protested bitterly every time a pro-choicer spoke out. In Massachusetts, some of Governor Weld's pro-choice delegate candidates lost in the caucuses. Governor Wilson's pledge to fight for the plank's removal set off angry calls for his removal as Dole's campaign co-chairman. Bay Buchanan threatened that any tinkering with the plank would be "an absolute retreat." Trying to be Daniel Webster, Ralph Reed floated a trial balloon for an innocuous change in the plank. He got shot down so fast by his ideological soul mates that he retreated before the ink was dry on the news story about the balloon.

On May 15, Dole startled the nation. He announced he was leaving the Senate to campaign full time:

> I will seek the bright light and open space of this beautiful country and will ask for the wise counsel of its people. . . . And some might find it surprising, given the view that Congress has been my life, but that is not so. With all due respect to Congress, America has been my life. . . . And the very least a presidential candidate owes America is his full attention—everything he can give, everything he has—and that is what America shall receive from me.

They were admirable words, but Dole's resignation wasn't going to help him. Maybe he really believed he could rescue his campaign, and rein in the Religious Right's intense pressure, by going to that amorphous group outside Washington—the people. But he was dead wrong. There was no time left to build a nationwide Dole movement. He could have best served the people by staying in Washington and doing what he did best.

It was in the Senate that Dole could fight for their interests. It was in the Senate that he could show them his strength and convince them that he would be a better president than Clinton. To win in November, he had to break loose from the Religious Right Republicans. Governors Beasley and Campbell and the Christian Coalition had delivered South Carolina to him. But Republicans outside the South, many of them pro-choice, had also worked for his nomination and represented a much larger proportion of the party's grassroots. This rank-and-file majority still wanted to follow him. But to energize them—and the deserters and disaffected—he had to lead his party away from extremism, from the backlash strategies. He needed political power to do this, and he needed to be bold.

Washington insiders argued that staying in the Senate would paralyze his ability to act. When he returned to Washington after winning the nomination, they said, Democrats purposely tied up legislation to make it difficult for him to lead. But this kind of partisan wrangling was nothing new, and certainly not to a consummate Senate professional like Dole. Moreover, even if the Republicans didn't have the sixty votes necessary to break a filibuster, they were still the majority. They controlled the Senate committees, the Senate floor, and the Senate calendar.

Dole could have proposed an agenda that trumped the traditional Republican positions Clinton had co-opted. He could have used it first to rally rank-and-file Republicans against extremism, then the nation. Infighting with the Gingrich revolutionaries would have been rough, but at least in the Senate, Dole would have been fighting on familiar turf.

The result of following this course could not have been any worse than the one he chose. At a minimum, he would have helped his beloved party. He would have stood up to the bullies who were trying to turn it into a safe harbor for bigots.

Resigning from the Senate shattered any opportunity Dole had to strike out in a new direction. In relinquishing one of the most powerful political offices in the land, he gave up the only power he had to break the rightists' hold over the GOP. Unlike George Bush, he didn't have a large network of people loyal solely to him to fight his battles in the field. Unlike Ronald Reagan, he had no ideological movement behind him. Dole's power was in the U.S. Senate.

Like King Lear, Dole deluded himself into believing the reputation of his good name and his long years of service would hold him in good stead. But the revolutionaries were not massing outside his fortress—they were within. By abandoning his powers, he became a prisoner of the right. Presiding over a fratricidal party and facing a country frightened by that party's intemperateness, he had no effective way to calm either his party or his country.

May 15 marked the end of Dole's political career, not just his congressional one. It was over. Within a week, the error was obvious. Seventy percent of Americans told pollsters his resignation would have no effect on their vote.

From that day on, the central focus of political action within the national GOP shifted away from Dole and to the question of who would win the advantage in the next five months. Who would lead the GOP into the twenty-first century? Would it be the theocrats and the New Right authoritarians, or would the other New Right men and women—the supply-siders and the libertarians—join with the old guard conservatives and moderates to finally challenge the self-righteous?

Throughout the campaign Dole kept trying to unite his party with gestures that went nowhere. Except for the one scrap of power he had left to leverage, his choice of a running mate, he was becoming almost irrelevant in the GOP civil war, as the episode of the wayward declaration of tolerance was to illustrate.

In an attempt to show some independence, Dole announced on June 6 that even though he would not change the 1992 abortion plank, he would support adding a declaration of tolerance to the platform. He failed to specify where in the platform this declaration would be placed. Traditionally, the party's platform reflects the nominee's wishes in those areas he considers important, and the convention respects those requests. But Dole controlled neither his party nor his convention. These were not traditional times. In a television interview four days later, Dole volunteered that the GOP's abortion conflict had been resolved. His declaration would be "in the abortion plank and not in the preamble. It seems to me if you want to make it clear to the people out there that we're tolerant, you make it—this is a moral issue, it's not like all the other things in the platform. It ought to be right up there where people can see it."

All hell broke loose. Pat Buchanan bullied Dole: "A declaration of tolerance for the idea that a woman has a right to choose whether to destroy her unborn child in the womb entails the negation and destruction of our party's pro-life stand. Any such declaration will be resisted at San Diego with all the resources at our command." The Christian Coalition threatened that it "might have to sit the election out." Pro-choicers were furious. Dole's so-called move toward reason and civility was a hypocritical hoax and in no way changed the substance of the party's intolerant position toward women's civil rights. Governor Weld had it right when he labeled Dole's tolerance language "a throwaway line."

The public pronouncements and private bloodletting continued unabated. Dole's clumsy efforts at mediating the discord brought no unity. As summer arrived, the Dole convention planners were afraid that San Diego would be more fractious than Houston. To diminish opportunities for the press to cover this ongoing civil war in even greater savoring detail, the RNC canceled the platform hearings for the first time in anyone's memory. The public could send its suggestions by fax or mail.

The convention Platform Committee meetings were only a month away when Dole threw in the towel. He dropped his previously "nonne-gotiable" position that there must be a tolerance declaration in the abortion plank. Dole and Platform Committee chairman Henry Hyde cut a deal.

They proposed a separate plank calling for tolerance and diversity on a variety of issues, including abortion and capital punishment. This declaration of tolerance was substantively meaningless since the anti-choice plank would not only stand but was being strengthened. It would now include a condemnation of "partial-birth abortions," and for the first time the party would urge prosecuting doctors who per-formed abortions.

Governor Weld minced no words: The new language "is not accept-able. . . . The so-called tolerance language in this draft is transpar-ently begrudging toward those who hold the pro-choice point of view." Susan Cullman said, "It's patronizing. We're not looking to be toler-ated," and Ann Stone commented that Hyde had "backed Bob Dole in to the corner and wrapped the human life constitutional amendment around his neck."

Buchanan didn't buy it either. "The language is inherently contra-dictory," he said. "You can't say abortion is simply a matter of personal choice or personal morality or personal consequence, [and] at the same time we're going to have a constitutional amendment to abolish it."

Ever the political fixer, Ralph Reed "unreservedly" backed the Dole–Hyde pact. And having bowed out of an active preconvention role in this battle, Governor Whitman said mildly, "I can fully support the new language on tolerance."

Dole's campaign had three problems to solve in San Diego. Could it fashion a platform Dole could run on? Could he select the person he wanted as his running mate without setting off a floor fight? Could the campaign staff control the televised proceedings?

Dole may have wanted an inclusive, tolerant party, but he was faced with over a third of the delegates ready to disrupt the proceedings if the party's "pro-life" plank was eliminated—or else "gutted"—by his abortion-specific tolerance language.

On the opening day of the Platform Committee deliberations, news polls showed that convention delegates were split three ways over whether to maintain the platform's call for a constitutional ban on abortion. According to the Associated Press, 41 percent wanted to retain the ban, 34 percent opposed it, and 25 percent didn't know or failed to answer the question. This suggested that the Religious Right was not as strong as it seemed. What the polls did not note was that Ralph Reed and his colleagues had a plan firmly in place should it become necessary to do battle on the convention floor: pagers and hand-held computers connected to a back-room operation on the twenty-first floor of the Marriott Hotel next to the convention hall, scores of volunteer coordinators, and enough delegates and money to make life difficult for Dole if he strayed off the reservation. The pro-choice side had nothing comparable.

As in the previous three conventions, the Platform Committee was stacked with New Right and Religious Right leaders and followers. With the exception of Pennsylvanian Elsie Hillman, there were no heavy hitters on the pro-choice side: no Wilson, no Weld, no Whitman, no Specter, no Pataki. None wanted to set foot in this particular swamp.

Yet an analysis of the 107-member Platform Committe indicated that twenty-seven of its members wanted to drop the abortion plank. This was enough to file a minority report. Under convention rules, the inclusion of a minority report in the Platform Committee proceedings would automatically bring it to the convention floor, where the delegates would have had to debate the plank before the television cameras and the world, as in 1976. The debate would have blown open the party's corrosive internal disagreements. While the pro-choice side would have lost such a debate, it would have won a public-opinion victory, giving it significant psychological leverage for its next battle with the right.

But the pro-choice coalition elected not to pursue this strategy. It sidestepped the Platform Committee deliberations, except for some amendments coordinated by Hillman, all of which were defeated. Instead, it pursued an ill-conceived six-state strategy. The press and the combatants in this struggle called it "the beginning of a floor fight over abortion," but their description was a pathetic misnomer. Unlike the minority report route, this six-state approach did not automatically force the convention to debate the issue. Rather, it was a cumbersome process whereby six states had to request the convention to suspend the rules in order to allow a matter not on the formal agenda to be considered. Then two-thirds of the delegates had to vote for the suspension before the question of whether to debate was even voted on.

Despite herculean exertions, and more resources and devoted volunteers than the pro-choice side had ever mustered at a convention, the six-state strategy was doomed. Governor Wilson would see that California, the largest pro-choice delegation, would be one of the six, and Weld would deliver Massachusetts. But the governors of New York, Connecticut, New Jersey, Illinois, Rhode Island, and Pennsylvania could not be depended upon. Their states had sizable numbers of anti-choice GOP legislators and active Catholic leaders who could make life politically difficult for the governors if they became too aggressively pro-choice.

Still, some Republican officials from these states, as well as others from Maine, Vermont, Delaware, Wyoming, Rhode Island, and Maryland, joined with the coalition in a strong effort to find six states willing to request the suspension of the rules. Maine senator Olympia Snowe, on the front line of the struggle, was rewarded for her integrity by being one of the party's few women federal officeholders not invited to speak to the convention.

In the end, the coalition failed to convince six states to request the suspension, but it would not have mattered. There weren't two-thirds of the delegates willing to cross either Dole or Ralph Reed. At best, thirty seconds would have been allotted to a voice vote on the suspension, and the exercise would have been over—with no debate.

The Religious Right got what they wanted: an even stronger GOP commitment to their agenda than four years before. They ran right over Dole, voting down the tolerance-language deal he had cut with Hyde. As journalists Jack Germond and Jules Witcover wrote, Dole "had his head handed to him in his very modest effort to have his party express explicit tolerance."

And what did the pro-choice coalition get for all its hard work? Nothing but an item in the appendix at the back of the platform that listed the amendments the committee had voted down. Their embarrassment did not match Dole's since they had started with so little and he so much; but despite the coalition's spin that it had done better than four years ago, the platform was a disaster for women's liberty, the pro-choice cause, and the GOP's effort to win women's votes.

I was standing next to Bay Buchanan when she declared the GOP platform was "the Buchanan platform." "[It] sounds as if they had Pat in the back room drafting this thing," she boasted. "We're considering asking Haley Barbour for royalties." She was right as far as social issues were concerned, although the committee had rejected her brother's populism.

But neither was it Bob Dole's platform. His much-ballyhooed new economic plan was a fresh version of Jack Kemp's supply-side credo. Dole the deficit cutter had transformed himself into a supply-sider.

On the social issues, the platform mirrored much of the two Pats' program. While Robertson and Buchanan were not addressing the convention, their words were right there in the platform. It criticized the UN and championed the repeal of gun-control laws like the Brady bill. It called for elimination of the Departments of Education, Commerce, Energy, and Housing and Urban Development; cuts in education and health care for the children of illegal aliens; and an end to America's long-standing tradition that children born in the United States are automatically citizens. It opposed affirmative action and gays in the military. It backed government-mandated, voluntary school prayer and the use of taxpayers' money for private and parochial education. As expected, the anti-abortion plank was the harshest ever. It was not a platform to win over America's center. It was the most radically right platform ever to be adopted by a national Republican convention.

The platform passed unanimously. Not one single delegate rose to object formally to its adoption. Later, Dole would say he felt no obligation to follow it. Barbour would add that he found platforms "meaningless" and never read them.

In the days before the convention opened, the right bullied Dole not to pick a pro-choice running mate. Robertson had tipped his hand three weeks earlier: "If Bob Dole does not pick a conservative, pro-life running mate, the Republican party will lose the House, lose the Senate, and lose the presidency." Buchanan said he would not endorse Dole unless he dropped support for a declaration of tolerance in the platform and selected a pro-life running mate such as Oklahoma senator Don Nickles, the chairman of the 1992 GOP Platform Committee.

Dole fooled them all. He kept his own counsel and chose a man most pundits thought he disliked. Jack Kemp was Dole's opposite: Kemp a product of the New Right, Dole a son of the Old Right.

Convention manager Paul Manafort, Dole's campaign manager Scott Reed, his campaign communications director John Buckley, and his campaign adviser Charlie Black had tried for years to make Kemp president. In 1988 Pat Robertson and George Bush had mowed them down. Now the Robertson forces were more powerful, Bush's people were scattered, and the New Right men and women were largely in Dole's camp. It was not the old guard whom Dole needed to check about his choice. He needed Pat Robertson's and Ralph Reed's approval if he was to avert disaster on the convention floor and the nation's television screens.

Hard feelings existed between Kemp and Robertson even though back in 1988 Robertson had called for one of Kemp's cure-alls, the flat tax. Ralph Reed had learned his politics in the Young Republican New Right and was a friend of the Kemp team—he'd been a Kemp supporter in Georgia in 1988 before Robertson hired him. Robertson was furious with Dole's choice, but after Ralph Reed smoothed the way, Robertson gave Kemp begrudging, tepid support.

Though hell hadn't frozen over, Buchanan also accepted Kemp and endorsed Dole. His campaign co-chair Schlafly, a 1988 Kemp leader, was pleased.

Kemp's selection was the fulfillment of the New Right's twenty-four-year-old dream. It was the culmination of years of work by an unholy alliance of New Right supply-siders and Religious Right political operatives, and the natural result of the ideological forces they had loosed in the seventies. Often disagreeing on issues and culturally far apart, these two ideologies were now formally joined in the cause of Kemp.

Now it was on to the television show. All the anger and pain of the last few years was supposed to be forgotten during convention week. Recruited by the Dole campaign, Mike Deaver, father of the Reagan era's effective smoke and mirrors technique, created a deceptive program that painted a glib picture of GOP unity, tolerance, and reasonableness. Reality took a backseat to distortion. Every minute was scripted to show contented mainstream moderates and conservatives with pro-choice Colin Powell, Susan Molinari, and Christine Todd Whitman in starring roles. Religious Right leaders either did not speak or were relegated to brief, innocuous statements. There was no repeat of Houston on television.

But underneath this harmonious surface was a convention that championed policies more right-wing than those adopted in Houston. More delegates subscribed to the Religious Right's worldview than ever before. Only 36 percent of the delegates were women, reflecting the leadership's inability to reward even its Christian right females. Inside the convention hall Dole's operatives banned both pro-lifers and pro-choicers from unveiling signs proclaiming their cause. By the third day, Religious Right delegates were chafing at Reed's acquiescing to the Dole camp's tight control. They had won the platform, yet their issues were seldom mentioned on the podium. They were tired of toning down their rhetoric, as directed by their leaders, when speaking to the press. Alan Keyes, the ideological favorite of the Christian right, expressed what many felt. "This has been a very scripted, Stalinist convention," he charged.

The Dole managers outlined five-minute speeches for women Republicans to deliver. Elizabeth Dole was the main attraction. If her husband won, she would be the first Republican First Lady since *Roe* to oppose a woman's right to choose. Knowing how proficient a performer she was, the managers gave her sixteen minutes to tell the nation why Bob Dole would make a good president. She never mentioned choice.

Watching her, I saw a woman who could easily be the GOP nominee in 2000. It was understandable why she was speaking on the night Dole was to be nominated and not on the night of his acceptance. She would have upstaged him. By now, she had become a favorite of the Christian Coalition, who admired her spiritual awakening in the late eighties and her sincere explanations of her faith in God.

The next night Dole swept away whatever goodwill his wife might have engendered among wavering women voters. Dark in tone, brutal in its criticism of Bill and Hillary Clinton and the baby-boom generation, his speech was at odds with the moderate image his staff was orchestrating. His one rhetorical gesture toward his now long-dropped battle for the GOP's heart and soul rang hollow. The words were almost right, but they were in ironic contradiction to his behavior of the past year.

> The Republican party is broad and inclusive. It represents many streams of opinion and many points of view. But if there is anyone who has mistakenly attached himself to our party in the belief that we are not open to citizens of every race and religion, then let me remind you: Tonight this hall belongs to the party of Lincoln, and the exits, which are clearly marked, are for you to walk out of as I stand this ground without compromise.

The Republican party of San Diego did not stand for individual liberty. It was neither broad nor inclusive. The 1996 platform was proof that the party of Lincoln had changed radically. Bill Weld summed it up on the convention's last day: "This has not been a fight about semantics. It is a fight about what it means to be a Republican."

He was right.

Between Labor Day and Election Day, the Republican presidential campaign never found itself. A CBS News/New York Times poll noted that only 18 percent of Americans expected any benefit from Dole's tax cuts.

He never convinced enough women that his party's years of neglecting them were over. Moderates and some old guard conservatives became Clinton Republicans. Religious Right leaders condemned Dole for not speaking out more on the "moral degeneration" of America. Robertson said there would have to be a "miracle from God Almighty" for Dole to win.

Long before the fall campaign, several national Republican conservatives and Religious Right strategists, believing that Dole would lose, had already decided to write off winning the presidency and to concentrate on retaining GOP control of the House and Senate.

In early summer, well before the convention, Gingrich and Trent Lott, who had taken over Dole's old job as majority leader, toned down their rhetoric, and began to work with the president. The House and Senate raised the minimum wage, and passed a controversial welfare reform bill that became a nonissue in the campaign when Clinton signed it. But not until after Dole failed to raise the right's social agenda —affirmative action, gays, gun control, abortion, school prayer—in the first presidential debate on October 6 did Barbour and Gingrich join the Religious Right in abandoning Dole.

The GOP Senate and House campaign committees worked to convince women who lived in swing areas that Republicans, too, wanted caring government. Aiming to make amends for shutting down the government, Republicans approved a budget that included Clinton's requests for more money for education and the environment. They passed legislation providing for more generous parental leave. They eliminated "drive-by" obstetrical deliveries by requiring insurance companies to pay for at least two days of hospital stay for the mother. These actions helped them win over the votes of those ubiquitous "soccer moms" in congressional races by ten percentage points, even as Dole lost them by seven. Their candidates were also helped by having closer connections to their constituents than Dole. Many women distrusted the Republican party but not their hometown member of Congress, who by and large didn't strike them as extremist.

Two weeks before the election, polls showed Republicans winning the Senate but losing the House. Then revelations about questionable Democratic party fundraising changed the campaign's direction. Undecided independents, a majority of them women, became disgusted by the scandal and voted Republican or didn't vote, thus helping the GOP to hold the House by a modest ten seats. It was the smallest House majority in forty-two years.

While the scandal alienated some potential Clinton voters, cutting the president's margin below his goal of 51 percent, it did not alter the presidential election outcome. Dole's campaign was too entwined with the messages of the Religious Right. While most voters did not view him as personally anti-women, his inability to stand up to Buchanan and Reed convinced many of them that he would give the Religious Right a major role in his administration. America is more conservative now than in 1980, but it is not the conservatism championed by the right. The majority of women want the government to have an effective role in their lives. They saw Clinton as a mainstream candidate who would help them. They did not believe this of Dole.

In fact, Dole's legislative record, apart from his anti-choice position, was actually in tune with the majority's view of government. But his presidential campaign fled from that record. In the end, Dole lost because his partnership with the New Right and the Religious Right frightened too many voters. Throughout the campaign the man from Kansas kept his dignity, causing most Americans to respect him even as they would not vote for him. But he could not overcome the chaos within the GOP, and he was defeated by the legacy of the disreputable, bankrupt backlash strategy that had enveloped the party to which he had devoted his life.

20

THE FUTURE OF THE REPUBLIC

On my desk lies a circular brass medallion, about two and a half inches in diameter, that was given to me by a friend whose father had received it in honor of his work for the Republican party. The medallion was struck in 1954 to commemorate the hundredth anniversary of the party's founding.

On one side are the faces of Lincoln and Eisenhower. On the other side are their words: "With malice toward none, with charity for all, with firmness in the right as God gives us to see the right . . ." from Lincoln's magnificent second inaugural address; and "In all things which deal with the people, be liberal, be human. In all those things which deal with the people's money or their economy, or their form of government, be conservative," which was Eisenhower's guiding philosophy for Republicans.

These words represent the bedrock of Republican philosophy. Except for the eras of FDR and LBJ in the case of Eisenhower's second tenet, the majority of American voters since the Civil War have found these principles compatible with their hopes for government. They have voted for candidates who stood for these views even if those candidates were Democrats, as in the case of Bill Clinton.

The Republican party of my youth no longer exists. While there are still pockets of Republicans scattered around America who reject the fundamental elements of the agenda of the Religious Right and the New Right, it is no longer possible to ignore the contradictions that since 1980 have subverted the party's traditional vision. These aberrant ideas have eaten at the national party, spreading like a cancer until now the only significant core of traditional belief uniting Republicans is the conviction that a free market is the best way to stimulate economic growth.

The party is split into numerous factions. The philosophy of the Religious Right and New Right supply-siders, who are dominant now, has little in common with Eisenhower's. The Religious Right's doctrine is neither humane nor liberal in its treatment of women and homosexuals. It harbors no charity toward those who disagree with its religious beliefs. The supply-siders' theory of how government is to be funded is not conservative; it is radical and irresponsible.

These ideologies have also done serious damage to the nation. Supply-side tax cuts during the Reagan years, with little corrective action during Bush's term, brought the American people an unprecedented additional federal debt of $3.5 trillion, larger than the total debt accumulated under all the nation's previous presidents combined. During this period when America was at peace except for the brief Gulf War, the nation's political leaders passed budgets that maintained high defense spending and entitlements while cutting taxes by 25 percent in three years. While the driving political force behind this foolhardiness was the Republican party, the Democrat-controlled House and Senate also voted for these reckless budgets.

Cutting this gargantuan debt down to manageable size has become one of today's greatest domestic challenges. While it is certainly good news to learn from the Office of Management and Budget's calculations that the federal deficit for 1997 will be about $37 billion, its lowest point relative to the nation's economic output since 1974, the decrease doesn't begin to slash the existing debt, which in 1997 was some $5.4 trillion. (The debt is the accumulated money, including at present a quarter-trillion dollars annually in interest, that the government owes on what it has borrowed to pay for years of deficit budgets.) And even though the Congress and the president agreed in 1997 to balance the budget for the first time in thirty years, they did not begin to confront the serious demographic tidal wave about to overwhelm Social Security and Medicare. In 2007, the baby-boom generation will begin to retire, straining the government's resources to the limit. If these problems are not solved now, the Congressional Budget Office projects that by 2020, "federal debt will rise at the rate of $1.4 trillion annually in today's dollars."

New Right leaders' indiscriminate attacks against the government are not helping. Although these leaders have backed down slightly from their earlier promises to eliminate most of the government's safety net, they still insist that the combination of tax cuts for the wealthy and government spending cuts affecting mainly the less well-off will benefit the majority of Americans. This is patently absurd. Punishing the poor, most of them women and children, castigating teachers, and weakening public education to aid private education—a few of many examples— sow resentment and fray the social fabric. Such actions do not bring domestic tranquillity; they needlessly pit Americans against one another, hindering the unity and sacrifice necessary to protect the nation's future—in this case, specifically cutting the debt.

The nation will be further undone if the Republican party continues to be a tool for furthering the Religious Right's political agenda. In a country as diverse as ours, the First Amendment's prohibition against the establishment of government-sponsored religion protects it from the sectarian strife so prevalent elsewhere in the world. To weaken this prohibition, as the followers and allies of Pat Robertson wish to do under the pretense of extending religious liberty, will harm Americans' liberty in ways never seen here before.

Four months after the 1996 election, the Religious Right reactivated its crusade to change the Constitution with another version of the Religious Equality Amendment, whose intent is to allow government-sponsored religion in public schools and other places. Republican congressmember Ernest Istook, Jr., of Oklahoma, with the backing of GOP House leaders, introduced this amendment, which says in part: "The people's right to pray and to recognize their religious beliefs, heritage or tradition on public property, including public schools, shall not be infringed." To launch the crusade for this change in the Constitution, the Christian Coalition announced it would spend over $2 million in radio and direct mail advertising and would rate lawmakers on how they stood on the amendment.

Istook's proposal stimulates exactly the kind of conflict the originators of the First Amendment sought to dampen. Lawmakers will now find themselves having to prove their piety by following the moral principles laid down by Istook and his confederates. Moves of this sort are not only a blatant attempt at political power; they divert time and resources from efforts to solve our pressing economic and social problems. The First Amendment already guarantees all Americans—including students in school—the right to practice their religious beliefs according to individual conscience. The nation's religious freedom is not in jeopardy except from people who wish to impose their religious convictions on those who disagree with them.

If the partnership between the theocrats and the supply-siders succeeds in dominating the GOP indefinitely, the country will face a stifling of the opportunities that have opened up in recent years for women, minorities, gays and lesbians, legal immigrants, and everyone else who is not an adherent of the fundamentalism preached by the Religious Right. Harbingers of this fundamentalist drive have already showed themselves. California's recent initiatives rolling back affirmative action and cutting schooling for the children of illegal immigrants are an example.

The prospect of further political action of this kind was launched in the spring of 1997, when the Religious Right opened a new front, moving from political education to direct political action. Although he remains president of the nonpolitical Family Research Council, Gary Bauer formed a new political action committee, the Campaign for Working Families (CWF), to elect "pro-family, pro-life, pro-free enterprise" candidates to the House, the Senate, and the White House. CWF is to be managed by the finance director of Pat Buchanan's 1996 presidential campaign. Ralph Reed announced he would be leaving the Christian Coalition to establish a political consulting business and create a "farm team" of similar candidates. Reed and Bauer thus freed themselves from the constraints imposed on their nonprofit tax-exempt educational organizations, which are prohibited by law from endorsing or contributing to candidates. Reed will be leading an openly political arm of the Religious Right movement, quiescent since the collapse of Pat Robertson's presidential candidacy in 1988. This will greatly increase Reed's ability to win more political power for himself and his cause. It is too early to tell whether the split within the Religious Right between Buchanan's followers and Reed's will weaken the theocrats' influence in the GOP. Regardless, these changes remain an unsettling omen of the Republican party's direction.

.   .   .

Over and over again lapsed Republicans like myself have been told that if they don't like what has happened to their party, they should leave it. In the past seventeen years, many have done so.

But leaving does not solve the deeper problem the nation faces in having one of its major political parties sanctioning a revolutionary course that can undermine its deepest traditions and cripple its economic might. Those who believe they can resolve the quandary by becoming a Democrat or independent fail to recognize the complexities of our political system. Unlike Western Europe, we are not a nation of strong party loyalties. Americans cross party lines not only in their voting but in their giving and volunteer activities, and they always have. Loyalty to a political party is not the answer to solving the nation's problems, but loyalty to a set of principles consistent with American constitutional ideals is. The issue is whether working within a party can bring about the furthering of those ideals.

A political party is a conduit for accomplishing a set of goals through politics. Those goals may be beneficial to the majority, to a minority, or to a few special interest groups. In the case of today's national GOP, a coterie of well-disciplined individuals with bountiful financial resources have taken over its leadership to further their own particular vision—a vision antithetical to the Republican party's traditional principles and, to those like me who believe in these principles, to the nation's greater good.

What would happen if those who oppose the GOP's latest versions of fundamentalism and Darwinism gave up on it? In 1992, and in greater numbers in 1996, some did. It did not mark an end to the party's power, although its congressional clout has diminished since its impressive victories in 1994. What if they should stay in the party? Is it realistic to believe they can change the direction the GOP has taken? They are not alone in this dilemma. Democrats are also engaged in a struggle, trying to decide whether to follow Clinton's new moderate course or to revive some version of their New Deal–Great Society legacy. Among traditionalists in both parties, as in much of the nation, there is a significant degree of disenchantment with the national political process, fueled by an out-of-control campaign finance system, and the old party loyalties are deeply shaken. Since neither party seems able to lead effectively, some are saying, perhaps it is time for a new political party, one that would be traditionally conservative fiscally and liberal on human rights issues—the Eisenhower philosophy on the medallion. This reasoning holds that it is time for fresh blood—the old parties have lost their reasons for being.

Is this a good idea? Feasible or blue-sky? Two factors mitigate against it, at least for now. Third-party development was dealt a blow in the spring of 1997 when the U.S. Supreme Court determined that states are not constitutionally required to allow candidates to appear on more than one party's ballots. Without the visibility and leverage that comes from forming fusion tickets with major parties, a third party has difficulty growing. The losing plaintiff in the case, the New Party, was supported by Perot's Reform Party.

In addition, the third-party route is entangled in the personality and the power dreams of billionaire Ross Perot. No one should forget that with his money, he has effectively built a small political party responsive to his whims and wishes, even as he denies this is so. To challenge the Religious Right and supply-siders through a third party would first require confronting Perot's own. Not only would it be a conflict not easily won; while the battle was being fought, the Religious Right and supply-siders would have an open opportunity to complete their takeover of the national GOP. If fiscal conservatives, old guard and moderate Republicans, pro-choicers, and New Right libertarians were all engaged in fighting Perot, there would be little effective opposition to the likes of Pat Robertson.

The argument has been made that since Perot's popularity sagged in 1996, the American people no longer take him seriously and he is therefore not a significant political player. This is unrealistic. In today's political arena, where the ability to gain national power is directly related to broad access to radio and television, Perot remains a power broker, openly or covertly, as long as he wishes to spend the money. It is always possible he could do what Pat Robertson did after his abortive presidential run in 1988—retreat behind a curtain, like the little man from Omaha in *The Wizard of Oz,* and find a Ralph Reed to front as the wizard.

Without a war chest comparable to Perot's, a third-party strategy is a mistake at the present time. If Perot should falter, this alternative should be revisited. But over the next few years, a more realistic course for traditional fiscal conservatives and those who cherish freedom and inclusiveness is to win back the leadership of the Republican party. They should mount a full-scale, well-financed New Center Republican movement running candidates against Religious Right and hard-line supply-side candidates in party primaries, caucuses, and conventions. To have any success, this challenge must get under way now. If it doesn't, the national GOP will continue with mounting vigor down the track laid out for it by the New Right and Religious Right in the Houston 1992 and San Diego 1996 platforms.

This New Center movement will need recruits, who can be drawn mainly from the ranks of independents. Polling data confirm that independents are ripe for a centrist cause that drops what they perceive to be the extremism of the national GOP and rejects the confused direction of the Democrats. Their number is substantial. As the Pew Research Center reports, "Thirty-one percent of Americans identify themselves as Democrats, 30 percent as Republicans and 39 percent as Independent or have no party affiliation." When independents are asked how they might lean, 46 percent choose Republican, 46 percent Democrat.

The policy road map for a New Center agenda lies in the profile of the attitudes of independents, which are similar to those of disaffected Republicans, and on most issues they fall between those of other Republicans and Democrats. Independents are more tolerant on sexual morality issues than are standard southern white evangelical Republicans. They are more pro-choice than either Republicans or Democrats. They favor affirmative action when it will increase job and educational opportunities for blacks, women, and other minorities. They are strongly in favor of environmental regulation, government aid for education, and gun control. They do not want to see a reduction in the rate of growth in Medicare spending, for which the Gingrich revolution has pushed.

Some observers have noted that these particular attitudes of independents sound more like a traditional Democratic agenda; therefore, why would they wish to work with New Center Republicans, rather than with Democrats?

It should be noted, first of all, that these are also the values of disaffected Republicans, who would form the core of a New Center GOP. For independents, the difference in appeal between the two parties has to do not only with social issues but with economics and the role of government.

In these latter two areas, independents are more in tune with the Republican disaffected and rank and file. Sixty percent of independents, compared with 71 percent of Republicans, believe that Congress should balance the budget. They also show a healthy distrust of big government. Fifty-three percent of independents, along with 71 percent of Republicans, believe that state government would do a better job of providing health benefits and long-term care to the poor, disabled, and elderly. Only 37 percent of Democrats support this position. Independents agree with Republicans that government regulations do more harm than good. Democrats disagree.

Second, the wing of the Democratic party that backs an activist federal government and deficit spending is still a major player in the party's leadership, despite Bill Clinton's positions to the contrary. As the race for the party's presidential nominee in 2000 heats up, this wing will try to regain ideological dominance.

Where will the independents go? To attract them, the Republicans will have to defeat the GOP extremists and push for an economic policy that eschews supply-side economics and aims to diminish the debt without unraveling the nation's safety net and infrastructure. The New Center would seek realistic balanced budgets similar in spirit, but unfortunately not in action to the budget agreed to in early May 1997 by President Clinton and the Congress. (Unfortunately, this spirit did not last. The final budget was an Alice-in-Wonderland document. Instead of taking advantage of the most robust economy in decades to balance the budget in 1998, the leaders stretched the date for balance to 2002. This politically expedient, economically unsound package of tax cuts and increased spending backloaded the budget's costs. Thus Americans will experience unnecessary hardship at about the time the inevitable recession arrives and Clinton and Gingrich are out of office.)

A necessary realistic balance would be sought between stimulation for the private sector to do what it does best—create wealth—and support for a fair, efficient, and prudent tax system that enables government to upgrade America's education, research, transportation, housing, and health and welfare systems while providing for an adequate defense, enhancing the arts, and protecting the environment. It would also tackle head-on the coming Social Security and Medicare crisis.

Government spending in recent years has not been channeled sufficiently into bolstering the nation's long-term prosperity. We have spent too much on transfer payments and not enough on building our capacity for higher productivity. Much ignored and recently maligned public works projects should be revisited. The New Center would encourage projects to improve public transportation and flood control and attack toxic waste dumps, polluted water, and outmoded sewage systems. Where such projects could be done more efficiently by the states, the New Center would encourage the federal government to be a secondary partner, as it was in the fifties and early sixties.

If prudently financed, these projects need not lead to unmanageable higher debt. According to historian Richard Striner of Washington College, "Recent economic studies—particularly the works of economist David Alan Aschauer—have suggested that an adequate level of investment in public infrastructure would stimulate 50 cents of private sector spending for every federal dollar spent. A booming economy investing in the physical necessities means greater prosperity, profits and earning power, which in turn would boost federal revenues. The converse of his argument is that lagging infrastructure spending over the past decades has impeded growth." Striner and Aschauer's approach could be the foundation for the New Center's answer to supply-siders.

The New Center would back revamping of the IRS and simplification of the tax code. It would reject a flat tax and elimination of the income tax, because such measures are unfair. It would support modification of capital gains and inheritance taxes, and it would be open to other tax cuts once the debt was in manageable shape and the country's infrastructure improved.

Fifty-three percent of independents are men and 47 percent are women. The New Center coalition would be composed of these new recruits, as well as centrist Democrats and old guard and moderate Republicans. It is likely that bringing even *some* of these men and women into the Republican party could effectively end the Republicans' gender gap. The movement would be unequivocally pro-choice, and by eliminating the party's contradictory insistence that it is the party of liberty except when it comes to women, the New Center would eliminate one of the root causes of the loss of centrist voters. In rejecting the Religious Right's agenda, it would signal to independents an end to this symbol of religious intolerance within the GOP. Unlike Bush and Dole, New Center leaders would not need to worry about the Religious Right deserting. Its political power would not depend upon them.

Winning back the women of America would necessitate the Republican party's facing reality—a commodity in short supply among its leaders in recent years. It would be hoped that New Center Republicans could accomplish this by convincing the party to come to terms with the myths it has used to attract backlash voters.

"Women agree with us but we don't communicate in their language" is one of the most pervasive of those myths. In the fall of 1996, as Clinton maintained his double-digit lead over Dole among women voters, Mary Matalin wrote that "conservatives can save their party and promote their philosophy not by changing their message but by conveying it in ways intelligible to women." (The subliminal text: Women aren't smart enough to understand plain old English.)

This insulting reiteration of a familiar New Majoritarian line was played out in 1996 just as it had been in previous years: at ladies' nights at national conventions, in the carefully staged appearances of women speakers and in their testimonials for television and radio, and in wifely praise of candidate husbands. Beneath these carefully packaged tactics was the underlying assumption that women communicate with women better than do men. The designated speakers were supposedly able to assure the women they addressed, in a way men couldn't, that the party spoke for their best interests.

Despite the outcome of the 1996 election, when it was clear even to those who previously would not acknowledge that the majority of American women were angry with the Republicans, the national Republican leadership has continued to follow the Matalin line that poor communication skills, not wrong policy, are the cause of the party's problems with women. (The leadership was following not only Matalin but a long-established tradition. From the very beginning of the republic, politicians of all stripes have been talking not to women but about and at them. Much of the time they have perceived women as they thought they should be, rather than asking women what they wanted. Until women had the vote, few politicians saw any reason to find out. Many of them have changed startlingly little since then.)

This thinking is the source of one of the most popular and persistent myths about how best to woo women voters and win their vote without antagonizing men: appeal to them through their concern for their families. Thus, women are viewed first as mothers and secondly as wives, but seldom as their own person. Seeking to respond to the backlash against women's striving for autonomy and equality, both parties have used the family as a hedge against the unpleasant reality of gender discrimination and its consequences. Lecturing mothers on staying home with their children is simpler than explaining why the richest nation in the world cannot solve its child-care crisis. It is easier to talk about saving unborn children than about protecting women from unwanted pregnancies.

In 1996 politicians' favorite euphemism for women's issues and women's needs was "the family." At the 1996 Democratic Convention in Chicago, family rhetoric was so ubiquitous that one had to wonder whether the Democrats even realized that some people may not be in anyone's family. Of course, not all women's issues are family issues any more than all men's issues are family issues.

One of the first things a New Center GOP must do is cut out euphemisms and evasions like these. Women should be addressed forthrightly and rationally. They don't need patronizing talk to define what they believe or who they are. Her family is a part of a woman, a very important part, but it is not her entire identity. She has a self, "a room of her own," just as a man does.

For years, "family values" was an honorable term, understood to signify that people care for their families. That changed with Dan Quayle. Picking up themes from the Religious Right, he politicized the words, charging that the moral glue holding the family together was dissolving because too many Americans ignored family values. If you were a woman, you practiced family values only by following the fifties version of happy domesticity and motherhood. You weren't practicing family values if you were pro-choice, if you used child care instead of staying home with your children, if you were divorced, if you were a lesbian mother, or if you sought an identity outside the home in addition to being a wife and mother. To place women in the apologetic position of having to say that they care deeply about their families, their children, their husbands, traps them in a snare set by those who attack women for not caring enough. The entire family values "debate" is an outright attempt to destroy the credibility of the goals of the women's movement.

To state what should be a given but has been corrupted by these destructive tactics, the women's movement believes in a morality that treats all human beings fairly. It believes in a family values ethic that respects women, men, and children equally. It venerates the family unit but rejects the authoritarian model as the "right" way to raise children. It stresses responsibility out of love, not guilt. It believes in freedom of religion and the right of each person to find his or her own religious experience without government dictates. Its beliefs are open and expansive, not exclusive and authoritarian. No one could know this after listening to the rhetoric of Religious Right women and men and those who have adopted their views.

In trying to explain the Republican party's women's problem, the New Majoritarians have perpetuated yet another myth. For the majority of women (apart from Religious Right women), they say, abortion is an irrelevant political issue and does not significantly affect the way they vote. Citing polling data, they point out that men and women do not differ very much on this issue—and they admit that the majority of both genders is pro-choice. But abortion as an issue never shows up as one of a voter's top priorities, they argue; peace, jobs, education, and crime prevention generally head the lists. Therefore, the New Majoritarians' tacticians have reasoned, responding to the pro-choice majority in order to win women's votes is politically counterproductive because even for this constituency, protecting legal abortion is not a priority. They add that the Republican party dare not alienate those loyal Religious Right women who claim to choose candidates solely for being pro-life.

This analysis is flawed. It is based on politics by polls alone. It fails to face up to the true nature of the issue, which is that regardless of a woman's position on abortion, she thinks about being a mother. The freedom to decide, perhaps with the counsel of others, perhaps on her own, is integral to every woman's sense of herself, whether or not she has articulated it. But it is not something that has been registered in political polling statistics. When the pollsters ask her to list the issues that concern her most, she will answer, "Jobs, health care, happy children, educational opportunity, no crime or drugs, peace." But she also thinks about whether she will have the freedom to fulfill her aspirations. The decision to have an abortion involves not only her emotional feelings but her economic condition. If her wish is to stay home with her children, she recognizes that its fulfillment will depend on how much money is being brought into the house. If she hopes for success in the work world, she knows this will depend on how she handles the strains of career and family. Whatever choice she makes, a woman considers her reproductive destiny when she is deciding her vote.

While the New Majoritarians are willing to acknowledge that abortion can be a wedge that may decide a close election, they will not admit that it really is a significant women's issue. At the same time, the Republican party's vehement opposition to a woman's right to choose has undermined women's trust in the party. Its failure to respect a woman's moral integrity by imposing its own edicts on her and making her feel immoral or criminal for decisions that are legal under the laws of the United States is at the heart of her disaffection with what the Republican party has become.

"Tax cuts bring families together" is another myth championed by the New Right, especially by the revisionist Independent Women's Forum, which rejects an equalitarian solution for eliminating gender discrimination. Lisa Schiffren, Forum member and former speechwriter for Quayle, criticized Dole and Kemp for failing to explain during the 1996 campaign "why lower taxes would do more to strengthen family values than would an expanded Family Leave Act." (Among other reasons,) she argued that "a tax cut that allows a mother to forgo working to rear her own children is far more significant than allowing her time off from work to attend a parent-teacher conference."

Few would argue that staying home if one can afford it or wishes to, and having to juggle the conflicting demands of family and work are the same. But Schiffren misses the point. Dole's proposed tax cuts would scarcely have helped the average family, while time provided by the Family and Medical Leave Act could at least enhance the quality of family life. Tax cuts by themselves do not necessarily make the best policy. If they are of the Reagan era variety, families will find their economic lives more insecure as high federal debt makes saving for college education and paying medical bills formidable. Rather, the crucial question is how average families will be affected by the sacrifices imposed by supply-side tax cuts.

In addition to her presumption that stay-at-home mothers are better mothers, Schiffren paints an unattainable picture for the majority of America's families. There are not enough adequately paying jobs for the average American family to be able to afford having one parent stay home with the children. It is only by their both working outside the home that most families have been able to make ends meet. It is the well-off who benefit from Schiffren's axiom.

(Her view does exemplify, however, the synergism between the goals of the supply-siders and the Religious Right, and it underscores why the two have been able to maintain their uneasy partnership. The moralists are happy because tax cuts keep Mom at home, and the supply-siders are happy because any tax cut is worthwhile.)

The gap between rich and poor Americans has increased. "The widening of inequality is beyond doubt," economist Paul Krugman has written. "It has been as firmly established by the evidence as the fact that smoking causes cancer." In the early nineties the economic security of the American middle class, the crucial ballast that keeps the nation stable, declined precipitously. According to Kevin Phillips, "survey after survey showed that middle-income ranks, while not precisely definable by dollars or purchasing power, had thinned by 8 to 15 percentage points of the nation's population from the days of John F. Kennedy, Lyndon Johnson, and Richard Nixon, an unprecedented decline." Despite a robust economy in certain sectors, low inflation, an overall increase in the gross domestic product, and in May and July 1997, the lowest jobless rate, 4.8 percent, since 1973, this gap remains the largest of all the world's democracies.

In the 1996 campaign, recognizing the precariousness of their existence, women with children—whether married, divorced, widowed, or single—took the Dole 15 percent tax cut proposal with a grain of salt. Despite supply-siders' belief that tax cuts were the way to a woman's heart, this proved once again not to be the case. Tony Fabrizio, Bob

Dole's chief pollster during the presidential campaign, admitted afterward that "post-election data would suggest it [the proposal] was ill-timed and ill-conceived."

Even as they identified themselves in polls as fiscal conservatives, women who voted against Dole knew that tax cuts without government spending cuts would mean higher deficits and more problems for their future and their children's. Today, American families are not being smothered by taxes; in fact, we have the lowest tax rates of any of the Western democracies. Families are being hurt by the federal debt, and by small raises, a disappearing job base for the unskilled and the high-school educated, retrenched health and pension benefits, lack of adequate, affordable child care, housing and transportation, too few educational opportunities, and low wages. As economics columnist Robert Kuttner has pointed out, while productivity increased by 1.2 percent in 1996, real wages went up by only 0.5 percent.

(But supply-side tax cuts have indeed had their benefits; they have enriched the wealthiest, brought huge salaries for CEOs, and increased profits for corporate shareholders. In the dream world of supply-siders, these profits trickle down to everyone, encouraging more investment and more jobs. In the real world, few full-time, livable-wage jobs have appeared for those most in need of them, and trickle-down economics is a fairy tale.)

Poor women and children are the centerpiece of another New Right myth. The claim is that under the new 1996 welfare reform law, most of the 12.8 million welfare recipients will find their way to a secure life. (It is important to remember that the majority of these recipients are women and children.) All who can will work, and those who are unable to work will be helped by private philanthropy or, in the most difficult cases, by the government.

Philanthropy was not able to shoulder the burden placed upon it when the government withdrew funds from social welfare programs in the 1980s. With the government no longer providing welfare for most of the poor, the private sector's burden increases. If past performance is any indication, women and children will not receive their fair share. According to a former leader of two national women's organizations, "only about 5 percent of philanthropic dollars go to help women and girls."

In the last two decades, poverty among women and children has grown. Children under eighteen now make up 25 percent of the population but 40 percent of America's poor, and almost half of all children who are poor live in households headed by women, according to the Census Bureau.

A study by the Columbia University Center for Children and Poverty reports that poverty among children under six rose sharply, from 18 percent in 1975 to 25 percent in 1994. The number of poor young children has grown nearly twice as fast in the suburbs as in the cities, and twice as fast among whites as blacks. Two-parent families with only one full-time worker constitute a sizable proportion of this increase, joining the ranks of those families headed by single young women with limited work skills.

The welfare law, with its starkly New Right agenda, will not improve the living situation of most of the poor. As soon as the economy sours and evidence piles up that there are not enough jobs available with wages sufficient to cover the costs of child care, health insurance, education, and transportation, and not enough private money to fill these needs, the fallacy on which this law is based will collapse of its own weight. At that point, Washington will intensively scrutinize the successful state government experiments to help the poor, as the country faces up to another national welfare crisis.

Seventy percent of American women under the age of sixty either work or are looking for work. The Institute for Women's Policy Research reports, "The wage gap between women and men, which had remained virtually constant from 1955 through the 1970s, began to decline in the 1980s. The ratio of women's annual earnings to men's for full-time, year-round workers increased gradually over the 1980s and early 1990s, reaching 72 percent in 1994 and falling slightly to 71.4 in 1995." This is better, but it isn't equity. Moreover, as the Institute points out, "nearly three-quarters of the reduction in the wage gap [between men and women] has been due to the falling earnings of men rather than improvement in women's earnings." If men's annual earnings had not dropped, women would have earned only 63 cents for every dollar men earned, rather than the 71 cents. According to the Census Bureau, the median annual earnings for a woman working full time in 1995 was $22,497, compared with $31,496 for men.

Women in America still do not have political or economic power at all commensurate with their numbers. In 1997 only 21 percent of them were state legislators, 11 percent U.S. House members, and 10 percent U.S. Senators; and just two, Republican Christine Todd Whitman of New Jersey and Democrat Jeanne Shaheen of New Hampshire, were governors. Among *Fortune* 500 companies, only 2.3 percent of the highest-ranking officers were women, and only one of the companies is headed by a female CEO.

Yet New Right women seem to have decided that women have made it. They argue that in most cases, job discrimination against women no longer exists, and that those who say that women earn less than men in comparable jobs are promoting women as victims. Of all the myths that have been floating around America and encouraged by some Republican party leaders, this myth is the most flagrant. Nevertheless, two female academics, endorsed by the New Right American Enterprise Institute and the Independent Women's Forum, argue that women's rights advocates have exaggerated women's economic condition. To back up their claim, they cite their research: "Among people ages 27 through 33 who have never had a child, women's earnings approach 98 percent of men's earnings."

Emphasizing that women earn the majority of associate, bachelor's, and master's degrees and 40 percent of doctorates, they argue that women start out with just as good a chance as men in the workplace, then falter because of their personal choices, such as having a child or not aspiring to long-term professional advancement. (This sounds reminiscent of Pat Buchanan's well-known quote that women are not endowed with the single-minded ambition to succeed.) They postulate that there is no such thing as wholesale discrimination against women in the workplace anymore; rather it is women's personal choices that cause them to earn less than men. According to this view, the glass ceiling does not exist; rather, women make themselves victims by opting out of the workforce.

They ignore the reason why women are the ones left to bear the professional cost of having children. They don't face the fact that working mothers must constantly accept the reality of fewer opportunities because affordable child care is unavailable. They fail to explain that a sexist corporate culture keeps many single-mindedly ambitious and competent women managers' careers stuck in midlevel jobs.

This statistical exercise is just one example of how the drive for women's equality has entered a new phase. Some women who have benefited from its successes and who claim to want opportunity for all now are organizing and speaking out to rein in action to help all women succeed. They are antifeminists masquerading as neofeminists, and they are perfect foils for those within the GOP who wish to cripple the political potency of the women's liberation agenda. The Independent Women's Forum was formed by women supporters of Clarence Thomas, including his wife, who were furious at women's support for Anita Hill. While IWF women reject the Religious Right's view that God meant for women to stay home, they also reject the belief that women face institutional sexism in achieving their goals. As libertarians, they believe government is the greatest impediment to a woman's professional success.

Another group, the Women's Freedom Network, differs only slightly from the IWF. Its board includes Harvard law professor Mary Ann Glendon, Vanderbilt political scientist Jean Bethke Elshtain, and conservative columnist Mona Charen, and it does acknowledge—unlike the IWF—that women have faced social and institutional barriers to full equality. But the Network also believes that women make themselves victims and, according to their statement of principles, that "Special state protections in areas such as employment, child care, the justice system and personal relations minimizes our accomplishments and undermines our present position of equality."

This latest direction in the gender war is not a backlash phenomenon but a mutation. New Right women are advocating many of the positions that Schlafly supports; however, they are no longer claiming, as Schlafly still does, that a woman's universe centers around being a wife and mother. They have accepted the feminist view that women should have the opportunity to follow their dreams. But their politics denies many women that chance.

The New Majoritarian strategy was conceived in part to take advantage of the backlash against the women's movement. Now, more than twenty-five years later, the backlash is not as overtly virulent and is no longer as effective a political tool. Even though gender and racial equity are still salient political issues, economic equity is fast becoming America's major domestic issue.

The power of a movement can be measured in part by the force of the anger directed against it. Despite twenty-plus years spent exploiting the backlash against the women's political movement, women have continued to make their way into leadership positions in business, boardrooms, labor unions, some religious institutions, and academia, as well as in the halls of government. The previously cited data make it clear that they still have a long way to go to attain genuine equality of opportunity, but as feminist activist Carol Reichert has said, "Women have been exercising the Nike principle—they're just doing it. They are not waiting for permission, validation or legislation to better their lives." They have organized a movement of enormous vitality, one that is changing the structure of power in America.

Since 1971 this political force has caused men in power to pay attention to its ideas. Some have been receptive, some have been angry, defensive, or hostile—but none have been unaware. Without the women's movement, the gains women have made would not have happened.

Long-range improvement for all of America's women can come only through political action. Individual women may be able to better their lives without engaging in politics, but none escape the society around them. As long as the country's institutions are sexist and women's rights and opportunities are marginalized, all women suffer. Most Americans will find it unacceptable that the dream that people who work hard and earn their own way will get ahead is being undermined. They will not long tolerate a situation in which the income of their fellow citizens in the top one-percent bracket is equal to that of the entire bottom 40 percent of the nation—and in which the gains of one of America's longest economic upswings have increased the wealth of its top 5 percent by 16 percent, while the income of those in the bottom 20 percent has dropped by 5 percent.

A New Center movement, either through the Republican party or a third political vehicle, can address this gross discrepancy by making economic equity the centerpiece of its agenda. Certainly women, as the ones most often on the bottom rungs of the economic ladder, will respond to such a call. A New Center goal for twenty-first-century American men and women can be found in the words of author Diane Johnson: "Everyone regardless of sex should have minimal 'rights': personal safety, autonomy in sexual and health matters, equal pay for equal work—conditions of basic fairness." Underscoring that these were the conditions more or less underpinning the Equal Rights

Amendment, Johnson notes that they were "pointedly refused by a society still unwilling to recognize either women or children as fully qualified citizens."

It is no accident that the states that rejected the ERA were also the states that formed the core of the New Majoritarian electoral strategy. But women are politically stronger and more adept now. A political movement that looks forward with hope and optimism, not back to fear and bigotry, has the potential for capturing not only the hearts of the majority of women but men of goodwill, who will recognize that the efforts of *all* Americans will be needed if we are to win the battle for economic security in the global marketplace. Despite the continuing rhetoric of divisiveness, the country is hungry for a new direction that treats all of us fairly.

Losing the White House twice has effectively ended the Republican war against women as a winning strategy. The Religious Right and the New Right now seek to consolidate their hold over the party and to wage the war in a different form. Gender will still be their decoy for winning power, and New Right women will be their cover for those who would accuse them of misogyny.

History has repeatedly proved that no democracy is secure, no honorable tradition permanent, simply because it is fair and just. Americans fought a civil war over the question of equality of opportunity, and they gave women the vote and passed civil rights legislation to further that quest. None of us, neither women nor men, should have to live harassed by the politics of fear and hatred. We cannot let those who reject their country's dream have our time, energy, or vote, no matter how precarious our economic condition or how pervasive our anger. Supreme Court Justice Louis Brandeis wrote that "the greatest dangers to liberty lurk in insidious encroachments by men of zeal, well-meaning but without understanding."

At the last millennium, women in most parts of the world were the property of men. They were prisoners to the religious doctrines and superstitions that kept them subservient, categorized in men's minds as either goddesses or whores. A thousand years later, America's women have not only been the guiding light for women around the world seeking opportunity; they and their male allies have been the political bastion against the right-wing sickness infecting their country's politics. They must continue to join forces as a new political movement is forged, and ensure that backlash bigotry no longer rewards its practitioners with power.

The Republican party may rise to the occasion and return to its honorable traditions. It may falter under the weight of its dominant factions. The Democratic party may extricate itself from its wasteful past. It may not.

Either way, the battle is joined.

NOTES

CHAPTER 1: THE CONFLICT OF PRINCIPLE AND EXPEDIENCY

Page 4: told well and in detail elsewhere: For a detailed analysis of race in contemporary Republican politics, see Thomas B. Edsall and Mary D. Edsall, *Chain Reaction: The Impact of Race, Rights, and Taxes on American Politics* (New York: W. W. Norton, 1991).

Page 6: woman is "man's equal": Alice S. Rossi, ed., *The Feminist Papers: From Adams to Beauvoir* (Boston: Northeastern University Press, 1973), p. 418.

Page 8: six normally Republican western states: Rebecca K. Leet, *Republican Women Are Wonderful: A History of Women at Republican National Conventions* (Washington, DC: National Women's Political Caucus, 1980), p. 5. All citations on women's progress in the party in this section come from Leet's account.

Page 10: "wormy food, open toilets": Dorothy Schneider and Carl J. Schneider, *American Women in the Progressive Era, 1900–1920* (New York: Doubleday, 1993), pp. 184–185.

Page 10: the Sheppard-Towner Act: Linda Witt, Karen M. Paget, and Glenna Matthews, *Running as a Woman: Gender and Power in American Politics* (New York: Free Press, 1993), p. 288.

Page 13: "go hunting where the ducks are": David A. Broder, "How Goldwater Did It," *Washington Star*, July 16, 1964.

Page 15: "The upcoming cycle of American politics": Kevin P. Phillips, *The Emerging Republican Majority* (New Rochelle: Arlington House, 1969), p. 465.

Page 16: bowing under pressure from labor leader George Meany: When the ERA was proposed by the National Women's Party in 1923, organized labor opposed it. Not until 1944, when Eleanor Roosevelt assured the Democratic party that the amendment would not hurt women's protective legislation, did the Democrats support the ERA. Meany opened up an old wound in 1964 by insisting support be dropped. States with ERA laws later proved that Meany was wrong.

Page 16: Catholics, a major linchpin of the New Deal coalition: Phillips, Ibid., pp. 166–175.

Page 17: "As early as 1970": Timothy A. Byrnes, *Catholic Bishops in American Politics* (Princeton, NJ: Princeton University Press, 1991), p. 65.

Page 17: "through their traditional relationships with urban machines": Ibid.

CHAPTER 2: TWO EMERGING AGENDAS

Pages 31–32: "child care should be available": New York Chapter, Ripon Society, letter to *Ripon Forum*, Jan. 14, 1972.

Page 32: "I would personally like to associate myself": *New York Times*, May 7, 1972.

Page 32: "a patent pitch for the Catholic vote": Ibid.

Page 33: "commit himself to name a woman": Bobbie Greene Kilberg, memo to Dr. Martin Anderson, June 22, 1972.

CHAPTER 3: THE LINE IS CROSSED

Page 40: The New Right is an amalgam of individuals: To understand the development of the new conservative and New Right movement through all its various phases, see John S. Saloma III, *Ominous Politics: The New Conservative Labyrinth* (New York: Hill and Wang, 1984).

Page 40: Viguerie had raised "about $7 million": Richard A. Viguerie, *The New Right: We're Ready to Lead* (Falls Church, VA: The Viguerie Co., 1981), p. 37.

Page 40: to seduce conservatives into leaving: Jerome L. Himmelstein, *To the Right: The Transformation of American Conservatism* (Berkeley: University of California Press, 1990), p. 83.

Page 42: a way "to provide an 'internal mechanism'": *Washington Post*, June 15, 1974.

Page 42: "proposal would, if adopted, thrust the Republican party": Ibid.

Page 43: "The lesson of the election for Republicans": *Chicago Sun-Times*, Nov. 8, 1974.

Page 46: White House aide speaking off the record: *Ripon Forum*, Dec. 15, 1974.

Page 47: Pat Buchanan proclaimed: *Washington Post*, Nov. 10, 1974.

Page 47: Bill Rusher criticized: *Human Events*, Sept. 21, 1974.

Page 47: A New Right colleague of Viguerie: *Human Events*, Oct. 19, 1974.

Page 48: The Democrats had their way of doing things: Political scientist Jo

Freeman has substantiated the cultural differences and style between Democrats and Republicans. See especially "The Political Culture of the Democratic and Republican Parties," *Political Science Quarterly* 101 (Fall 1986), pp. 327–356.

Page 48: We announced we'd work with existing Republican groups: Republican Women's Task Force proposal, May 16, 1975.

Page 48: but as Clarke Reed told Bobbie Kilberg: Minutes summary, first meeting of Republican Women's Task Force, Apr. 18, 1975.

CHAPTER 4: AN EMBOLDENED NEW RIGHT

Page 49: Maryland senator Charles Mathias charged: *Congressional Quarterly*, Nov. 15, 1975.

Pages 50–51: newspaper publisher William Loeb: Jules Witcover, *Marathon: The Pursuit of the Presidency, 1972–1976* (New York: Viking, 1977), p. 58.

Page 52: "Women's lib is a total assault on the role": Jane J. Mansbridge, *Why We Lost the ERA* (Chicago: University of Chicago Press, 1986), p. 104.

Page 53: Dorothy Collins summed up their relationship: Unpublished reporter's notes for *People* interview, Jan. 1981. Author's files.

Page 53: "At first she did not see it": Ibid.

Page 54: A hero to many Americans, Ervin was hailed: Donald G. Mathews and Jane Sherron DeHart, *Sex, Gender, and the Politics of the ERA* (New York: Oxford University Press, 1990), p. 52.

Pages 54–55: he "even placed his franking privilege": Ibid., p. 51.

Page 55: "As he expected politicians to act like gentlemen": Ibid., p. 43.

Page 55: "The minister who argued that his church's tax-exempt status": Ibid., p. 172.

Page 55: Those ERA opponents who believed family life had been undermined: Ibid.

Page 55: "forced busing, forced mixing, forced hiring": Ibid., p. 173.

Page 57: One opponent dressed up "as an outhouse": Lisa Cronin Wohl, "The ERA—What the Hell Happened in New York," *Ms.* (Mar. 1976), p. 64.

Pages 57–58: Journalist Jane O'Reilly answered these charges: Jane O'Reilly, "The Bogus Fear of ERA," *Nation*, July 8–15, 1978.

Page 58: polls consistently showed that Catholics were more likely: Mansbridge, *Why We Lost the ERA*, p. 15.

Page 58: if the ERA were passed, the "Catholic church could be required": *New York Times*, Mar. 2, 1975.

Page 59: Schlafly insisted the ERA would put sex discrimination: Ibid.

Page 59: A few evangelical Protestant churches: Ibid.

Pages 59–60: the four supposedly most progressive counties in New Jersey: *New York Times*, Nov. 8, 1975.

Page 60: He did not agree with *Roe v. Wade,* he announced: Ibid., Feb. 4, 1976.

Page 61: *The Washington Post* editorialized: *Washington Post,* Feb. 11, 1976.

Page 61: a flyer that quoted Ford as suggesting: Witcover, *Marathon,* p. 411.

Pages 61–62: "I've always been a Democrat": Ibid., p. 419.

Page 62: "There is a deep, fundamental split on the political right": Pat Buchanan, "Civil War in the Republican Party," *Human Events,* May 22, 1976.

Page 63: Republican women "will be allowed to vote, occasionally": *New York Times,* July 28, 1976.

Page 63: Republicans "don't have women positioned correctly": Ibid.

Page 64: he directed the attorney general to review the U.S. Code: NWPC Republican Women's Task Force newsletter, July 1976.

Page 64: He also stated that while he supported the ERA: Ibid.

CHAPTER 5: A TIME OF ACCOMMODATION

Page 69: the nomination now hinged on Ford's winning: Jules Witcover, *Marathon: The Pursuit of the Presidency, 1972–1976* (New York: Viking, 1977), pp. 468–470.

Page 72: sponsored by member Bob Dole: Barbara Gunderson, letter to author, Sept. 1, 1976.

Page 76: "The inclusion of an anti-abortion plank": *Official Report of the Proceedings of the Thirty-first Republican National Convention.* See pp. 303–309 for the full debate.

Page 79: engineered what *The New York Times* described as: *New York Times,* Aug. 17, 1976.

Page 79: "I consider it immensely more important": Ibid.

Page 79: *Ms.* magazine quoted White House counsel Bobbie Kilberg: *Ms.* (Nov. 1976), p. 19.

Page 80: The bishops said they "were encouraged": *MacNeil-Lehrer Newshour,* Sept. 15, 1976.

Page 80: "What I really fear is, for instance": Ibid.

Page 80: Ford's campaign manager James Baker reinforced: Ibid.

Page 80: the use of contraceptives to minor children: President Ford Committee advertisement, *Globe* (Sioux City, IA), Oct. 14, 1976.

Page 81: "I'm still not sure that things didn't work out for the best": Lyn Nofziger, *Nofziger* (Washington, DC: Regnery Gateway, 1992), p. 207.

Page 81: "Had Mr. Ford carried Delaware and Ohio": *New York Times,* Nov. 10, 1976.

CHAPTER 6: THE BACKLASH BREAKS OUT

Page 86: ". . . [J]ust below the surface, the Republican party": *Buffalo Evening News,* Nov. 6, 1976.

Page 87: In 1977 Viguerie was bringing in at least $25 million: Alan Crawford, "Richard Viguerie's Bid for Power," *The Nation,* Jan. 29, 1977, p. 105.

Page 87: Louis Ingram, a former member of the Capitol Hill chapter: Ibid., p. 106.

Page 88: James Buckley noted that "the Viguerie people": Ibid.

Page 88: Arthur Finkelstein, one of the New Right's strategic gurus: *Ripon Forum,* Dec. 15, 1977.

Page 89: The majority argued that the issue: *Washington Post,* June 21, 1977.

Page 89: In sharply worded dissenting opinions: Ibid.

Pages 89–90: Justice Thurgood Marshall added his own: Ibid.

Page 90: Cartoonist Herblock summed up the New Right's philosophy: *New York Times,* June 22, 1977.

Page 90: President Carter endorsed the Court's ruling: *Washington Post,* July 3, 1977.

Page 90: Democratic women issued a statement: *Daily News,* July 19, 1977.

Page 90: Other Democrats criticized Carter: *New York Times,* July 29, 1977.

Page 91: Packwood told his colleagues: *Washington Post,* July 3, 1977.

Page 91: Brooke called the ban "nothing": *New York Times,* June 28, 1977.

Page 91: Hyde lashed out at once: *Washington Post,* July 8, 1977.

Page 94: As Megan Rosenfeld wrote: *Washington Post,* Dec. 2, 1977.

Page 97: The Imperial Wizard of the United Klans: *Christian Science Monitor,* Sept. 29, 1977.

Page 97: that it "was a poor idea" and feared a brawl: *Washington Post,* Nov. 18, 1977.

Pages 97–98: "So here we are, the faces and voices": IWY commissioner Liz Carpenter speech, delivered at the national IWY convention, Houston, TX, Nov. 19, 1977.

Page 98: the all-white Mississippi delegation: *Washington Post,* Nov. 20, 1977.

Page 99: Unfurling banners with giant color photos: Lucy Komisar, "Feminism as National Politics," *The Nation,* Dec. 10, 1977.

Page 99: "I never had been opposed to civil rights": Betty Friedan, "The Women at Houston," *New Republic,* Dec. 10, 1977.

Page 101: Extreme-right California congressmember Robert Dornan: GOP for ERA press release, Nov. 19, 1977.

Page 101: "the great tragedy": *Human Events,* Dec. 10, 1977.

Page 101: When Gloria Steinem was told: *Washington Post,* Nov. 23, 1977.

Page 101: He called the delegates "a gaggle": GOP For ERA press release, Nov. 19, 1977.

Page 102: David Broder wrote prophetically that: *Washington Post*, Nov. 22, 1977.

Page 102: Elly Peterson was a former chairman: *Washington Post*, Nov. 21, 1977.

CHAPTER 7: THE SUCCESSFUL TRIAL RUN

Page 105: New Right leader "[Paul] Weyrich disguised the fact": E. J. Dionne, Jr., *Why Americans Hate Politics* (New York: Simon and Schuster, 1991), p. 230.

Page 105: Weyrich created the name Moral Majority: Ibid.

Page 107: As Howard Phillips declared, "Organize discontent": James P. Gannon, "Coalition Politics on the Right," *Wall Street Journal*, Jan. 3, 1978.

Page 107: Her messages alienated many people: Jane J. Mansbridge, *Why We Lost the ERA* (Chicago: University of Chicago Press, 1986), p. 104.

Page 107: "stopped our momentum dead": Ibid., p. 137.

Page 108: Campaigning as "the candidate of middle-class people": *New York Times*, Nov. 9, 1978.

Page 108: "Newt will take his family to Washington": *Washington Post*, Dec. 19, 1994.

Page 108: A Gingrich campaign official described the strategy: Ibid.

Page 110: But this was often not the case during the ten-year ERA battle: Ibid., pp. 165–177.

Page 111: Ostensibly, Packwood left the committee: Lee Roderick, *Leading the Charge: Orrin Hatch and 20 Years of America* (Carson City, NV: Gold Leaf Press, 1994), p. 127.

Page 112: In 1978 Packwood opposed Hatch for the chairmanship: Ibid., p. 128.

Page 112: Brock hailed Republican gains: *New York Times*, Nov. 9, 1978.

Page 113: Out in Iowa, Roger Jepsen: *The American Political Report* (Bethesda, MD: American Political Research Corp.), Nov. 10, 1978.

Page 113: and as Crisp said: Mary Crisp speech to Planned Parenthood Western Conference, Portland, Oregon, May 5, 1994.

Page 114: In New York, the Right-to-Life party: *Political Animal* (Torrance, CA), Jan. 29, 1979.

Page 114: Only some 16 percent of the Republican candidates: *New York Times*, Nov. 9, 1978.

Page 115: In a most uncharacteristically crude public remark: *Congressional Quarterly*, Apr. 28, 1979, p. 775.

Page 115: Weyrich angrily attacked Brock for not encouraging: Ibid.

Page 116: in June 1978 he had warned conservatives: Ibid., Aug. 5, 1978, p. 2,027.

CHAPTER 8: WINNING THE BRASS RING

Page 117: "Feed them spaghetti and the feminist line": Republican Women's Task Force Newsletter (Jan.–Feb. 1979).

Page 119: "We saw him as a moderate": Mary Louise Smith, interview, Nov. 30, 1994.

Page 119: Further, he wrote: Republican Women's Task Force, 1980 GOP Presidential Questionnaire, released Jan. 17, 1980.

Page 120: "This statement shows a complete lack": Susan McLane, letter to George Bush, July 16, 1979. Author's files.

Page 120: As she told me: Susan McLane, interview, Oct. 1, 1995.

Page 122: political reporter Jim Perry read the Bush strategy: "To George Bush, Seeking Presidency Seems Almost a Duty," *Wall Street Journal*, July 6, 1979.

Page 122: Describing him as "a possible back-up on a Reagan ticket": "Will a Conservative Capture the 1980 GOP Nomination?" *Human Events*, Feb. 17, 1979.

Page 122: "I think Bush is pretty conservative": "Bush Acquires Top Conservative Operative," *Human Events*, Mar. 3, 1979.

Page 122: Six weeks later, the campaign hired: *Washington Post*, Apr. 20, 1979.

Page 122: Snider liked "the way he talks": Ibid.

Page 123: Bush was his man: *Washington Post*, May 4, 1979.

Page 123: Anderson's campaign manager said that "it hadn't occurred": Michael McLeod, interview, Jan. 6, 1995.

Page 127: he had let his father-in-law, Dr. Loyal Davis: "The Leader He Was, the Leader He Wasn't," *Washington Post*, Apr. 26, 1980.

Pages 127–128: Bill Rusher, never one to mince words: "Will Reagan 'Trim Toward the Center' for 1980?" *Human Events*, Oct. 13, 1979.

Page 130: "We got sidetracked in our presidential plans": Michael McLeod, interview, Jan. 6, 1995.

Page 132: "Riponites are hardly of a single mind": "A Word from the Editor," *Ripon Forum* (May–June–July 1980).

Page 133: "I never endorsed Anderson": *Washington Post*, July 7, 1980.

Page 133: "I hired a professional": Mary Crisp, interview, Oct. 12, 1995.

Page 134: Judy Mann caught our group's frustration: Judy Mann, "GOP Feminists Seek Way to Support Reagan," *Washington Post*, May 30, 1980.

Page 134: "I think there's a lot of feeling among a number": Ibid.

Page 135: Roger Semerad, who was supervising the platform hearings:

Martin Gruberg, "Women at the National Party Convention" (Oshkosh, WI: Unpublished manuscript, 1980), p. 8. Author's files.

Page 135: He added that Platform Committee chair John Tower: Ibid.

CHAPTER 9: REAGAN'S NEW REPUBLICAN BEGINNING

Page 142: "It was a revival of the oldest chestnut": Sidney Blumenthal, *The Rise of the Counter-Establishment: From Conservative Ideology to Political Power* (New York: Times Books, 1986), p. 167.

Page 142: Say's Law posited that: Ibid., p. 168.

Page 142: It was the perfect economic doctrine for Reagan: Ibid., p. 170.

Page 147: As Alice Tetelman remembers, "We didn't think we had": Alice Tetelman, interview, Nov. 30, 1994.

Page 147: "Reagan at Odds with Conservatives on ERA Platform Plank": *Washington Post*, July 4, 1980.

Page 147: It included almost word for word the statement: Ibid.

Page 147: "Obviously, the Governor accepts what comes out": Ibid.

Page 147: "Reagan would prefer a platform plank which opposed": Ibid.

Page 147: Schlafly announced that she was "shocked": Ibid.

Page 147: Roy Brun, the Louisiana Platform Committee delegate: Ibid.

Page 148: To drop the ERA plank, he told the committee: Ibid.

Page 149: Kathy Wilson couldn't get Moral Majority Alaska delegate: Washington, DC: Republican Women's Task Force Newsletter, Aug.–Sept., 1980.

Page 149: State legislator John Leopold: *Wall Street Journal*, July 9, 1980.

Page 149: As Rebecca Leet remembers: Rebecca Leet, interview, Apr. 20, 1995.

Page 150: Californians Nancy Chotiner and Lorelei Kinder: Alice Tetelman, interview, Nov. 30, 1994.

Page 150: The goal for all: Ibid.

Page 151: "We applaud our presidential candidate's pledge": Author's personal notes from 1980 Republican National Convention.

Page 152: Surely the legal profession would be outraged: The American Bar Association *was* outraged. In early August it roundly criticized the Republican court-packing plank and overwhelmingly reaffirmed "its commitment to the appointment of judges qualified on the basis of merit and renounces any appointment process repugnant to that concept."

Page 154: District of Columbia delegate Jan Evans asked for a vote: *Washington Post*, July 10, 1980.

Page 154: Afterward, for public relations reasons, the Reagan team: Ibid.

Page 154: "Although our party has presented the outward": Ibid.

Page 155: *The New York Times* reported incorrectly that she had: *New York Times,* July 10, 1980.

Page 155: Reagan attacked her personally: Judy Mann, "GOP Got in Its Time Machine and Returned to the 50's," *Washington Post,* July 11, 1980.

Page 155: Mary Louise Smith said, "Yes, the ball game's over": *New York Post,* July 10, 1980.

Page 156: sent Reagan a letter asking to meet with him: Letter to Governor Reagan, July 10, 1980, signed Margaret Heckler, Andrew H. Card, Jr., John Leopold, Doris M. Russell, Patricia R. Stuart, Phillip C. Clark, Nancy B. Chase, Astrid Hanzalek. Author's files.

Page 157: Maybe the Platform Committee delegates believed: *New York Times,* July 10, 1980.

Page 157: But as Martin Anderson said, the Reagan camp: Ibid.

Page 157: an estimated twelve thousand ERA advocates: Martin Gruberg, "Women at the National Party Conventions," unpublished manuscript, 1980, p. 12.

Page 157: "My party has endorsed the Equal Rights Amendment": *Washington Post,* July 15, 1980.

Page 158: "[the] most outrageous I have ever seen": Ibid.

Page 159: "As the discussion started, I'm looking at this man": Alice Tetelman, interview, Nov. 30, 1994.

Page 159: Smith recalls that "our hopes were very high": Mary Louise Smith, interview, Nov. 30, 1994.

Page 159: After the meeting, Reagan issued a statement: *New York Times,* July 16, 1980.

Page 160: Afterward, Smith told the press, "We came away": *Daily News,* July 16, 1980.

Page 160: Heckler was also diplomatic, though with a somewhat: Ibid.

Page 160: Only task force chair Curtis was blunt: *New York Times,* July 16, 1980.

Page 161: Heckler expressed the sentiments of people like Milliken: Bill Peterson, *Washington Post,* July 15, 1980.

Page 161: Pennsylvania's young lieutenant governor, William Scranton III: Martin Schram, *Washington Post,* July 15, 1980.

Page 162: Said Milliken: "The day will never come": Ibid.

Page 162: "More than anything else he [Bush] wanted to be president": Anonymous interview with author, Dec. 1994.

Page 162: At his first joint news conference with Reagan: David Broder, *Washington Post,* July 18, 1980.

Page 163: Reagan stated his assurance that Ambassador Bush: Pro-Life Impact Committee press release (Marlene Elwell contact), July 17, 1980.

Page 164: "The forces that started working in our politics in the 60s": M. Stanton Evans, "The Reason for Reagan," *Human Events*, Aug. 2, 1980.

CHAPTER 10: THE "WOMEN'S PROBLEM"

Page 166: "The source of Reagan's inspiration was less": Lou Cannon, *President Reagan: The Role of a Lifetime* (New York: Simon and Schuster, 1991), p. 97.

Page 168: Farenthold urged feminists to "abandon party ranks": Sissy Farenthold endorsement speech, Oct. 1980.

Page 169: the Reagan team picked up on the same arguments: Reagan campaign literature, "Women's Rights. Who Cares?"

Page 169: Before September 21 Carter had been leading: *New York Times*, Oct. 1, 1980.

Page 169: "false and misleading accusations have been made": Reagan–Bush Committee news release, Oct. 14, 1980.

Page 170: "I haven't figured out yet why": Lyn Nofziger, *Nofziger* (Washington, DC: Regnery Gateway, 1992), p. 246.

Page 170: a Gallup survey showed that "36 percent of the voters": Austin Ranney, ed., *The American Elections of 1980* (Washington, DC: American Enterprise Institute for Public Policy Research, 1981), p. 166.

Page 171: Jerry Falwell said it had registered four million: *New York Times*, Nov. 11, 1980.

Page 171: As political analyst William Schneider wrote: Ranney, *Elections*, p. 248.

Page 171: Election analyst John Robinson of Cleveland State University: *Christian Science Monitor*, July 14, 1980.

Page 172: Most surveys reported that men had given Reagan: Nelson W. Polsby and Aaron Wildavsky, *Presidential Elections*, 6th ed. (New York: Charles Scribner's Sons, 1984), p. 165. See CBS News/*New York Times* exit poll data, Nov. 1980.

Page 172: Differences between men and women began to show up: Center for the American Woman and Politics, "The Gender Gap" (New Brunswick, NJ: Eagleton Institute of Politics, 1994).

Page 174: The former Moral Majority executive director, the Reverend Robert Billings: *New York Post*, Feb. 21, 1981.

Page 175: New Right money man Joseph Coors vetoed: Helene von Damm, *At Reagan's Side: Twenty Years in the Political Mainstream* (New York: Doubleday, 1989), p. 133.

Page 177: "there were obstacles. One of the biggest was": Ibid., p. 267.

Page 177: Kassebaum publicly criticized the White House's attitude: Ibid.

Page 178: They claimed she had used her "Republican leadership positions": "Mary Louise Smith for Treasurer?" *Human Events*, June 10, 1981.

Page 178: They ridiculed her for organizing a women's advisory board: Ibid.

Page 179: it was "disappointed and concerned that overall representation": "Civil Rights Update," U.S. Commission on Civil Rights (July 1983).

Page 180: to which Episcopalian Barry Goldwater angrily responded: Cannon, *President Reagan*, p. 805.

Page 180: "In nominating Ms. O'Connor, the White House has left": "O'Connor Choice: Why, Mr. President?" *Human Events*, Aug. 1, 1981.

Page 180: When Orrin Hatch endorsed her because he believed: Lee Roderick, *Leading the Charge* (Carson City, NV: Gold Leaf Press, 1994), p. 168.

Page 181: "For the first time, an administration moved the decision-making": von Damm, *At Reagan's Side*, p. 214.

Page 181: "there was a strong institutional pride among the lawyers": Ibid., p. 213.

Page 181: Von Damm interceded to see that "the Reagan Revolution": Ibid., p. 212.

Page 181: She insisted her office did make "an effort to find": Ibid., p. 214.

Page 181: By Meese's count, Reagan appointed "almost half": Edwin Meese III, *With Reagan: The Inside Story* (Washington, DC: Regnery Gateway, 1992) p. 316.

Page 182: Every major national women's organization attacked: National Women's Political Caucus, press release, Mar. 26, 1981.

Page 182: "if the fertilized egg were constitutionally a person": Rhonda Copelon, "Danger—A 'Human Life' Amendment Is on the Way," *Ms.* (Feb. 1981).

Page 183: In March the president told the press he thought: *New York Times*, Apr. 22, 1981.

Page 184: In July 1981 pollster Louis Harris reported that: Ruth Mandel, "How Women Vote: The New Gender Gap," *Working Woman* (Sept. 1982).

Pages 184–185: "Women make less than men in every job": Linda Tarr-Whelan, "Women's Issues and the Women's Vote," Apr. 21, 1982, speech in Washington, DC.

Page 185: "women's votes elected the Democratic governors": Ruth Mandel, "The Power of the Women's Vote," *Working Woman* (Apr. 1983).

Pages 186–187: A Justice Department memo to the White House's: Robert A. McConnell memo to Kenneth Duberstein, Dec. 23, 1982.

Page 187: Reagan's popularity dropped to 35 percent: Cannon, *President Reagan*, p. 274.

Page 187: arguing that the gap between men's and women's economic: Mandel, "Power of the Women's Vote."

Page 189: Instead, Faith Whittlesey, who would be expected to be responsible for such implementation: Peggy Simpson, "Faith Whittlesey, Presidential Assistant," *Working Woman* (Oct. 1983).

Page 189: "She's the only person here who says there isn't a gender gap": Ibid.

Page 191: We didn't know whether to laugh or cry: Ronald Reagan quote from Hager, Sharp, and Abramson pamphlet for BPW, Washington, DC, Aug. 2, 1983.

CHAPTER II: "TEACH THEM A LESSON"

Page 194: Lansdale said Reagan's opposition to abortion: Peggy Simpson, "A 'Sophie's Choice' for Republican Women," *Working Woman* (Sept. 1984).

Page 194: "We heard from many women office holders": Maureen Reagan, *First Father, First Daughter: A Memoir* (Boston: Little, Brown, 1989), p. 301.

Page 195: As Louis Harris reported in a study: *New York Times,* Dec. 3, 1983.

Page 196: "Occasionally in life there are moments": Geraldine Ferraro, acceptance speech, Democratic National Convention, San Francisco, July 19, 1984.

Page 197: "I'm thirty-six years old. I'm a Republican": Geraldine Ferraro, *Ferraro: My Story* (New York: Bantam Books, 1985), p. 319.

Page 198: As Mondale said, "She was tough": Jules Witcover, *Crapshoot: Rolling the Dice on the Vice Presidency* (New York: Crown, 1992), p. 323.

Page 199: As Pamela Curtis told the press: *Dallas Morning News,* Aug. 13, 1984.

Page 200: one "special Gallup poll done for *Newsweek*": Jack Germond and Jules Witcover, *Wake Us When It's Over: Presidential Politics of 1984* (New York: Macmillan, 1985), p. 413.

Page 204: the national press "stopped harassing me": Ferraro, *My Story*, p. 182.

Page 204: The National Right-to-Life Committee: Michele McKeegan, *Abortion Politics: Mutiny in the Ranks of the Right* (New York: Free Press, 1992), p. 99.

Page 204: An audiotape from a New Right leadership institute: Ibid.

Page 205: "I can only say that Geraldine Ferraro has said": Ferraro, *My Story*, p. 222.

Page 205: "Religious leaders and other citizens should speak out": Ibid., p. 227.

Page 206: Scranton's Catholic bishop attacked her: Ibid.

Page 206: threatened "to pull all the Catholic kids": Ibid., p. 232.

Page 207: Columnist Richard Reeves described what was happening: Ibid., p. 234.

Page 208: Reagan won "more votes for his Republican candidacy": Gerald Pomper et al., *The Election of 1984: Reports and Interpretations* (Chatham, NJ: Chatham House, 1985), p. 60.

Page 208: The gender gap "ranged from four to nine percentage points": Ibid., p. 101.

Page 208: in a year when the top of the ticket had been so popular: Ibid.

Page 209: The proportion of women voters exceeded that of men: Center for the American Woman and Politics, "Sex Differences in Voter Turnout Fact Sheet" (New Brunswick, NJ: Eagleton Institute of Politics, 1994).

Page 209: Democratic pollster Dotty Lynch reported that: Peggy Simpson, "What Happened in '84: Did Women Make a Difference?" *Working Woman* (Feb. 1985).

Page 209: As Rosalie Whelan of the National Women's Education Fund: *Washington Post*, Nov. 8, 1984.

Page 209: As Thomas Mann, executive director: Simpson, "What Happened."

CHAPTER 12: THE COALITION CRACKS

Page 211: In 1985 Richard Viguerie's business fell apart: Jerome L. Himmelstein, *To the Right: The Transformation of American Conservatism* (Berkeley: University of California Press, 1990), p. 201.

Page 211: he became solvent: Ibid.

Page 212: television evangelists Jim and Tammy Bakker: Sidney Blumenthal, *Pledging Allegiance* (New York: HarperPerennial, 1990), p. 69.

Page 213: "Reagan does not need anyone to the right": Michael K. Deaver, *Behind the Scenes* (New York: William Morrow, 1987), p. 182.

Page 214: the line aptly described by Bob Teeter: Jane Mayer and Doyle McManus, *Landslide: The Unmaking of the President, 1984–1988* (Boston: Houghton Mifflin, 1988), p. 6.

Page 219: "Without the women's vote, Republicans": *Christian Science Monitor*, Nov. 7, 1986.

Page 219: "of the twenty-three Christian Right candidates": Michele McKeegan, *Abortion Politics: Mutiny in the Ranks of the Right* (New York: Free Press, 1992), p. 105.

Page 219: Paul Weyrich bluntly called the elections: *Conservative Digest* (Jan. 1987), p. 50.

Page 219: Viguerie's monthly New Right propaganda magazine: Ibid.

Page 222: "the president could advance his entire social agenda": Ethan

Bronner, *Battle for Justice: How the Bork Nomination Shook America* (New York: W. W. Norton, 1989).

Page 223: Specter was bothered "that Bork seemed selective": Ibid., p. 270.

Page 223: When he called Bork to tell him, Bork said: Ibid., p. 311.

Page 224: Bork and his followers were wrong to charge later: Ibid., p. 341.

Page 224: "George Bush has become a Reagan Republican": Robert K. Dornan, "Why My Choice Is George Bush," *Insight,* Apr. 14, 1986.

Page 226: "with an annual increase in world population": Barbara Mosbacher, letter to Frank Fahrenkopf, Jr., Oct. 9, 1985.

Page 226: Back in February 1986, at the annual Conservative: *New York Times,* Feb. 2, 1986.

Page 227: "created political cells masquerading as mere voter-education brigades": Jack W. Germond and Jules Witcover, *Whose Broad Stripes and Bright Stars? The Trivial Pursuit of the Presidency, 1988* (New York: Warner Books, 1989), p. 83.

Page 227: "We saw the hand of God going before us": Allen D. Hertzke, *Echoes of Discontent: Jesse Jackson, Pat Robertson, and the Resurgence of Populism* (Washington, DC: Congressional Quarterly Press, 1993), pp. 140–41.

Page 228: "one of the most frightening pieces of legislation": *Presidential Candidates Information Project,* NWPC Republican Task Force (Aug. 1987).

Page 228: "the wonderful process of mortality tables": Ibid.

Pages 228–229: "Bush . . . appeared before two dozen evangelical preachers": Germond and Witcover, *Whose Broad Stripes,* p. 151.

Page 229: "We are bigger than Robertson though": Hertzke, *Echoes,* pp. 144–45.

CHAPTER 13: VALUABLE WEAPONS: BUSH'S POLITICAL WOMEN

Page 233: Linda DiVall, who was just coming into: *Boston Globe,* Aug. 23, 1987.

Page 233: Bush declared before a "safe" NFRW crowd: *New York Times,* Sept. 20, 1987.

Page 236: Lee Atwater and Robertson's campaign manager: *New York Times,* Apr. 28, 1988.

Page 236: They had fashioned a lucrative consulting business: Art Levine, "Publicists of the Damned," *SPY,* Feb. 1992.

Page 237: Jo Ann Gasper, a convert to Roman Catholicism: Michele McKeegan, *Abortion Politics: Mutiny in the Ranks of the Right* (New York: Free Press, 1992), p. 114.

Page 239: Even Bennett's wife participated: Fred Barnes, "Baby Face-Off," *New Republic,* May 8, 1988.

Page 239: "day-care centers as about as beneficial to children": Ibid.

Page 239: report that concluded there was no child care crisis: Ibid.

Page 239: Bush was "prepared to let the 1988 Republican platform": *New York Times,* Apr. 28, 1988.

Page 240: I told Walter Robinson: *Boston Globe,* June 5, 1988.

Page 241: women might not be "easily appealed to": Ceci Cole McInturff, memo on organization of Office of National Voter Coalitions (Spring 1988).

Page 242: "a combination of substantive policy references": Ceci Cole McInturff and Connie Newman, memo to the vice president, re: women (June 1988).

Page 243: Bush "should *always* be introduced by a woman": Ibid.

Page 243: Bush's press secretary, Sheila Tate, laid out the Bush campaign line: *New York Times,* June 19, 1988.

Page 243: "we're not running around and dealing with a lot": Ibid.

Page 243: Ethel Klein, who had prepared the report: Women's Agenda Conference Report release, June 14, 1988.

Page 245: the Bush campaign would "adopt the 1984 platform": *Newsday,* June 26, 1988.

Page 247: but it was "close to the $2.5 billion called for": *New York Times,* July 25, 1988.

Page 247: Phyllis Schlafly, who had derided the ABC bill: Mary Frances Berry, *The Politics of Parenthood* (New York: Viking, 1993), p. 180.

CHAPTER 14: VICTORY WITHOUT HONOR

Page 250: "One of the ironies of American politics is that": Richard Reeves, "GOP—Well-Oiled Machine," *Daily News,* Aug. 21, 1988.

Page 250: The data indicated that by now, more than: Mary Frances Berry, *The Politics of Parenthood* (New York: Viking, 1993), p. 171.

Page 253: "What I object to is the implication of these words": Marjorie Bell Chambers, statement to GOP Platform Committee, Aug. 10, 1988.

Page 254: "Have you ever faced a teenage kid who is the victim": *Times-Picayune* (New Orleans), Aug. 11, 1988.

Page 256: The committee's PAC chairman, Gerald Meyer, had said: *Washington Post,* Oct. 6, 1980.

Page 257: "We need to be very careful about this confusing of political": Ibid.

Page 257: The charges against Bauman: *Washington Post,* Oct. 3, 1980.

Page 258: Bush said "he supported": *New York Times,* June 29, 1988.

Page 258: "I don't think that's what is intended here at all; therefore": Ibid.

Page 259: For several years Dannemeyer had been carrying on: Michael Barone and Grant Ujifusa, *The Almanac of American Politics 1988* (Washington, DC: National Journal, 1988), p. 168.

Page 260: Black had been specific: *Times-Picayune* (New Orleans), Aug. 12, 1988.

Pages 260–261: Humphrey also said he wanted "assurances from Mr. Bush": *New York Times,* June 30, 1988.

Page 261: "Phil is a cinch to get nominated because every woman": Jon Margolis, "Phil Crane: A Conservative Runs Against Reagan," *New York,* Mar. 26, 1979.

Page 263: Two-thirds were white Protestant men, and almost three-quarters: *Los Angeles Times,* Aug. 17, 1988.

Page 263: He accused Dukakis of letting "murderers out on vacation": Jack W. Germond and Jules Witcover, *Whose Broad Stripes and Bright Stars? The Trivial Pursuit of the Presidency, 1988* (New York: Warner Books, 1989), p. 162.

Page 264: "I am against supplying birth control aids to minors": George Bush for President statement on social/family issues: Family planning. Author's files.

Page 265: "I haven't sorted out the penalties, but": *New York Times,* Sept. 26, 1988.

Page 265: "I think what the vice president is saying is that he's": Germond and Witcover, *Whose Broad Stripes,* p. 433.

Page 265: The American Medical Association said: *New York Times,* Sept. 27, 1988.

Page 266: In 1958, when abortion was illegal, "eighteen states": Ellen Goodman, "The Real Penalties of a Retreat into History," *Newsday,* Oct. 4, 1988.

Page 266: "It's tempting to ask what it says about Bush": Michael Kinsley, "An Instant Philosopher," *Washington Post,* Sept. 29, 1988.

Page 266: "Two-thirds of women in the labor force": Gerald M. Pomper, *The Election of 1988: Reports and Interpretations* (Chatham, NJ: Chatham House, 1989), p. 122.

Page 268: A comprehensive interpretation of the election: Ibid., p. 132.

Page 268: Men gave Bush 56 percent to 44 percent: Nelson W. Polsby and Aaron Wildavsky, *Presidential Elections,* 8th ed. (New York: Free Press, 1991), p. 337.

CHAPTER 15: PRO-CHOICERS FIGHT BACK

Page 270: in the words of conservative legal scholar Bruce Fein: *New York Times,* Jan. 24, 1989.

Pages 270–271: the executive director of the National Right to Life Committee: *Newsweek,* July 17, 1989.

Page 272: raising the level of acrimony and hate: Ann Baker, interview, Oct. 5, 1995.

Page 272: He appealed for funds: *Atlanta Journal*, Aug. 10, 1988.

Page 273: He boasted about his twenty-five arrests in seven cities: *San Jose Mercury News*, Nov. 15, 1988.

Page 274: according to a detailed account of the case in *Ms.*: Rhonda Copelon and Kathryn Kolbert, "Imperfect Justice," *Ms.* (July/Aug. 1989), p. 42.

Page 274: Fried claimed that the Court's 1965 *Griswold* decision: David J. Garrow, *Liberty and Sexuality: The Right to Privacy and the Making of Roe v. Wade* (New York: Macmillan, 1994), p. 675.

Page 274: Frank Susman, the lead attorney for the pro-choice side: Ibid.

Page 276: and proclaimed, "it's going to take": *The Columbia* (SC) *State*, Aug. 12, 1989.

Page 278: "You know how he deals with it": Michael Kramer, "The Abortion Issue—Again," *Time*, Nov. 25, 1991.

Page 279: Eddie Mahe, the New Right Reagan strategist: *St. Louis Post-Dispatch*, July 5, 1989.

Page 279: in a September 1989 interview with David Frost: *Public Affairs Action Letter*, PPFA (Planned Parenthood Federation of America), Sept. 15, 1989.

Page 280: Maryland Democrat Steny Hoyer underscored: *Daily News*, Oct. 26, 1989.

Page 280: Nancy Johnson labeled the legislation "deeply": *New York Times*, Oct. 31, 1989.

Page 280: Marge Roukema said it was hard to "go against": Ibid.

Page 281: Richard Viguerie was cage-rattling again: *New York Times*, Nov. 15, 1989.

Page 282: Atwater got to work. First, he reintroduced: Michael Kramer, "Building a 'Big Tent' Around Abortion," *Time*, Feb. 5, 1990, p. 18.

Page 282: "Lynn Martin would no doubt vote": "Early Campaigning Tests Abortion Foes' Muscle," *Congressional Quarterly*, Mar. 10, 1990, p. 769.

Page 283: *Buffalo News* cartoonist Tom Toles laid out: Tom Toles cartoon, *Buffalo Evening News*, May 25, 1992.

Page 283: Atwater told her that the party would never change: Alan Pell Crawford, "Pro-Choice PACs at War in GOP," *Legal Times*, Mar. 16, 1992.

Page 284: One letter said (with an overabundance of exclamation): Undated Republicans for Choice letter, received by author May 1990.

Page 285: Her first priority was to identify pro-choice Republicans: Crawford, "Pro-Choice PACs," p. 17.

Page 285: polls taken in December 1989 indicated that 92 percent: Penn and Schoen Associates poll, privately commissioned, released Jan. 1990.

Page 287: "I can understand people saying that. . . . I think it's wrong":

Jack W. Germond and Jules Witcover, *Mad as Hell: Revolt at the Ballot Box, 1992* (New York: Warner Books, 1993), p. 36.

Page 288: Valerie Syme of the Abortion Report: *New York Times*, Dec. 15, 1990.

Page 288: "the issue tends to have the greatest impact at the state level": Ibid.

Page 288: Six gubernatorial winners, in Maine, California: Ibid.

CHAPTER 16: FAITHFUL FRIEND OF THE RIGHT

Page 291: Bauer, now heading a New Right group: Mary Frances Berry, *The Politics of Parenthood* (New York: Viking, 1993), p. 185.

Page 292: Libertarians were upset because the vouchers: Ibid., p. 190.

Page 292: On August 14 Bush delivered a fiery speech: H. Norman Schwarzkopf, *It Doesn't Take a Hero* (New York: Bantam Books, 1992), p. 316.

Page 292: By the time the six-month buildup was completed: Ibid., p. 391.

Page 293: "the highest recorded since the June 1945 rating": Jack W. Germond and Jules Witcover, *Mad as Hell: Revolt at the Ballot Box, 1992* (New York: Warner Books, 1993), p. 50.

Page 293: "John Sununu contributed more than any other": Ibid., p. 35.

Page 294: "do not significantly impinge on the doctor-patient relationship": David J. Garrow, *Liberty and Sexuality* (New York: Macmillan, 1994), p. 685.

Page 294: One barbed drawing showed a family-planning clinic: Anna Quindlen, "Rust, Roe and Reality," *New York Times*, July 17, 1991.

Page 295: The administration was taking to heart Gary Bauer's words: *Washington Post*, July 21, 1991.

Page 296: Quayle had weighed in, trying his hand at being Atwater: *Washington Post*, Oct. 9, 1991.

Page 297: He fired National Endowment for the Arts chairman: Germond and Witcover, *Mad as Hell*, p. 234.

Page 297: Phyllis Schlafly and her Republican National Coalition for Life: The name National Coalition for Life was a play on Crisp's National Coalition for Choice. The unaware could easily be confused into thinking its acronym, RNC for Life, stood for Republican National Committee for Life.

Pages 297–298: Ken Ruberg of the Republican Mainstream Committee: Founded by Mary Louise Smith, John Buchanan, and Jim Leach in 1984, the Mainstream Committee is a national coalition of moderate Republicans working for arms control, environmental protection, women's and civil rights, and government fiscal restraint. Its membership is modest, made up mainly of Ripon and task force people.

Page 300: The show's executive producer, Diane English: Germond and Witcover, *Mad as Hell*, p. 397.

Page 300: he launched an attack on the "cultural elites": Ibid., p. 398.

Page 301: "In theory, *Roe v. Wade* is still on the books": Barbara Hinkson Craig and David M. O'Brien, *Abortion and American Politics* (Chatham, NJ: Chatham House, 1993), p. 326.

Page 301: Weddington characterized the ruling: Ibid.

Page 301: "some anti-abortion leaders say that a ruling": *Wall Street Journal*, Aug. 23, 1991.

CHAPTER 17: THE COLLAPSE OF BUSH

Page 305: Mosbacher briefly laid out for the press: Barbara Mosbacher statement, Houston, TX, Aug. 10, 1992.

Page 305: the New Right supply-siders succeeded in pulling a fast one: All material about the Platform Committee and the 1992 convention are from the author's notes taken during the committee's deliberations and from the official convention proceedings.

Page 315: Black grew worried: Mary Matalin and James Carville, *All's Fair: Love, War, and Running for President* (New York: Random House, 1994), p. 295.

Page 316: recalled Jim Lake, Bush's communications director: Jack W. Germond and Jules Witcover, *Mad as Hell: Revolt at the Ballot Box, 1992* (New York: Warner Books, 1993), p. 441.

Page 316: Rich Bond had told the Republican National Committee: Rich Bond remarks, Houston, TX, Aug. 12, 1992.

Page 319: According to a study done by Emory University professor: Alan I. Abramowitz, "It's Abortion, Stupid: Policy Voting in the 1992 Presidential Election," delivered to the American Political Science Association, Washington, DC, Sept. 2–5, 1993.

Page 320: political scientist Gerald Pomper: Gerald M. Pomper, *The Election of 1992* (Chatham, NJ: Chatham House, 1993), p. 142.

Page 323: political campaign chroniclers Jack Germond and Jules Witcover: Germond and Witcover, *Mad as Hell*, p. 413.

Page 323: Lake agreed with Teeter and Black that: Ibid.

CHAPTER 18: THEOCRATS GET A PLACE AT THE TABLE

Page 327: "the party of gunk, gun clubs, and granny-bashing": Kevin Phillips, "The Rise and Folly of the GOP," *Washington Post*, Aug. 6, 1995.

Page 329: men voted 57 percent Republican to 43 percent Democratic: Karlyn H. Bowman, "The Gender Factor," *America at the Polls, 1994* (Storrs, CT: Roper Center, 1995), p. 52.

Page 329: a process of "financialization" that was reducing "the connection": James Fallows, "The Republican Promise," *New York Review of Books,* Jan. 12, 1995.

Page 330: An assessment of gender-voting numbers found that: *WISH List News* (Jan. 1995).

Page 330: were elected to the Senate in open seats: Kay Bailey Hutchison was first elected in June 1993 in a special election to fill a vacancy opened by the resignation of Lloyd Bentsen.

Page 331: The only southern woman in the freshman class: Jennifer Gonnerman, "The Femi-Newties," *Village Voice,* Jan. 31, 1995.

Page 332: WISH did well in 1994, raising $370,000: Eliza Newlin Carney, "That Was the Year That Wasn't," *National Journal,* Nov. 19, 1994, p. 2,751.

Page 332: Dedicated to helping "women who support the right-to-life": Ibid.

Page 333: RENEW's executive director, Karen Roberts: Hanna Rosin, "Invasion of the Church Ladies," *New Republic,* Apr. 14, 1995, p. 20.

Page 335: John Green, an academic expert on the religious: *New York Times,* Sept. 10, 1995.

Page 336: In May 1995, when the Christian Coalition announced: *Washington Times,* May 18, 1995.

Page 336: Wisconsin Republican state chairman David Opitz: Ibid.

Page 336: "Any survey research you or I have seen": *New York Times,* Apr. 12, 1995.

Page 338: The contract "sets the hurdles too low": *Washington Times,* May 20, 1995.

Page 338: "I believe we really ought to be bold": CNN, *ID Weekend,* May 20, 1995.

Page 338: had played a "vital part" in bringing "a revolution": *USA Today,* May 18, 1995.

Page 338: "we are committed to keeping faith with": *Wall Street Journal,* May 18, 1995.

Page 339: "embodies a radical vision for regulating": *New York Times,* May 17, 1995.

Page 339: Bob Dole announced that he would work: *Washington Post,* May 18, 1995.

Page 340: When Randall Terry called for "restructuring": *Dallas Morning News,* July 15, 1993.

Page 340: As Reed said, "We issue no ultimatums": *Washington Times,* May 18, 1995.

CHAPTER 19: THE CHAOS OF THE GOP

Page 342: For the first time in the nation's history: In 1980 feminist leader Eleanor Smeal first labeled the *difference* between how men and women viewed a particular candidate, party, or issue as the gender gap. Since then the gender gap has often been calculated by comparing the difference between a candidate's percentage vote from women with the candidate's percentage vote from men. Figured this way, Clinton's gender gap in 1996 was 11 percent, the highest in presidential polling history. This should not be confused with the point spread between women's votes for Clinton and Dole, which was 16 percent.

In 1996 some analysts calculated the gender gap in a different way. They subtracted the percentage of men voting for Dole from those voting for Clinton and then did the same calculations for women. The gap was the difference between these two calculations. Figured this way the gender gap was 17 percent.

The use of the "gender gap" label for gauging how men and women react politically is a tool of limited value in understanding gender politics. The term was overworked and misunderstood in 1996 and should be replaced by the more easily understood point-spread approach to explain gender voting.

Page 342: As for the men: All election statistics are from exit poll data taken on Election Day, Nov. 5, 1996, collected by the Voter News Service and cited by CBS News/*The New York Times*.

Page 344: After the 1994 election: Using the 1994 election as proof, Barbour pointed out that *white* women had given GOP House candidates 53 percent of their vote. But he didn't tell the whole story. Women voters of all races had backed Democratic House candidates by 54 percent, and while Republicans did have a huge advantage among southern white women, they had no similar advantage anywhere else. White women's vote in the East was the converse. In the Heartland and the West, where Republicans generally do well, the party's problems with women were as serious as they had ever been. White women in these regions voted for the GOP House candidates by such narrow margins as to make the outcomes a statistical tie. The party had conceded African-American women to the Democrats. A detailed analysis of the 1994 women's vote can be found in Everett Carl Ladd, ed., *America at the Polls, 1994* (Roper Center Data Book, 1995), p. 52.

Page 346: "Women are not endowed by nature": quoted in *New Republic*, Mar. 18, 1996, p. 17.

Page 347: Just as in Iowa: All primary election information comes from CBS News/*New York Times* polling data unless otherwise cited.

Page 347: but was forced to step down: *New York Times*, Feb. 17, 1996.

Page 347: "He's a populist": *New York Times*, Feb. 23, 1996.

Page 348: "They don't want him to redefine": *New York Times*, Feb. 22, 1996.

Page 349: Dole would be the: *USA Today,* Mar. 8, 1996.

Page 349: "Overall, the survey showed": *Philadelphia Inquirer,* Mar. 15, 1996.

Page 350: Several polls found: Greenberg Research Memo; survey done Mar. 20–24, 1996. The margin was 19 percentage points among women, 6 among men.

Page 350: While a majority of women thought: Ibid.

Page 350: the nearly 12 million people: *New York Times,* Mar. 31, 1996.

Page 351: According to ACOG: *FPA* [Family Planning Advocates] *Legislative Update,* Albany, NY, Mar. 5, 1997.

Pages 351–352: Ralph Reed described: *New York Times,* Mar. 23, 1997.

Page 352: On April 10, in an emotional ceremony: *San Francisco Chronicle,* Apr. 11, 1996.

Page 352: America's Catholic bishops: National Conference of Catholic Bishops press release, Apr. 16, 1996.

Page 352: Ralph Reed threatened: Christian Coalition press release, Apr. 10, 1996.

Page 352: In a highly unusual action: AP wire, Apr. 19, 1996.

Page 352: A journalist for the conservative: Josette Shiner, *Capitol Gang Sunday,* CNN, Apr. 21, 1996.

Page 353: The Republican Coalition for Choice: The word *National* had been dropped from the title, but the organization remains a national coalition of pro-choice Republicans.

Page 355: Indeed, Catholics preferred: *Los Angeles Times,* Apr. 19, 1996. Data based on *Los Angeles Times* April 13–16 telephone poll.

Page 355: *Los Angeles Times* reporter: Ibid.

Page 355: "The challenge for Republicans": *Weekly Standard,* Apr. 29, 1996.

Page 355: "So who's Bill Kristol?": *Face the Nation,* CBS News, Apr. 21, 1996.

Page 356: Bay Buchanan threatened: *New York Times,* May 4, 1996.

Page 358: Seventy percent of Americans: *Newsweek,* May 20, 1996.

Page 358: His declaration would be: *Inside Politics,* CNN, June 10, 1996.

Page 358: "Any such declaration": Buchanan campaign press release, June 11, 1996.

Page 359: it "might have to sit the election out": *Washington Times,* June 12, 1996.

Page 359: Governor Weld had it right: *New York Times,* June 8, 1996.

Page 359: Governor Weld minced no words: *Boston Globe,* July 13, 1996.

Page 359: Susan Cullman said: *Washington Times,* July 13, 1996.

Page 359: Ann Stone commented: *Chicago Tribune,* July 13, 1996.

Page 359: "The language is inherently": *Face the Nation*, CBS News, July 14, 1996.

Page 360: Ever the political fixer: Christian Coalition press release, July 12, 1996.

Page 360: Governor Whitman said: *Philadelphia Inquirer*, July 13, 1996.

Page 361: But the governors of New York: Even in Connecticut, considered the most pro-choice state in the nation, with a well-organized pro-choice Republican group led by Woody Bliss and Republican Coalition for Choice co-chair Jennifer Stockman, the wife of supply-sider and Reagan's first federal budget director David Stockman, the delegation wouldn't back the pro-choice effort.

Page 362: As journalists Jack Germond and Jules Witcover wrote: *Baltimore Sun*, Aug. 7, 1996.

Page 362: "the Buchanan platform": *Washington Times*, Aug. 6, 1996.

Page 363: "If Bob Dole does not pick": *Washington Times*, July 19, 1996. Robertson recommended four anti-choice men for Dole's running mate: California attorney general Dan Lungren, Missouri governor John Ashcroft, Ohio congressmember John Kasich, and Wal-Mart president David Glass.

Page 363: Buchanan said he would not: *Chicago Tribune*, Aug. 1, 1996.

Page 364: "This has been a very scripted": *USA Today*, Aug. 15, 1996.

Page 365: Bill Weld summed it up: *Boston Herald*, Aug. 15, 1996.

Page 366: These actions helped them win: "Anatomy of the Women's Vote in the '96 Election," Celinda Lake and Stan Greenberg, *The Polling Report*, Nov. 18, 1996.

CHAPTER 20: THE FUTURE OF THE REPUBLIC

Page 369: an unprecedented additional federal debt: Peter G. Peterson, *Facing Up* (New York: Simon and Schuster, 1993), p. 358.

Page 369: While it is certainly good news: *New York Times*, Aug. 7, 1997.

Page 369: (The debt is the accumulated money): If the federal government had not had to make interest payments on the debt in 1997, *New York Times* reporter David E. Sanger wrote, it would have run a $172 billion surplus, about half the cost of paying for that year's Social Security benefits. "Instead, those interest payments will cost the government $247 billion, or $20 billion less than the entire defense budget." *New York Times*, May 2, 1997.

Page 369: If these problems are: Jason Epstein, "White Mischief," *New York Review of Books*, Oct. 17, 1996.

Page 370: Republican congressmember Ernest Istook: *New York Times*, May 9, 1997.

Page 371: The nation's religious freedom: On June 25, 1997, the Supreme Court declared unconstitutional the 1993 Religious Freedom Restoration Act.

Unlike the Istook amendment, which has the potential to enable government establishment of religion, the act attempted to protect religious observance from governmental intrusion. Supported by a broad coalition of religious and civil liberties groups, the act aimed to guarantee that governments at all levels could "not substantially burden" religious observance without proving a "compelling need to do so."

Page 374: As the Pew Research Center reports: The survey placed respondents in party categories based on how they identified themselves, not their party registration. "Republicans: A Demographic and Attitudinal Profile," Pew Research Center for the People and the Press, Aug. 7, 1996. All data on independents in this section comes from the Pew Center.

Page 375: This politically expedient: These tax breaks would increase the deficit by an estimated $200 billion in ten years with a majority benefiting the top 20 percent of American's families. In an egregious lack of courage and bowing to the pervasive influence of the family values lobby, they agreed to a $500 child tax credit. It is the most misguided element in the budget, giving short-term minimal tax relief to parents, while adding to the federal debt. Future generations will have to pay for this folly.

Page 376: According to historian: Richard Striner, "Uncle Sam's Red Ink," *Washington Post Weekly,* Apr. 18, 1997.

Page 377: In the fall of 1996: Mary Matalin, "Women Do Support the GOP," *Los Angeles Times,* Sept. 29, 1996.

Page 377: The designated speakers: These tactics are not unique to Republicans, but the Democrats' policies have generally been more helpful to more women.

Page 380: Lisa Schiffren, Forum member: Lisa Schiffren, "Nixon's GOP Will Always Be a Loser," *New York Times,* Nov. 9, 1996.

Page 381: "The widening of inequality": Paul Krugman, "The Wealth Gap Is Real and It's Growing," *New York Times,* Aug. 21, 1995.

Page 381: According to Kevin Phillips: Kevin Phillips, *Boiling Point: Democrats, Republicans and the Decline of Middle-Class Prosperity* (New York: Random House, 1993), p. 3.

Page 381: Despite a robust economy: A former chief economist for the Labor Department reports: "We are in danger that when this economic upswing ends, it will be the first recovery on record in which the real wage of the median worker fell." From 1989 to 1997, the median worker's wage dropped 5 percent, and in 1996 the real median weekly wage for full-time employees increased by only 0.3 percent. Alan B. Krueger, "The Truth About Wages," *New York Times,* July 31, 1997.

Page 381: Tony Fabrizio, Bob Dole's: Dan Balz, "Those Feuding Republicans," *Washington Post Weekly,* Mar. 3, 1997.

Page 382: As economics columnist: Robert Kuttner, "An Irrational Action," *Washington Post Weekly*, Apr. 7, 1997.

Page 382: According to a former leader: Susan Lowell Butler, "Once More Unto the Gender Gap," *Nation*, Aug. 26–Sept. 2, 1996, p. 2.

Page 382: Children under eighteen now make up: U.S. Census Bureau, #P23–193, "How We're Changing: Demographic State of the Nation," Mar. 1997.

Page 382: A study by the Columbia University: Lawrence Aber et al., "One in Four: America's Youngest Poor," National Center for Children in Poverty, Columbia University, New York: Jan. 1997.

Page 383: The ratio of women's annual earnings: "The Wage Gap: Women's and Men's Earnings," Institute for Women's Policy Research, July 1996.

Page 383: According to the Census Bureau: Census Bureau, "How We're Changing."

Page 383: Among *Fortune* 500 companies: "The 1996 *Catalyst* Census of Women Corporate Officers and Top Earners," *Catalyst*, Oct. 1996.

Page 384: To back up their claim: Diana Furchtgott-Roth and Christine Stolba, *Women's Figures: The Economic Progress of Women in America* (Washington DC: American Enterprise Institute, 1997).

Page 386: They will not long tolerate a situation: Ronald Steel, "The Hard Questions," *New Republic*, Feb. 10, 1997.

Page 386: A New Center goal for: Diane Johnson, "What Do Women Want," *New York Review of Books*, Nov. 28, 1996.

BIBLIOGRAPHY

Abramowitz, Alan I. "It's Abortion, Stupid: Policy Voting in the 1992 Presidential Election." Unpublished manuscript. Atlanta: Emory University, 1993.

Abramson, Paul R., John H. Aldrich, and David W. Rohde. *Change and Continuity in the 1992 Elections,* rev. ed. Washington, DC: Congressional Quarterly Press, 1995.

Anderson, Martin. *Revolution.* New York: Harcourt Brace Jovanovich, 1988.

Anti-Defamation League. *The Religious Right: The Assault on Tolerance and Pluralism in America.* New York: Anti-Defamation League, 1994.

Bakashian, Aram, Jr. *The Candidates—1980.* New Rochelle, NY: Arlington House, 1980.

Balz, Dan and Ronald Brownstein. *Storming the Gates: Protest Politics and the Republican Revival.* Boston: Little, Brown, 1996.

Barone, Michael. *Our Country: The Shaping of America from Roosevelt to Reagan.* New York: Free Press, 1990.

Bashevkin, Sylvia. "Facing a Renewed Right: American Feminism and the Reagan/Bush Challenge." *Canadian Journal of Political Science* (Dec. 1994).

Bellant, Russ. *Old Nazis, the New Right and the Republican Party.* Boston, MA: South End Press, 1988.

Bennet, David H. *The Party of Fear: From Nativist Movements to the New Right in American History.* Chapel Hill: University of North Carolina Press, 1988.

Bernstein, Richard B., with Jerome Agel. *Amending America.* New York: Times Books, 1993.

Berry, Mary Frances. *The Politics of Parenthood: Child Care, Women's Rights, and the Myth of the Good Mother.* New York: Viking, 1993.

————. *Why ERA Failed: Politics, Women's Rights and the Amending Process of the Constitution.* Bloomington, IN: Indiana University Press, 1986.

Black, Gordon S., and Benjamin D. Black. *The Politics of American Discontent: How a New Party Can Make Democracy Work Again.* New York: John Wiley and Sons, 1994.

Blanchard, Dallas A. *The Anti-Abortion Movement and the Rise of the Religious Right.* New York: Twayne, 1994.

Blumenthal, Sidney. *The Rise of the Counter-Establishment: From Conservative Ideology to Political Power.* New York: Times Books, 1986.

————. *Pledging Allegiance: The Last Campaign of the Cold War.* New York: Harper Perennial, 1991.

————, and Thomas Byrne Edsall, eds. *The Reagan Legacy.* New York: Pantheon Books, 1988.

Brodie, Fawn M. *Thaddeus Stevens: Scourge of the South.* New York: W. W. Norton, 1959.

Bronner, Ethan. *Battle for Justice: How the Bork Nomination Shook America.* New York: W. W. Norton, 1989.

Brookhiser, Richard. *The Outside Story: How Democrats and Republicans Reelected Reagan.* Garden City, NY: Doubleday, 1986.

Brown, Clifford W., Jr., with the Ripon Society. *Jaws of Victory.* Boston: Little, Brown, 1973.

Byrnes, Timothy A. *Catholic Bishops in American Politics.* Princeton, NJ: Princeton University Press, 1991.

Cannon, James. *Time and Chance: Gerald Ford's Appointment with History.* New York: HarperCollins, 1994.

Cannon, Lou. *President Reagan: The Role of a Lifetime.* New York: Simon and Schuster, 1991.

Center for the American Woman and Politics. "Sex Differences in Voter Turnout Fact Sheet." New Brunswick, NJ: Eagleton Institute of Politics, 1994.

————. "Women in Elective Office 1994." New Brunswick, NJ: Eagleton Institute of Politics, 1994.

————. "The Gender Gap." New Brunswick, NJ: Eagleton Institute of Politics, 1994.

Craig, Barbara Hinkson, and David M. O'Brien. *Abortion and American Politics.* Chatham, NJ: Chatham House, 1993.

Crawford, Alan. *Thunder on the Right: The New Right and the Politics of Resentment.* New York: Pantheon, 1980.

Deaver, Michael K., with Mickey Herskowitz. *Behind the Scenes.* New York: William Morrow, 1987.

Dionne, E. J., Jr. *Why Americans Hate Politics*. New York: Simon and Schuster, 1991.

Dodson, Debra L., and Lauren D. Burnbauer. *Election of 1989: The Abortion Issue in New Jersey and Virginia*. New Brunswick, NJ: Eagleton Institute of Politics, 1990.

Dole, Bob, and Elizabeth Dole, with Richard Norton Smith. *The Doles: Unlimited Partners*. New York: Simon and Schuster, 1988.

Drew, Elizabeth. *Election Journal: Political Events of 1987–1988*. New York: William Morrow, 1989.

———. *Campaign Journal: The Political Events of 1983–1984*. New York: Macmillan, 1985.

———. *American Journal: The Events of 1976*. New York: Vintage Books, 1978.

Dugger, Ronnie. *On Reagan: The Man and His Presidency*. New York: McGraw-Hill, 1983.

Edsall, Thomas Byrne, and Mary D. Edsall. *Chain Reaction: The Impact of Race, Rights, and Taxes on American Politics*. New York: W. W. Norton, 1992.

Faludi, Susan. *Backlash: The Undeclared War Against American Women*. New York: Crown, 1991.

Felsenthal, Carol. *The Sweetheart of the Silent Majority: The Biography of Phyllis Schlafly*. Garden City, NY: Doubleday, 1981.

Fenwick, Millicent. *Speaking Up*. New York: Harper and Row, 1982.

Ferraro, Geraldine A., with Linda Bird Francke. *Ferraro: My Story*. New York: Bantam Books, 1985.

Freeman, Jo. *The Politics of Women's Liberation*. New York: David McKay, 1975.

Friedan, Betty. *The Second Stage*. New York: Summit Books, 1981.

———. *The Feminine Mystique*. New York: Dell, 1964.

Garrow, David J. *Liberty and Sexuality: The Right to Privacy and the Making of Roe v. Wade*. New York: Macmillan, 1994.

Germond, Jack W., and Jules Witcover. *Mad as Hell: Revolt at the Ballot Box, 1992*. New York: Warner Books, 1993.

———. *Whose Broad Stripes and Bright Stars? The Trivial Pursuit of the Presidency, 1988*. New York: Warner Books, 1989.

———. *Wake Us When It's Over: Presidential Politics of 1984*. New York: Macmillan, 1985.

Gienapp, William E. *The Origins of the Republican Party, 1852–1856*. New York: Oxford University Press, 1987.

Gilder, George. *Wealth and Poverty*. New York: Basic Books, 1981.

———. *Sexual Suicide*. New York: Quadrangle, 1973.

Gingrich, Newt. *To Renew America*. New York: HarperCollins, 1995.

Githens, Marianne, Pippa Norris, and Joni Lovenduski. *Different Roles,*

Different Voices: Women and Politics in the United States and Europe. New York: HarperCollins, 1994.

Green, Fitzhugh. *George Bush: An Intimate Portrait.* New York: Hippocrene Books, 1989.

Greenberg, Stanley B. *Middle-Class Dreams: The Politics and Power of the New American Majority.* New York: Times Books, 1995.

Griffith, Elizabeth. *In Her Own Right: The Life of Elizabeth Cady Stanton.* New York: Oxford University Press, 1984.

Grimes, Ann. *Running Mates: The Making of a First Lady: A Penetrating Look at Private Women in the Public Eye.* New York: William Morrow, 1990.

Gruberg, Martin. "Women at the National Party Conventions." Unpublished paper. Oshkosh: University of Wisconsin, 1980.

Henry, Sherrye. *The Deep Divide: Why American Women Resist Equality.* New York: Macmillan, 1994.

Herron, Jerry. *After Culture: Detroit and the Humiliation of History.* Detroit: Wayne State University Press, 1993.

Hertzke, Allen D. *Echoes of Discontent: Jesse Jackson, Pat Robertson, and the Resurgence of Populism.* Washington, DC: Congressional Quarterly Press, 1993.

Himmelstein, Jerome L. *To the Right: The Transformation of American Conservatism.* Berkeley: University of California Press, 1990.

Hofstadter, Richard. *The Paranoid Style in American Politics and Other Essays.* New York: Vintage, 1964.

Hunter, James Davison. *Culture Wars: The Struggle to Define America.* New York: Basic Books, 1991.

Jamieson, Kathleen Hall. *Beyond the Double Bind: Women and Leadership.* New York: Oxford University Press, 1995.

Jepson, Dee. *Women Beyond Equal Rights.* Waco, TX: Word Books, 1984.

Johnson, Haynes. *Divided We Fall: Gambling with History in the Nineties.* New York: W. W. Norton, 1994.

———. *Sleepwalking Through History: America in the Reagan Years.* New York: W. W. Norton, 1991.

Kazin, Michael. *The Populist Persuasion.* New York: Basic Books, 1995.

Klatch, Rebecca. *Women of the New Right.* Philadelphia, PA: Temple University Press, 1987.

Klein, Ethel. *Gender Politics: From Consciousness to Mass Politics.* Cambridge, MA: Harvard University Press, 1984.

Kolb, Charles. *White House Daze: The Unmaking of Domestic Policy in the Bush Years.* New York: Free Press, 1994.

Ladd, Everett Carll, ed. *America at the Polls 1994.* Storrs, CT: University of Connecticut Press, 1995.

Leet, Rebecca K. *Republican Women Are Wonderful: A History of Women at Republican National Conventions.* Washington, DC: National Women's Political Caucus, 1980.

Lind, Michael. *Up from Conservatism: Why the Right Is Wrong for America.* New York: Free Press, 1996.

Lipset, Seymour Martin. *Emerging Coalitions in American Politics.* San Francisco: Institute for Contemporary Studies, 1978.

Lubell, Samuel. *The Hidden Crisis in American Politics.* New York: W. W. Norton, 1970.

Mandel, Ruth B. *In the Running: The New Woman Candidate.* New Haven: Ticknor and Fields, 1981.

Mansbridge, Jane J. *Why We Lost the ERA.* Chicago: University of Chicago Press, 1986.

Matalin, Mary, and James Carville. *All's Fair: Love, War, and Running for President.* New York: Random House, 1994.

Mathews, Donald G., and Jane Sherron DeHart. *Sex, Gender, and the Politics of ERA: A State and the Nation.* New York: Oxford University Press, 1990.

Mayer, Jane, and Jill Abramson. *Strange Justice: The Selling of Clarence Thomas.* Boston: Houghton Mifflin, 1994.

Mayer, Jane, and Doyle McManus. *Landslide: The Unmaking of the President, 1984–1988.* Boston: Houghton Mifflin, 1988.

McKeegan, Michele. *Abortion Politics: Mutiny in the Ranks of the Right.* New York: Free Press, 1992.

McWilliams, Wilson Carey. *The Politics of Disappointment: American Elections 1976–94.* Chatham, NJ: Chatham House, 1995.

Meese, Edwin, III. *With Reagan: The Inside Story.* Washington, DC: Regnery Gateway, 1992.

Miller, Kristie. *Ruth Hanna McCormick: A Life in Politics, 1880–1944.* Albuquerque: University of New Mexico Press, 1992.

Morris, Celia. *Storming the Statehouse: Running for Governor with Ann Richards and Dianne Feinstein.* New York: Charles Scribner's Sons, 1992.

National Women's Political Caucus. "On Women's Political Progress." Washington, DC: National Women's Political Caucus, June 1995.

———. "Perception and Reality: A Study Comparing the Success of Men and Women Candidates." Washington, DC: National Women's Political Caucus, September 1994.

Nelson, Michael, ed. *The Elections of 1992.* Washington, DC: Congressional Quarterly Press, 1993.

Nofziger, Lyn. *Nofziger.* Washington, DC: Regnery Gateway, 1992.

Noonan, Peggy. *What I Saw at the Revolution: A Political Life in the Reagan Era.* New York: Random House, 1990.

Paige, Connie. *The Right to Lifers: Who They Are, How They Operate, Where They Get Their Money*. New York: Summit, 1983.

Peterson, Peter G. *Facing Up: How to Rescue the Economy from Crushing Debt and Restore the American Dream*. New York: Simon and Schuster, 1993.

Phelps, Timothy, and Helen Winternitz. *Capitol Games: Clarence Thomas, Anita Hill and the Story of a Supreme Court Nomination*. New York: Hyperion, 1992.

Phillips, Kevin. *Boiling Point: Democrats, Republicans, and the Decline of Middle-Class Prosperity*. New York: Random House, 1993.

———. *The Politics of Rich and Poor: Wealth and the American Electorate in the Reagan Aftermath*. Harper Perennial, 1990.

———. *Post-Conservative America: People, Politics, and Ideology in a Time of Crisis*. New York: Vintage Books, 1983.

———. *The Emerging Republican Majority*. New Rochelle, NY: Arlington House, 1969.

Polsby, Nelson W., and Aaron Wildavsky. *Presidential Elections: Contemporary Strategies of American Electoral Politics*. 8th ed. New York: Free Press, 1991.

———. *Presidential Elections: Strategies of American Electoral Politics*. 6th ed. New York: Charles Scribner's Sons, 1984.

Pomper, Gerald M., et al. *The Election of 1996*. Chatham, NJ: Chatham House, 1997.

———. *The Election of 1992*. Chatham, NJ: Chatham House, 1993.

———. *The Election of 1988: Reports and Interpretations*. Chatham, NJ: Chatham House, 1989.

———. *The Election of 1984: Reports and Interpretations*. Chatham, NJ: Chatham House, 1985.

Powell, Colin, with Joseph E. Persico. *An American Journey*. New York: Random House, 1995.

Pringle, Henry F. *Theodore Roosevelt*. San Diego, CA: Harcourt Brace, 1984.

Rae, Nicol C. *The Decline and Fall of the Liberal Republicans: From 1952 to the Present*. New York: Oxford University Press, 1989.

Ranney, Austin, ed. *The American Elections of 1980*. Washington, DC: American Enterprise Institute for Public Policy Research, 1981.

Reagan, Maureen. *First Father, First Daughter: A Memoir*. Boston: Little, Brown, 1989.

Reagan, Nancy, with William Novak. *My Turn: The Memoirs of Nancy Reagan*. New York: Random House, 1989.

Reeves, Richard. *American Journey*. New York: Simon and Schuster, 1982.

Regan, Donald T. *For the Record: From Wall Street to Washington*. New York: Harcourt Brace Jovanovich, 1988.

Reichley, A. James. *The Life of the Parties: A History of American Political Parties.* New York: Free Press, 1992.

Republican National Committee. *Official Report of the Proceedings of the Republican National Convention for 1972, 1976, 1980, 1984, 1988, 1992.* Washington, DC: Republican National Committee.

Rhode, Deborah L. *Justice and Gender.* Cambridge, MA: Harvard University Press, 1989.

Ries, Paula, and Anne J. Stone, eds. *The American Women, 1992–93: A Status Report.* New York: W. W. Norton, 1992.

Roderick, Lee. *Leading the Charge: Orrin Hatch and 20 Years of America.* Carson City, NV: Gold Leaf Press, 1994.

Rossi, Alice S. *The Feminist Papers: From Adams to Beauvoir.* Boston: Northeastern University Press, 1973.

Rusher, William A. *The Coming Battle for the Media: Curbing the Power of the Media Elite.* New York: William Morrow, 1988.

———. *The Rise of the Right.* New York: William Morrow, 1984.

Saloma, John S., III. *Ominous Politics: The New Conservative Labyrinth.* New York: Hill and Wang, 1984.

Scammon, Richard M., and Ben J. Wattenberg. *The Real Majority: An Extraordinary Examination of the American Electorate.* New York: Coward-McCann, 1970.

Schieffer, Bob, and Gary Paul Gates. *The Acting President.* New York: E. P. Dutton, 1989.

Schneider, Dorothy, and Carl J. Schneider. *American Women in the Progressive Era, 1900–1920.* New York: Doubleday, 1993.

Schwengel, Fred. *The Republican Party: Its Heritage and History.* Washington, DC: Republican Heritage Foundation, 1987.

Shea, Daniel M., and John C. Green, eds. *The State of the Parties: The Changing Role of Contemporary American Parties.* Lanham, MD: Rowman and Littlefield, 1994.

Smith, Hedrick. *The Power Game: How Washington Works.* New York: Random House, 1988.

Speakes, Larry, with Robert Pack. *Speaking Out: The Reagan Presidency from Inside the White House.* New York: Charles Scribner's Sons, 1988.

Stacks, John F. *Watershed: The Campaign for the Presidency, 1980.* New York: Times Books, 1981.

Tarr-Whelan, Linda, and Lynne Crofton Isensee. *The Women's Economic Justice Agenda: Ideas for the States.* Washington, DC: National Center for Policy Alternatives, 1987.

Taylor, Paul. *See How They Run: Electing the President in an Age of Mediocracy.* New York: Alfred A. Knopf, 1990.

Tilly, Louise A., and Patricia Gurin. *Women, Politics, and Change.* New York: Russell Sage Foundation, 1992.

Times Mirror Center for the People and the Press. *The New Political Landscape.* Los Angeles: Times Mirror, 1994.

Verba, Sidney, and Gary R. Orren. *Equality in America: The View from the Top.* Cambridge, MA: Harvard University Press, 1985.

Viguerie, Richard A. *The New Right: We're Ready to Lead.* Falls Church, VA: Viguerie Co., 1980.

Von Damm, Helene. *At Reagan's Side: Twenty Years in the Political Mainstream.* New York: Doubleday, 1989.

Wenz, Peter S. *Abortion Rights as Religious Freedom.* Philadelphia: Temple University Press, 1992.

Whitaker, Robert W., ed. *The New Right Papers.* New York: St. Martin's Press, 1982.

White, F. Clifton. *Suite 3505: The Story of the Draft Goldwater Movement.* New Rochelle, NY: Arlington House, 1967.

White, Theodore H. *America in Search of Itself: The Making of the President, 1956–1980.* New York: Harper and Row, 1982.

———. *The Making of the President, 1972.* New York: Atheneum, 1973.

Wills, Garry. *Reagan's America.* Garden City, NY: Doubleday, 1985.

Witcover, Jules. *Crapshoot: Rolling the Dice on the Vice Presidency.* New York: Crown, 1992.

———. *Marathon: The Pursuit of the Presidency, 1972–1976.* New York: Viking, 1977.

Witt, Linda, Karen M. Paget, and Glenna Matthews. *Running as a Woman: Gender and Power in American Politics.* New York: Free Press, 1993.

Woodward, Bob, and Carl Bernstein. *The Final Days.* New York: Simon and Schuster, 1976.

ACKNOWLEDGMENTS

For nearly twenty-five years, in the struggle to convince the Republican party to advance the rights of women, I have fought alongside women and men who showed great courage and integrity under difficult circumstances. We have argued, we have disagreed, we have agreed. All have been an inspiration to me, and their ideas have enriched this book.

First, I want to thank those Republicans who stood up in the beginning and the many who gave me help in remembering. These pioneers included: Catherine East, Chris Topping Milliken, Maureen Drummy, Pamela Curtis, Pat Bailey, Connie Newman, Constance Cooke, Charlotte Conable, Elly Peterson, Helen Milliken, Pat Goldman, Sheila Greenwald, Bobbie Kilberg, Betsy Griffith, Susan McLane, Ann O'Laughlin, Alice Tetelman, Nancy Hunt, Colleen McAndrews, Sharon Macha, Susan Catania, Cathie Bertini, Jill Ruckelshaus, Janet Luhrs, Jean McKee, Phyllis Weinberg, Patsy Richter, Muriel Siebert, Fran Leavenworth, Ginny Cairns Callen, Kaye Phillips, Evelyn Cunningham, Audrey Rowe, Roy Goodman, Bill Green, Nancy Thompson, Mary Stanley, Barbara Gunderson, Ann Peckham, Victoria Toensing, Victoria Markell, Alice Heyman, Tara Duffy, Rebecca Leet, Barbara Franklin, Rosemary Ginn, Millicent Fenwick, and Peggy Heckler.

Joining them later were those who fought the good fight during the Reagan and Bush years: Kathy Wilson, my sister-in-law Gayle Melich, Dianne Davis, Mary Dent Crisp, Darlee Crockett, Nancy Sternoff, John Deardourff, Susan Cullman, Wilma Goldstein, Lowell Weicker, Julie Belaga, Arlen Specter, Ellen Harley, Mary Louise Smith, Elsie Hillman,

Eileen Padberg, Nan Bostick, and Harriet Stinson and the members of Californians for Choice.

It is easier to speak out once others have, but those who first take up an unpopular cause show special character. The founders of the New York State Republican Family Committee are such people: Mary Curley, Barbara Gimbel, Pauline Harrison, Barbara Mosbacher, and Frances Reese. Their sense of right and wrong, and their belief in me, launched a rebellion within our party that goes on to this day. I will always treasure the ten years we spent together in the trenches, and I thank them for kindnesses too numerous to mention. I also owe special thanks to the committee's board and its leaders, Mary Baily Wieler and Dorothy Sprague, for their patience and cooperation during the early days of writing this book. They never wavered in their support, and I am most grateful for that, as well as for their friendship.

The Republican women officeholders who have fought for women's issues and continue to do so are heroines in this drama. Caught between their loyalty to the party and their commitment to women's rights, they have acted with courage and conviction in often-difficult situations. I am grateful for the time we have spent together, and I also thank those among them who talked to me specifically about this book. Those Congressmembers, past and present, include Nancy Johnson, Connie Morella, Susan Molinari, Lynn Martin, Jan Meyers, Sue Kelly, Claudine Schneider, Pat Saiki, Nancy Kassebaum, and Olympia Snowe. The state and local legislators are Pat McGee, Fran Sullivan, Cecile Singer, Mary Goodhue, and Penny Zeplowitz. I especially appreciate the consideration given to me by New Jersey Republicans Christine Todd Whitman, the governor, and Marge Roukema, the dean of the state's congressional delegation.

I thank those who ran for public office but were defeated by the New Right: Arliss Sturgelewski, Norma Paulus, Mary Estill Buchanan, Liz Hager, Mary Alice Ford, and Joan Bozer. They bore the brunt of misogynist politics and held their ground honorably.

I have also been blessed by friends in the broader women's movement who over the years have shared their ideas and provided facts for this book. Thanks to May Del Rio, Shirley Gordon, Donna Lieberman, Anne Davis, Ruth Mandel, Ida Schmertz, Betsy Wright, Rosalie Whelan, Barbara Kelleman, Janet Bode, Dotty Lynch, Karen Paget, Ruth Sabo, Gale Brewer, Irene Natividad, Sharon Rodine, Ethel Klein, Emily Tynes,

Linda Tarr-Whelan, Kathy Bonk, Marcia Greenburger, Lael Stegal, Wendy MacKenzie, Nancy Duff Campbell, Judy Lichtman, Ann Baker, Annie Bower, Heidi Hartmann, and Marie Wilson, who provided an introduction to my publisher.

Professional women journalists have been a valuable source of information. I particularly thank Illinois reporter Linda Witt for explaining her state's politics, CBS News executive Kathie Frankovic for deciphering the mysteries of the disenchanted centrist voter, *Washington Post* columnist Judy Mann for her good sense, reporter Eileen Shanahan for breaking down the barriers, and my gifted friend Peg Simpson, who shared her vast knowledge of the women's movement.

Professor Howard Gillette of George Washington University provided friendship and insight as he perceptively unraveled the mystery of what happened to the moderate Republicans. John Topping and Mike McLeod generously explained the intricacies of third-party candidacies. I will miss our Ripon Society colleague, Dan Swillinger, who carried on a twenty-four-year dialogue with me on this subject until his death before the book's completion. His widow, Lois, and son, Patrick, know how much I treasure the help he gave to many of us in the women's movement. Robert Pennoyer, an honorable man of the John Stuart Mill school who guided the Ripon Society lawsuit, has long been an advocate for women's liberation. I am deeply grateful for his help in conceptualizing this book.

When the women's political movement began in 1971, there was almost no information available on political women. Today there are many sources. One of the best, in my judgment, is the Center for the American Woman and Politics, and I appreciate the help of Ruth Mandel and Debbie Walsh and her staff in providing me with detailed statistics and analysis on women's political progress. Political scientists Jo Freeman and Sylvia Bashevkin generously discussed their excellent continuing research on the women's liberation movement.

I want to thank Susan Carroll and Alice Tetelman, who gave me sage advice about analyzing the 1996 campaign, and Darlee Crockett for moral support during 1996. Also, Jodi Armstrong and Lara Tabac were most helpful in typing the drafts for the revised edition.

I thank with special gratitude those who patiently read the book's early drafts and painstakingly worked with me to make them better: Michael Brewer, Julia Kagan, Celia Morris, Joseph Persico, Carol Reichert, and Susan Russell. Their friendship and encouragement have sustained me not only during the writing of this book but through many years of political war.

Charity Kelly was my assistant through the preparation of the book's first draft, and I am especially grateful for her tenaciousness, energy, loyalty, and her welcome perspective on the younger generation.

Ann Harris, my editor at Bantam, believed in this book from the first time we discussed it. I admire not only her professionalism and quick intelligence but her warmth and kindness. We shared a similar vision as she guided me sensitively through the editing. An author could not wish for more; she is the best. Ann's assistant, Samantha Howley, has also been first rate, and I thank her for her competence and good cheer.

In the end, it is family that most shapes one's life. My mother and father sent me out on this political journey very early, and I thank them for doing so and for their unwavering love and faith in me. I have never regretted the path I chose. I am also blessed with loving and politically astute siblings, Michael, Nancy, and Robert, and their spouses Gayle, Lex, and Katie. For all your years of affection and advice, my thanks.

My husband, Noel, and our children, Karla and Evan, have lovingly sustained me. Karla not only provided welcome editorial criticism but stepped in at the last minute to finish typing the manuscript. I also thank her friend Peter Mendelsund and Evan's friend Alexandra Messore for extra moral support.

Noel's love, support, and quick, insightful mind have eased my political struggle and helped me remember that smelling the flowers is as important as winning elections. I have no words for his unselfish devotion. I am honored to be his wife.

November 7, 1995
Updated September 24, 1997

INDEX

ABOUT THE AUTHOR

TANYA MELICH, whose roots in the Republican Party run long and deep, has been a party official, served in many GOP campaigns, and co-founded the Republican women's movement. With broad experience in elections and politics, women's concerns, the media, corporate public affairs and public policy research, she speaks frequently on these issues and has published op-ed pieces in numerous national newspapers and magazines.